INFANT BEHAVIOR,

ITS GENESIS AND GROWTH

INFANT BEHAVIOR

ITS GENESIS AND GROWTH

BY

ARNOLD GESELL

PH.D., M.D., SC.D.

*Director of the Clinic of Child Development and Professor of
Child Hygiene in Yale University*

AND

HELEN THOMPSON, PH.D.

*Research Associate in Biometry
The Yale Clinic of Child Development*

ASSISTED BY

CATHERINE STRUNK AMATRUDA, M.D.

*Research Pediatrist
The Yale Clinic of Child Development*

FIRST EDITION

GREENWOOD PRESS, PUBLISHERS
NEW YORK

PREFACE

Investigations as well as infants grow. The present volume has its roots in earlier studies which are briefly outlined in the opening chapter. We must at once acknowledge our indebtedness to earlier associates who helped to set in operation general principles and methods of procedures; namely, Mrs. Margaret Cobb Rogers, Miss Elizbeth Evans Lord, Miss Ruth Wendell Washburn, and Dr. Marian Cabot Putnam. Through its diagnostic and advisory service, the clinic has fortunately been able to build up relations of confidence and friendliness in the community. This has resulted in excellent cooperation from the parents of New Haven who, through themselves and through their infants, have made a generous contribution to our scientific undertaking.

We have benefited in numerous ways from the cooperation of other departments of the School of Medicine; and of social agencies, including the Visiting Nurse Association and the Bureau of Vital Statistics. In the home visits and interviews we had the assistance of Miss Glenna Bullis and of several graduate students. We wish also to make grateful acknowledgment to Miss E. Elizabeth Allis for assistance in the preparation of manuscript.

This publication is based upon periodic developmental examinations of normative infants throughout the first year of life. The stenographic protocols of the observations entailed a large amount of painstaking analysis which was carried through by a group of assistants especially trained and supervised for the task: Miss Helene Mallay, Miss Helen Richardson, Miss Charlotte Peck, Miss Georgina Johnson, and Mrs. Harriet Lange Rheingold. Mrs. Esther Upjohn Shipley, over a period of three years, developed a detailed familiarity with the data and rendered valuable service in connection with the analysis of the normative cinema records. These records were made with the active cooperation and helpful advice of Professor Henry Marc Halverson, Research Associate in Experimental Psychology.

Extensive cinema records, both normative and naturalistic, have been codified in *An Atlas of Infant Behavior* which portrays in action photographs the forms and early growth of human behavior patterns. The present volume bears an organic relation to

the systematic delineations of the Atlas. A forthcoming volume by
the present authors, entitled *Norms of Infant Development*, will set
forth in monographic detail the basic data of the normative survey,
the specific procedures used in the developmental examinations,
and biometric conclusions and applications.

The present volume deals mainly with findings and genetic
interpretations. The results of the normative survey are reported
in six chapters and sixty sections. Chapter Three, which constitutes
the core of the book, summarizes the behavior characteristics
displayed in twenty-five different situations, instituted at fifteen
age levels from four through fifty-six weeks. The newborn infant
was not included in our systematic observations. The period
immediately after birth involves medical, nutritional, and environmental complications and so many highly variable factors that it
requires special techniques for adequate study. We have not,
however, been unmindful of the importance of the neonatal period
and (in Chapter Four) have indicated its genetic relations to the
fetal and later postnatal period.

For perspective and orientation, the reader may find it profitable to read Chapter Four in advance of Chapter Three. Chapter
Four deals in an inclusive manner with The Ontogenetic Patterning
of Infant Behavior and provides a general overview of the developmental trends and of the entire range of age levels.

We hope that the reader will not be dismayed by the minutiae
of the tables and the multiplicity of the behavior items. This book
deals primarily with the detailed structuralization of early behavior
growth. The researches were not directly concerned with the
concept of general ability or of intelligence, but with the nature
of developmental sequences. Mental growth is a process of progressive behavior patterning, which may be investigated from the
standpoint of developmental morphology. The action systems of
embryo, fetus, and infant undergo orderly changes of pattern,
which are so consistent that we may be certain that these changes
are governed by mechanisms of form regulation comparable with
those which are being defined by the science of embryology. Must
we not, therefore, approach the phenomena of infant behavior
with the same minute interest in structured form which the disciplines of embryology and anatomy require?

New Haven, Connecticut,
 September, 1934.

CONTENTS

INFANT BEHAVIOR

Its Genesis and Growth

Chapter One

A DEVELOPMENTAL STUDY OF THE FIRST YEAR OF LIFE

A Summary Account of Methods and Objectives

§1. Development of the Normative Project

THE present volume and the associated volume *Norms of Infant Development* report the results of a normative survey of the first year of life. This survey was inaugurated in 1927, after a preliminary developmental study of five normal infants. The latter study served to refine the research procedures for the more comprehensive normative survey. Both studies were made under the auspices of The Yale Clinic of Child Development.

The clinic, established in 1911, has long been concerned with the preschool period of childhood. Our early work was conducted in close association with the pediatric and well-baby clinics of the New Haven Dispensary. This led to an interest in problems of developmental diagnosis. Infants who came to the conferences for physical examinations were also brought to our clinic and were examined from time to time by psychological methods. Binet and Kuhlman had recently indicated the applicability of intelligence age concepts to early age levels. This was a point of departure for our exploratory studies of the total behavior of the growing infant. These studies were made from the standpoint of developmental pediatrics and were based on the premise that the developmental status of the infant should be diagnosed and supervised in terms of behavior as well as of bodily conditions. Intelligence was presumed to be but a partial aspect of a total complex of behavior growth. For such developmental diagnosis more comprehensive norms of behavior development were essential.

Accordingly in 1919 a normative charting of the behavior development of normal children was undertaken for the period from birth to six years of age. This preliminary normative investigation took account of ten age levels as follows: 0, 4, 6, 9, 12, and 18 months; 2, 3, 4, and 5 years. This calibration of age levels gave recognition to the rapid rate of early infant development. Some

50 children were investigated at each age. The survey attempted to include the total development of the infant without specific stress on intelligence. Therefore the observations and examinations took account of the following major fields of behavior maturity: *motor development*, including posture, locomotion, prehension, and drawing; *language development*, including vocabulary, word comprehension, conversation, and reproduction; *adaptive behavior*, including visual-motor functions, imitation, recovery of objects, comprehension, discriminative performance, apperception, completion, number concept; *personal-social behavior*, including reaction to persons, personal habits, initiative and independence, play responses, acquired information.

In securing the normative data in these fields, simple procedures and devices were used. The child was seated in a high chair, or on his mother's lap, confronting an adjustable table. On this table objects were placed to elicit his attentional regard, prehension, manipulation, and exploitiveness, and his responsiveness to gesture, demonstration, and command. An effort was made to keep the examination situation simple and natural. For this reason such homely objects as the cup, spoon, rattle, ball, ring, and string became part of the testing paraphernalia. A dozen red, one-inch, wooden cubes proved to be very serviceable and they were used as standard test devices throughout the whole range of age levels. To define better the nebulous characteristics of the 9 months old infant, we added a tiny pellet (7 mm. in diameter) to provoke his increasing refinement of prehension. These simple objects have shown themselves technically suitable for clinical and also for experimental purposes.

The normative results of the survey were codified into a developmental schedule embracing about 150 different normative items. Although many of the results were of preliminary character, they impressed us forcibly with the wealth and variety of behavior patterns of the human infant. The genetic and clinical significance of the first year of life became increasingly apparent in the application of the preliminary norms of development.

When requisite grants were made through the generosity of the Laura Spelman Rockefeller Memorial in 1926, we projected an investigation concentrated on the period of infancy. Beginning in 1926, as already indicated, the clinic staff made an intensive, coordinated study of five normal infants. Behavior inventories and examinations and physical measurements were made at lunar-month intervals throughout the first year of life. The 16 mm. cinema was systematically used for the purpose of recording the development and for refining its analysis. It soon became apparent that detailed biogenetic study of individual infants required more numerous and precise norms of behavior growth.

§2. THE PROJECT IN OUTLINE

Therefore in 1927 a systematic normative program was projected embracing 15 age levels from 4 weeks through 56 weeks. Although custom and our own earlier studies favored the use of solar-month intervals, it was decided to conduct all the normative observations on a lunar-month basis. The advantages of the lunar month may be summarized as follows: (a) The lunar month is of uniform length (solar months vary as much as 11 per cent); (b) the lunar-month interval permits reappointments on a fixed day of the week; (c) it makes for greater comparability of data from diverse workers and in diverse fields; (d) it makes for greater statistical accuracy; (e) it is in harmony with the scientific movement for calendar revision; (f) it is in closer correspondence with biological and physiological cycles. The adoption of the lunar month reflects our respect for the age factors which are so important during the most rapid periods of mental growth.

The normative significance of the data was protected by a scrupulous regard for the chronological age of the subjects. With very rare and minor exceptions each child was examined within two days of the exact age by the lunar-month calendar. The age factor was further controlled by excluding all infants who had a definite history of prematurity or postmaturity of birth, or who suffered from any severe disease or nutritional handicap.

To strengthen further the normative validity and the developmental comparability of the data, the infants were carefully selected to constitute a homogeneous group from the standpoint of socio-economic status and educational background of parents and race. The parents of the infants were all born in the United States and their grandparents were of northern European extraction. Only those infants were included whose parents were of middle status with respect to occupation, schooling, avocational interests, home equipment and household furnishing. The fathers' occupations gave ratings from 4.98 to 11.74 based on the Barr Scale of Occupational Intelligence. Details concerning the selection of subjects are elaborated in the accompanying normative volume.

The general character of home conditions is briefly indicated by the following percentages based on cases reporting on the several items: 79 per cent rented an apartment; 11 per cent rented a house; 10 per cent owned a house. The average number of rooms was 4.69; the average number of people living at home 4.02. In 42 per cent of the households the laundry was sent out; in 52 per cent, no outside domestic help was employed. Fifty-eight per cent read one daily newspaper; 19 per cent had a piano; 40 per cent had a victrola; 62 per cent had a radio. Ninety-nine per cent attended church; 43 per cent were Protestant; 49 per cent were Catholic. Thirty-three per cent owned an automobile; 91 per cent attended the movie theater; 43 per cent had vacations.

All told, 107 different infants were studied; 58 girls and 49 boys. Many of these were seen repeatedly; 7 were examined at lunar-age intervals from 4 through 56 weeks. The total number of examinations was 524. An extended cinema record was made of one-third of these examinations; for 82 per cent a partial cinema record was made.

The records for each case and visit included the following: (a) Data in regard to family conditions and parentage, secured through a home investigation; (b) information in regard to the infant's behavior routine, supplied by parental interview; (c) birth and health history; (d) physical measurements; (e) stenographic report of the developmental examination (and supplementary cinema records); (f) a clocked record of the events and observations which occurred while the child was at the clinic. The protocols will be described in more detail in Sect. 5.

Each normative inventory at the clinic at each of the 15 age levels required a full half day. The basic systematic observations were secured through the normative or developmental examination, which will be described in detail in following chapters. The devices and materials of this examination were similar to those which had been used in the earlier preschool survey, including the red cubes, the bell, rattle, ring and string, pellet, etc. The setting of the examination, however, was more carefully controlled and the procedures for administering the test materials were defined in greater detail. No effort was made to alter the character of the examination by employing more technical devices. It was felt that more useful and significant results would come through a maximum utilization of simple materials congenial to the environment and experience of the infant.

In the interests of standardization and experimental control the infant was examined in a "clinical crib." This crib simulates a household crib in its general outlines but is equipped with an adjustable platform, panels, and side rails. It carries at its head end a container for the psychological test materials. Details and specifications for this apparatus are given elsewhere.

For the postural behavior situations the infant was placed on the platform of the crib, which was covered with a blotter, softened at the early ages by an underlying pad. At 12 weeks and at later ages, whenever the infant required support in the sitting position, he was placed in a small adjustable chair of the morris type. With the youngest infants a canvas belt which encircled the child's trunk at the diaphragm was used. This supportive band was secured at the back of the chair. For older infants a single canvas strap athwart the diaphragm was used. When the infant had acquired independent sitting control he sat on the blotter on the platform confronting a table top which rested on the side rails of the crib. Upon this table top the various stimulus objects were placed in accordance with specified procedures.

It will be evident from this introductory summary that the normative survey was designed to preserve a high degree of experimental control. Many informalities were set aside to insure certain basic uniformities of procedure. The arrangements at the clinic and the general observation policy, however, placed a premium upon an optimal emotional adjustment and a maximum of natural behavior on the part of the infant.

Questions of statistical reliability and other biometric considerations will be considered more technically in a monographic volume. It is sufficient to point out here that the value and the validity of the findings must rest primarily on the accuracy and detail of the original observations and on the homogeneous, median character of the group of infants investigated. The normative survey was not a study of an unselected or random population. The survey was not concerned in a restricted way with the psychometry of intelligence. We were interested in the establishment of norms as instrumental aids for the analysis of the processes of behavior growth and for the characterization of developmental status. The norms are representative of a biologically and sociologically median group. They express general developmental trends and sequences. Derived as they were, the norms are specificative formulations which may be used to define the characteristics and maturity values (in normative terms) of observed behavior. The genetic import of the norms is further indicated in the following discussion of the underlying concepts which guided the normative investigation.

§3 UNDERLYING GENETIC CONCEPTS

The basic objective of the normative investigation was a study of the products and the processes of mental growth. We shall use the terms growth and development interchangeably. This is for convenience and also because it seems impossible to maintain a consistent distinction which would identify growth with augmentation and development with differentiation. From the standpoint of biology one can scarcely conceive of pure increase without some concomitant change of conformation and configuration. Mental growth, at least, is not hyperplasia. Even though the term growth is strongly associated with the idea of dimensional increase, it is desirable to make this excellent monosyllable do service in the discussion of problems of genetic psychology.

From a genetic standpoint the "mind" as well as the body grows. Ignoring metaphysical issues, we may in a monistic sense regard growth as a single function of the living organism. Changes in somatic size, structure, and shape constitute the phenomena of physical growth. Comparable changes in the organization and reactions of the organism as a behavioral entity constitute the phenomena of mental growth. Fundamentally these phenomena are inseparable. In any event it is impossible from the standpoint of genetic science to regard the psyche as a manifestation so unique that it is independent of the laws of growth and of the same developmental morphology which molds the visible organism.

Growth is a process of progressive differentiation and systematization which organizes the individual throughout a changing life cycle. Thus stated, the concept of growth applies equally to mental and to physical forms. Mental growth, like physical growth, is a morphogenetic process which produces progressive pattern. The psychological individual, like the physical individual, is patterned. He is the sum and the concatenation of all his behavior forms. His capacities, his modes and trends of behavior, and the ontogenetic sequence of his reaction systems all are patterned. His psychological make-up has a consistent organic structure constituted of action patterns. In infancy at least he must be construed from the standpoint of developmental morphology.

When does this ontogenetic patterning of the human individual begin? It is always difficult to establish an absolute zero, and the paucity of our knowledge makes the effort premature. It may be suggested, however, that even from a behavioral point of view, this zero must lie near the time of conception. When the embryo is but 4 mm. long and 3 weeks old, the heart begins to beat. When the embryo is less than 2 months old the neuromuscular system is already sufficiently advanced to make rhythmic movements of trunk and extremities possible. At 2 months, the embryo has been observed to respond reflexly to a light touch of the skin, the "reflex" irradiating over the whole body and involving head and trunk. Mental growth we are obliged to believe is then already under way, for although no one can assess the psychological essence of such primitive behavior, it is impossible to hold that it is in a biological sense nonmental.

Irradiated mass reaction is characteristic of early stages of maturity, but as early as the third month the fetus displays some capacity for circumscribed response. In embryos of this age mouth movements by lowering and lifting the chin occur with stimulation of the lips and tongue. During the fourth and fifth months complicated postural mechanisms are in the making. Stimulating the toe evokes a diagonal or trot reflex. Thoracic movements respiratory in character occur as early as the fifth month. By the sixth month the neuromuscular equipment has advanced so far that a child prematurely born in this month has at least a slender chance of survival. It is as though nature hastened to bring the most vital functions to relative completion against this very contingency. The viability of the prematurely born infant strengthens the thesis that the same morphogenetic processes which fashion the fetus project themselves into the postnatal sectors of the life cycle. In many significant ways the premature neonate continues to grow as though he were still a fetus.

Normally human gestation covers a period of 40 weeks, but birth with survival has been known to occur as early as 24 weeks and also as late as 48 weeks. This makes a range of variation amounting in extreme to 6 lunar months. Variation within a range of 3 lunar months is common. These facts show the genetic importance of the problem of age with all its interesting relativities.

Time in the Newtonian sense flows at a uniform rate. It is simply duration. But time in a biological sense becomes a relative rather than a uniform reality when it is considered in terms of the morphogenetic events which occur within a life cycle. Time ceases to be simply duration; it is age. An age is a position in a life cycle, which cycle has a beginning and an end. A stage is a degree of progression in such a cycle.

Chronological age is a conventional or statutory value in terms of duration computed from birth. This value may be projected against the life cycle, and one may think of age as a moment in a life cycle, the life cycle being a continuum of ages or stages. It is evident, however, that an age and a stage are not identical and that the relationship between age and stage must vary among individuals as it varies between species. Thus arises the whole problem of age and maturity.

The relationship between statutory age and biological stage raises interesting questions concerning the philosophy and significance of developmental norms. By definition, statutory age can be measured only in clock intervals, that is, in astronomer royal units. A biological stage, however, can be expressed or "measured" only in terms of the products of growth. These two sets of units are in two different worlds of discourse and in a sense the twain can never meet. But one may always solve a paradox by not recognizing it or by inventing a reconciliatory fiction. Therefore we superimpose the calendar cycle of ages on the organic cycle of stages and designate the stages in terms of ages. Soon we find ourselves talking about the behavior values of age and the age values of behavior. Thus the twain meet after all.

This is permissible because we do not have at our disposal an absolute mensurational unit for computing growth. Perhaps it is also necessary because growth is patterning and cannot be reduced to purely energic, or linear, or dimensional concepts. Patterns can be appraised only with the aid of patterns. A developmental norm therefore is a pattern, or indicator of pattern, specified with sufficient concreteness to serve as a standard of comparison in the analysis and estimate of a given pattern of growth.

In a specification sense one might derive a useful set of norms from a careful study of one individual infant. If the infant were happily selected, a single case might be as good as a hundred. Indeed, it would be much better than a hundred poorly selected cases, for by premise "happily selected" means normatively representative or typical. In complicated genetic phenomena there is only a very limited safety in mere numbers. As already indicated, we have aimed to increase the validity of our norms by deriving them from a homogeneously selected group and by formulating the norms comparatively on the basis of their incidence in the individual and their collective trend in a homogeneous group of individuals.

This argument should not be construed as a rejection of more elaborate statistical approaches. We simply wish to clarify our suggestion that, for the analysis of developmental conditions, the specificative value of a norm comes foremost. We must have some specific standard of reference by which we can identify what we observe in the complex output of the infant's behavior. Having identified, we can appraise with due caution in terms of normative trends, ascertained by the study of a normative group. Trends are probabilities of varied magnitude. Some of them are obscure and unreliable; others are certainties. As we approach the certainties, analytic diagnosis (in terms of specificative norms) also approaches prediction.

The application of concrete norms in the identification of observed behavior is a process of matching. Among an array of norms we look for the best fit. Other things being equal, the more numerous and graduated the norms, the better the chance for a good fit. If the reader should contend that this is mere approximation, and that science demands measurement, it might be answered that all measurement is a form of comparison. Only the perfect comparison is a perfect measurement. One may measure aspects of prehension in the units of physical science, that is, on an absolute scale in units of time and space; but the patterns of prehension, temporal and spatial, can as yet be "measured" only in the comparative terms of normatively ascertained patterns.

It would, therefore, be dogmatic to push too far distinctions between descriptive and quantitative methods of approach. At the present stage of our knowledge when the data are complex, descriptive formulas do justice to the complexity. Numerical or quantitative devices inadequately supported, lead to oversimplification. General deductions must rest on detailed findings. We need detailed normative criteria which will serve to classify and order the specific data under observation. This office, it is hoped, the norms which are offered in the present volume may in a measure fulfill.

§4. BEHAVIOR CATEGORIES AND PATTERNS

The normative investigation was particularly concerned with those visible forms of behavior which could be elicited under the controlled conditions of a developmental examination supplemented by interview. The fields of behavior that were surveyed in this manner subdivide into the seven following categories:

A. Postural Behavior:
   (1) Supine; (2) prone; (3) sitting; (4) standing and other bodily orientations.
B. Locomotion:
   (1) Rolling; (2) creeping; (3) walking; (4) climbing and other bodily translocations.
C. Perceptual Behavior:
   (1) Tactile; (2) visual; (3) auditory; (4) anticipatory and selective regard.
D. Prehension:
   (1) Approach; (2) grasp; (3) release.
E. Adaptive Behavior:
   (1) Manipulation; (2) self-initiated combining and exploitive behavior; (3) induced behavior; (4) autonomous learning.
F. Language Behavior:
   (1) Subphonetic; (2) vocalizations; (3) vocal signs; (4) words; (5) gesture.
G. Social Behavior:
   (1) Reactions to persons; (2) responsiveness to gesture and speech: (3) socialized learning and habituations.

The present volume will treat each of these basic categories, with especial emphasis upon the first five. A *behavior category* is here defined as a classification group which comprises objectively similar and genetically related behavior items. A *behavior item* is a specific phase or distinguishable feature of behavior. The foregoing categories were established for their convenience in analyzing the growth and status of infant behavior. It is not assumed that the categories are mutually exclusive; both dynamically and developmentally the contrary is assumed. The relationship between locomotion and posture is very close; likewise the relations between posture and prehension. We would even hold with Coghill that in all behavior there is concealed posture. Indeed, the concept of posture can be applied in the interpretation of higher forms of adaptive behavior.

The expression *behavior item* deserves further discussion. A *pattern of behavior* is a configured response which can be described specifically in terms of a given situation. A *behavior item* is an aspect or a component of a pattern ascertained by direct observation or by subsequent analysis. Being a product of analysis, it is assumed that the item is not an entity in nature. It is an aspect of a pattern. To a considerable extent this same limitation applies to the concept of pattern. A pattern, as pattern, is not a circumscribed entity in nature. It always has a context, and this context if analyzed can in turn be reduced to constituent patterns. But since contexts also have contexts, it follows that perhaps the only pattern which has full integral status is the organismic pattern, which is the individual himself. Pattern categories therefore can be arranged in a gradient from minute differentiated areas of behavior like the reflex wink to complex coordinations like prehension and to the yet more inclusive patterns which correspond to the entire personality or large sectors of it.

There are also patterns of genetic sequence. Behavior as it matures follows an orderly progression, and this progression when expressed in lines of genetic sequence can be envisaged as pattern. It is desirable to use the term *pattern* in this flexible manner even though the resultant patterns become too multitudinous for complete inventory. In a pervasive organismic manner all the patterns of behavior are consolidated in the individuality of the infant himself, and the distinctive concatenation of his behavioral predispositions is an expression of superpattern. In this sense every individual has a unique biogenetic pattern.

The connotations of the terms *function, behavior pattern, behavior item* will vary with context. For theoretical safety we shall not assume the existence of a function as a well-defined entity but shall stress the objective reality of the pattern forms and pattern phases or items. Although patterns are variable with respect to their specific details and with respect to their duration in the life career of the infant, we regard them as having a substantive existence which makes them subject to descriptive inventory.

A *behavior situation* is a complex combination of stimulus factors which evoke patterns of response. The external aspects of the behavior situation and the behavior responses themselves constitute the sole data for actual observation. Functions are at best inferences drawn from such observations. Generally conceived, grasp is a function; specifically, it is always a pattern. The pattern may be described in terms of the mechanics of the act of seizure, including a description of the posturing and participation of all of the digits. But the pattern may also be described in terms of antecedents and sequelae, including the stimulus, the approach upon the object, and manipulation of it. Similarly, sitting is a function only in the sense that grasp is one; the chair or the platform is the *situation*. Sitting is related to standing, as manual closure is related to digital prehension.

A *modality of behavior* is a trend in configuration and in sequence of response which can be described in general terms and is predicated on the similarity of patterns of behavior in similar situations. A modality is in the nature of a paradigm or norm abstracted from numerous observations or records of behavior.

When so generalized a modality tends to become synonymous with the term *function*. This usage is permissible if the function is regarded as a generalization rather than as specific biological entity. In the present analysis of our data we have used the concept of function for purposes of exposition and discussion but we have tried to cleave consistently to the more tenable and secure concept of developmental morphology. In biogenetic analysis, the validation of functional continuities and correlations will become a problem of critical importance.

Accordingly, manifestations of behavior are set forth in the substantive terms of behavior patterns and behavior items. Although these patterns are more or less transient and always subject to dynamic inflections it is assumed that they have structured reality. They are expressions of the attained architecture of the organism rather than fortuitous symptoms of formless functions or forces.

As already noted, in order to do justice to the complexity of the behavior patterns we used stenographic and cinematographic methods of recording. When these records were subjected to analysis they yielded, after a process of elimination, a total of over a thousand behavior items. For all of these items we have ascertained frequency values in terms of their incidence in the normative groups studied. Many of the items covered the whole gamut of age levels from 4 weeks through 56 weeks; all of them covered two or more age levels; and for each of them a trend value is made apparent by the tables of percentages. These numerous items constitute the basis for the discussion of behavior growth in various behavior fields. Some of the items are more interesting, more dramatic, and more significant than other items. We have not, however, presumed too much on our capacity to interpret, and therefore have included in the tables items which occurred with comparative infrequency. It does not follow that such items have no normative usefulness in the interpretation of growth conditions.

Even apparently trivial and inconspicuous behavior items may be highly indicative in a genetic sense.

It should be reemphasized here that the behavior situations were not set up with the idea of devising performance tests to secure a statistical array of successes and failures on which to base a psychometric scale. The situations were designed to evoke characteristic behavior with all its natural limitations. It was the total tide of behavior rather than eventual success of performance which concerned us. We were quite as interested in the anticipatory as in the culminating phases of the behavior; and almost more interested in approximations than in complete adaptations.

For this reason many of the "test" materials were administered to a child whose abilities were far too immature to meet the requirements of the test from the conventional standpoint of successful performance. Take for example the formboard, perhaps the most sophisticated article in the battery of stimulus objects. The formboard was presented to 20 weeks-old children even though they can have only the most rudimentary command of its geometry. However, even the 20 weeks-old infants gave outward token of some perception of spatial factors. We were interested in that nascent *some*, and the task was to chart the cumulative progress which finally led to discriminative response to the circular hole.

From a sheer development point of view, the infant never fails. He is at every age interesting, complex, and competent. His aggregate behavior is always an index of his developmental status. Therefore the primary inventory of behavior at each examination was made as inclusive as possible. The normative survey was concerned in a genetic sense with the total phenomena of mental growth. The normative data were approached from this genetic point of view.

§5. THE DATA

The concepts and general principles just outlined guided the analysis and organization of the normative data. It is now in order to examine more closely the nature of these data and the methods of their treatment, reserving the monographic details for the volume on *Norms of Infant Development*.

A full set of protocols for each child included the following:

1. *The Descriptive Home Record.* This form supplied the name, address, and birth date of the infant; name, date of birth, race,

occupation, education, and descriptive remarks for the father, mother, maternal grandfather and grandmother, paternal grandfather and grandmother, and siblings; ownership or rental of apartment or house; the number of rooms, servants, and persons in the house; books, magazines, newspapers, piano, victrola, radio; membership in clubs; attendance at church, concerts, lectures, sports, the theater; ownership of an automobile; summer vacation; family physician; general characterization and remarks.

2. *History Interview.* This record detailed the birth history of the child and nutritional and medical history.

3. Record of the domestic *behavior day* covering the daily routine of the infant at the time of the examination. This record listed in order in hours and minutes the major events of a 24 hour day from morning waking, bath, feeding, etc., through the night's sleep.

4. *Anthropometric Measurements.* The measurements made at each examination covered the following items: *Height:* vertex, suprasternal, symphysium; *diameters:* biacromial, mesosternal, iliocristial; *girth:* head, chest; *weight; teeth; asymmetry; complications;* and *general comments.*

5. A *behavior interview record* included the conversational report of the mother's observations in the fields of motor, language, adaptive, and personal-social behavior.

6. *Record of Behavior Day at the Clinic.* This record detailed the time of various events occurring during the course of the visit at the clinic from arrival to departure.

7. *A Stenographic Record of the Normative Examination.* This verbatim record covered the entire course of each developmental examination including marginal time entries, stating the time of occurrence and the duration of all of the observed behavior situations.

8. *Maturity ratings* made on the Yale infant development schedule.* These ratings covered about a dozen items at each age level in the fields of motor, language, adaptive, and personal-social behavior. The ratings were made as an aid to defining and clarifying points of observation.

9. *Cinema Records.* Extended cinema records were made of most of the infants from 8 to 16 weeks of age and of seven special

---

* GESELL, A., *Infancy and Human Growth*, Chap. VI, An infant development recording schedule, New York: Macmillan, 1928.

photographic cases from 8 through 56 weeks. Partial cinema records depicting prehension and manipulation were made of 82 per cent of the cases.

10. *A general summary sheet* which assembled, with a special view to later biogenetic study, observations, estimates, and ratings under the following headings:

Complicating factors: infant; parent; home; clinic.

Ratings: Gross motor; fine motor; language; adaptive; personal-social.

Comparative estimates: General outlook; energy; emotivity; perceptivity; assertiveness; sociability.

Classification and file items.

Maximum attainment: Gross motor; fine motor; language; adaptive; personal-social.

Characterization and special impressions.

Follow-up and predictive items.

The normative investigation comprised 107 different infants and a total of 524 examinations. All of the records were entered on letter size (8.5 by 11 inches) paper, most of them typewritten. For the entire group of subjects these data consist of some 5,564 pages. As already indicated, the basic data for the normative study were embodied in the stenographic behavior reports. On the average these stenographic reports required a little less than four single-spaced, typewritten sheets. All told, a typical stenographic report for 15 age levels for one child, or for a group of children spanning these age levels, amounted to approximately 50 pages or more. The estimated number of pages for the entire group of normative infants totals over 2,000. These stenographic records embrace all of the developmental behavior situations systematically observed beginning ordinarily with the supine, spontaneous behavior in the younger infants, and concluding with the observation of postural and personal-social behavior with the older infants. The nature of these records as dictated by the examiners is illustrated by random citations as follows:

Name J ... F ...   Girl   Age: 4 weeks
Examined: At home (on portable examination table)   Date: June 7
Behavior Situation

9:15. *Supine Spontaneous: Infant was asleep when we arrived. Was taken up by Examiner.* Wakes up slowly. Placed on the table. She starts to fuss when undressed but quiets and lies quietly on the table. She lies with her head

* * *

turned toward the left. Sneezes. Raises the left arm vertically in the air. Legs extended. Lies with head in midline. Lies in t-n-r, head to left. Right hand fisted on the chest. Left extended down to the side. Legs externally rotated, flexed. Rolls pelvis to the left. Extends both arms down to side. Looks fixedly at left. Starts. Both arms at side. Clasps them together, over the chest. Begins to fuss. Assumes t-n-r position. Turns head from left to right and back again. Now the right hand is open at the occiput. Makes windmill movement with left arm.

9:19. *Dangling Ring: Dangling ring is presented in the midline as she lies in the left t-n-r. Ring brought into line of vision.* She fixes ring momentarily as it is in line of vision. Fixes ring again and again as *it is brought into line of vision.* Follows it with eye turning for about 20° repeatedly toward the midline. Does not follow it completely to side. She follows it up to head of table extending her head and rolling her eyes. Then follows it down to shoulder level. Looks away.

9:21. *Round Rod.*

* * *

Name: J ... F ...   Girl   Age: 24 weeks
Examined: In photographic dome   Date: November 6
Behavior Situation
11:31. *Pellet.*

11:33. *Bell: Is presented.* Extends left hand, fans the fingers, pushes the bell out of reach. *Put into near median position,* she sweeps bell in with left hand in pronate attitude, brings the handle to the mouth. Mouths the handle vocalizing while so doing. She seizes the bell between the thumb and digits by clasping it palmarwise at junction of handle and bowl. While chewing the bell she inspects the surroundings and then stares forward. She slumps decidedly to the right while in the chair. She now withdraws the bell and looks at it only momentarily and then brings it back to the mouth, chews it. She also brings up the free right hand, thrusts the fingers into the mouth. Fingers of the right hand are flexed and rest on the table. Later they finger and flex upon the rim of the bowl. She is now holding the bell with both hands, chewing handle rather vigorously, staring forward. The arms are sharply flexed at the elbow. In transferring to the right hand, the bell drops to the platform.

11:36. *Ring and String:* Looks at the Examiner's hand, then at the string and then at the ring. Straightens the body, lifts the left hand and strains toward the ring. The regard shifts from the ring to the string. There is no persistent approach upon the ring and string. *Presented in midline.* Looks again at ring, then at string, extends left hand, looks to Examiner, looks at ring. Fusses audibly. Left hand touches string but she does not pursue the contact. Looks at ring and string and now while looking toward the right her hands rest on the string and she flexes without regard and momentarily prehends the string.

11:41. *Formboard.*

* * *

Name: J ... F ...   Girl   Age: 48 weeks
Examined: In photographic dome   Date: April 24
Behavior Situation
10:51. *Pellet and Bottle.*
10:54. *Bell:* With both hands she approaches the bell placing hands pronate on table and secures bell in left hand, turns bell up, immediately fingers clapper first with left and then with right. Holding in right hand by bowl, waves it. Attention goes back to clapper, pokes with her thumb. Turns bell over, holds by handle in left hand, waves it. Bell does not ring. Then with right index finger flexes the finger so that she pushes the clapper about. Transfers bell to right hand holding it inverted, waves it, rings it, listens. Waves it, rings it, listens. Transfers to left hand and again displays the same performance. *The Examiner demonstrates the ringing of the bell.* She picks up the bell by the handle with right hand, immediately transfers to left holding by bowl, waves it not ringing it. Takes by handle with right hand, holds and pokes at clapper. *Second demonstration.* Again approaches with right hand, transfers to left, waves it, transfers back to right, waves it. During third demonstration she looks to Examiner, smiles. Immediately approaches bell with right hand, transfers to left, holds bell on side, pokes clapper, transfers to right, pokes at clapper, back to left, drags on table.
During the interval Examiner places hand on table and J. places the bell on Examiner's hand.
10:58. *Ring and String:* Looks toward ring, glances momentarily at string, prehends string twice pulling the ring a short distance each time. Picks up ring, waves it. Attention goes to string. Fingers it with right hand, then transfers ring from hand to hand, bringing it in contact with the table top. Carries to platform at right, releases there. Brings it back to table top, releases there. Vocalizes. Reaches toward string, starts to prehend that, is unsuccessful. *Ring and string are removed.*
10:59. *Ring, String, and Bell.*

In terms of individual age levels, as already indicated, the number of protocols included in the study totals 524. When all of these protocols were in hand a systematic analysis of the data was undertaken with the help of several research assistants. The original narrative records were read and reread repeatedly in order to establish familiarity with the prevailing consistencies in the behavior characteristics reported. After considerable preliminary exploration and trial and error, the total behavior episode was reduced to a list of separate items of behavior. Only those items were listed which had definite status in the dictated report. Frequency values expressed in percentage of the cases observed were ascertained for all of the items included in this basic ledger listing. This list was then subjected to further scrutiny and all items of a doubtful or ambiguous character were eliminated. After this winnowing, the most useful and reliable items remained. These items are reproduced in the normative tables printed elsewhere in this volume and in elaborated form in the monographic volume. All counted, the items which appear in these tables total 1,024. For example, for the supine spontaneous situation there are 69 items; for the dangling ring, 49 items; for the bell, 78 items; for the ring and string, 37 items.

The nature of these items is illustrated by a few samples from the bell situation, samples which correspond in part to the specimen dictated record which has just been placed before the reader.

Item	Percentage Frequency at 24 Weeks	Percentage Frequency at 48 Weeks
Regards bell....................................	100	100
Regards consistently............................	77	100
Approaches with one hand......................	62	93
Grasps promptly................................	69	97
Grasps with right hand only....................	45	59
Holds with both hands..........................	35	7
Pokes clapper..................................	7	65
Pulls clapper...................................	0	10
Brings bell to platform.........................	3	24
Waves or rings bell only after demonstration.......	10	15
Waves or rings both before and after demonstration.	0	73
Vocalizes.......................................	14	24

From the foregoing summary it is apparent that the basic data of the normative survey consist of typewritten reports of the behavior as dictated by the examiners while the behavior was actually in progress. A complete, true organic picture of the reactions of the infant to any situation can be secured only by a detailed narrative report of the entire course of the behavior or by a cinematographic rendering which virtually reproduces the behavior in its original integrity. For the age levels from 4 to 16 weeks, the associated cinema records were extensively used to identify and to define the patterns and phases of response. At all ages both preliminary and concurrent study of the cinema records served to direct observations and to refine subsequent analysis. Because of the close association of the cinema records and the normative research, a summary statement may now be made concerning the relation of cinematography to the analysis of behavior patterns.

§6. CINEMATOGRAPHY AND THE ANALYSIS OF BEHAVIOR PATTERNS

The wealth and complexity of infant behavior are beyond human description. But this behavior by reason of its very manifoldness calls for systematic charting. With the powerful aid of cinematography, such charting comes within the range of possibility, particularly if the cinema records are supplemented by other forms of investigation and inventory.

The cinema registers completely and impartially; it sees everything with instantaneous vision; and it remembers infallibly. It preserves in correlated combination the movements of members and of the whole. It registers in their simultaneous totality the attitudes of head, trunk, arms, legs, eyes, fingers, and face. It crystallizes any given moment of behavior in its full synthesis and permits us to study this moment as a frozen section of behavior pattern. By multiplying the moments, the cinema reconstitutes the entire reaction event and permits us to study a whole episode of behavior manifestations.

But in the service of genetic research the cinema can do still more. It can chronicle succeeding days, months, or years and bring them into seriation. Thus the cinema makes available for study (*a*) the behavior moment; (*b*) the behavior episode; and (*c*) the developmental epoch. When the cinema records are subjected to minute analysis, they open deep vistas in the detailed mechanics of behavior. When the cinema records are viewed in broader perspective, they reveal configured trends and sequences in the ontogenetic cycle. Growth thus becomes a complicated form of motion which may be studied in terms of time and space.

An analytic interest in the study of motion is not peculiar to recent science. The artist has always had a keen perceptiveness for significant phases of motion in bodily action and posturing. Painter and sculptor try to catch the most salient attitude. The engineer or scientist may be interested in the entire sequence of attitudes. Gilbreth invented the magster as a device for picturing the dynamic elements at the basis of various forms of skill.

A chronophotograph is a record of a moving object taken for the purpose of exhibiting successive phases of motion. In the modern cinema seriated chronophotographs are represented by the individual photographic frames of the flexible film. In the 16 mm. cinema, these frames number 40 per foot; a foot is durationally equal to 2.5 seconds. In the 35 mm. film, these individual frames number 16 per foot; a foot is durationally equal to 1.0 second. Each individual frame of the cinema film registers a discrete phase of a behavior event.

The films of the Yale Clinic of Child Development have been assembled into a photographic research library. The contents of the films have been catalogued by library methods and can be consulted by chapter and verse. These films have formed the basis for various publications listed in the subjoined bibliography, including *An Atlas of Infant Behavior: A systematic delineation of the forms and early growth of human behavior patterns*, illustrated by 3,200 action photographs. This *Atlas*, in conjunction with the present volume, can be made to serve as a source book for the minute study of the genetic patterning and the mechanisms of infant behavior.

Volume One of the *Atlas* (Normative Series) may be consulted for detailed photographic delineations of the behavior of infants in the 24 normative situations which are discussed in Chap. III of the present volume. Time values and accompanying text reconstruct the behavior patterns in dynamic sequence. These pictorial delineations provide typical specimens of behavior for objective study.

Volume Two of the *Atlas* (Naturalistic Series) portrays the behavior of normal infants in the situations of domestic life: feeding, bath, play, sleep, parent-infant relations, and social reactions to other children and to adults.

The normative volume of the *Atlas* is based entirely on the 16 mm. cinema records mentioned in Item 9 of the normative protocols. The selection of these photographs was a long process of sifting, accomplished by means of movieolas and other projection devices operated by motor and by hand. The projection desk chiefly used in the analysis of the 16 mm. films throws a succession of small images on a viewing glass. By turning a crank the images may be viewed in full or slowed motion, forward or reverse. By arresting the crank, any frame may be studied as a stilled pattern phase and the whole record may be subjected to frame-by-frame dissection.

Cinema analysis, therefore, is an objective method of behavior research which was made possible only by the invention of the flexible film and other modern photographic techniques. Cinema analysis is a form of biopsy which requires no removal of body tissue from the living subject. Yet it makes possible a study of the structuralization of the child's living behavior. It permits us to bring this behavior without any deterioration into the laboratory for searching dissection. This dissection is equivalent to a microscopic examination of the histology and the function of an organ *in vitro*. Anyone clinically or scientifically interested in the genetic problems of infancy may study records of behavior pattern with

FIG. 1.—Cinema analysis.

the same minute interest in structured form which the disciplines of embryology and anatomy demand.

The following publications deal with photographic research methods and with investigations made by means of cinema records and related studies. Subject matter which concerns the behavior

situations discussed in Chap. III of the present volume is indicated
by reference in parentheses to the appropriate section.

CASTNER, B. M.: The development of fine prehension in infancy, *Genetic Psychology Mono-graphs*, vol. 12, no. 2, pp. 105–193, 1932. (*Cf.* Sec. 26, *Pellet Behavior.*)

GESELL, A.: *The Mental Growth of the Preschool Child*, Chap. XII, New York: Macmillan, 1925. 447 pp.

————: *Infancy and Human Growth*, Chap. III, New York: Macmillan, 1928. 418 pp.

————: The developmental morphology of infant behavior pattern, *Proceedings of The National Academy of Sciences*, vol. 18, no. 2, pp. 139–143, 1932.

————: *An Atlas of Infant Behavior: A systematic delineation of the forms and early growth of human behavior patterns*, illustrated by 3,200 action photographs, in two volumes. Vol. I: *Normative Series* (in collaboration with Helen Thompson and Catherine Strunk Amatruda), pp. 1–524; vol. II: *Naturalistic Series* (in collaboration with Alice V. Keliher, Frances L. Ilg, and Jessie Jervis Carlson); pp. 525–922. New Haven: Yale University Press, 1934.

GESELL, A., and THOMPSON, H.: Learning and growth in identical infant twins. An experimental study by the method of co-twin control, *Genetic Psychology Monographs*, vol. 6, no. 1, pp. 1–123, 1929. (*Cf.* Sects. 19, *Cube Behavior*, and 13, *Stair Climbing Behavior.*)

HALVERSON, H. M.: An experimental study of prehension in infants by means of systematic cinema records, *Genetic Psychology Monographs*, vol. 10, nos. 2, 3, pp. 107–286, 1931. (*Cf.* Sect. 19, Cube Behavior.)

————: A further study of grasping, *Journal of Genetic Psychology*, vol. 71, pp. 34–64, 1932.

————: The acquisition of skill in infancy, *Journal of Genetic Psychology*, vol. 73, pp. 3–48, 1933. (*Cf.* Sect. 26, *Pellet Behavior.*)

McGINNIS, JOHN M.: Eye movements and optic nystagmus in early infancy, *Genetic Psychology Monographs*, vol. 8, no. 4, pp. 321–430, 1930. (*Cf.* Sect. 16, Visual Regard.)

RICHARDSON, HELEN M.: The growth of adaptive behavior in infants: An experimental study at seven age levels, *Genetic Psychology Monographs*, vol. 12, nos. 3, 4, pp. 195–360, 1932. (*Cf.* Sect. 29, *Ring and String Behavior.*)

CHAPTER TWO

THE NORMATIVE OBSERVATIONS

Arrangements and Procedures for Conducting the Investigation

§7. THE BEHAVIOR SITUATIONS

THE preceding chapter has outlined the general plan of the investigation and the underlying concepts which determined the fields of observation and the treatment of the data. It remains to characterize in a general way the behavior situations and the examination materials. The specific discussions of these situations and materials will appear in separate sections of the following chapter but, for perspective, the total array of behavior situations should have an introductory review.

Twenty-four major behavior situations were included in the normative survey. Roughly classified into three groups these situations are listed below approximately in the order in which they will be treated in the main sections of the present volume:

A. Posture and Locomotion (Normative Crib Situations):
    1. Supine behavior (4 to 40 weeks).
    2. Prone behavior (4 to 56 weeks).
    3. Stair climbing (40 to 56 weeks).
    4. Sitting (4 to 52 weeks).
    5. Standing and walking (4 to 56 weeks).
B. Early Perception and Prehension (Supine Situations):
    6. Dangling ring (4 to 28 weeks).
    7. Rattle (4 to 28 weeks).
C. Perceptual, Prehensory, and Adaptive Behavior (Sitting Situations):
    8. Table top (12–56 weeks).
    9. Consecutive Cubes (12 to 56 weeks).
    10. Massed Cubes (16 to 56 weeks).
    11. Tower Building (44 to 56 weeks).
    12. Cup (12 to 36 weeks).
    13. Spoon (16 to 36 weeks).
    14. Cup and Spoon (32 to 56 weeks).
    15. Cup and Cubes (32 to 56 weeks).
    16. Pellet (12 to 56 weeks).
    17. Pellet and Bottle (32 to 56 weeks).
    18. Bell (16 to 56 weeks).

19. Ring and String (28 to 56 weeks).
20. Ring, String, and Bell (32 to 56 weeks).
21. Paper and Crayon (36 to 56 weeks).
22. Performance box (40 to 56 weeks).
23. Formboard (20 to 56 weeks).
24. Ball play (40 to 56 weeks).
25. Mirror (40 to 56 weeks).
D. Supplementary Behavior Fields (Data secured by incidental observation or parental report):
26. Vocalizations (4 to 56 weeks).
27. Social and domestic behavior (4 to 56 weeks).
28. Play opportunities (4 to 56 weeks).
29. Feeding habits (4 to 56 weeks).
30. Toilet habits (4 to 56 weeks).

FIG. 2.—Home examination table.

For each of the foregoing situations a table of normative behavior items is assembled in Chap. III. Including the supplementary subdivision *D*, a total of 1,108 items are listed.

The physical arrangements for the normative examinations were kept essentially similar for all of the age groups. Most of the infants four and six weeks old, and a few 8 weeks-old children, were examined in their homes on a portable canvas table (20 by 33 in.). The portability of this table made it possible to establish relatively uniform conditions for the observations of the infant who was at these ages predominantly in the supine position.

At 8 weeks of age and at all the subsequent age levels the infants were brought to the clinic for their examination and for the cinema record. These examinations were conducted in the photographic dome or in a small examining room (approximately 8 by 12 ft.) similarly equipped.

The photographic dome has been described in more detail elsewhere.* It is pictured in the accompanying illustration. Al-

Fig. 3.—The photographic dome.

though the dome was primarily designed for systematic cinema recording of behavior, it proved very well adapted for the conduct of the normative examinations. The bare and almost unconfigured walls of the dome and the marked dispersion of the illumination which, filtered through glass and tissue paper screens, served to reduce the distractions of the physical surroundings to a minimum. The warmth and soft brightness of the interior made the dome congenial to the infant when his clothes were removed. All the infants were examined in the nude (or with band and diaper) to

* GESELL, A., *Infancy and Human Growth*, New York: Macmillan, 1928.

give ample scope for their movements and to make more complete
the photographic record of their behavior.

The dome was encased in 16-mesh white painted wire screening
with one-way vision properties. This screen not only provided
ample ventilation for the interior but segregated from the infant
the observers and stenographer stationed in the darkened exterior
of the dome. In the great majority of instances the mother also
took her station behind the one-way vision barrier where she was
completely concealed from the child's view but could intimately

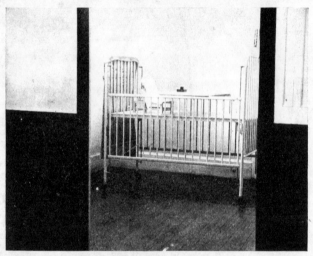

Fig. 4.—Normative observation crib with one-way-vision screen panels.

watch his behavior. To the mother the infant was visible; to him,
she was invisible. This one-way vision control served effectively
to keep the social distractibility of the surroundings to a minimum.

Similar control was attained in the normative examination
room, which was also illuminated with a soft, diffused light,
filtered through tissue paper. The walls were bare and of light
neutral tint. One wall consisted of a series of one-way-vision screen
panels behind which the mother and recorder took positions.

The physical and social arrangements served to direct the
infant's attention toward the immediate environs of the crib and of
the table top and to make the observations from child to child and
from age to age highly comparable.

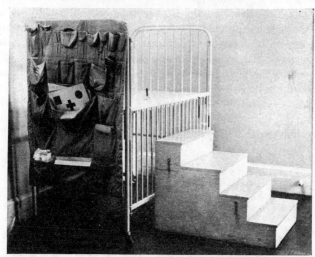

Fig. 5.—Normative observation crib with staircase and container bag for test materials.

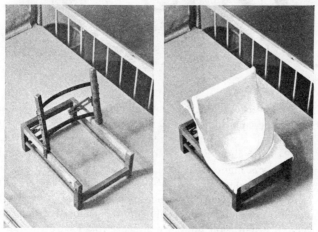

Fig. 6.—Examination chair, showing removable canvas covering.

The clinical crib and its accessories need but brief description here. They are depicted in the accompanying illustrations, and detailed specifications may be found in the monographic volume. The crib was of a modified domestic type equipped with a solid platform raised 30 inches from the floor level—that is to say, the adult's floor level; for the crib platform itself was the infant's floor level. On it he lay prone or supine, crept, stood, or sat. If he needed mechanical support he was placed in an adjustable chair of the morris type with removable (and washable) canvas covering and canvas belt. The wooden platform was softened and kept

Fig. 7.—Developmental test materials.

sanitary by an absorbent gray blotter and cotton or cellulose pad. For the youngest infants up to 12 weeks of age a resilient mattress with deep cellulose padding covered with canvas was provided.

From 24 through 56 weeks of age a large part of the normative examination was made with the infant seated in front of a table top which rested on the adjustable side panels of the crib. This table top became the working surface upon which the infant wrought his behavioral exploits. The table top was painted a light gray, with several orientation lines which served to locate the lanes of activity and the standard median position where most of the stimulus objects were first placed (see Fig. 8). The near median position is located at a point midway between the standard median position (s.m.p.) and the near edge of the table top (see Fig. 9).

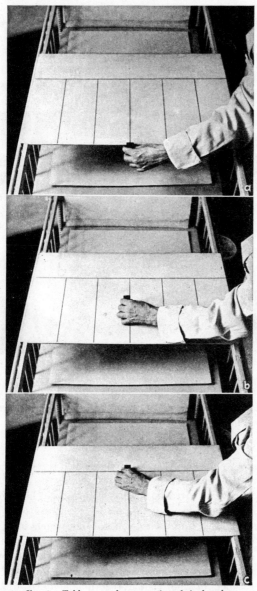

FIG. 8.—Table top and presentation of single cube.

The standard maneuver by which the examiner placed the objects on the table top will be presently described. Prevailingly the examiner took an inconspicuous position near the head end of the crib, which carried the container bag with the pockets from which the examination materials were withdrawn. Before, during, and after the presentation of each object, the examiner dictated his

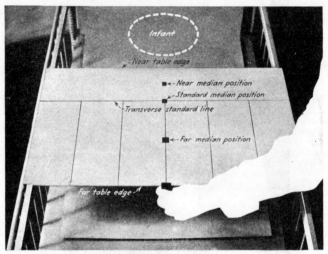

Fig. 9.—Location points of examination table.

observations in an impersonal, subdued, narrative recital, keeping a cordial but not effusive working relationship with the infant.

§8. STIMULUS FACTORS AND STIMULUS VALUES

It remains to characterize in a general way the stimulus values of the normative examination as a whole. And here we enter at once upon hazardous ground, for it is easy to lose the solid footing of description in a precarious pursuit of interpretation. The very term *stimulus values* implies interpretations which in a scientific sense may often be gratuitous and beyond demonstration.

Great is the gulf between infant and adult. It is impossible for us to reconstruct in psychological detail the perceptual and the emotional essence of the visible reactions evoked by stimulus objects. Stimulus, response, receptivity, reaction, perception, all are difficult concepts to apply in characterizing any given behavior event. Even the classic formula of stimulus-response does not solve our problems nor should it prescribe our theories. Receptivity is a tenuous abstraction apart from the effector mechanisms and from the total reaction of the organism. Receptivity must almost be identified with reactivity. Anticipatoriness, which is such an important aspect of stimulus "values," is most fundamentally a motor or effector phenomenon. The stimulus value of any object proves to be highly contingent upon the total current and acquired reaction trends of the particular organism, which here means a unique, individual infant. The stimulus values, accordingly, are products of adult analysis; they reside not so much in the objects as in the make-up and predispositions of the reacting subject. This is doubly true when the reacting subject is also a rapidly growing one. For this reason it is safer to use the vaguer term *stimulus factor* in preference to the term stimulus value. Having made our reservations, we shall use both terms somewhat interchangeably. The visible behavior patterns are the objective data which alone can be described with full security. Nevertheless, the genetic changes in these patterns can be better appreciated if we attempt to relate them to the physical and personal properties of the external environment in which the behavior forms itself.

In summary, the major external stimulus factors of the normative examination included the following: (*a*) the clinical crib with its impinging platform and accessible side rails and panels; (*b*) the table top with its succession of test objects; (*c*) the surrounding, relatively unconfigured, diffusely illuminated walls of the room; (*d*) the audible dictation of the examiner's report; (*e*) the variable physical presence of the examiner. On occasion the examiner came into full view and established brief social contact with the infant, but most of the time the examiner was only in marginal or partial view. The examiner's providing hand with which he presented the enticing test object and the examiner's invading hand with which he took away the object—these were typically the most recurring incidents in the total stimulus situation.

In appraising the stimulus significance of any object or environment, it is always necessary to take full account of the developmental naivete of the infant. What to the adult is a matter of course may be for the infant, quite naturally, a thrilling novelty. The very platform on which he lies, the chair on which he sits for the first time, the table top which he pounds, have to him values which we can scarcely envisage, because even on a purely perceptual level such experiences are by us taken so completely for granted. They have sunk into secondary, automatic levels.

Likewise with the physical and geometric properties of common objects such as those which figure in the normative examination materials. Because these objects are far from familiar to the infant, we shall make a simple analysis of their stimulus characteristics in the following chapter to remind ourselves how these characteristics may operate in the reactions of the infant. It has already been noted that the objects are simple and homely rather than technical. But analysis will show that these unpretentious articles embody a very inclusive range of physical, topographic, and geometric properties—basic properties in the child's material environment. Many shapes, sizes, weights, and consistencies are represented in the total battery of materials. Sizes range from the tiny pellet 7 mm. in diameter to the formidable performance box approximately 20 by 20 by 40 cm.

This box is so large from the infant's point of view that it frequently tempts him to stand upright when it is placed before him on the table top. He seizes the upper edge of the box to pull himself to the erect position. From our oversophisticated notion of the performance box, we were of the opinion that the three holes for rod insertion were its chief attribute as a test object, but the infant has called our attention to other stimulus values. In fact an adequate account of the stimulus significance of any one of the objects among the normative materials could only be constructed through a study of the child's reaction under stated conditions and at varying ages. Our very familiarity with the simple objects which are used for the developmental examination makes it necessary for us deliberately to point out their physical construction and their potential perceptual properties. For the infant an object may have progressive novelty, that is, a novelty which does not weaken but which continues because each lunar month in the first year of life bestows increasing capacities of response.

Textures as well as sizes have a wide range in the examination materials. Textures range from the hard unyielding surface of the table top to the pliancy of the string and the paper. Auditory values are produced by the resounding of the table top to the impact of the child's hand, or to the object in his grasp. The rattle, bell, performance box, paper, cup, and spoon, also resound each in its distinctive way to his manipulations and percussions.

The examination objects were usually presented singly in order to circumscribe the area of the behavior response. But the objects were also presented in close consecutiveness as in the three cubes, or in combination as in the massed cubes, or simultaneously as in the side by side presentation of the pellet and bottle. These simple variations in numerical and spatial relationships introduce a large variety of permutations in the stimulus possibilities of the test situation.

A wide diversity of forms is represented in the linearity of the string, the right angularity of the edges of the cubes, the sphericity of the ball, the circularity of the ring, etc. The important geometric relationship of container and contained is embodied in the cup and cube situation, in the pellet and bottle, in the block insertion of the formboard, and in the rod insertion of the performance box. Elementary principles of the lever and of tool utilization are incorporated in the small hand bell with its pendant clapper, in the crayon and paper, and other situations.

To the naive observer these simple objects take on the guise of playthings or toys, and much of the infant's activity may indeed be called play activity. But play is the infant's work, and only studious analysis of the patterns of his motor response can reveal the psychological import of the things which he manipulates in this work of his. The infant addresses himself to these simple objects seriously. We must take them seriously, too, if we are to learn their significance in his developmental psychology. They are not "mere" toys. They are touchstones which disclose his perceptual and exploitive capacities. Although his responses show similarities from age to age, close analysis of his behavior patterns discloses subtle adaptations to the distinctive qualities of these objects. These distinctive adaptations are a clue to his advancing maturity. He is eager and tireless in his exploitations of the objects. Though ruses are sometimes necessary to detach him from what he holds in hand, he takes versatile satisfaction in the variety of the objects. He may play or work with them a full hour without ennui. This certifies to the "stimulus values" of the normative observation materials. It was not necessary to resort to artificial procedures in order to "motivate" the infant and to make the materials enticing. They carried their own enticement, which is an extroverted way of saying that the infant has an ingrained propensity to exploit his physical environment.

§9. GENERAL OBSERVATION PROCEDURES

As a preface to the account of the individual behavior situations it will be advisable to formulate a broad statement concerning the general procedures of the normative observations as a whole. As already stated in the previous chapter, the investigation was undertaken from an experimental, exploring standpoint. A consistent effort was made to keep the situations on a systematic, standardized basis so that the resultant data might yield to comparative treatment. The individual behavior situations were not set up as a series of psychometric tasks. They were instituted to release evidences of developmental changes in behavior pattern.

The behavior situations were reasonably controlled, but they were not rigidly confined to a restricted field of reaction. The total tide of behavior was brought within the scope of observation. To this extent the procedure was naturalistic in method, although the observer's attention was necessarily focalized on selected features of behavior. And toward this end the examiner supplied a running dictation to keep abreast of all the behavior as it occurred. For example, if the infant averted his gaze to the surroundings or to his feet and hands, it was reported. If the child turned away from the test object to explore the rear of the crib or to manipulate the side panels, or to erect himself to a standing position, these reactions were not only tolerated but were fully recognized in the dictated report as the natural expressions of the child's true behavior equipment.

This method of reporting the observations overcomes the disadvantages of preconceived emphasis. The dictated reports of behavior were kept on a plane of neutral impartiality. Although certain preconceptions undoubtedly led to false emphasis, this method of report protected the potential claims of those data which could prove their importance only after exhaustive analysis of the records.

We adopted the attitude that all behavior manifested was potentially significant from the standpoint of genetic interpretation. Had we delimited the observation situations too strictly by experimental definition, or had we relied too much upon psychometric concepts of success and failure, we would have prejudiced the observations from the very start and would have missed the unforeseen developmental data.

To a very limited extent did the audible dictation prove to be a distracting factor, because the infant, having made an adjustment of general confidence, readily accepted the examiner's vocalizations as a natural part of the total situation. Indeed at all ages the examiner's voice tended to operate as a socializing factor which gave reassurance and continuity to the whole period of observations.

The experimental control of the behavior situations was not pushed to an artificial extreme which might endanger the emotional reactions of the infant. Every effort was made to secure optimal emotional conditions in both infant and parent; this was done on the assumption that the systematic and experimental value of the data would be enhanced by a protection of all factors which made for favorable personality adjustment. That we succeeded in realizing this ideal to a marked degree is shown by the excellent and almost uniform cooperation received from the parents and by the sustained output of creditable performance on the part of the infants.

Vigorous and rebellious crying occurred in a very small proportion of the infants observed. In some of these cases, interestingly enough, the emotional pattern was such that the normative examinations were nevertheless carried through successfully on a piecemeal basis. Such an infant "worked" satisfactorily for a short period, fretted, was soon appeased, and then "worked" again for a short period. That the normative situations made an almost universal appeal to the infants is proved with overwhelming statistical evidence by the records. The number of instances of complete resistance, either active or passive, was amazingly small. Occasionally it was amusing to see how an infant exploited the test materials with unabated effectiveness while he was still in the throes of a temporary emotional disturbance.

Fretting and fussing were noted and recorded even when the manifestations were extremely mild and fleeting. At every age level there were from 17 to 41 per cent of the infants who showed no fussing whatsoever. And in the great majority of the remaining infants the fussing was transient.

The adequacy of the infant's behavioral attitude and of the observational conditions is best reflected in the great rarity of instances in which the normative examination had to be postponed or abandoned. In a total of 524 visits there were only 12 instances

in which the infants were returned to the clinic on the second day
to complete the examination, and then the consideration sometimes was one of practicability rather than necessity.

Preventive precautions were taken to secure satisfactory adjustment at the clinic. In the preliminary home visit the baby's daily
schedule had been determined. The appointment at the clinic and
the examination at home were planned to fit into this schedule.
Accordingly, from 85 per cent to 95 per cent of the infants from
12 to 44 weeks of age were seen in the afternoon. At 4 and 6 weeks
of age from 89 to 97 per cent of the infants were observed in the
morning. From one-fourth to one-third of the infants from 48 to
56 weeks of age were also seen in the morning. From one-half to
three-fourths of the infants of all age levels were fed at the clinic
prior to the normative examinations. Frequently the infants were
also placed in the crib for a period of rest or sleep. These arrangements served to promote a favorable initial adjustment to the
total situation.

Care was also taken to reassure the confidence of the mother
and to encourage her interest. The general aim of the whole investigation was explained to her and she was freely invited to observe
the examination. Usually her observation station was behind a
one-way-vision screen which offered full visibility but concealed
her completely from the infant. If the child was highly dependent
upon the mother, the mother was permitted to take an inconspicuous position near the head of the examining crib outside of
the direct vision of the infant. In any event it was the mother who
undressed the child and wrapped the blanket around him and
carried him to the examining crib where, under the direction of the
examiner, she placed the infant on the platform or in the examining
chair. The mother was therefore closely associated with the examination without actively participating during the period of more
formal observation. The examiner's dictation served to establish a
measure of detachment on the part of the mother during the
examination.

At the 4 and 6 weeks age levels the normative examinations
were made in the home out of deference both to the mother and to
the infant. Except in hot weather the examination was usually
made in the kitchen, which had been previously warmed for the
occasion. It may be said at this point that the locus of the normative
examination, whether at home, in examining room, or in photographic dome, had only a minor effect upon the flow of behavior.

At 8 weeks of age, however, it was observed that the infants just recently fed tended to bask so contentedly in the diffuse light of the dome that this possibly had a depressor effect upon the degree of activity. At all later ages, the conditions of the dome examination tended to operate in a stimulating direction. Although the cameras were well concealed and silenced, there were a few children at the more advanced age levels who showed marked sensitivity to sounds.

The special arrangements for the home examination may be briefly summarized. The examiner brought a portable examining table pictured in Fig. 2. This examining table was approximately 20 inches wide and 33 inches long. If the baby was awake, he was placed in the supine position on the canvas examining table and his clothes were gently removed, with a possible exception of the abdominal band. Here, as at the clinic, the mother usually undressed the infant. If the baby was asleep, he was permitted to sleep unless he was in any event routinely awakened at that time. When placed on the examining table, the infant's spontaneous behavior was first noted; the examination then proceeded in accordance with schedule.

At 8 weeks of age the infants were examined at the clinic and at this age, and at 12 weeks, the infant was placed upon a specially constructed canvas frame which lay athwart the platform of the crib and was upholstered with layers of cellulose to a thickness of about four inches. Beginning with the age of 12 weeks, and at subsequent age levels through 28 weeks, all of the infants were also placed in the chair for part of the examination. At 32 weeks 85 per cent, and at 36 weeks 46 per cent, of the infants were placed in the chair for the examination. These percentages declined to 0 at 56 weeks. It should be said, however, that in a few instances infants were placed in the examining chair not because they needed its support but because the chair helped to adjust them more satisfactorily to the table-top situations. The percentage of children who were not placed in the chair but who sat on the platform for the entire examination rose from 21 per cent at 32 weeks to 100 per cent at 56 weeks.

Whenever possible the infant was allowed to sit on the platform confronting the table top without the use of the chair. If the infant showed any signs of fatigue from sitting, or any evidence of imbalance, he was put in the examining chair for the remainder of the examination. Incidentally we should stress the importance of safeguarding the infant even after he has apparently attained the ability to sit alone without support. Two things may happen to such an infant. The child may balance himself quite competently say for twenty minutes, and then for reasons of fatigue he suddenly fails in his control and may topple over. Or he may "forget" himself and lunge either to the side or completely backwards. Such a backward lunge is obviated if the child sits near the rear of the crib. The lateral falls can be intercepted only by the vigilance of the examiner or the attendant. It is well not to presume too much on the sitting competency even of a 40 weeks-old infant.

The duration of the examination varied in general with the maturity of the infant. Individual variations arose out of differences in personality and special circumstances. Postural maturity also tended to have an effect upon the length of the examination. In general, the average length of the examination rose from a quarter of an hour at 4 weeks to approximately half an hour at 20 weeks. After 20 weeks, the examination consumed approximately three-fourths of an hour.

The course of the examination likewise varied somewhat with the age and postural capacities of the infant. At the younger age levels the examination always began with an observation of the behavior in the supine position. At 4, 6, 8, 12 and 16 weeks this was followed by the dangling ring situation which in turn was followed by the rattle, except for one group of 16 weeks-old infants in which this order of ring and rattle was reversed. The routine of the procedure is summarized in the accompanying chart. The chart also indicates the scope of each behavior situation. The order of procedure indicated was strictly adhered to except in a small number of instances, when photographic or other requirements made slight changes desirable. It should be added that the standard order of procedure was the empirical outgrowth of previous clinical experience with the method (see Fig. 10).

Slight variations in procedure also were introduced in the observations of the advanced postural reactions in infants 32 weeks of age and older. These observations occurred after removal of the table top, when the child had the freedom of the crib, and they were conducted in a more informal manner, the child being encouraged to take the lead and to assert his postural capacities.

In the table-top situations the established procedure was closely followed but not in a stilted manner. Effort was made to have the course of the examination run fluently, merging one situation into the next by smooth transitions. We attempted to

ROUTE SCHEDULE FOR NORMATIVE EXAMINATIONS

Read across to ascertain the ages at which a given situation was used.

Read down from the top of any given age column to ascertain the sequence of situations at that age.

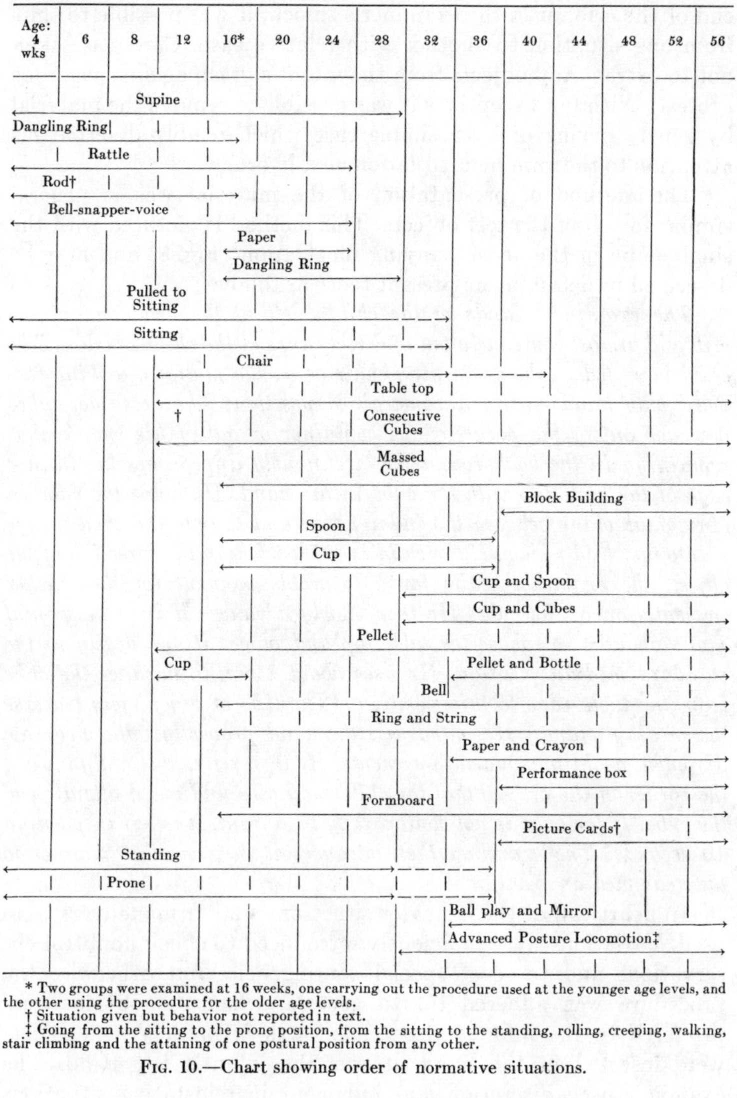

Age: 4 wks	6	8	12	16*	20	24	28	32	36	40	44	48	52	56

Supine

Dangling Ring

Rattle

Rod†

Bell-snapper-voice

Paper

Dangling Ring

Pulled to Sitting

Sitting

Chair

Table top

† Consecutive Cubes

Massed Cubes

Block Building

Spoon

Cup

Cup and Spoon

Cup and Cubes

Pellet

Cup

Pellet and Bottle

Bell

Ring and String

Paper and Crayon

Performance box

Formboard

Picture Cards†

Standing

Prone

Ball play and Mirror

Advanced Posture Locomotion‡

* Two groups were examined at 16 weeks, one carrying out the procedure used at the younger age levels, and the other using the procedure for the older age levels.

† Situation given but behavior not reported in text.

‡ Going from the sitting to the prone position, from the sitting to the standing, rolling, creeping, walking, stair climbing and the attaining of one postural position from any other.

FIG. 10.—Chart showing order of normative situations.

avoid the attitude of setting tests in sharp installments and aimed
at unity and continuity in the examination session. By keeping the
examination material readily accessible in the container bag at the
end of the crib, or in the examiner's smock, it was possible to shift
from one situation to another with relative ease. Care was taken
not to extract any objects from the infant's grasp against vigorous
protest. With few exceptions it was possible to remove the material
by gently prying or by a simple ruse which readily diverted his
attention to the imminent situation next in order.

The method of presentation of the material was in general
similar for all of the test objects. This method is pictured with the
single cube in the accompanying illustration (Fig. 8) and may be
described in detail in the present tense as follows:

*The examiner stands at the child's left at the head end of the
crib and almost completely out of direct range of the child's vision. The
child is seated in the examining chair or on the platform looking forward with hands in an unconstrained position. The examiner takes
the cube out of the pocket of the container or out of his smock and,
remaining in the background, he circuitously approaches the farther
edge of the table top with the cube in his hand. He holds the cube in
horizontal plane between the index finger and thumb and then brings
it into the child's view. If the child is not looking in the direction of the
object, the examiner waits for a favorable moment for the further
presentation of the cube. He then slowly advances it in a horizontal
plane about 2 in. above the table top and places it noiselessly in the
standard median position. He uses about 2 sec. to advance the cube
from the table edge to this position. (The tips of his fingers traverse
the median plane.) He withdraws the hand promptly with moderate
dispatch, avoiding sudden movements. He then retreats slightly toward
the corner of the crib so that the child may give undivided attention to
the cube. If the cube is not contacted by the infant, it is left in position
10 seconds. The examiner then advances it in a similar manner to
the near median position.*

In nearly all of the behavior situations similar maneuvers were
used. Variations were judiciously introduced to check doubtful observations and to meet special contingencies but otherwise the
procedure was adhered to. In general, when the objects were
proffered to the infant neither hand was favored. When objects
were inserted in the hand, it was the infant's left hand. The
examiner used discretion and judgment in reinstating situations
if the conditions were abnormally altered by fortuitous reactions.

The specific procedure for the individual behavior situations will be presented in the following chapter. The formulations will be made in the past tense and may be regarded as concise descriptions of the experimental conditions of the systematic normative observations. A more extended and technical specification of the procedures in the present tense will be found in the monographic volume.*

As a final precaution, it should again be emphatically stated that the procedures as outlined do not cover all of the technicalities and safeguards which were instituted in the conduct of the study. Every care should be taken with regard to the physical safety of the infant. His manipulation of the objects and his activities in the crib must be vigilantly watched. Precautions must also be taken with respect to the cleanliness of all the observational test objects and the sanitariness of the arrangements. Behavior observations of infants should not be too freely attempted by the amateur. No diagnostic work with infants, and particularly infants of tender age, should be undertaken apart from medical auspices and medical safeguards.

* *Norms of Infant Development.*

CHAPTER THREE

NORMATIVE CHARACTERISTICS OF INFANT BEHAVIOR

Its Growth as Revealed by the Normative Survey

§10. POSTURAL BEHAVIOR IN GENERAL

POSTURE is behavior. Postural patterns are behavior patterns. To be sure, these patterns are influenced by bodily size and proportions, by joints and ligaments, and even by the abdominal viscera. But primarily they are determined by the maturity and organization of the infant's central neural equipment. The positions, the stances, the motor attitudes which he assumes are net resultants of a complicated system of reflexes and reaction trends which vary from age to age. Posture is not the manifestation of a discrete set of abilities which increase "as the child grows stronger."

It is quite unwarranted to relegate posture to a secondary status in the psychology of the infant. It is sounder, at least from a genetic standpoint, to interpret postural behavior by the same principles which we apply to so-called higher orders of behavior. The adaptive aspects of postural adjustments should be recognized and conversely the effect of postural control on adaptive behavior, even on insight, should not be overlooked.

There is more danger in using the category of posture too narrowly than too broadly. For purposes of discussion the term will be made to refer chiefly to translocations of the entire body and changes in the orientation of the body or its members. But since the body participates as a whole in most of the reactions of the infant, we may look for mechanisms of posture in his subtle as well as gross activities. In a sense there is a postural aspect, overt or concealed, in all of his behavior. Theoretically also the concept of posture may be extended to parts of the body as well as the total physique. We may speak of leg posture, of head posture, digital posture, and even of ocular posture. In the early development of eye-hand functions, and particularly in prehensory approach, postural factors are of great importance.

It is impossible to separate the mechanisms of prehension completely from those of posture. It is equally impossible to separate posture from locomotion, for locomotion is an alternating, repetitive series of postures. Adequately coordinated, the seriation results in pivoting or in propulsion, forward, backward, sideward, or upward. A more limited coordination results in "mere" postural activity, like bouncing, wriggling, kicking, head rolling, etc. When the postural reactions are discriminatingly directed to the solution of a problem or the overcoming of an obstacle, postural activity blends into adaptive behavior.

So much for the pervasiveness of postural behavior. When next we inquire, Whence comes all this postural behavior? we raise important theoretical issues concerning the whole subject of stimulus factors.

At the outset a simple distinction, though by implication a difficult one, should be made between postural energy and postural ability. Postural activity entails many calories. The debilitated infant, therefore, husbands energy by reducing his postural activity. Likewise timidity, so often associated with debility, depresses postural behavior. Such reduction of activity should not be confused with intrinsic retardation or inferiority of postural abilities. The abilities depend more on developmental organization than on energy availability.

In the healthy child postural reactiveness is largely determined by his developmental maturity. The intensity of his bodily activity, as well as its pattern, is a function of the ripeness of his postural equipment. At critical stages of nascency his postural propensities are well-nigh irrepressible. He seems to be under an urge to assume new attitudes, to lift his head, to sit up, or to propel himself forward. He combats the confinements of space and gravity. Surely the primary stimulus factor here arises intrinsically from the process of growth itself.

Consequently the infant will often appear to engage in postural activity for its own sake. He may be comfortably seated in front of the table top of the crib and suddenly pivot about or rise to his feet as though under an obtruding impulse which will not be denied. Likewise his creeping and early walking often are quite unpremeditated. He simply goes somewhere, but apparently with no objective other than locomotion itself.

Yet it is surprising how soon and how perseveringly he will use his immature postural abilities in an instrumental way, or combine them with some other ability. Even during the act of pulling himself up in the play pen he will reach through the palings to grasp at the same time a toy which interests him. Thus he combines a matured with a maturing pattern of behavior. He will hold and carry a toy even when he can scarcely maintain his balance. When creeping he will support himself on all threes while he uses his fourth extremity to drag or manipulate an object. These simple observations have more than trivial import. They show that the infant is manifesting neither a highly generalized instinct nor a highly specific one. In posture as elsewhere he is bringing varied forms of behavior into functional relationship to serve his developmental needs.

Postural behavior therefore presents an almost paradoxical mixture of certainty and of contingency. Nothing is normally more certain than the prediction that the newborn infant will some day assume an erect posture and walk; but there are impressive individual differences with respect to the time schedule and the style schedule which he will follow as he "learns" to walk like a man.

These individual differences raise further, complicated questions concerning stimulus factors. Some children have great native caution, others have equally great abandon. These personality differences influence postural behavior. Some children have been much restrained by the restriction of clothes, by severe falls, or by parental interference. Other individual differences may have a physiological or specific hereditary basis. The effect of rickets and other nutritional conditions on motor activity is well known. The tonicity of the muscular system influences postural patterns. If infants are roughly divided into two bipolar groups, those who are definitely of an extensor type prove to make a better showing on the posture development schedules. There can be no doubt that constitutional traits express themselves in infancy in differences in motility, notably in the sphere of posture and locomotion.

Many other factors could be listed to show how the trends of postural development are inflected by associated circumstances. So ubiquitous are all these factors, both remote and immediate, that they could not be brought under complete control in the normative investigation. Nevertheless, a systematic effort was made to secure inclusive data on postural behavior at each of the age levels from 4 through 56 weeks. Postural situations were instituted well in advance of the ages where full performance was expected. Care of course was taken not to prolong novel postures and to postpone certain observations to the end of the examination. All observations were reported chiefly in positive, descriptive terms in order to establish the developmental forerunners and components of the more mature behavior.

In principle no distinction was made between postural situations and "nonpostural" situations. Similar pains were taken to observe adopted procedures. As an experimental test, placing a child in the prone position to elicit his postural reactions has as much status as placing a cube before him to evoke visual attention and prehension. It was found that exactness of procedure and adequate rapport with the child were no less important in the postural situations than in the more refined behavior situations. Even slight changes in the way in which a child was held and handled, or oriented to a new position, introduced changes of motor set which influenced the postural response. When a child is lifted, he tends increasingly with age to assume a rather labile state of multiple readiness, so that he can promptly adjust to any position in which he may be placed. This makes room for many variables. Apparently innocent environmental factors prove to have considerable power. Accordingly it was found that the method of administering lures to induce posture, needs careful attention from the examiner. The lure was most effective when placed just outside of the child's reach. Ruses must sometimes be used to increase the enticement of the lure, which proves that the stimulus factors are not in fixed equilibrium but are subject to inflection. For example, if the examiner wishes to induce rolling from supine to prone he should hold the lure at an optimum level and position. If the lure is so placed that the child reaches sideward for it, the attitude of the arm nearest the lure may physically interfere with rolling, whereas if the lure is moved further headward this difficulty is removed. Weariness, contentment, and general maturity may also affect the response. When the child is ready to creep he is more ready to adopt a prone position. Sometimes an added social stimulus will be a deciding factor, and an immobile child will then creep or toddle toward the receiving hands of his mother at the end of the crib.

When one attempts to recapitulate all of the stimulus factors which may enter into the production of postural behavior, the list becomes formidable. These factors, external and internal, include fatigue, nutrition, antecedent experiences, vitamins, term of gestation, constitutional trends and specific hereditary determiners, emotional characteristics, the distance of the lure, the pressure of the assisting hands of the examiner, the texture and hardness of the mattress in the younger infant, the pull of gravity, the visual goals, the inner urges, motivational excitants, and other factors too numerous to catalogue. In spite of all these variables, consistent and lawful trends asserted themselves in the normative data. These trends will be considered in detail in connection with individual situations. It is noteworthy that developmental trends did become so evident. It means that the general course and sequence of postural behavior are after all governed by intrinsic growth factors. The contingencies are limited by certainties. The ontogenetic certainties are assured by maturation and are expressed in developmental drive. The effectiveness and *modus operandi* of the extraneous contingencies are delimited by the attained organization of these certainties.

These maturational certainties are partly expressed in the cephalocaudad "law" of development. It has been amply demonstrated both in man and in infrahuman vertebrates that the course of developmental organization in general proceeds in an anteroposterior direction and from proximal to distal segments. This law or principle is frequently mentioned in subsequent discussions; but we do not assume that it operates in a symmetric and uniform manner. It is a descriptive formula which reveals interesting exceptions that can be explained only in terms of less generalizing concepts. The principle of "from fundamental to accessory" has a similar status in the interpretation of infant behavior.

Postural behavior does not constitute a separate or secondary set of phenomena which can be successfully isolated for scientific study. Posture must be analyzed in relation to its contexts. And in a great number of behavior situations, posture itself contributes to the context. To the adult, postural behavior is so automatic that he easily forgets its primary and often dominating status in the life of the infant. Genetically the mechanisms of postural behavior are extremely complex. It takes time to perfect them and, above all, it takes time to weave them into complicated relations with the mechanisms for other forms of behavior. This is one reason why human infancy is so prolonged, and why a kitten walks earlier than a baby.

§11. SUPINE BEHAVIOR

(4 weeks–40 weeks)

The Situation

FIG. 11.—Supine behavior, 6 weeks and 24 weeks.

The mother or examiner placed the infant on his back upon the platform of the examining crib. In accordance with the procedure, which was uniform for most of the situations, the examiner took a place inconspicuously at the rear left corner of the crib and observed the course of the infant's spontaneous behavior for a period of three minutes. No further stimulus was supplied in this situation. A lure (rattle, tricolored rings, or bells) was used from 24 weeks on to induce pivoting and rolling to the prone position.

Stimulus Factors

When one attempts to appraise the possible stimulus factors which operate in the production of supine behavior patterns, the complexity of this whole behavior field at once becomes apparent. Superficially the spontaneous supine behavior situation appears to be the simplest in the entire developmental schedule, but analysis discloses the presence of numerous stimuli, external and internal, whose relative force changes from age to age.

The platform or mattress on which the infant lies is the basic external stimulus factor. The snug impingement of an extensive surface against his back may well afford him a positively agreeable experience at the early age levels. The 28 weeks-old infant, however, exhibits a kind of intolerance for the passive supine position and a preference for other postures.

The attitude in which an infant holds his head influences his supine posturing. The rotated sidewise position of the head is

part of the tonic neck reflex and the pressure sensations aroused
by this head attitude are an important stimulus factor for inducing
and maintaining the total postural response. When the head becomes active and seeks the mid-line position more frequently,
the tonic neck reflex tends concomitantly to dissolve. These correlations suggest that the stimulus importance of the proprioceptors changes with the maturity of the infant. As his head and
eyes gain in mobility, visual factors influence his behavior more
powerfully. For this reason he also becomes more sensitive to
lures, which wield an increasing effect upon his postural attitudes.

In spite of all of these inflectional factors, the trends of development indicate that the patterns of movement and of attitude are
primarily determined by the maturity of the controlling neuromuscular system. Even if the environment were heavily weighted
with social and perceptual inducements, it would be impossible
to produce in the infant of 8 weeks the patterns of supine behavior
which he so readily assumes at 20 weeks.

Behavior Trends

In spite of the apparent simplicity of the supine situation, the
patterns of observed behavior are difficult to characterize in
totality. It is impossible to bring the whole child under comprehensive observation and yet his entire physique must of necessity be
accounted for in a full description of the behavior flow. This flow
is continuously affected by changes in the stimulus factors, both
internal and external, and the various subsidiary fields of activity
undergo corresponding shifts of emphasis. It is this fluctuation in
the condition of equilibrium or lack of sustained focalization which
makes the behavior seem somewhat random and elusive.

A close study of this behavior, however, shows that it is in no
sense inchoate but is integrated and systematized. Repeated
inspection of the cinema records of supine behavior convinces one
that the observed items of behavior are significantly correlated
and that even though there are shifts of emphasis the child is
reacting as a unit. Comparative study of cinema records at advancing age levels affords convincing proof that there is a systematizing
postural behavior mechanism which is organically continuous
throughout advancing age levels. To secure the most intimate
familiarity with supine behavior it is necessary to study such
cinema records repeatedly, to see the reactions of the infants

SITUATION: SUPINE (Su)

Su	Behavior items	4	6	8	12	16	20	24	28	32	36	40	44	48	52	56
1	Head predominantly rotated	100	97	93	84	20	0									
2	Head predominantly rotated to same side	72	64	79	69	33										
3	Head in mid position only momentarily	44	11	25	15	0										
4	Head maintains mid position	53	36	48	62	76	100									
5	Head predominantly in mid position	0	4	7	15	67										
6	Rotates head perceptibly	66	61	54	69	71										
7	Rotates head from one side to the other	38	32	29	38	57										
8	Lifts head	0	0	0	0	11	13	10	35	16	33	68				
9	Arms prominently in t-n-r position	100	97	93	64	30	0									
10	Face arm ex. lat. or flexed forearm vertical	56	75	71	60	—										
11	Occiput arm at occiput, shoulder, or chest	81	68	64	56	29										
12	Arms symmetrical	38	43	25	62	63										
13	Arms prominently symmetrical	19	18	21	40	63										
14	Arms ex. lat. or flexed, forearm vertical	25	32	46	35	54										
15	Arms extended laterally, or at side of trunk	38	25	25	23	34	28	40	35	22	13					
16	Arms flexed	62	46	57	56	68	57	48	35	25	8					
17	Arms predominantly flexed	0	16	40	31	59	45	44	19	9						
18	Arms flexed, hand beside·head	31	21	14	20	27	8	28	5	4	—					
19	Arms flexed, hand on chest	19	11	14	24	17	15	5	5	4						
20	Arm extended	81	89	82	64	53	57	41	55	55	46					
21	Arm predominantly extended	0	0	12	12	7	35	8	35	17	3					
22	One arm extended	59	75	64	44	25	20	10	23	48	29					
23	Arm extended vertically or laterally	25	21	32	31	34	11	28	35							
24	Arm ex. at side of body or directly footward	31	32	18	20	14	35	36	35	52	29					
25	Arms extended	44	32	32	28	31	40	35	42	16	20					
26	Arms in windmill motions	25	7	11	8	0	0	0	0	0	0					
27	Hand predominantly closed	100	100	92	72	63	31	30	21							
28	Hands predominantly closed	66	83	92	52	35										
29	Hand predominantly open	33	16	16	50	59										
30	Hands predominantly open	0	0	8	28	35	69	70	79							
31	Hand at mouth	41	21	29	24	38	15	20	0	8						
32	Face hand at mouth	38	11	21	12	0										
33	Fingers or scratches body	9	18	32	40	39										
34	Hands in contact, arms flexed	16	4	11	28	47	33	14	8	0						
35	Hands active in mutual fingering	0	0	8	27	32	15	10								
36	Hands engage at distance from chest	0	0	0	0	12	20	10	5	—						
37	Grasps foot	0	0	0	0	0	8	28	35	8						
38	Pulls foot to mouth (r)	0	0	0	0	4	10	24	31	44	8					
39	Leg predominantly flexed	90	100	93	92	81	57	68	48	5	19					
40	Legs acutely flexed at knees and hips	32	29	32	29	46	48	36	35	26	17					
41	Legs flexed, heels on platform	81	79	89	72	55	57	52	52	36	50					
42	Legs flexed, outwardly rotated	91	93	97	96	94	79	72	43	45	22					
43	Leg extends briefly	65	82	57	42	32										
44	Legs ex. on platform more than briefly	3	0	0	0	9	24	36	—	4	4					
45	Legs extended and lifted more than briefly	3	4	0	4	2	21	28	54	65	42					
46	Both legs active	69	75	71	80	96										
47	One leg independently active	35	54	64	58	24										
48	Face leg more active than occiput leg	19	36	39	19	0	0	0	0	0	0					
49	Feet engage	19	18	25	23	38	21	36	30	18	12					
50	Lifts leg from platform	72	86	82	77	70	71	84	87	86	72					
51	Leg, flexed, lifts and lowers	53	61	61	42	33										
52	Kicks	22	29	54	58	40	36	28	35	41	31					
53	Lifts head and shoulders	0	0	0	0	0	7	7	15	8	20	63				
54	Lifts head, shoulders, and feet	0	0	0	0	0	0	3	4	8	13	16				
55	Rolls or swings pelvis	35	25	57	58	32	21	7	8	8	4					
56	Pivots	7	0	0	0	29	28	21	4	17	—					
57	Arches back	3	7	0	8	8	7	17	4	—	8					
58	Bounces hips	0	0	0	0	4	0	10	4	—						
59	Progresses headward (r)	38	35	37	50	43	27	17	0	4						
60	Rolls to side	39	21	29	12	50	59	62	54	54	68					
61	Rolls to prone	0	0	0	0	0	3	17	19	29	38	42				
62	Rolls to prone or attains sit. with slight ass.	0	0	0	0	0	3	17	19	28	54	68				
63	Rolls to prone or attains sitting	0	0	0	0	0	3	17	19	28	42	58				
64	Stares vacantly	59	4	0	0	0	0	0	0	0	0	0				
65	Fixates definitely	19	88													
66	Stares at window or wall	75	52	45	44	17										
67	Regards Examiner	63	71	63	84	81	53	41	42	24	13					
68	Regards hand	0	0	15	24	5	7	7	—	—	—					
69	Facial expression attentive	22	68													

Extended laterally means at right angles to body.   (r) = report.

In all normative tables, percentages of **50** *and above are printed in* **bold face.** *Frequencies less than 50 which have indicative import are printed in italics.*

themselves, and to analyze reflectively the data provided both by photography and by direct observation.*

Since the task of verbal description is difficult, it will be necessary to describe separately the behavior patterns of different parts of the infant's body. Incidental comment will be made to remind us that these parts do not function independently but always in some dynamic and genetic relationship with all other parts. It does not follow that this dynamic relationship between varied portions of the body is equally strong at all ages and at all moments, for there is continuous shifting in the whole pattern of tensions. We shall consider in order: the head, arms, hands, trunk, and legs, stressing the growth changes in behavior patterning throughout the gamut of age levels. The synthetic correlation of the developmental data in these varied subdivisions must be left largely to the reader. It is proper enough to begin with the head, for, in general, neuromuscular organization proceeds cephalocaudally, that is, from head to foot. Moreover, the head postures at the early stages play an almost decisive role in shaping the total patterns of the infant's supine attitudes and reactions.

The Head.   There are three forms of head activity to be considered: rotation from left to right and right to left; fixation of the head in a side or mid position; lifting of the head from the platform. Head lifting was not observed in any normative infants from 4 through 12 weeks of age, but they displayed to a variable degree the other forms of head activity. At least two-thirds of the infants at all ages rotated the head perceptibly. At 8 weeks the percentage fell below two-thirds because, at that age, the infants under the conditions of the examination were more than ordinarily quiescent. The amount of head activity during the period of observation showed an increasing trend from age to age up to 16 weeks.

The degree of head turning showed a similar increase. This reaction, however, is unquestionably affected by the shape of the head as well as by the maturity of the infant. Round-headed infants rotate the head through a longer arc and also rotate it more frequently. When round-headedness was combined with extensor habitus, the amount of head activity was conspicuously increased. At all ages from 4 to 16 weeks, about one-quarter of the infants proved to be active head turners. On the other hand,

---

* A careful study of the delineations in the *Atlas of Infant Behavior* will serve to make concrete the details which are developed in the following summary.

a group of equal size showed little or no head turning. In the latter group there were marked cases of long-headedness. It did not, however, follow that the active head turners were more competent in following with eyes and head a moving object like the dangling ring. If anything the quiescent group ultimately made a better showing in ring following. These behavior contrasts between the long- and the round-heads will be developed in the discussion of the dangling ring and rattle situations in which the infant also displayed his supine behavior characteristics.

When the 4 weeks-old infant is lowered and placed on the horizontal platform, his head promptly assumes a side position which brings the chin near to the shoulder. Indeed, such a position was assumed by 100 per cent of the normative group. At 4 weeks approximately one-third of the cases seemed to have a definite preference for the right side during the period of observation, another third preferred the left side, and the remainder assumed either right or left side position with apparently equal ease and comfort. Although it is not suggested that these preferences persist throughout a full hour, or a full day, or a full week, they do assert themselves very definitely and impress their influence on the total behavior picture for considerable periods. Characteristically the 4 weeks-old infant lies prolongedly with his head fully turned to the side. He does turn it occasionally as far as the mid position, but maintains the latter position only very briefly. No 4 weeks-old infant held the head predominantly in the mid position and only a few did so at 6, 8, and 12 weeks. At 16 weeks, however, two-thirds of the children maintained a mid position of the head predominantly. This simple item is developmentally of great importance because it is correlated with numerous behavior patterns which genetically concern perception, prehension, and general postural control.

Conversely, from 84 to 100 per cent of children at 4, 6, 8, and 12 weeks of age kept the head predominantly in the side position. At 16 weeks one child in five showed this head posture; and at 20 weeks no child assumed it. In two-thirds or more of the cases through 12 weeks the head remained rotated to the same side during the period of observation. The side position of the head is seldom as marked at 12 weeks as at the earlier age levels, and the position is more accurately described as being semi-left or semi-right. This fact is itself an indication of increasing mobility of head posture. The 4 weeks-old infant not infrequently displays a degree of mobility which seems to be greater than that at 6, 8, and 12 weeks. This is a primitive form of mobility not identical with the directed head control displayed at 16 weeks. It may be said that certain behavior items at the 4 weeks level not infrequently resemble those observed at 16 weeks but they arise out of a different neuromotor basis and have a more primitive genetic significance. Even with these qualifications, there is a definite developmental trend toward facile head movements. About one-third of the infants accomplished complete or nearly complete head rotation through an arc of 180° at the age levels up to 12 weeks. At 16 weeks over half (57 per cent) rotated the head completely from one side to the other.

One item of behavior in the 16 weeks-old infant is not shared by his juniors at 4, 6, 8, and 12 weeks: namely, lifting the head. At 16 weeks 11 per cent, and at 28 weeks 35 per cent, of the infants lift the head. At 16 weeks this head lifting occurs only during social stimulation; at 28 weeks it occurs without social stimulation probably as part of the urge to sit up. At 32 weeks only 16 per cent lifted the head, but this is partly due to the fact that the infant at this age rolls to his side and pushes himself to a sitting position by his arm. Lifting the head forward increases again after this age until at 40 weeks 68 per cent of the infants lift the head and shoulders as a preliminary adjustment to sitting up without rolling over.

Arms and Hands. The transition from head to arms is a simple one because in the mechanisms of supine behavior the head, as already suggested, plays a determining role. The side position of the head so definitely seen at 4 weeks produces the tonic neck reflex—a postural reflex which involves all four extremities with most pronounced effect upon the arms. The "face" arm (namely the arm toward which the infant is facing) is in a condition to flex and extend and move about while the occiput arm is held flexed and relatively immobile close to the shoulder. Reversals occur with change of head position. If the face is turned to the right, the right arm is typically extended at right angles to the body on the platform, the left arm is flexed and the left hand is near the occiput. Variations from this classical picture are observed but the pattern is universal at 4 weeks; almost universal at 6 and 8 weeks; present in two-thirds of the children at 12 weeks; in one-third of the children at 16 weeks; and quite out of the picture at 20 weeks. These decrements are correlated with the changes in pattern of head activity which have already been described. At 6 weeks the pattern is highly stereotyped. The disappearance of the tonic neck reflex attitude at 20 weeks is correlated with the free ranging mobility of the head at this age. This does not mean that the tonic neck reflex mechanism has dropped out of the child's neurological constitution; doubtless in his versatile activity he frequently assumes for imperceptible periods the attitude corresponding to the immature tonic neck reflex, but such posturing is so transient and so lost in the multitude of other patterns that it escapes observation. It probably persists in some latent form.

Very frequently at the early age levels the tonic neck reflex attitude can be induced by the examiner through manipulation of the child's head posture and can be reversed from left to right by altering the head station. In one striking instance we elicited this postural reflex repeatedly without even touching the child. We passed the hand slowly across his field of vision. His head moved in obedience. When the hand was moved to the right, the child assumed a rightward tonic neck reflex position; when the hand was moved to the left, he assumed almost with jumping-jack precision the leftward tonic neck reflex attitude. When our hand was immobilized in the mid line to induce a mid-position fixation, the child assumed a symmetrical pronate attitude of the flexed arms as though he were under mechanical control. These phenomena were in no sense miraculous; they occurred because both the maturity level and current physiological state of the infant were peculiarly propitious.

The tonic neck reflex keeps the arms of the infant at 4, 6, 8, and 12 weeks laterally at the head and chest levels. Nearly all of the movements take place above the waist level and the arms remain in a more or less constricted sphere of activity. Up to 12 weeks the face arm is characteristically found resting on the platform; both forearms show a tendency as the child develops to move from a position in the lateral vicinity of the head to a lateral position in the vicinity of the chest, and finally, at 16 weeks, to a position which brings the hands nearer to the mid plane. From 20 weeks through 32 weeks the arms show an increasing tendency to be projected below the waist line toward the feet.

As a result of this postural trend, the hands frequently come to the mouth at 16 weeks (52 per cent). This same tendency leads to symmetrical attitudes of the arms in almost two-thirds of the children at 12 weeks and at 16 weeks. At the latter age, the arms are predominantly in symmetrical orientation. Both arms may then rest in lateral extension on the platform at right angles to the body with or without forearm flexed and directed vertically (54 per cent). It will be noted incidentally that these arm attitudes are favorable to, or preparatory to, the closing-in reaction upon a dangling object.

Prior to 4 weeks, innervation of the arm is mostly at the shoulder and the predominant activity consists of internal and external rotation. The arm is sharply flexed. At 4 weeks, the flexion is already less sharp and there is some independent movement at the elbow and a greater degree of extension at the forearm. The arms also show more abduction and supination.

At the younger age levels, a symmetrical attitude is not characteristically maintained except during periods of relaxation or sleep, when the arms at either side of the head rest semiflexed with the hands loosely closed, palms turned up. This relaxed attitude is frequently seen when the child is asleep and also just before he goes to sleep or while he is waking. Under these conditions, the head may be in the side position without inducing the tonic neck reflex attitude in the arms. The symmetrical attitude with the hands in the cephalic position is again seen with frequency at 16 weeks (29 per cent) and at 24 weeks (28 per cent). At 20 weeks the infant is characteristically active. He extends both arms upward into the air or outward in the lateral direction (40 per cent); and, in 35 per cent of the infants, the arms were predominantly in full extension. At 24 weeks the infant shows some preference for the cephalic position; he extends the arms less frequently and also brings them less frequently to the mid plane. During extension the arms are out or down at the side. The general behavior picture is more relaxed. This tendency toward symmetrical activity displays itself also in prehensory situations. The child makes a simultaneous approach upon an object and often attains it by a closing-in or corralling action.

At 28 weeks the infant is again more active; extension comes into greater prominence; the arms show a tendency to reach footward as well as upward. At 20 weeks, the hands may come occasionally to the thigh or abdomen. At 24 weeks the hands tend to touch the knee sometimes and to snatch at or scratch the foot. At 28 weeks, foot seizure is still more common because both legs and arms show increased mobility. At 32 weeks, the arms are characteristically extended down at the side. Broadly speaking it may be said that the arms are predominantly flexed prior to the 16 weeks age level and that thereafter they tend to become predominantly extended.

Associated with these changes in the posture and spontaneous activity of the arms are changes in eye-hand functions which express themselves in changes of prehensory approach and grasp. Once more the 4 weeks infant presents a pseudo-exception to the trends noted. The 4 weeks-old infant displays symmetrical arm activity in vertical windmill movements (38 per cent). These movements are rarely seen at subsequent ages except in moments of distress or of emotional disturbance and are often associated with crying. The windmill reaction characteristic of the 4 weeks infant consists of a succession of tremulous, jerky movements of both arms over the head down over the face and chest. Often the range of the occiput arm is somewhat less than that of the face arm, but the form of the pattern is similar and the movements tend to be crudely symmetrical. Even in the 4 weeks-old infant windmill movements are more pronounced during crying and fussing.

Shoulders and arms are in general innervated before the hands. From 4 through 16 weeks it is highly characteristic for one or both hands to be predominantly closed. The latter age marks a transition period, for at the next three age levels seven or eight children out of ten keep their hands predominantly open ready to grasp with increasing promptness any object which may come within their scope. The 4 weeks-old infant again presents a partial exception to the rule, for, although characteristically his hand remains fisted, it opens actively during the extensor activity of windmill movements.

In the supine situation the infant does not have much opportunity to grasp, but at 8, 12, and 16 weeks one-third or more of the infants finger or scratch their own bodies. "Pulling" at blanket or dress is frequently observed by mothers in infants 12 weeks of age. At 16 and 20 weeks the hands often become active in mutual fingering (27 and 32 per cent). At 28 and at 32 weeks, it is common for the infant to grasp his own foot (28 and 35 per cent). With each age his ability to make an extensory thrust seems to increase. His arms become more rangy so that when his hands engage in mutual fingering at 20 weeks, they are more raised from the body than at 16 weeks.

Trunk Movements. It might seem logical to pass from arm movements to a discussion of leg movements. Actually, however, the "wave" of development travels from head to toes and, for genetic reasons, it is more logical to consider next the movements of the trunk. Although the legs are active throughout the course of development, the neuromotor organization of the trunk may be regarded as primary to that of the legs.

The trunk movements are dependent upon the maturation of the central nervous system and associated changes in the axial musculature and gross topographic anatomy. At the earlier stages of development, the trunk tends to react as a whole, that is, as a barrel or cylinder. The 4 weeks-old infant has very meager innervational control of parts of the trunk. When the legs are flexed, his back becomes quite convex and when the back is thus rounded, the infant rolls because his back offers only a small supporting surface area. With activity, the center of gravity moves beyond this small contact area and the infant consequently rolls toward the side. This rolling is usually sudden and often startles the infant, sometimes into crying. Typically he rolls toward the side and, if the displacement is slight, he rolls back toward dorsal, and may oscillate again to the side. Very few infants held the side position when they attained it. These somewhat exceptional infants roll completely to the side and are with difficulty replaced in the flat supine position.

After 4 weeks, the trunk becomes more relaxed and the back is less rounded. Rolling to the side is seen with rare frequency at 6, 8, and 12 weeks. At 16 weeks and the subsequent age levels, from five to seven children out of ten roll to the side. The trunk gives increasing evidence of intrinsic mobility and differential control of parts and also increased correlations between the fore body and the hind body. At 16 weeks, the infant turns his head and shoulders to the side; the hind body follows and partially adjusts to this movement.

The infant seems to enjoy activity and, when the examiner restores him to the supine position, the infant frequently resumes the side position of his own initiative. Infants may roll either to the right or to the left; or both to the right and to the left. Rolling or swinging of the pelvis is relatively frequent at 4 and 6 weeks and occurs in more than half of the children at 8 and 12 weeks of age. Thereafter as a specific item, it undergoes decline and almost reaches the vanishing point at 36 weeks. This is partly due to the fact that rolling of the pelvis comes into dynamic relation with other modes of activity like leg extension, and this coordination results in pivoting at 16, 20, and 24 weeks; in arching of the back (17 per cent at 24 weeks); and in bouncing of the hips (10 per cent at 24 weeks).

The Legs. Flexion and outward rotation of the legs with the knees widely separated are highly characteristic of all ages from 4 to 28 weeks. Although there is a tendency toward increasing flexion with outward rotation at the hips with age, there is also a trend toward increased extension both of legs and arms from 16 weeks on. Up to that age more than brief extension of the legs on the platform was very rare. At 20 and 24 weeks somewhat prolonged leg extension (on the platform) becomes more common. At 28 and 32 weeks the legs are not only extended but lifted from the platform (54 per cent and 65 per cent). Kicking of varied patterns, bilateral, unilateral, symmetric, or alternate, occurs at all ages, but is especially prominent at 8 and 12 weeks. At 28 weeks and still more at 32 weeks, kicking is a vigorous performance. Both legs participate and are brought against the platform with considerable force.

Supine behavior patterns are not unrelated to patterns of postural behavior in associated fields. Although supine and prone behavior patterns lie at opposite poles, they must be genetically and dynamically brought into relationship. Indeed, the varied supine patterns of head, arms, trunk, and legs just summarized suggest a preliminary organization of equipment which is prerequisite for progression in the prone position. It is significant that the infant's ability to roll to the prone position does not assert itself strongly until these preparatory stages of supine behavior have been traversed. Although many of the arm and leg postures apparently serve no practical end, they seem to be developmentally essential in the same manner that fetal coordinations forerun the neonatal. When arms and legs are brought into adequate functional cooperation with trunk movements, the infant accomplishes increasingly complex postural readjustments and orientations.

At 24 weeks 62 per cent roll to the side but only 17 per cent of the infants rolled to the prone and attained a sitting position with little or no assistance. At 40 weeks, 68 per cent of the infants were able to attain the sitting position from supine without assistance. At that age either the infant rolls to the prone and pushes himself back to the sitting position or he rolls to the side and pushes himself on his arm until he sits. Pivoting was not observed at 6, 8, and 12 weeks, but occurs at every age level thereafter, most frequently at 16 weeks and at 20 weeks (29 per cent). If the legs extended when the pelvis was swung, pivoting resulted; but often the pelvis swung back to mid position before leg extension occurred and then no change in position followed. Leg activity produced headward progression in over one-third of the infants at 4, 6, and 8 weeks; in one-half at 12 weeks, and in two-fifths at 16 weeks. Thereafter such progression becomes infrequent.

Perceptual as well as locomotor changes manifest themselves in the supine situation. At 4 weeks the regard of the infant is characteristically a vacant stare. The eyes may be directed toward a window or toward a wall, but focalization of the fixation is difficult to determine. Such vacant staring was noted in 59 per cent of the 4 weeks infant, in only 4 per cent at 6 weeks, and was not noted at any subsequent age level. Contrariwise, definite fixation was noted in 19 per cent at 4 weeks but in 88 per cent at 6 weeks. Thereafter definite fixation becomes universal. Staring in the direction of a window or wall undergoes steady decrease from 75 per cent at 4 weeks to 17 per cent at 16 weeks. At 4 weeks the infant, if anything, elects to stare at surroundings in preference to the examiner. From 6 weeks through 28 weeks, however, the examiner is frequently regarded and particularly so at 12 and at 16 weeks. But at 36 weeks the examiner suffers a new kind of disregard due to the infant's preoccupation with his own activities.

The facial expression of the infant is usually impassive at 4 weeks; at 6 weeks it is more alert; at 8 weeks it is still more attentive, and smiling is very frequently observed. The perceptual equipment has so far advanced that at 8 weeks as many as 15 per cent of the infants pay shallow, fleeting regard to their own hands. At 12 weeks at least one child in four regards his hand.

The supine infant displays activity in several different members which function quasi-independently and also in correlation. However difficult to describe, none of the behavior can be characterized as truly random, although some forms of it appear to be more adaptive and teleological than others. Sometimes the activity in the supine situation seems to have an irrational aspect. At all age levels from 4 to 24 weeks, headward progression was observed in many children. This kind of propulsion would seem to have no rationale in the infant's developmental economy, but not infrequently one observes supine sliding used as a locomotor technique on the nursery floor. If the infant did not soon come into full possession of new prone patterns of behavior, it is possible that this would become a normal mode of locomotion which might even get social sanction.

At 16 weeks of age, anticipations of prone behavior declare themselves in the supine situation. Later on, sitting propensities also assert themselves. For this reason much of the activity of the infant in the supine situation wears the guise of an effort to escape from this very posture. Only at the earliest age levels does he seem to accept the position with complacence; he expresses himself at first in throaty vocalizations and later in cooing, gurgles, bubbles, and chuckles.

§12. PRONE BEHAVIOR

(4 weeks–56 weeks)

The Situation

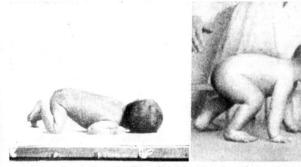

FIG. 12.—Prone behavior: 4 weeks and 52 weeks.

The examiner held the infant in ventral suspension and then slowly lowered him to the prone position, adjusting the infant's arms and, if necessary, the head in the process. The examiner then dangled a lure in front of the infant to secure visual fixation and to induce head lifting. The same lure was then moved on the platform to elicit reaching and pivoting in clockwise and counterclockwise directions.

At the older age levels, the infants were given an opportunity to reveal postural reorientation from the prone to a sitting position and from a sitting to the prone position. The lure was again used to elicit crawling or creeping behavior and to induce rolling from supine to prone position. If the infant did not lift his head at the early age levels, the examiner gently rotated the head to mid position to induce lifting.

Stimulus Factors

Stimulus factors operate in the prone position in the same complex manner that they operate in the supine situation. The embarrassment of free vision adds further complication. Prone behavior is of interest chiefly as postural and locomotor behavior. For the 4 weeks-old infant the prone situation is almost an unnatural one. Even when he is held in ventral suspension with ample support under the mid trunk, his whole physique sags and droops in a hapless manner which suggests that his neuromuscular system is far from prepared for such postural exigencies.

When the 4 weeks-old infant is placed prone on the platform the tactile stimulus factors assume importance. His weight impinges on his knees, stomach, chest, and face. Apparently it is the facial stimulus which is most effective and his chief response is rotation of the head. At later ages, when his head is lifted the tactile stimulus factors are more confined to his trunk and extremities. By the age of 12 and 16 weeks he accepts the prone position with equanimity, for he has improved command of his head posture. At subsequent ages he may take more or less active satisfaction in the bodily locomotor activity which the prone situation makes possible. Individual and even temperamental differences apparently play a role in determining the amount of satisfaction which a child takes in the prone position. Some children are consistently intolerant of the position and escape either by vigorous crying protest or by bodily struggle. Not infrequently mothers report negative behavior of this kind. Home experiences and conditioning factors may be responsible for some of these cases. Some mothers deny floor opportunity to the infant and it is possible that some of the infants who are reported not to creep may never have had full opportunity to do so.

The patterns of prone behavior are chiefly influenced by the maturity of the neuromuscular system, though some allowance must be made for emotional and personal factors. The normative data show unmistakable trends in the basic maturational processes. The gravitational center of the infant's stance shifts its position in a consistent manner which reveals the presence of potent growth laws.

Locomotion consists in a rhythmic alternation or succession of postural changes. This zigzag in attitudes leads to forward or backward propulsion. It also enables a creature to extricate itself from threatening entanglements in which it has been caught. Zigzagging push and pull is an important escape mechanism. It is foreshadowed in certain diagonal reflexes of the human fetus. It is somewhat erroneous to say that the infant is under the spell of a general locomotor drive which propels him forward, because at certain ages his behavior results in circular motion and even in retrogression. At 40 weeks of age more than one child in four in the prone position regressed rather than progressed. Effective forward locomotion depends upon an effective correlation of postural attitudes assisted by both internal and external stimulating factors. The changing postural attitudes of the prone infant are chiefly symptoms of the stage of organization of his neuromuscular system. To what extent these changes are also conditioned by topographic relationships in his skeletal system is a problem which needs further study. It is quite possible that the activities themselves have some molding, regulative effect upon these anatomical changes.

Behavior Trends

Here, as in the discussion of supine behavior, it is advisable to treat in turn four anatomical subdivisions and, following the law of developmental progression, we shall proceed from head and arms to trunk and legs. It will be difficult to keep these subdivisions separate because in prone behavior, even more obviously than in supine behavior, the organism reacts as a unit; each member adjusts in relation to another.

The Head. In ventral suspension as well as in full placement upon a horizontal surface, the head tends to assume a characteristic attitude in response to gravitation forces. One infant in five at the age of 4 weeks shows some degree of head compensation during ventral suspension. The completeness and duration of this reaction increase steadily with age. Not until the age of 16 weeks do all of the children show well-defined head compensation during ventral suspension. At the moment of placement on the horizontal platform, about half of the children at 4 weeks react with head rotation. Such head rotation was observed in only 9 per cent of the children at 16 weeks. It may be interpreted as a protective or escape response. Even under conditions of modern life it probably has some survival value in preventing imminent suffocation. When the infant is 8 weeks old, raising the head slightly is the preferred reaction; 56 per cent of infants at that age hold the head for a

SITUATION: PRONE (Pr)

Pr	Behavior items	4	6	8	12	16	20	24	28	32	36	40	44	48	52	56
1	(Ventral suspension) Head compensates....	19	69	67	80	100										
2	(Placement) Head rotates................	53	52	44	12	9										
3	(Placement) Head in mid position........	47	48	56	88	89	87	97	96	100						
4	Lifts head momentarily..................	63	75	57	25	25	19									
5	Holds head lifted sustainedly............	23	39	54	71	73	83	82	87							
6	Lifts head to Zone 1....................	88	100	89	100	100	100									
7	Lifts head to Zone 2....................	47	86	79	81	93	87	97	96	100						
8	Lifts head to Zone 3....................	3	10	14	46	54	81	97	90	100						
9	Lifts head to Zone 4....................	0	0	0	0	0	23	28	61	69	100					
10	Raises upper chest......................	3	14	36	48	68	72	86	81	96	100	100				
11	Arms flexed............................	100	100	100	100	88	83	65	67	14	10					
12	Arms flexed, close to chest..............	67	100	60	50	26	35	3								
13	Arms extended..........................	0	0	4	8	16	50	74	56	80	90					
14	Lifts hand.............................	31	16	21	8	57										
15	Lifts arm and hand.....................					8	12	26	36	21	23	20				
16	Scratches platform.....................	6	24	21	20	13	54	20	11	—	—	7				
17	Legs flexed and adducted (Kneels)........	94	82	71	15	8	0									
18	Hips raised............................	100	82	85	69	29	17									
19	Legs flexed, outwardly rotated...........	3	24	46	57	37	28	32	0	7	7	3				
20	Legs flexed only at knees................	19	24	11	23	53	66	52	58	24	30	10	7	4	3	
21	Legs extended or semiextended...........	44	69	50	85	74	75	68	55	45	40	20	7	4	3	
22	Legs extended..........................					54	41	45	26	41	33	10	7	4		
23	Rests on forearms......................	6	24	57	67	82	72	35	24	7	4	4	—			
24	Rests on hands.........................	3	0	0	4	16	32	65	67	93	96	96	100	—		
25	Rests only on knees, abdomen, chest, head.	92	73	50	10	14	5									
26	Rests only on knees, abd., chest, forearms..	8	24	46	53	19										
27	Rests only on thighs, abd., chest, forearms.	0	4	21	26	70	62	39	42	10	7	7	11	—	3	
28	Rests only momentarily on abd. and chest.	8	4	11	10	7	38	16	23	17	7					
29	Rests only on thigh, abd., chest, hands.....					4	13	52	71	62	73	60	41	35	33	40
30	Rests only on thighs, lower abd., hands....	0	0	0	0	4	13	6	38	28	48	32	38	15	—	
31	Assumes creeping position................					—	9	7	7	17	23	43	63	73	77	80
32	Assumes quadrupedal position.............									10	3	3	26	15	18	7
33	Rolls to side or supine...................	6	7	4	8	13	26	40	30	29	35	32	14	—		
34	Rolls to side only.......................	6	7	0	8	10	9	19	14	4	3	16	4			
35	Rolls to supine.........................	0	3	4	0	4	17	21	11	25	37	23	14	0	—	
36	Flexes legs in crawling movements........	84	79	64	19	13	3	6	3	—						
37	Flexes leg drawing up knee..............					0	0	23	23	35	37	57	59	77	83	87
38	Pivots.................................	13	13	46	24	19	20	33	34	60	70	77	95	96	97	
39	Regresses.............................	0	3	0	0	4	3	—	—	3	7	28	5			
40	Progresses.............................	13	17	4	4	2	0	0	0	17	17	40	54	81	87	100
41	Crawls................................					—	—	—	0	3	17	7	13	3		
42	Creeps................................								17	17	30	46	65	80	80	
43	Attains supine or sitting.................	0	3	4	0	4	17	21	11	27	30	57	68	83	94	83
44	Pushes upward and backward to sitting....									3	3	30	57	83	94	

brief period lifted in the mid position. This percentage rises steadily until at 24 weeks and thereafter virtually all of the infants hold the head lifted more or less sustainedly in the mid position. Momentary head lifting is characteristic of the 4, 6, and 8 weeks age levels. Eight weeks may be regarded as the transitional age level because at that age over half of the children also exhibit sustained head lifting in addition to momentary head lifting. Energy and fatigue factors of course affect this response but here as in many other behavior patterns the most important factor is the maturity of the neuromuscular equipment. Incidentally it is by no means a simple practical or theoretical matter to draw a sharp distinction between fatigue and immaturity. For example, when the tender, 4 weeks-old infant for a brief moment lifts his head a few degrees during the short journey of ventral suspension, is his failure to erect his head more sustainedly due to physiological fatigue or to neurological incompleteness?

Head behavior is a key to the total patterning of prone behavior. When all the attendant conditions are normal and typical, it is possible to make an inferential reconstruction of the general postural behavior picture from a profile of the head station. Careful plotting of the alignment of the head at advancing age levels would reveal significant development trends. At the age of 4 weeks 88 per cent of the children lift the head to Zone 1; that is, the chin barely clears the platform. At 6 weeks an equal number of the children lift their heads to Zone 2, an inch or more above the platform. This ability becomes well-nigh universal by 16 weeks. At that age also over half of the infants lift the head to Zone 3, in which attitude the plane of the countenance is almost perpendicular to the platform. This ability becomes almost universal at 24 weeks. At 28 weeks 61 per cent of the children, and at 36 weeks 100 per cent of the children, rear the head to Zone 4. At this age level the plane of the countenance, because of head retraction, may make an obtuse angle with the horizontal plane of the platform.

Closely associated with these head movements are alterations in the postural control and attitudes of chest, arms, hands, and more secondarily of hips and legs and feet. The influence of head behavior upon the total reaction picture suggests very strongly that growth is a process of progressive consolidation and individuation rather than a linking of discrete behavior components.

The Arms. In ventral suspension the arms of the 4 weeks-old infant sometimes droop as haplessly as his head, perhaps even more so since we have already noted an occasional infant who raises his head a bit during ventral translation through space. But at the age of 6 weeks the arms and legs, as well as the head, participate in the ventral suspension response. As the child grows older both the arms and the legs come into increased extension and assume attitudes anticipatory of those which will be displayed when the infant lodges on the platform.

For the ages from 4 to 12 weeks, the arms are flexed and held relatively close to the body when the infant is in prone position on the platform. At 8 and 12 weeks the upper arms are more or less passively lifted by the pull of back extension. Some of the weight of the body presses upon the forearms. It is probable that at these ages the upper arm and shoulder are sufficiently innervated to contribute at least a fraction of active support to the body. At 16 weeks and later this innervation extends into the forearm. Even at 16 weeks the hands are occasionally seen to lift from the platform. At 20 weeks the child's arms definitely extend at the elbow and he may scratch the platform. The hands assume a more predominantly open attitude. Full extension of the arms occurs in nearly all children at 36 weeks and at subsequent age levels. At 28 weeks about one child in three was able to lift the arm and hand in response to a lure, maintaining partial balance during the lifting reaction.

Concomitant with these changes in arm posture, there is a change in the relations of chest and abdomen to the platform. At 16 weeks 82 per cent of the infants rest their forearms on the platform. It is difficult to infer the exact distribution of weight from mere inspection. Approximately two-thirds of the children at 12 weeks and almost three-fourths of the children at 20 weeks rest on the forearms. At 24 weeks, however, two-thirds of the children rest their weight on the hands—this because the arms are now characteristically in full extension. At 32 weeks 93 per cent of the children, and at 44 weeks 100 per cent of the children, rest the body weight on the hands. The significance of these percentages is revealed in changing postural attitudes of the trunk which will be next considered.

The Trunk. As already suggested, the postural attitude of any portion of the infant's physique tends to involve or influence the total body stance. Accordingly, the changes described for movements and attitudes of head and arms are reflected in changes in the region of the trunk. When the 4 weeks-old infant is placed in the prone position, the pelvis is elevated, the knees are close to each other, and the child quite involuntarily approximates a devout attitude of prayer. The main axis of the trunk slopes downward toward the head. At 6 weeks and at 8 weeks this main axis of the trunk lies nearly parallel to the platform. From 12 weeks to 32 weeks the trunk shows a concave arching due to the progressive erection of the head and upper chest. At later age levels, during both pivoting and creeping, the main axis of the infant's trunk tends to remain parallel to the platform. Even in the quadrupedal attitude, resting on palms and soles, he adjusts the flexion at the knees so that he will not pitch forward during the progression. At the earliest age levels, the trunk tends to react as a unit (one might say as a barrel) but as the child grows older, the pelvis and the upper trunk show a more autonomous mobility which displays itself in pivoting, creeping, and other postural readjustments. In ordinary language we say that the child becomes more agile. This agility is an expression not so much of increased expertness as of an increased flexibility which neurologically is based upon individuation and differentiation of specific patterned abilities.

In general, the fulcrum of prone activities shifts from head to foot as the child grows older. This shift is in some way related to the cephalocaudad principle of developmental organization. At the age of 36 weeks to 40 weeks the (normative) infant has slight control over his center of gravity, owing to limitations in his arm and leg attitudes. His arms and legs are active, but this activity results in a circular motion, or pivoting. The fulcral area remains in a middle position and the infant remains where he is. Locomotion still lies in the future.

The Legs. At 4 and 8 weeks the legs are flexed at the hips and the knees, the knees resting on the platform. During this period, ineffective crawling movements are observed. Crawling may be distinguished from creeping. In crawling, the infant's abdomen contacts the platform. In creeping, his abdomen is lifted above the platform and he rests on feet, hands, and knees. At 12 weeks, although the legs are sometimes flexed at the hips and knees, they assume an attitude of pronounced outward rotation. The pelvis lies closer to the platform. The infant maintains a frog-like attitude. At 16 weeks the legs are extended at the hips and flexed at the knees, the feet being frequently raised from the platform. This attitude is common through 28 weeks.

Only rarely does the infant approximate a creeping position prior to 36 weeks. Thereafter an increasing number assume this position. At 44 weeks 63 per cent of the children assumed a well-defined creeping position, and 26 per cent assumed a quadrupedal position. There are many variations of the details in the stances assumed. In the fully defined quadrupedal position, the infant rests on all fours with hands and feet in full plantigrade relation to the platform. This does not mean, however, that in actual locomotion this attitude will be maintained, for different children use varied techniques at different ages and also within a short space of time at any one given age. They bring a forearm, hand, knee, and foot into diverse unilateral and bilateral relationship with the platform. An infant may creep on hands and feet, on hands and knees, or on hands and knee and foot, etc.

Nature not only abhors a vacuum, but also abhors stationariness in the infant. Even though he may have no well-defined directional sense or destination, he tends to expend his bodily energy so that he will get into new orientation with his environment. Only toward the end of the first year of life does he creep forward in a well-defined and purposeful manner. The stages by which he reaches this performance may now be rapidly reviewed.

The 4, 6, and 8 weeks-old infant rests predominantly on knees, abdomen, chest, and head. At 12 weeks the head is slightly raised and the forearms come into play to contribute a supporting base. At 16 weeks the infant raises the upper chest as well, rears his head to a vertical position, extends the hips, and brings the thighs into contact with the platform so that he rests on thighs, abdomen, lower chest, and forearms. This position remains characteristic until 24 weeks when the child extends the arms and rests on hands, thighs, abdomen, and lower chest. At 20 weeks the back is usually arched in such a way that the weight is sustained more or less evenly by arms, legs, abdomen, and chest. At 24 weeks, if the child attempts to rest on his hands, he readily loses his balance and rolls to the side. At 28 weeks he has acquired better lateral equilibrium. He may even lift his hand toward a lure, but he cannot pivot toward it. At 32 weeks he can pivot about on his abdomen, both clockwise and counterclockwise, to secure the lure. At 36 weeks he pushes upward and backward on his arms in an aborted effort to advance; instead, he often rolls to the side. At 40 weeks he maintains better balance, but he is almost as likely to regress as to progress when he becomes active. However, if he wishes, he can escape from the prone position either by rolling to the supine position or by pushing himself to a sedentary position. At 44 weeks he pushes back with his hands, draws up his knees, and assumes a creeping posture. He manages to propel himself forward, although his creeping technique may not be well established until the age of 48 weeks or later. At 48 weeks, two-thirds of all of the infants of the normative group crept forward on the platform of the crib.

§13. STAIR CLIMBING BEHAVIOR

(40 weeks–56 weeks)

The Situation

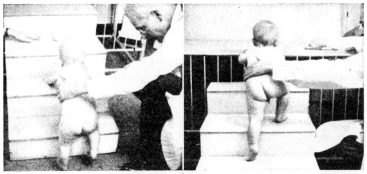

FIG. 13.—Stair climbing behavior: 40 weeks and 56 weeks.

With the movable staircase in position, the examiner lifted the infant and placed his feet in front of the first tread. The child was permitted to bend forward and to rest his hands on the second tread. Lending support when necessary, and occasionally holding the child's foot after it was planted on a tread, the examiner placed a lure of bells, rattle, or ring on an advanced tread to induce climbing.

Stimulus Factors

Climbing up the experimental staircase onto the platform of the crib presents a problem intermediate between creeping and walking. The stimulus factors in this intermediate situation comprise elements which are common to both creeping and walking but which are also distinctive. The staircase is both an obstacle and an opportunity. As he confronts it for the first time at 40 weeks, what can the infant do? The examiner has placed him in a favorable stance, put his feet on the floor and his hands on the second tread, and has even placed a lure enticingly near on the tread above. Often the infant stays planted in his position, unable to go forward, upward, or backward. Gravity, assisted by the extensor action of his extremities, keeps him almost immobile. He may lift his foot for a few inches, he may sway his pelvis, but he makes no further conquest of his environment. Sometimes he may cry out of his helplessness, or sink ingloriously to a sedentary position. Or he may shift to a full creeping attitude on the floor and creep or cruise around the staircase, achieving a partial round-about solution even though he by no means scales the summit.

When he attempts actually to climb, visual factors begin to play a directive role. If it is not too accessible, he reaches for the lure. The lure becomes more than a vague incitement. Its position determines the general direction in which he will exert his locomotor drive. It serves to lift the line of effort upward, but it can do this only when intrinsic developmental forces have supplied the essential power to lift the feet. In other words, the incitement power of the visually perceived lure is limited and in a measure produced by the ripeness of the infant's motor abilities. Visual, tactilemotor, and kinesthetic factors thus come into closely interwoven and repercussive relationships.

SITUATION: STAIRCASE (Stc)

Stc	Behavior items	4	6	8	12	16	20	24	28	32	36	40	44	48	52	56
1	Surmounts first tread...................											18	36	63	74	88
2	Surmounts second tread................											—	—	50	74	82
3	Surmounts third tread.................													31	65	77
4	Surmounts fourth tread................													31	39	53
5	Reaches crib platform................													31	39	53

Behavior Trends

Climbing is not dependent upon specific previous practice. Not a few children in our normative group, to the amazement of their mothers, exhibited their first climbing on the experimental staircase. As early as 44 weeks one child in three surmounted the first tread. At 48 weeks this number was almost doubled and half the infants climbed the second tread as well. Two-thirds of the infants surmounted the third tread at the age of 1 year, and over half reached the crib platform at 56 weeks.

The gradation in these percentages is almost as regular as that of the treads of the staircase. It suggests that the quantity as well as the pattern of activity is governed by maturity factors. Though lures could induce the performance, they did not determine the length of the performance. It does not follow that because a child can climb one tread, he can assuredly climb two treads, even though one tread seems no more difficult than another. In its nascent stage, the infant seems to be parsimonious with the display of a talent. It is only when the ability is well established that the infant displays it prodigally. When he has reached that stage he will not only climb the staircase once but he will do so repeatedly and with keen enjoyment if given the opportunity. Most of the infants in the normative group had not arrived at that stage at 56 weeks. Once more it is hard to draw a distinction between fatigue and immaturity. Is the apparent indifference to the second and third treads due to spent power (inadequate energy availability), or is the impulsion itself weak because the neuromotor foundation of the pattern is meager (inadequate structure)?

To what extent visual factors determine the infant's performance constitutes an interesting speculative problem. He probably has no insightful visual perception of height and depth to regulate his climbing effort. He may envisage the lure as a goal and by sustained striving he reaches it because each tread becomes a platform for further effort. But he has no apprehension of the staircase as a construction or as an apparatus. He simply climbs it. It is not perception of the staircase which makes him climb. It is climbing which aids him to define and deepen the perception. Perhaps we have in this relationship a paradigm of the mechanism of higher orders of behavior, even those in the conceptual sphere of reasoning.

The mechanics of stair climbing presents so many aspects of genetic interest that the subject would repay detailed analysis. At the most nascent level the infant merely lifts one heel. He does not even raise the whole foot from the floor. Later he lifts the foot to increasing height. Indeed in the immature phase he lifts it to lavish heights, which results in an amusing degree of overstepping. Interestingly enough even when he is able to lift his foot without making a forward thrust, or if he sets it plantigrade on the first tread, he may yet lack the ability to shift his weight to this foot to permit a corresponding elevation of the other foot. This failure is not due to lack of physical strength or to lack of command of balance but probably arises out of a certain inflexibility of his torso already noted in the prone situation. His trunk in the present stance tends to behave as a partially immobilized cylinder. Even when he strains forward toward the lure he does it by reaching and by pulling his fore body forward by the force of his arms. His hind body can sustain weight but cannot exert aggressive leverage. Consequently he stays put. This is his predicament at 40 weeks.

Eight weeks later he is in possession of a new flexibility which makes it possible for him to "zig" and to "zag." He swings his pelvis first left, then right, and with proper correlation he brings his arms and also his hind quarters into play. Thus by a modification of pivoting and of creeping patterns he makes an ascent. His technique is quadrupedal, a kind of clambering. He pulls with his fore extremities; he pushes with his hind extremities. Climbing is a variant of creeping at 48 weeks.

Another 8 weeks later, at 56 weeks, he shows a palpable increment of competency and assurance. Is this increment merely an augmentation or strengthening of the ability which he displayed at 48 weeks? There are similar components in his performance at these two age levels but there is a significant difference in pattern. This difference is not one of degree but one of kind. The arms play a much lesser role in the advanced performance. His technique is less quadrupedal and more bipedal. Climbing has become a variant of walking and looks more like ambulation than clambering. The infant is nearer to an erect posture. He comes closer to adult performance. Sometimes he even scales two treads with one alternating stride, without planting both feet on the first tread before taking the second.

The patterns of descent constitute another story, one which we have not investigated in detail. The story is so distinctive that it cannot be explored by viewing a cinema of stair climbing in reverse. For, from the standpoint of behavior mechanisms, descent is not simply a reversal of the process of ascent.

§14. SITTING BEHAVIOR

(4 weeks–52 weeks)

The Situation

The younger infants were placed athwart the crib in the supine position. The examiner confronted the child and, after establishing rapport, took hold of the infant's hands and arms (as described in detail elsewhere) and, exerting cautious, gradual traction, pulled the child slowly to the sitting position. This maneuver was modified in accordance with the age and the motor capacities of the infant. Placing a hand on either side of the infant's chest, the examiner steadied the sitting infant for a moment of observation. The examiner next rotated the position of the infant so that the infant's feet faced toward the foot of the crib. The examiner then partially or completely withdrew his supporting hands to determine the possibility of momentary passive sitting. If the infant sat independently, the examiner retreated partially out of view and placed a lure on the platform at the left or right to induce clockwise or counterclockwise pivoting.

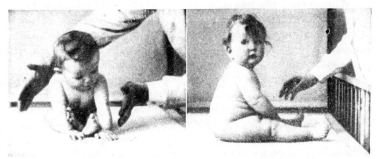

Fig. 14.—Sitting behavior: 28 weeks and 36 weeks.

Infants who showed adequate independent sitting control were permitted to sit on the platform of the crib during the course of the table-top situations later described. All infants 12 weeks of age or older without adequate independent sitting control were placed in the examining chair for all or part of the examination. This examination chair carried a broad canvas belt which was secured across the infant's chest and abdomen. The support of a special bandage which also encircled the trunk was used when necessary with the youngest infants to keep them for a brief period without sideward leaning in the examining chair.

Stimulus Factors and General Considerations

Sitting is a complicated form of behavior which man shares with humbler vertebrates but which he acquires by slow degrees and somewhat late in the cycle of growth. Developmentally, sitting is an intermediate, transitional phase between the supine and the upright posture, but it is always retained as an economical substitute for standing. Although sitting is a natural ability, it is in its early stages highly dependent upon props and aids supplied by the infant's elders. To explore the normative development of sitting it therefore became necessary to make observations of the behavior under three different conditions, namely: (a) the child was raised to a sitting position by traction on his arms; (b) the child was placed on the platform (equivalent to the floor), the examiner's hands supplying or withholding support as needed; (c) the child was placed in a chair with the support of a transverse canvas belt. These three situations are so closely related that they will be considered together.

What moves the infant to sit up? There is no simple answer. Here, as in so many fields of behavior, the relationships between stimulus and response are so intimately reciprocal that it is almost impossible to distinguish between cause and effect. From a genetic standpoint, sitting is not a simple, well-defined ability, but is the cumulative, integrated end result of a long developmental process which traces back to the fetal period. Although the fetus does not in any sense ever assume the sitting posture, his postural mechanisms and the associated labyrinth reflexes undergo a basic organization which is essential to the matured sitting response. The fetus is in a fluid medium and suffers changes of position to which he is in a measure actively responsive. The neonate likewise makes a slight degree of active postural response to handling. He does not remain completely passive to the numerous manipulations which arise out of infant care. He doubtless experiences in some way sensations of translation or change of position and surprisingly early he reacts positively to being held in a sitting position in the lap. If external signs are not altogether deceptive, he enjoys at 8 weeks an experience something in the nature of a thrill in connection with his early sedentary orientations. To what extent such pleasurable reaction is due to distance receptors or to kinesthetic ones, we can only speculate.

At 16 and at 20 weeks of age, the supine infant not infrequently lifts his head. This bit of behavior simulates trying to sit up, but it must be interpreted with caution. The impulse may arise chiefly out of an individuation process and may not mean that the infant is seeking either new perceptual experiences or an upright posture. However, such head activity is at least an early herald of sitting ability and when somewhat later the shoulders as well as the head lift, the behavior seems to be more clearly a developmental component of sitting. The head takes a developmental lead in the attainment of sitting, but there are exceptional instances in which the torsal control seems more advanced than head control.

The pulled-to-sitting situation tested the elementary aspects of the infant's sitting behavior. Our purpose was to determine the most rudimentary postural reactions, taking great care not to impose upon the child's capacities. The procedures in this situation must be followed with extreme caution, particularly when head control is immature and when the arms make no flexor response to the pull. Stimulus factors vary greatly. The response of the young infant is heightened by a slight, preliminary, tentative traction on the arms before his full weight is pulled up. The reactions are also heightened by establishing social rapport. Indeed the situation was utilized as a basis for observing the social responsiveness of the infant. It is noteworthy that personality factors affect even the character and completeness of a "simple" postural response in a very young infant. The general tonicity of the muscular system likewise exerted an important influence. In some cases when the infant is of the extensor type, a pull on his arms may stimulate extension to such a degree that he does not flex at the hips. He extends his legs and remains immobile at the pelvis so that, as he is pulled, he either slides along the platform or is reared to a standing position. As the child is pulled upward and forward, gravity pulls him downward and this becomes a further stimulus for active tension.

In the passive, induced sitting position, the infant at certain stages leaned forward with hands on the platform. The stimulus factors which operate in this position include the pressure stimulation from the platform, the pressure and kinesthetic stimulation derived from the weight on his own arms and hands, the enlarged perceptual horizon, and the sense of balance. The sense of imbalance was not permitted to reach the level of fear. Some infants were more compliant to postural manipulation than others.

When an infant is placed in a chair which snugly conforms to his back and buttocks, the pattern of stimulus factors takes on important changes. If he does not experience too much nostalgia from his isolation in the chair, he is likely to have a heightened sense of security from the snugness of the back and seat, and also from the belt applied across or around his trunk.

Infants as young as 12 weeks were placed in the adjustable, canvas-back, morris chair as a standard part of the normative examination. This is a tender age for any kind of sitting, but the infant in this instance was firmly ensconced by a broad canvas band which encircled him at the diaphragm. With this degree of support, the 12 weeks infant not only tolerates but often positively enjoys the sitting situation for brief periods which may be lengthened to ten minutes, depending on his muscular vigor and maturity. As the infant grows older these periods increase until the age of 36 weeks when over half of the infants were able to sit alone without the aid of a chair throughout the required part of the examination. At 44, 48, and 52 weeks only one or two infants were placed in the chair. At 12 to 24 weeks all of the infants needed the chair; at 28 weeks about nine-tenths of them were placed in the chair. Thirty-two weeks marks the transitional period. At this age many infants could sit alone for part of the examination, but at this age balance is still precarious. An infant may maintain efficient independent balance for over 15 minutes and then, without warning, topple. Such sudden loss of control is characteristic of a certain maturity level and is also affected by personality factors. Vigilance on the part of the examiner is especially importance in all observations of postural behavior.

The effect of the chair on the sedentary control of the infant can be summarized in a brief paragraph. At 12 and 20 weeks, three-fourths of the infants slumped to the side; at 28 weeks, less than one-third. Forward straining against the band occurred not infrequently at 20 and 24 weeks. At 16 weeks 33 per cent, and at 24 weeks 100 per cent, held the head steady. At 16 weeks and at 20 weeks head rotation is wanting or very restricted. At 28 weeks three-fourths of the infants maintain an erect body position and all of them rotate their heads freely.

The stimulus factors of the chair, however, go beyond the field of posture. At the earlier age levels (12 to 24 weeks) there is an element of novelty in the chair situation which makes for heightened activity and heightened emotions. New perceptual horizons spread before the infant. We have been impressed by the vividness with which young infants react to chair placement and how competent they are to adopt a separate station outside the mother's lap.

The major stimulus factors which operate in the development of sitting behavior patterns include the following: (a) intrinsic, maturational factors, (b) perceptual factors, (c) physiological factors like fatigue and illness, (d) personality characteristics.

Of all these factors, the first mentioned are the most potent. Physiological and personality factors, however, have a marked influence upon the manner in which the sitting abilities are manifested and the prodigality with which they are displayed. The personality factor of caution is important. Some infants are much more startled by insecure support than others. Some infants are so cautious that they greatly restrict their movements. The more audacious infants seem almost to be thrilled by losing balance and engage recklessly in postural activity.

Behavior Trends

The growth of sitting behavior patterns shows a marked tendency to follow the law of developmental progression. These patterns bring into successive prominence head, arms, trunk, and legs. It will, therefore, again be convenient to sketch in turn the developmental sequences characteristic of each of these anatomical regions. It is, of course, understood that this progression does not proceed on an installment or linkage plan. To some degree the total physique of the child is always involved in his reactions at each and every age level. However, it can be readily shown that the process of developmental individuation goes from head to foot.

The Head. The reactions of the head constitute the most important item of observation in the pulled-to-sitting situation. In the great majority of infants (84 to 72 per cent) from 4 to 16 weeks of age, the head lags to some degree. At 20 weeks one-third, and at 28 weeks only one-tenth, of the infants showed any head lag.

SITUATION: PULLED TO SITTING (SiP)

SiP	Behavior items	4	6	8	12	16	20	24	28	32	36	40	44	48	52	56
1	Head lags..........................	84	76	82	85	72	35	15	10							
2	Head lags completely.................	34	23	14	8	0	0	0	0							
3	Head lags completely or markedly........	44	45	46	27	8	6	0	0							
4	Head lags markedly...................	9	21	32	19	8	6	0	0							
5	Head lags mod., slightly, or only initially.	41	31	36	58	64	32	15	10							
6	Head lags moderately or slightly........	9	10	32	42	40	9	0	0							
7	Head lags initially only...............	31	21	4	15	25	23	15	10							
8	Head compensates or lags only initially...	47	45	21	31	52	93	96	97							
9	Head compensates.....................	16	24	18	15	28	70	81	87							
10	Back extends.........................	26	17	7	19	17	—	—	—							
11	Pulled with difficulty.................	—	—	25	32	13										
12	Pulled easily........................	0	0	0	0	27	50	57	70							
13	Assists Examiner by pulling self forward..	0	0	0	0	8	18	42	50							

SITUATION: SITTING (Si)

Si	Behavior items	4	6	8	12	16	20	24	28	32	36	40	44	48	52	56
1	Head sags..........................	74	56	54	12	0										
2	Head only momentarily erect............	35	37	14	0	0										
3	Head bobbingly erect...................	16	46	57	56	10	0	0	0	0	0	0	0	0	0	0
4	Head set forward..................	13	15	32	36	41	16	9	3	0	0	0	0	0	0	0
5	Head steadily erect.....................	3	4	0	24	53	75	91	100	100	100	100	100	100	100	100
6	Head erect when leans forward...........	0	0	8	12	12	56	65	73	82	86	94	100	100	100	100
7	Back extends.......................	23	11	21	12	9	—	—	—	—	—	—	—	—	—	—
8	Back rounded uniformly................	92	91	71	57	13	17	8	0	0	0	0	0	0	0	0
9	Back lumbar curvature.................	0	5	29	43	76	—	—	—	—	—	—	—	—	—	—
10	Body erect, supported.................					25	50	62	79	—	—	—	—	—	—	—
11	Body erect...........................	0	0	0	0	0	3	30	58	67	77	88	97	94	100	96
12	Body erect moment or less than minute....	0	0	0	0	0	3	27	36	27	6	0	0	0	0	0
13	Body erect one minute or more..........	0	0	0	0	0	0	3	21	39	72	88	100	100	100	100
14	Sits with slight or no sup. (mom. or better)	0	4	7	36	46	88	91	94	100	100	100				
15	Sits only momentarily leaning forward.....	0	0	0	12	11	28	41	27	6	0					
16	Sits only mom. or less than one minute....	0	0	0	12	11	31	56	64	39	20	0	0	0	0	0
17	Sits one minute or more.................	0	0	0	0	0	3	6	24	61	80	100	100	100	100	100
18	Sits for ten minutes (approximately).......	0	0	0	0	0	0	0	0	21	57	80	97	91	95	100
19	Sits for indefinite period................	0	0	0	0	0	0	0	0	21	46	66	97	85	93	100
20	Falls...................... ...	100	100	100	92	80	75	84	69	58	54	23	20	6	0	0
21	Falls forward........................	67	77	77	81	72	64	42	25	12	23	0	0	0	0	0
22	Falls sideward........................	0	23	36	10	4	13	50	49	40	34	17	3	0	0	0
23	Falls backward......................	13	10	18	15	20	3	6	9	30	11	14	13	6	0	4
24	Leans forward passively...............					94	93	74	69	55	29	3	0	0	0	0
25	Leans sideward......................	0	23	36	10	12	16	56	51	46	49	17	3	0	0	0
26	Leans forward or sideward actively.......	0	0	0	0	0	0	3	22	45	74	86	80	80	83	64
27	Sits unsteadily......................	—	—	—	7	9	27	27	30	40	20	3	0	0	0	
28	Sits leaning forward....................	0	0	0	12	11	31	47	58	49	26	3	0	—	—	—
29	Sits unsupported......................	0	0	0	12	11	34	62	88	100	100	100				
30	Uses hand for support.................	—	—	—	7	47	44	42	33	11	0	0	0	0	0	
31	Grasps or plays with feet................	0	0	0	0	0	19	35	30	6	3	0	0	0	0	0
32	Erects self from leaning forward..........	0	0	0	0	0	6	18	36	40	80	94	100	91	100	100
33	Turns to side and maintains balance.......	0	0	0	0	0	0	0	0	9	26	74	67	76	66	76
34	Pivots.............................	0	0	0	0	0	0	0	0	3	11	40	45	65	58	60
35	Attains prone......................	0	0	0	0	0	0	0	0	21	29	52	57	59	69	56
36	Attains sitting from prone..............	0	0	0	0	0	0	0	0	28	20	28	71	65	57	93
37	Attains creeping or quadrupedal position...	0	0	0	0	0	0	0	0	6	6	29	53	53	59	40
38	Pulls to standing.....................	0	0	0	0	0	0	0	0	0	9	28	36	62	73	85
39	Lowers self.........................	0	0	0	0	0	0	0	0	0	11	19	42	54	67	70
40	Attains standing independently...........	0	0	0	0	0	0	0	0	0	3	3	21	16	27	45
41	Attains standing independently (r)........	0	0	0	0	0	0	0	0	0	9	3	24	19	29	52

SITUATION: SITTING IN CHAIR (SiC)

SiC	Behavior items	4	6	8	12	16	20	24	28	32	36	40	44	48	52	56
1	Placed in chair........................				100	100	100	100	92	85	46	28	7	7	4	
2	Head erect and steady.................				0	33	67	100	100							
3	Head turns freely....................				0	0	16	60	100							
4	Body slumps to side...................				79	79	69	57	31							
5	Body leans forward....................				10	14	35	33	26							
6	Body erect...........................				0	10	28	47	72							

At all ages, even at 4 and 6 weeks, there are a few infants who do not manifest head lag. These early exceptions may be due to a general hypertonicity or to a flexor tendency sufficiently strong to embrace the cervical musculature. Complete or marked head lag was noted in almost half of the infants at 4, 6, and 8 weeks. At 12 weeks and at 16 weeks moderate, slight, or only initial head lag was the rule. As the child grows older, the head shows increasing power to compensate. The percentages for head compensation rise sharply from 28 per cent at 16 weeks to 70 per cent at 20 weeks, to 87 per cent at 28 weeks.

The degree of head postural control is further indicated by the head station and head mobility displayed when the infant, after being pulled forward, is given an opportunity to sit with and without support on the platform. At 4 and 6 weeks the head sags forward; at 8 and at 12 weeks it is held bobbingly erect. At 16 weeks it is held more steady, but tends to be set forward. At 20 weeks the head erects itself in a compensatory way even when the trunk leans forward; the head is more mobile; the neck is physically and functionally more prominent; the infant can retract the head and turn it to the side in the sitting position. At 24 weeks, under the stress of passive sitting (maintained by leaning forward and resting some weight on the hands), the head becomes somewhat immobilized, but at 28 weeks the mobility and control return.

Versatility of head movements steadily increases with age as the stability and mobility of the trunk are coordinately perfected. At 4 and at 6 weeks one-third of the infants held the head erect for a moment. At 12 weeks all the children held the head erect more than momentarily. At 20 weeks no child held the head bobbingly unsteady. At 28 weeks all the children held the head steadily erect when the trunk was upright. At 44 weeks all the children held the head erect when the trunk leaned forward.

The Arms. Changes in the reactions of the arms show a progression comparable to those of the head. Even at 4 weeks the infant may contribute some slight tensing of the shoulder musculature as he is pulled to the sitting position. This contribution and the cooperative tension of arms increase with age. At 12 weeks, when positive social rapport is established, the infant definitely responds with increased tension of the arms as he is pulled forward. At 16 weeks he not only participates but he may even anticipate with tension at the shoulders. At 20 weeks nearly all the infants manifested obvious pleasure in the situation, and half of them were pulled up into position with ease. At 28 weeks 70 per cent of the children were pulled to the sitting position with ease and half of them assisted the examiner to a considerable degree by pulling themselves forward. Not until 40 weeks are 58 per cent of the infants able to assume the sitting stance from the supine position without some assistance from the examiner.

The following tabulation outlines, somewhat schematically chiefly on the basis of cinema records, the behavior trends with respect to the attitudes and activity of the arms when the infant is in the sitting stance. It should be emphasized, however, that there are numerous individual variations which arise out of bodily and behavioral factors.

From 4 to 8 weeks the arms are flexed and raised well above the platform.

At 12 weeks the arms extend somewhat passively at the sides and may come to rest on the platform as the infant leans forward.

At 16 weeks and at 20 weeks the arms are more active. The infant flexes them or lifts them from the platform while he is supported. This new capacity is secondary to the more advanced head control.

At 20 weeks almost half of the infants place their hands on the platform or leg, as a more or less active response to leaning forward.

At 24 weeks the arms are extended at the sides, but less passively. They rest on the platform and serve as props. They set wide apart.

At 28 weeks the arms and hands continue to serve as props, but they are held closer together. The trunk tends to lose balance at this age in spite of the propping arms.

At 32 weeks the arms come still closer together but trunk control is so advanced that the child can elevate one arm while he props himself with the other.

At 36 weeks the arms are no longer needed as props and they are free to reach for lures.

At subsequent age levels the range and versatility of arm movements are further augmented by the increased mobility of the trunk.

The Trunk.   Just as the body as a whole illustrates a cephalo-caudad trend of development, so the neuromotor organization of the trunk itself proceeds antero-posteriorly. At early ages the upper half of the trunk (the fore body) is more mobile and shows more tonus than the lower trunk. At 4 weeks the entire trunk is relatively flaccid. As already suggested there is a trace of shoulder response when traction is exerted but the back offers no resistance to the examiner's pull. Occasionally, especially at 4 weeks, the infant may suddenly extend the back. Under these conditions or when flexion at the hip is resisted, pulling to the sitting posture is difficult and sometimes impossible. In the induced sitting posture the infant is extremely flaccid. The head sags forward and the curvature of the back is continuous with the curvature of the cervix and cranium. This curvature is so uniform and continuous that it is reminiscent of the postural curvature which the infant maintains in utero.

At 6 weeks the back is still rounded but there is more muscular tonus and reaction on handling of the child. There is a slight straightening of the upper thorax or cervical spine so that in the sitting position the fetal configuration is less pronounced. At 8 and at 12 weeks the cervical spine is somewhat straighter and the head is held up, but the thoracic spine still shows curvature. At 16 weeks the cervicothoracic spine is more nearly straight and the curvature is more restricted to the lumbar segments. This lumbar curvature, however, has also undergone some reduction and is not so pronounced as it was at the earlier age levels.

The general trend of development in the conformation of the back is further indicated by the following percentages. In 92 per cent of the infants at 4 weeks the back was uniformly rounded. Such rounding was observed in only 8 per cent of the children at 24 weeks and in no child at 28 weeks. Lumbar curvature was not observed at 4 weeks, and was noted in 43 per cent of the children at 12 weeks and in 76 per cent of the children at 16 weeks of age. With increasing age the trunk tends to assume a straight alignment so that at about 44 weeks lumbar kyphosis is disappearing to be ultimately replaced by a lumbar lordosis.

These gross morphological changes are associated with developmental changes in behavior patterns. Indeed we may suppose that to a considerable extent the molding of the trunk of the infant is synchronized or identified with changes in the forms of the neuromotor patterns.

The trunk acquires independent control by the same slow developmental gradations which characterize the acquisition of head control. Independent head station, however, is attained long before independent trunk control. At 16 weeks the trunk was held erect by only one child in four even when the examiner offered sufficient support to prevent full loss of balance. At 28 weeks eight children out of ten held the trunk erect under these conditions. At 32 weeks two-thirds of the children, and at 52 weeks all of the children, held the trunk erect.

In the induced sitting position the trunk typically leans forward at the age of 24 weeks. The child is relatively helpless and although he supports the trunk in this leaning position he manifests no further command over it. At 28 weeks the hands come closer together and the trunk does not lean forward to the same degree. The child now shows a slightly greater capacity to flex and extend the trunk, but he can not maintain lateral balance. At 32 weeks he may hold the trunk erect momentarily without support from his own hands or those of the examiner. The upper trunk at this age is definitely more mobile than the lower trunk. At 36 weeks the trunk control is so far advanced that three-fourths of the infants can actively lean forward or sideward. An equal number can erect themselves to an upright sitting position after leaning forward. Leaning at this age is an active innervation whereas at 16 and at 20 weeks virtually all of the children lean forward in a purely passive manner.

The capacity to twist or rotate the trunk is becoming better defined at 36 weeks. In this torsion the upper trunk is still the predominant component. At subsequent age levels the lower trunk assumes a larger share in the act of torsion and in other postural adjustment including pivoting. Pivoting, however, is dependent not only upon trunk mobility but also upon the coordinated assistance of the legs which are at this time gaining a greater independence and adopting new responsibilities.

The Legs.   From 4 to 20 weeks of age the legs of the infant are relatively passive. At the earliest age levels they flex in a reflexive manner when the child is pulled to the sitting position. At these ages the legs behave almost like flippers, the mobility being largely restricted to the upper segment of the leg. At 20 weeks the legs show a more defined independent mobility when the child is supported under the arms by the examiner. But when the child is in the passive sitting stance, the legs revert to their earlier helplessness. At 24 weeks outward rotation of the legs is conspicuous. The legs serve as passive stabilizers or outriggers. The hands, like the legs, spread wide apart to maintain this squatlike attitude. The configuration of the child takes on the aspect of a low, ungainly pyramid with a very broad base. At subsequent age levels this pyramidal disposition of his anatomical mass alters; the apex of the pyramid becomes higher and the base contracts. But typically it is not until the age of 32 weeks that the infant assumes a truly active sitting stance. He is now able to innervate his legs actively, both the upper and the lower segments. He actively draws the legs out and flexes them at the knees. At 36 weeks the angle between the legs contracts and the sitting stance approximates to that of the adult.

When this stance and the correlated equilibrium have been attained, the legs assume new importance in the child's economy. He no longer needs his legs as outrigger props. He can use them to attain the prone position and to pivot about on the platform. Sometimes, especially at 36 weeks of age, he goes from sitting to prone by falling forward. At a later age he may go from prone to sitting by pushing upward and backward (30 per cent at 40 weeks). Some of the normative infants were reported to hitch about in a sitting position on the floor rather than creep. Pivoting is accomplished in two ways: (*a*) by pushing with one heel; (*b*) by leaning on one hand and swinging one leg toward the hand and then alternately replacing hand and leg in this manner.

At 44 weeks we witness a high degree of leg activity which is independent of sitting. Seventy-one per cent of the children at 44 weeks and 93 per cent of the children at 56 weeks are able to attain the sitting position independently from the prone position due to the newly acquired effectuality of their legs. A similar number of children are able to attain the creeping or quadrupedal position from the sitting position. And at 48 weeks almost two-thirds are able to pull themselves to a standing position. At 52 weeks an equal number lower themselves to the sitting position, having attained the standing. But only half of the children even at 56 weeks of age are able to attain the standing position independently, that is with no fulcrum but the floor.

Thus while at the neonatal period the legs were in the nature of superfluous appendages, and while at 24 weeks they simply served as passive props, at 40 weeks they become active instruments for translocation and readjustment of posture. They cease to be appendages of the trunk; they become prime movers to reorient the trunk and to propel it both horizontally and vertically into new environmental fields.

This review of the developmental progression of sitting behavior reveals how interwoven are the numerous patterns of behavior and how closely related are postural, locomotor, and adaptive forms of behavior. By way of summary we may list the outstanding normative frequencies which indicate the emergence of both partial and integrated control in the field of sitting behavior.

Except for very rudimentary head and shoulder tensions, the 4 weeks-old infant cannot be credited with any obvious sitting abilities. Only one-third of the infants at 4 weeks of age hold the head erect even momentarily. At 12 weeks, however, over half of the infants hold the head bobbingly erect. At 20 weeks from two-thirds to three-fourths of the children hold the head steadily erect whether seated in the adjustable chair or on the platform between the supporting hands of the examiner. At 28 weeks the trunk as well as the head is held erect by the majority of infants. It is not held erect steadily, that is to say, for a minute or more, until the age of 36 weeks when approximately three-fourths of the children manifest this ability. Normatively, however, 32 weeks may be regarded as the age when the infant begins to sit independently. Sixty-one per cent of the children in the normative group sat independently for a minute or more at 32 weeks; 80 per cent at 36 weeks; and 100 per cent at 40 weeks.

As the child grows older the ability to sit continuously for more prolonged periods increases. Even at 36 weeks the majority of the infants were able, with recurring unsteadiness, to sit for ten minutes or more. At 56 weeks about all the infants sat for an indefinitely prolonged period.

Maintenance of balance is achieved slowly. Normative percentages show very steady incrementations with respect to this aspect of sitting behavior. At 8 weeks 100 per cent of the infants, at 28 weeks 70 per cent, at 32 weeks 58 per cent, at 36 weeks 53 per cent, of the children showed a tendency to fall or topple. This tendency was entirely absent at 52 weeks. It is significant, however, that although independent sitting ability has been attained at 32 and at 36 weeks, over half of the children at those ages show a definite tendency to imbalance. Under the conditions of the normative observations the predominant tendency up to 24 weeks is to fall forward; though from 4 to 8 weeks an increasing proportion of the children fall sideward, probably due to extensor tendencies and leg activity. After 16 weeks an increasing number of children fall to the side. At 24 and at 28 weeks there is a still more marked tendency (50 per cent) to fall sideward; at these ages it will be recalled the trunk is seeking a more erect position. At 32 weeks there is a transient tendency (shown in 30 per cent of cases) to fall backward.

To a considerable degree sitting behavior retains passive characteristics up to 32 weeks of age. At that age over half of the children lean forward passively. Developmentally the infant squats in a flaccid manner before he sits upright in an active manner. This squatting must be differentiated from active sitting. Our percentages show that passive sitting momentarily or better with slight or no support occurs in 36 per cent of the children as early as 12 weeks and in 88 per cent of the children as early as 20 weeks. At 24 weeks 62 per cent and at 28 weeks 88 per cent of the infants sit without support in squat-like attitude.

In this squatting, passive and active elements are combined. Accordingly from 42 per cent to 47 per cent of the infants from 20 through 28 weeks of age use their hands for support in the sitting position. Full balance is not acquired until the age of 40 weeks when three-fourths of the children can turn to the side and still maintain their equilibrium. At that age only one-fifth of the children sat with imbalance. At 44 weeks no child manifested imbalance in the sitting position. The ability to sit, like so many other infant abilities, is built up by degrees and not with dramatic suddenness.

§15. STANDING AND WALKING BEHAVIOR

(4 weeks–60 weeks)

The Situation

FIG. 15.—Standing behavior: 4 weeks and 44 weeks.

Placing a hand on either side of the thorax, the examiner lifted the infant to a standing position and supported him with hands under the axillae. The infant confronted the examiner. The examiner then gradually released this support, allowing the soles of the infant's feet to contact and then to press the platform.

If the infant supported his full weight, the examiner cautiously withdrew support to determine control of balance. For further determinations, the infant was permitted to seize the side rail with one hand. If the postural control was adequate, the child was permitted to grasp the rail with two hands. The examiner used a lure to elicit cruising either to right or to left. The same lure was used to determine the infant's capacity to lower himself from the standing to the sitting position. In the sitting position the examiner attempted to induce independent assumption of the erect posture. If the child stood effectively with support, the examiner assisted him to release hold of the side rails, confronting him at the distant end of the crib and eliciting stepping or walking movements, lending support only so far as necessary.

At the early ages, the examiner gently swayed the trunk to determine head compensation.

Stimulus Factors

Standing and walking, in many respects, constitute the most difficult postural problem of infancy. Many normal infants do not attain independent standing ability in the first year of life. It takes a full year to lay the basis for this achievement. In order to explore the full range of the developmental antecedents of standing this behavior situation was instituted at all age levels beginning with the fourth week.

In quadrupedal animals the act of standing is somewhat simpler than it is in the human infant. Subcortical neural centers control the mechanisms of standing so completely that a decerebrated quadruped can maintain a standing position by the reflex action of its musculature. Similar mechanisms operate in man but the difficulties of equilibrium greatly complicate bipedal standing. The upright posture represents a comparatively late attainment in racial evolution and partly for this reason it comes late in the cycle of the infant's development. In his ontogenesis man has not completely short-circuited quadrupedal phases of posture and of locomotion.

A comprehensive list of the stimulus factors which appear in the inception and control of standing and walking would include the following: (1) tactile impressions, arising chiefly in the soles of the feet; (2) muscle, joint, and tendon impressions conveyed through the proprioceptors; (3) changes of position communicated

through the otoliths of the semicircular canals; (4) changes in
rate of body movement reported by the ampullae of these canals;
(5) visual perception of supporting surfaces, of goals, and obstacles;
(6) visual and auditory perception of lures; (7) imitative responsiveness; (8) inner urges and drives; (9) tactile and visual
perception of the examiner's supporting hands.

It would, of course, be futile to attempt to assess the relative
importance of these many factors. They vary with age as well as
with individuality. They are further modified by physical conditions like fatigue and illness. Standing makes heavy demands
upon the infant's energy. Retardation in standing associated with
rickets is a protective factor. Some infants further protect themselves with caution. Here temperamental differences as well as
previous experiences with falls and bumps assert themselves.
One infant may be overcautious; another may be reckless; although on the whole the infant shows a noteworthy tendency to
temper his performances to his fundamental capacities and
needs.

Since the examiner was always at hand to lend support when
necessary, no undue demands were made on the infant in placing
him in a standing posture. At the earlier age levels, notably at
16 and 20 weeks, the infants enjoyed the postural manipulation
and showed positive pleasure in the supported standing situation.
At 28 weeks only 9 per cent, and at 36 weeks only 12 per cent, of
the children showed any protest or discomfort. At 32 weeks,
however, 46 per cent expressed discomfort by brief fretting. This
latter percentage is significant, for 32 weeks is a nascent period
in which about one-half of the infants could not support their
entire weight; whereas at 36 weeks 91 per cent were able to do so.

Brief mention should be made of the young infants of extensor
type who respond with marked extensor movements in the posture
situations. There was at least one such infant at each of the age
levels from 4 through 16 weeks. The extensor infant makes a
fictitiously good showing in the standing situation and shows a
neuromuscular predilection for "standing" as opposed to sitting.

Early sitting offers more thrill to the infant than does early
standing. Sitting up in contrast to lying down brings with it new
perceptual and social horizons, particularly when the infant sits
in a high chair or at table level where he can more nearly see his
elders eye to eye. Mere standing does not bring with it an equally
revolutionary reorientation and enrichment of visual impressions.

When, however, standing gives way to walking, the upright posture takes on new values.

Whence comes the propensity to stand? In reply one may adduce inner urges or drives. But whence come the drives? Surely not from some occult force which wells up suddenly in some vague, instinctive manner. There comes a time when the infant seems to be under an impulsion to grasp the rail of his pen and to pull himself upright. This may look like a dramatic and even saltatory change in his behavior; but it is essentially the seasoned end product of a long process of ontogenetic patterning which now comes to a partial culmination in performance. But the developmental preparation proceeded by slow degrees.

The normative percentages show an impressively steady and gradual incrementation with respect to the critical items: (a) *Supports a fraction of weight* (from 19 per cent at 4 weeks to 100 per cent at 56 weeks); (b) *Supports entire weight* (from 28 per cent at 20 weeks to 100 per cent at 56 weeks). Standing and walking are the result of incrementations and progressive correlations of numerous contributive abilities which are finally integrated into one working system. From one point of view, the specific drives of the infant are the symptomatic consequence or correlate of the maturing of these abilities. There is no general drive to stand; there is a host of abilities, and the following summary will attempt to indicate how these abilities finally lead up to the consummation of standing.

Behavior Trends

Standing is for the infant a difficult neuromuscular feat; but its ontogenesis is in principle quite similar to that of prehension or of poking. Standing is a complicated form of muscular motion which through the oscillation of checks and counter checks overcomes the pull of gravity. To a considerable degree the ontogenesis of standing has already been summarized in connection with sitting behavior; for sitting is an intermediate stage or halfway phase in the assumption of the upright posture. However, the procedures of the normative survey aimed to induce standing responses by suspending or placing the infant in a perpendicular position. Therefore his reactions to this orientation must be separately detailed for the full range of ages. As in the other posture situations, it is convenient to formulate this summary by anatomical divisions from head to foot.

SITUATION: STANDING (St)

St	Behavior items	4	6	8	12	16	20	24	28	32	36	40	44	48	52	56
1	Head sags	73	52	36	4	0										
2	Head extends	23	16	7	8	5										
3	Head erect only momentarily	30	14	8	0	0										
4	Head sags or erect only momentarily	77	55	44	4	0										
5	Head bobs or set forward	23	28	52	48	33										
6	Head bobbingly erect	17	21	32	17	0										
7	Head set forward	12	7	20	35	33										
8	Head set forward or steadily erect	10	21	44	78	95										
9	Head steadily erect	3	14	24	48	62										
10	Head compensates when swayed	3	14	47	41	75										
11	Legs flexed, do not extend	56	32	30	21	19	23	7	9	8	—	—	3			
12	Legs extend briefly	42	54	52	64	59	66	50	28	21	22	12	3			
13	Legs extend recurrently	0	10	15	24	34	50	31	31	14	13	15	19	0	0	4
14	Hips flex, legs flex or extend	100	90	81	66	70	69	50	56	52	53	40	32	31	26	
15	Hips flex, legs held extended	15	25	25	8	31	22	22	37	41	33	23	13	23		
16	Supports no weight	77	62	41	43	32	28	15	17	14	3	0	3			
17	Offers very slight resistance	61	73	52	25	27										
18	Supports a fraction of weight	19	38	53	50	61	72	72	78	83	94	97	97	97	98	100
19	Supports a large fraction of weight	3	14	23	32	22	53	53	75	83	94	97				
20	Supports a large frac. of wt. more than mom.	0	0	0	0	4	31	41	53	76	82	91	94	97	98	100
21	Supports entire weight	0	0	4	8	2	28	28	44	55	91	94	97	97	98	100
22	One foot engages the other	10	3	4	12	27	13	19	19	17	9	9	3	2		
23	Feet apart four inches or more			5	8	13	3	0	3	17	18	24	23	28	43	22
24	Toes flex	85	86	86	64	36										
25	Feet rest with soles on platform	92	77	61	61	59	84	78	81	62	62	85	87	97	96	100
26	Feet inverted					29	5	26	12							
27	Stands on toes	3	10	26	38	38	38	28	31	31	50	18	29	6	7	
28	Stands on toes, weight not supported	3	10	26	38	38	32	32	9	3						
29	Stands on toes, weight supported					0	6	9	22	28	50	18	29	6	7	
30	Rises to toes, supporting weight						6	3	9	7	31	3	16	6	7	
31	Lifts foot	23	10	41	60	59	34	41	31	28	28	40	52	69	81	88
32	Lifts foot without supporting entire weight	23	10	41	60	59	21	28	15	18	0	3				
33	Lifts foot while supporting entire weight					0	13	13	16	10	28	40	48	69	81	88
34	Stepping movements not supporting weight	3	3	7	28	38	22	16	16	14	6	3	7			
35	Bounces						13	13	25	7	9	12	19		2	4
36	Is placed standing					100	100	100	100	97	62	51	44	19	7	8
37	(Hands supported) Balance inadequate									34	64	45	38	31	12	
38	Stands only when both hands are supported								14	31	21	19	22	9	8	
39	Stands holding side rail							6	14	25	51	58	72	80	44	
40	Stands independently (without support)										9	10	22	33	68	
41	Attains st. with E's assistance or independ.								3	28	49	56	75	74	76	
42	Attains standing independently									3	3	21	16	27	45	
43	Pulls to st. holding side rail or independently								3	9	28	36	62	73	85	
44	Attains standing independently (r)									9	3	24	19	29	52	
45	Lowers self using support										11	19	42	54	67	70
46	Cruises or walks using support										16	24	39	72	82	88
47	Walks using support										3	6	16	47	63	80
48	Walks only when both hands supported											3	10	31	26	16
49	Walks independently												3	3	26	44
50	Responds pleasantly to situation					35	34	33	28	31	24	15	13	13	9	—

Note: St 43 and 45, at 44 weeks. Some children are placed standing and lower themselves though they do not pull themselves to standing.

The Head. The reactions of the head in the standing situation are comparable to those which have been outlined for the sitting situation. The support of the examiner's hands under the axillae tended to make head station more stable in young infants. Although the infant does not stand with or on his head, the head normally participates in the total reactions of trunk, arms, and legs and retains a regulative role both in the development and in the dynamics of standing. This role is partly accomplished through attitudinal reflexes which originate in the end organs of sight and of equilibrium. The attitudinal reflexes of body and extremities are responsive to changes in head attitudes. The reverse also is true. When the head attitudes are predominantly determined by the visual and static senses, the child at last is able to balance himself and to step forward. Not until the head is ready to assume this leading role in the total body control does he command the upright posture. To this extent, the infant stands and walks with his head!

At 4 weeks the head sags forward; the chin rests on the chest. Head extension occasionally occurs. Such extension is momentary but well defined; and is more frequent at 4 weeks than at subsequent age levels. At 6 weeks the head still sags but to a lesser degree. It shows more prolonged tone, but wavers very readily both laterally and antero-posteriorly when the trunk is slightly swayed in these directions by the examiner.

At 8 weeks the improved tonus shows itself in recurrent compensatory extensions to overcome sagging. There is not much tonicity at the neck. Consequently the head either sets forward and /or is held bobbingly erect. At 12 weeks crude head bobbing is less frequently seen. In a neurological sense the head still bobs, but so smoothly and subtly that 48 per cent of the infants are credited with holding the head steadily erect. Steadiness of the head and of the bodily frame is accomplished by a check and counter-check process essentially similar to bobbing. In one-third of the cases the head still sets forward both at 12 and at 16 weeks.

Sixteen weeks again marks a transitional period in head control. At this age the neck rather than the shoulders supports the head; two-thirds of the infants hold the head steady and erect when the trunk is somewhat tilted. Head compensatory movements are more prompt and vigorous, and three-fourths of the infants compensated to the swaying manipulations of the examiner. Put in more mechanistic terms, the head at 16 weeks has an enduring tonicity and static responsiveness which make it relatively resistant to quick changes in space. The head can stand but the infant cannot—yet

At 20 weeks the head begins to display more freedom of move ment. Then and at several succeeding age levels the infant rotates flexes, and extends it with increasing facility when he is well supported by the examiner's hands. But toward the end of the first year, while the infant is acquiring independent support, he again moves his head with more restraint and wariness. This, as already suggested, is due to the fact that the head is assuming a determining role in his postural behavior. Through the visual-static receptors the head modulates and in a measure initiates the complex of attitudinal reflexes which result in standing and presently in walking. Therefore the infant clearly circumscribes his head activity during the early stages of standing and walking. Later, when he is more expert, the head will reassert freedom and facility of movement on a higher level of integration.

The Arms.   The arms play a definite though not conspicuous role in the development of standing and walking. Our observations were chiefly directed to the legs and to the infant's ability to sustain and to balance his body weight. But a few incidental findings based on the normative examinations and cinema records will serve to remind us that the arms are involved in the genetic patterning and in the ultimate mechanisms of standing and walking. At 4 and at 6 weeks the arms droop as flaccidly as the head. At 8 weeks they exhibit more tone. At 12 weeks they flex and are drawn up toward the chest. At 16 weeks they show more range and independence of movement. Even during the standing situation we have seen an infant bring his hands together at the mid line and inspect them. It is noteworthy, however, that although this infant was supporting part of his weight in the standing position, he posturally collapsed (in the examiner's hands) as soon as he fixed his regard on his own hand. This means, of course, that the arms have by no means attained autonomy. Indeed, they always retain some share in the mechanism of standing and walking.

At 28 weeks arms and legs show a tendency to function together. Bouncing reactions and flexions at the pelvis, which often occur in the standing situation at this age, involve arm as well as leg activity. Even under the partial restraint of the examiner's hold upon the infant's chest, the infant tends to lift his arms when he flexes his legs or when he extends them. This is a kind of jumping-jack reaction, not at all surprising when the long phyletic association of the anterior and posterior extremities is recalled.

Both phyletically and ontogenetically upright standing consists in the suppression of the supportive function of the arms and an augmentation of that of the legs. We must not forget that even the human infant as a rule stands on all fours before he stands on his two feet. At 40 weeks 43 per cent, and at 44 weeks 63 per cent, of the infants assume a creeping or a quadrupedal position. One month later, at 48 weeks, an equal proportion of the infants (62 per cent) assume a bipedal position with and without the assistance of a physical support on which to pull and lean. In general it might be said that for a whole month the infant uses his arms on a par with his legs for standing. Thereafter he places the burden on his legs and uses his arms to steady the burden and to cruise. At 44 weeks he cannot cruise because he cannot readjust his arms with foot lifting. He lifts his foot and puts it back again.

Cruising is anticipatory walking. Or it is reminiscent creeping, for cruising is a quadrupedal form of progression in which the arms still serve their ancient locomotor function, but against a vertical rather than the horizontal plane. Not until the arms are completely released from this menial function does the infant truly walk. Even then the arms participate in the swings of his toddling and of his mature stride. These arm movements and posturings are reminders of man's quadrupedal estate; they are also physiological balancing components of bipedal locomotion.

The Trunk. Reactions of the trunk in the standing situation are comparable to those which have been outlined for the sitting situation. To some extent, indeed, they are parallel, for sitting is an intermediate phase of standing from a mechanical and genetic point of view. The trunk, therefore, tends to react as if it were in the sitting station except that the partial suspension and pressure on the legs inevitably impose distinctive features on the patterns of response. Since the basic developmental changes in the trunk behavior have already been outlined, they will be only briefly indicated here.

At 4 weeks the trunk is highly flaccid and tends to assume a fully rounded configuration. Even at 8 weeks the back comes only slightly and briefly into extension. At 12 weeks the more enduring muscular tone so essential to standing asserts itself. With advancing age the trunk becomes more upright, manifesting persistent tonus in the upper segments earlier than in the lower segments. We have already indicated changes in the station of the head, which at first sits somewhat laxly on the shoulders and later becomes erect. This is due to changes in the spinal alignment and the spinal musculature. At 12 weeks the cervical spine is relatively straight; at 16 weeks the cervicothoracic spine is also more nearly straight and the head rides more freely above the shoulders. Momentary erectness of the trunk in the standing situation is observed at 16 weeks, and more persistent erectness at 20 weeks. At 28 weeks there is an occasional tendency to throw the trunk backward. At this age the child is able to erect his trunk from the leaning forward position with but slight assistance from the examiner.

As in the sitting situation, so in the standing, the trunk begins to exhibit more mobility in the last quarter of the first year. The child shows a tendency to rotate the shoulders when supported by the hands in the standing position. This rotational mobility is brought into requisition at 44 weeks and at 48 weeks in connection with cruising. At this age the mobility involves the lower as well as the upper trunk.

The trunk musculature does not of course develop independently of that of the lower extremities. However, one gains the impression that, prior to the attainment of standing, the legs and the trunk are incompletely coordinated. The child does not fail to stand alone for lack of strength but he fails because the trunk and leg musculature are not in organic functional relationship. When they come into such relationship he is more firm and agile on his feet and he is ready to stand if the head, as already indicated, assumes the requisite regulative control.

Standing, therefore, furnishes an excellent example of the unitary nature of the developmental organization. Analytically it is possible to discern more or less distinctive patterns in individual segments of the body. But these patterns are not discrete. Only when they are brought into highly correlated combination do they produce the intricate performance of standing. We can scarcely picture the complexity of this developmental organization. The problem is especially complicated by reason of the fact that almost at the same time that the child is acquiring his ability to stand, he is also passing through the quadrupedal cycle of behavior so that the trunk must come into functional relation not only with the vertical bipedal mechanisms of standing but also with the horizontal mechanisms of creeping. It is surprising that these two sets of patterns do not more obviously conflict in the actual behavior of the infant.

The Legs and Feet. The legs show a fairly consistent tendency to straighten by extension at the knee throughout the gamut of age levels. The 4 weeks-old infant makes only slight extensions at the hip and knee. At 4 weeks, however, over half of the infants flex the legs without extension. From 4 to 24 weeks all leg extension was relatively brief. The legs flex recurrently in half of the infants at 20 weeks of age and in a minority of the infants at all age levels from 6 to 44 weeks. Flexion at the hips with the legs either extended or flexed was universal at 4 weeks and shows a consistently decreasing trend to 26 per cent at 52 weeks of age. Sometimes the legs were also held in extended position in association with flexion at the hips. This item rose to a peak frequency of 41 per cent at 36 weeks. These various postures of the legs arise from a diversity of stimulus factors, and some of the attitudes have no direct relationship to the mechanisms of standing, particularly when assumed before the infant's feet contact the platform.

There is one behavior item, however, which shows a highly consistent trend throughout the entire range of ages and this has a significant bearing on standing performance, namely, the item *Supports a fraction of weight*, which rises from a frequency of 19 per cent at 4 weeks to 100 per cent at 56 weeks. A large fraction of the weight is supported by three-fourths of the children as early as 28 weeks, but at that age about half of the infants support this large fraction only momentarily. At 32 weeks of age over half of the children (55 per cent) support their entire weight, and at 36 weeks 91 per cent support the entire weight. We may, therefore, regard 36 weeks as the age when in a normative sense the infant's bodily frame, though not his neuromuscular maturity, permits him to assume the standing station. At this age he is stiffer at the knees than at the hips. He leans forward maintaining leg extension when the examiner relaxes support. His tendency to flex at the hips shows that the vertical trunk is still in meager functional association with the legs. In a developmental sense the infant is not so much weak at the knees as weak at the pelvis.

Leg activity is relatively slight at 4, 6, and 8 weeks. Flexion of the toes and plantar flexion of the foot are the most prominent reactions. At 12 weeks there may be extension and flexion of the ankle; the toes remain curled; the foot may lift one or two inches from the platform. The legs flex more or less passively as soon as the weight is relaxed by the examiner's supporting hands.

At 16 weeks the interesting phenomenon of stepping movements occurs with relative frequency. It was found in 38 per cent of the normative group and with lesser frequency at 12, 20, 24, 28, and

32 weeks. The phenomenon is highly exceptional at 4 and 6 weeks. At 16 weeks this movement is excited by the pressure of the foot onto the platform. While making stepping movements the infant sustains slight or no weight. He takes delight in this activity and if the examiner, sustaining the infant's trunk vertically, moves it forward through space at an adjusted speed, the child paces across the platform in a manner which astonishingly resembles walking progression. But it is fictitious; the infant does not transport his own body, the examiner does it for him.

At 40 weeks, however, under similar circumstances, comparable stepping movements result in a pushing of the trunk against the examiner's hands. The child sustains his weight and on his own power paces across the platform, the examiner simply steadying the locomotion. This is true assisted walking. These stepping movements tend to be exaggerated; the child steps higher than necessary and he may fling his leg in a goose-step manner. At 20 weeks the arms as well as the legs become more active. Leg activity consists in more sporadic flexion and extension. At 28 weeks the leg activity often takes on a bouncing character (25 per cent). This is a manifestation of the new flexibility at the pelvis. It is, however, a rather generalized reaction in which the arms participate.

The attitude of the feet on the platform undergoes changes with growth. Although at all ages the soles of the feet usually come into full contact with the platform, the toes display a well-defined response through the first 12 weeks. The toes react with a sustained grasp-like flexion. At 16 weeks the soles of the feet are everted so that only the outer edges come into contact with the platform. A similar attitude of the feet was observed in the supine situation when the legs are outwardly rotated. At 36 weeks when leg extension is well defined, the infants often rise to the toes. A similar rise to the toes without sustaining full body weight is not infrequent from 8 through 24 weeks. Through 16 weeks the feet are close together as they rest on the platform. Sometimes they are so close that they contact each other. After 16 weeks the feet show a tendency to separate and the distance between them widens. Although at 36 weeks they are often close to each other, they again show a tendency to separate. The child at this age makes his balance more secure by widening his base in this manner. As he acquires facility in walking, the feet again approximate each other more closely. At 36 weeks the normative infant tends to remain riveted to the spot on which he stands. The legs flex at the pelvis and he passively bends in divers directions without being able to correct his stance by adjustment of the legs and feet. At about 40 weeks of age, however, he begins to lift his heel and at 44 weeks and thereafter he shows an ability to lift his feet from the platform. Lifting of the foot was also present at 12 weeks and at 16 weeks but this earlier ability had no immediate relationship to walking. From 28 weeks to 56 weeks from 69 to 88 per cent of the children were able to lift one foot while supporting their entire weight.

The transition from self-supported standing to free standing, to independent walking is genetically a gradual one, even though performance finally manifests itself with apparent suddenness. The saltatoriness is fictitious and rests upon the assumption that the child's behavior falls into only two categories—that he either stands or stands not; that he either walks or walks not. It must now be clear that he approximates walking and standing by slow degrees, through incrementations and synergetic correlation of many abilities. The attainment of self-balance is the culminating factor.

This attainment also is reached by gradual organization rather than quick efflorescence. At first the examiner supplies all of the steadying balance, contributing as much foot-pound energy as the child himself would have to expend in the process. Standing is an antigravity contest. As the infant acquires power to sustain his weight, he supplies a slowly increasing amount of self-balance. The examiner expends less energy and supplies restraint only at critical moments. These critical moments decrease in number with maturity. Investigated by precise quantitative methods the progress in self-balance would probably reveal a mathematically perfect gradient.

At 40 weeks the infant can stand holding the side rail. At first he stands rather helplessly moored. He does not venture to release even one hand. He may lift a foot, or he may lift only the proximal segment of his foot, his heel. Later he cruises and for brief moments he may relax his hand hold. With the graduated assistance of elders or by his own devices he "learns" to walk. It is evident that "learning" is a process of developmental patterning in which the static controls gradually become incorporated with a growing postural equipment. Even though the labyrinthine apparatus of equilibrium is formed in the fetal period, walking must wait ontogenetically until the basic neuromotor apparatus is ripe and ready.

Summary

Standing, therefore, proves to be a complicated form of behavior presupposing many preparatory stages which involve both the progressive utilization and the integration of preexisting behavior mechanisms. The developmental sequence proceeds somewhat as follows: (*a*) supine posture, (*b*) assisted sitting, (*c*) stepping when held in suspension, (*d*) independent sitting, (*e*) weight supported when held, (*f*) pulling self to standing, (*g*) weight supported with physical prop, (*h*) cruising, (*i*) standing momentarily, (*j*) independent standing, (*k*) independent steps, (*l*) toddling, (*m*) walking, (*n*) running.

A tabular summary of characteristic behavior items in age sequence follows. Selected items are assigned to the age at which they first appear with normative frequency.

4 weeks	Head sags; legs flex without extension; toes flex
6 weeks	Legs extend briefly
8 weeks	Head bobs or sets forward; supports fraction of weight
12 weeks	Head sets forward or steadily erect; lifts foot
16 weeks	Head steadily erect; compensates on swaying
20 weeks	Legs extend recurrently; supports large fraction of weight momentarily
28 weeks	Supports large fraction of weight more than momentarily
32 weeks	Supports entire weight
36 weeks	Stands on toes
40 weeks	Stands holding to side rail
44 weeks	Pulls to standing independently or with assistance
48 weeks	Pulls to standing independently or with grasp of rail; lowers self using support; cruises
52 weeks	Walks using support
56 weeks	Attains standing station; stands independently, and walks almost independently

§16. DANGLING RING BEHAVIOR

(4 weeks–28 weeks)

The Situation

The infant lay in the supine position. The examiner with circuitous approach brought the dangling ring above the infant's lower chest. If no positive response occurred, the examiner moved the ring into a line of vision, right or left depending upon head position. The ring was then bobbed gently in the visual fixation field. When the infant fixated, the examiner moved the ring slowly through an arc of 180°. In a similar manner, starting at the infant's eye level, the examiner advanced the ring in the median plane beyond the infant's head and then in the opposite direction toward the infant's toes to elicit visual pursuit. At the 12 weeks age level the ring was held above the sternum for a long period to elicit incipient or delayed response. If the infant did not contact the

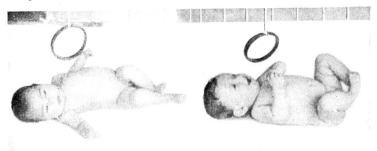

Fig. 16.—Dangling ring behavior: 8 weeks and 20 weeks.

ring, it was moved toward his left hand to facilitate grasp. If grasp did not occur the examiner placed the ring into the infant's palm.

Stimulus Factors

The dangling ring was a natural observation device for use at the lower age levels. The suspended ring is a prototype of the most primitive infant toy. To dangle an object before the infant is an almost instinctive expression of parental playfulness. By a similar playful approach the mother also brings her face hoveringly over the infant to stimulate his immature visual powers. The dangling of an enticing object before his upward gaze is not only a token of a social relationship, but is also a tacit recognition of the psychological individuality of the infant. Particularly when the infant lies in the crib not sustained by the mother's arms, a dangling presentation becomes a revealing test for elementary perception and prehension.

The geometry of the dangling ring is simple. It consists of a vertical line terminating in a circle. We use ordinary twisted string to suspend a bright red embroidery ring approximately four inches in diameter. To what extent the geometry of the dangling ring is duplicated in the subjective perception of the infant one can only speculate. At the earliest stages of response it is reasonably sure that he does not see a complete circle and a vertical line. He may, however, be sensitive to the disruption of a neutral background by a straight streak and by the hollow hoop. To the simple configuration of circle and line must be added the examiner's hand which holds the end of the string. The close juxtaposition of hand, string, and ring creates for the young infant a problem in perceptual discrimination and offers him an early opportunity for exploratory inspection. His eyes travel from one focal point to another. In the rivalry of the three stimulating foci the hand often proves most powerful.

The ring slowly rotates as it hangs pendant. The optical stimulus values of the ring are multiplied or accentuated in some unknown way by this slow twirling motion. With no entrance into his sensorium, can we even guess how he subjectively apprehends this motion? It is, however, objectively indicated that the dangling ring has a greater potency than the rattle in eliciting early perceptual response. Even though the stimulus of the rattle is reinforced by slight motion and sound, it does not at the earlier age levels (4 to 8 weeks) make so strong an appeal as the ring. We are inclined to believe that the difference in stimulus value arises out of the large amplitude, the defined contour, and the kaleidescopic gyration of the ring.

Another stimulus factor of great importance at the younger ages is the transit of the ring across the field of vision. This slow arc-like motion from left to right and return, and from head to foot and return, simultaneously compounds with rotation. Sometimes, to induce regard, the ring is also slightly bobbed in a perpendicular plane, which adds a third component of motion. The optimum distance of the ring from the eyes of the infant and the rate of its movement were empirically established in each case. Five seconds were usually consumed in traversing the arc of 180°. This is a favorable rate for eliciting ocular adjustment. The dependence of perceptual behavior on various factors of distance, speed, and direction of movement calls for further investigation by precise experimental methods. The genetic aspects of adaptation to these factors are numerous.

In the last half of the first year the dangling ring situation becomes too elementary for the infant's powers of perception and prehension; the supine orientation irks him and he prefers to strike out on a horizontal plane. In a different guise, however, the ring was kept in the observation procedures for the age levels subsequent to 28 weeks. The ring was no longer dangled but was placed with the attached string flat on the table top. The child was seated confronting the table top. In their absolute physical qualities, the ring and string of course remained unchanged, but their stimulus values were greatly altered by this arrangement. The altered effect upon the perceptual and exploitive reactions of the infant will become apparent in the discussion of the ring and string situation.

Behavior Trends

Regard. In spite of its potent stimulus values, as many as 77 per cent of the infants at 4 weeks of age disregard the ring when it is suspended in the mid plane. Infants at this age, it will be recalled, nearly always lie with head averted. But at 16 weeks, only 14 per cent of the infants disregard the dangling ring in this plane. Thereafter prompt regard becomes practically universal; the head now favors the mid position.

Delayed regard for the ring is the rule at all age levels up to 16 weeks. At 16 weeks about one child in four manifests delayed regard. From the standpoint of duration three different types of regard may be distinguished for the age period from 4 weeks to 28 weeks: momentary, prolonged, and sustained regard. Momentary regard is relatively frequent at 4, 6, and 8 weeks. Prolonged regard is characteristic of 12 weeks and 16 weeks; at the latter age, 87 per cent of the children stare with a marked fixation which apparently signifies a vivid visual experience. In spite of the intentness of this regard, the ring does not receive sustained attention throughout the period of observation. Only 17 per cent of the infants at 16 weeks were credited with consistent regard. Such regard rises steadily throughout the subsequent age levels reaching 90 per cent at 28 weeks. At 16 weeks, however, 93 per cent of the infants shifted the regard. In order of frequency this shift was to the examiner (64 per cent), to the examiner's hand (48 per cent), to the infant's own hand (19 per cent), and to the surroundings (13 per cent). These "distractions" assert themselves at all age levels. Regard for the examiner's hand is especially conspicuous at 6, 8, and 12 weeks in frequencies of 64, 61, and 77 per cent. The infant's own hand has most distractive power at 16 weeks; very rarely an infant pays regard to his own hand as early as 6 weeks and as late as 24 weeks.

SITUATION: DANGLING RING (RD)

RD	Behavior items	4	6	8	12	16	20	24	28	32	36	40	44	48	52	56
1	Regards after delay	77	54	64	65	27	13	14	5							
2	Regards immediately	26	46	36	35	68	97	96	95							
3	Regards momentarily	53	85	71	38	35										
4	Regards prolongedly	47	43	29	62	87	47	38	5							
5	Regards consistently					17	26	59	90							
6	Disregards in mid plane	77	39	46	46	14										
7	Regards in mid plane	29	61	54	54	86										
8	Regards in mid plane (long head)	22	25	12	50	83										
9	Regards in mid plane (round head)	32	75	70	56	88										
10	Regards ring in hand					66	82	100	100							
11	Regards string					7	13	46	53							
12	Shifts regard	94	100	100	96	93	46	38	41							
13	Shifts regard to surroundings	75	68	61	35	13	16	14	5							
14	Shifts regard to Examiner's hand	28	64	61	77	48										
15	Shifts regard to Examiner	41	54	57	65	64	27	24	27							
16	Shifts regard to hand	0	4	7	8	19	5	3								
17	Follows past mid plane	44	62	50	58	84										
18	Follows past mid plane (lg.h.)	20	33	25	37	83										
19	Follows past mid plane (rd.h.)	55	75	60	67	77										
20	Follows approximately 180°	16	43	46	50	68										
21	Follows approximately 180° (lg.h.)	0	11	25	25	83										
22	Follows approximately 180° (rd.h.)	36	55	55	61	62										
23	Approaches	0	0	11	12	62	89	96	100							
24	Approaches after delay					58	30	19	9							
25	Approaches promptly					32	66	81	91							
26	Arms increase activity	0	4	11	42	64										
27	Arms separate	0	0	4	15	17	19	7								
28	Approaches with one hand	0	0	4	12	20	24	39	55							
29	Approaches with both hands	0	0	0	0	50	76	82	77							
30	Approaches with arms flexed	0	0	0	12	44	60	54	14							
31	Hands come together	0	0	0	8	20	38	11	5							
32	Contacts ring	3	4	4	15	43	81	100	100							
33	Dislodges ring on contact	3	4	4	8	20	35	28	5							
34	Grasps	0	0	0	8	22	73	96	100							
35	Grasps after delay						75	46	14							
36	Grasps interdigitally						61	45	7							
37	Retains entire period					20	19	40	65							
38	Holds with both hands					10	33	56	67							
39	Hand opens and closes on ring					30	11	10	14							
40	Brings ring to mouth					38	58	82	74							
41	Free hand to mid plane					25	51	56	84							
42	Transfers					3	18	41	74							
43	Drops					78	56	41	32							
44	Drops immediately					42	32	7	0							
45	Regards dropped ring					10	37	43	100							
46	(If drops) pursues dropped ring					7	16	29	100							
47	(If drops) resecures dropped ring					7	5	29	60							
48	Rolls to side	3	4	8	4	35	42	38	18							
49	Frets	9	14	4	8	27	23	32	21							

Note: Ring not placed in hand at early age levels.
Rd 28 and 29. If child drops ring, it may be represented. Infant may, therefore, approach with one hand on one presentation and with both hands on another presentation.

It is of course impossible to reconstruct the discriminativeness of early perceptions in their subjective aspect. Objective signs indicate that the string is unperceived or only slightly regarded until the age of 16 weeks, when 7 per cent of the infants evidently fixated upon the string when it suspended the ring or when they themselves held the ring. This proportion rises steadily to 53 per cent at 28 weeks. The selective regard for the string in the ring and string situation at later ages likewise undergoes interesting developmental changes.

At the early age levels, the dangling ring proved to be especially useful for the determination of the oculomotor control as expressed in eye following. It will be recalled that the ring was presented in the mid line; held in suspense over the chest; was then moved directly into the infant's line of vision; and, once the ring was perceived, it was moved in a curving plane from side to side and from head to foot to elicit visual following. With this procedure the item *Follows the ring past the mid plane* shows a progressive increase from 44 per cent at 4 weeks to 84 per cent at 16 weeks. Headward and footward following matures earlier and is present to some extent at all the ages studied, the frequencies ranging from 80 to 100 per cent.

Although the normative findings show a general and regular increase with age, it was discovered that within a given age group there were striking individual differences. These differences deserve a special comment and tentative discussion. Of 32 infants studied by Dr. Catherine Strunk Amatruda at 4 weeks of age, ten were distinguished by the shape of the head: the occiput was very prominent, the head having a long antero-posterior diameter. The ten obvious and outstanding cases were called long-headed and the remainder were arbitrarily called round-headed. These terms will serve for the following discussion but, since cephalic measurements were not made, the classification is not strictly equivalent to a technical determination of dolichocephalic (cephalic index up to 74.9) and brachycephalic (cephalic index 80 and above).

It was at once apparent that the long, protruding occiput made head turning very difficult, and analysis of the abilities involving head rotation from age to age revealed that the performance of the long-headed infants lagged consistently behind that of the round-headed infants until 16 weeks, when there is no discernible difference in behavior. At this age likewise the head formation observed earlier had become so changed that many of the long-headed infants could no longer be identified by inspection. This difference in performance was studied in relation to other possible selective factors including sex, health, and emotional adjustment but all of these factors were eliminated as probable explanations.

Up to 16 weeks of age in general a marked and consistent difference showed itself in the long-headed versus the round-headed groups with respect to the following items: *Regards in mid plane, Follows past mid plane, Follows approximately* 180°. These differences in rotational mobility are readily summarized by a comparison of the average number of degrees through which the dangling ring was followed at the five age levels in question. Although the figures must not be interpreted too precisely, their trend is unmistakable and conform to the clinical impressions.

	Round-headed	Long-headed
4 weeks	118°	68°
6 weeks	142°	102°
8 weeks	123°	80°
12 weeks	140°	100°
16 weeks	152°	154°

Similar analytical comparisons were made with regard to head rotation and visual fixation in the spontaneous supine and the rattle situations, and similar trends asserted themselves up to the age of 16 weeks. Even initial regard in the mid plane is augmented by round-headedness at 4, 6, and 8 weeks. The maximum percentage for mid-plane regard is 75 per cent at 6 weeks for the round-heads and 25 per cent for the long-heads. Following past the mid plane showed comparable ratios which need not here be detailed.

Following to the extent of 180° ranged from zero per cent at 4 weeks to 25 per cent at 12 weeks for the long-head group. For the round-head group the percentages ranged from 36 at 4 weeks to 61 at 12 weeks, a palpable difference. At 16 weeks the difference had been completely resolved and indeed the long-heads were then in the ascendancy for maximum following. The incrementation in eye following is not completely expressed by this increase in range of movement. There was a correlated increase in the quality of the following movements which became more smooth, more prompt, and more competent with age.

If findings like the above become established, it is probable that head conformation exerts significant influence upon postural, perceptual, and prehensory behavior, as well as upon oculomotor behavior in the first trimester of infancy.

Prehension. Sixteen weeks appears to be a critical age not only from the standpoint of visual perception, but also from the closely correlated standpoint of prehensory adjustment, for it is at this age that 62 per cent of the infants make definite approach movements upon the ring as opposed to 0, 11, and 12 per cent of the infants at the three preceding age levels. In the three succeeding age levels the percentage rises to 100. For the age range from 6 weeks to 28 weeks, therefore, the curve for approach movements shows a rapid rise from 0 per cent to 100 per cent. Approach, however, is still in a nascent stage at 16 weeks, for only 32 per cent approach promptly and 58 per cent after delay. At 20 weeks the relationships are reversed: only 30 per cent approach after delay, whereas 66 per cent approach promptly. At 28 weeks promptness of approach was noted in 91 per cent of the infants.

At the age levels prior to 16 weeks, approach movements cannot always be distinguished from increased arm activity. Such increase of activity on sight of the ring is not observed at all at 4 weeks and in only 4 per cent of the children at 6 weeks. But these frequencies rise to 42 per cent at 12 weeks and to 64 per cent at 16 weeks. The nature of this increased arm activity varies with age and doubtless also with personality characteristics. The movements are frequently abrupt and sporadic. Sometimes they are definitely preceded by a comparable period of diminished activity and of almost complete immobilization. Sometimes the activity eventuates in a separation of the arms which is somewhat paradoxical, for prehension requires closure upon its objective. Such separation of the arms, however, occurred in 15 per cent of the infants at 12 weeks, 17 per cent at 16 weeks, and 19 per cent at 20 weeks. The genetic relationship of paradoxical abduction to true adductive approach movements merits further analysis. These movements are not so contradictory as they seem; even in adult embrace arms fling out before they close in.

Approach with one hand constitutes still another pattern which undergoes a rather regular developmental increase from 4 per cent at 8 weeks to 55 per cent at 28 weeks. *Approach with both hands* is the most frequent pattern. Such definite approach was noted in 50 per cent of the children at 16 weeks, in 76 per cent at 20 weeks, in 82 per cent at 24 weeks, and 77 per cent at 28 weeks. A comparable pattern is designated *Hands come together*. In this reaction the hands do not definitely close on the ring; they simply contact the ring or penetrate it; but usually they come together outside the ring and without contacting it. This type of hand approximation occurs in 20 per cent of the children at 16 weeks and in 38 per cent of the children at 20 weeks, with lesser frequencies at 24 weeks and 28 weeks.

Contact of the ring may occur more or less fortuitously in exceptional cases at 4, 6, and 8 weeks. Contact occurs in 15 per cent of the children at 12 weeks, in 43 per cent at 16 weeks, in 81 per cent at 20 weeks, and in 100 per cent at 24 weeks.

The bilateral approach at 20 weeks is characteristically vigorous though it sometimes exhibits a labored and leaden slowness. It frequently results in a marked dislodging of the position of the ring on contact. Successful grasp, however, takes place in 73 per cent of the cases at 20 weeks as compared with only 22 per cent of the cases at 16 weeks, and in only 8 per cent at 12 weeks. By 24 weeks grasp is nearly universal. Grasping at 20 weeks, however, is not perfected, for 75 per cent of the infants grasp only after delay; while at 28 weeks only 14 per cent show delay in their grasping. The delay in grasp at 20 weeks is comparable to the delay in approach noted at 16 weeks. Lacking adaptive hand orientation, interdigital grasp is very frequent at 20 weeks. It occurs in 61 per cent of the infants at that age as compared with 7 per cent at 28 weeks.

Retention and manipulatory exploitation of the ring are dependent upon a substratum of prehensory capacity. Accordingly we find that the percentage of children who retain the ring in one hand during the entire period of observation rises from 20 per cent at 16 weeks to 65 per cent at 28 weeks. Holding the ring with both hands during the situation also rises from a frequency of 10 per cent to 67 per cent in this age range.

Since 16 weeks is so transitional in the organization of prehensory patterns, it is not surprising that the number of children who open and close the hands somewhat rhythmically upon the ring occurs with a maximum frequency (30 per cent) at this age. This is another paradoxical association of apparently contradictory patterns comparable to the fling-out and close-in of the arms. Alternate hand opening and closing were observed in 14 per cent of the children as late as 28 weeks.

Once the ring is seized its preferential route is to the mouth, and mouthing rises from a frequency of 38 per cent at 16 weeks to 82 and 74 per cent at 24 and 28 weeks. The manipulations characteristically involve both hands. As a matter of fact, the relatively large size of the ring (especially large if we remind ourselves of the diminutive dimensions of the infant) favors the participation of the free hand. This free hand comes to the mid plane during manipulation in 25 per cent of the infants at 16 weeks, 51 per cent at 20 weeks, 56 per cent at 24 weeks, and 84 per cent at 28 weeks.

It is a very interesting and significant fact that, although the free hand is in the mid zone with such frequency at these age levels, actual transfer does not occur with comparable frequency. The frequencies for transfer at corresponding ages are 3 per cent at 16 weeks, 18 per cent at 20 weeks, 41 per cent at 24 weeks, and 74 per cent at 28 weeks. From this ratio of frequencies we may conclude that bilateral grasp, bilateral manipulation, and hand-to-hand transfer arise developmentally as partially individuated patterns. Accordingly these patterns remain partially merged and do not become well differentiated and coordinated until about the age of 28 weeks.

For similar reasons, dropping of the ring occurs with a high frequency of 78 per cent at 16 weeks and a low frequency of 32 per cent at 28 weeks. So intermittent is prehension at 16 weeks that 42 per cent of the infants drop the ring immediately, whereas immediate dropping is rarely or never observed at 24 and 28 weeks.

If the ring is dropped it is pursued by 29 per cent of the infants at 24 weeks and 100 per cent at 28 weeks. All or most of these infants are successful in resecuring the ring when it is dropped. Rolling to the side is a pattern of postural activity which intrudes itself at 16, 20, and 28 weeks of age. It does not much alter the patterns of exploitation. Even though the infant rolls to the side he continues the exploitiveness in which he is engaged. But in the concealed process of growth some correlation is being established between these postural and manipulative patterns so that in due time they will be under full voluntary initiation and voluntary coordination.

§17. RATTLE BEHAVIOR

(4 weeks–28 weeks)

The Situation

The infant lay in the supine position. The examiner with circuitous approach brought the rattle above the infant's lower chest. If the infant fixated on the rattle it was held there for 5 additional seconds. If not, the examiner gently activated the rattle (by twirling it between index finger and thumb). If the infant did not then regard the rattle it was brought into the visual field, right or left depending on head position. When visual regard was secured, the examiner immobilized the rattle and held it so for 5 seconds. The examiner then moved the rattle toward the face hand, touching the dorsum of the digits if the hand was partly closed. He inserted the rattle handle into this hand if open, or he pried the fingers back to effect insertion. Having observed the infant's responses after grasping, the examiner took the rattle again and moved it slowly toward the occiput hand (repeating the procedure just described). These particular maneuvers were limited to infants who were in the tonic neck reflex postural attitude with face hand in extension.

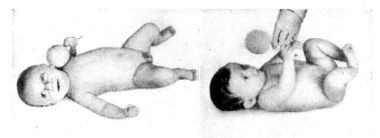

Fig. 17.—Rattle behavior: 12 weeks and 20 weeks.

At 12 weeks and at subsequent age levels the examiner held the rattle above the sternum for some time if necessary to elicit delayed spontaneous grasp. If grasp did not ensue he moved the rattle within a few inches of the left hand to evoke grasp. If grasp did not occur he inserted the rattle into the hand to observe the subsequent manipulation for approximately three minutes.

Stimulus Factors

It is natural that we should have included the rattle in our complement of test objects. The rattle is one of the most ancient and universal of all infant toys. It rivals the ball. Indeed, a frequent type of rattle is a hollow, sound-producing ball with a handle. Prototypes of the modern nursery rattle have been found among the remains of very early cultures. The model used in our normative observations was made of celluloid with a slender handle terminating in a loop. Physically the features which were significant from the standpoint of stimulus values were the lightness of weight, the sphericity of the bowl, one half of which was blue (or pink), the other white; and the contained gravel which gave a mild frictional or percussive sound on movement.

The procedures used in the presentation of the rattle served in some measure to define the stimulus factors which were operative in determining behavior, but the exact role of the sound cannot always be ascertained from the data. The rattle was first presented without sounding, but it was mildly agitated by the examiner if sight alone did not provoke response. The rattle was presented only to infants in the supine position. If the child could not secure the rattle unassisted, its handle was brought near his hand, was touched to his fingers, or, as a last resort, was inserted in the palm. The rattle thus became a device for defining the prehensory capacities of the infant, under graded stimulus conditions.

When does the infant "shake" the rattle "in order to" produce the sound? Probably at a later age than the optimistic parent and even the adultomorphic examiner unwarily supposes. Even an infant of very tender age presents a plausible picture of absorbed rattle play which is very deceiving. Does he really play the rattle, using the verb transitively? Our normative data throw light on this interesting psychological question, because all the infants who were observed in the rattle situation were also previously observed in the supine situation. During the latter situation, the infant was subjected to no specific stimulation and his free, spontaneous action patterns asserted themselves. These patterns could be compared with those for rattle play. On making a comparative analysis of the patterns for the five age levels from 4 to 16 weeks, it was found that possession of the rattle had no influence, or only a very slight influence, on the observable behavior. Opening and closing of the fingers (on the rattle handle) and mouthing were increased, but otherwise the patterns of manipulation and exploitation were much the same, whether or not the infant's hand was empty. The examiner might also remove the rattle, but the infant would continue to wave and brandish his arms, as indeed he had done before the rattle was ever presented.

This simple and oft substantiated finding has general significance for the whole problem of stimulus factors throughout the period of infancy. Our conventional stimulus-response concepts often make us ascribe an undue stimulus power to an external object which in reality may influence the course of action no more than the sparrow influences the veering of the weather vane upon which it happens to perch.

There comes a time, of course, when the sound produced by the rattle has a repercussive effect upon movements which the infant makes during the act of sound production. Very gradually he becomes a prime mover in the utilization of the rattle. The movements are first of all mainly endogenous in origin; slowly they become associated with visual-auditory components which become stimulus factors; and these components of themselves tend to set up the movements by which they were initiated in the first instance. In this circularity of endogenous movement, reaction, and response we have the basis for that anticipativeness which ultimately makes the infant a true *agent* in the utilization of the rattle. He reaches this level by slow and gradual developmental processes which are suggested below in the summary of rattle behavior.

The rattle was presented only at the eight age levels up to 32 weeks. The reader who wishes to gain an impression of the patterns of rattle play at subsequent age levels may find their partial equivalent in the older infants' behavior in the bell situation. The hand bell is a rattle with a visible sound mechanism.

Behavior Trends

Regard. It will be recalled that the rattle was at first presented noiselessly and held in suspense for five seconds over the child's chest. The rattle was then gently sounded if no visual regard occurred. If still unheeded, the rattle was brought into the direct visual field and if necessary was again sounded. Infants who continued to disregard had yet further opportunity to fixate upon it, for the rattle was touched to the hand or inserted into the palm. These progressive stages in the presentation of the rattle served to differentiate ascending levels in the organization of perception.

As many as 41 per cent of the infants 4 weeks old fail to regard the rattle at all. This percentage falls to 24 at 6 weeks and to 0 at 20 weeks. Of those who look at the rattle, approximately one-third at 4, 6, 8, and 12 weeks give spontaneous regard when the rattle is held without sounding in the mid plane. Strikingly enough, at 16 weeks this proportion rises sharply to 69 per cent. At 28 weeks prompt spontaneous regard in the mid line is well-nigh universal. Delay in regard is highly characteristic from 4 through 12 weeks and occurs in approximately three-fourths of all the infants who manifest any regard. There is more than an even chance that the regard will also be only momentary at these ages. Even at 16

SITUATION: RATTLE (Ra)

Ra	Behavior items	4	6	8	12	16	20	24	28	32	36	40	44	48	52	56
1	Does not regard	41	24	22	8	4										
2	(If r.) r. only in line of vis. or when shaken	70	68	67	68	28										
3	Regards after delay	43	48	54	72	35	24	21	6							
4	(If regards) regards after delay	77	72	78	72	41										
5	Reg. in mid plane (spon. or after shaken)	46	44	35	62	95										
6	Regards in mid plane (lg.h.)	16	16	14	16	100										
7	Regards in mid plane (rd.h.)	56	56	40	80	94										
8	Regards spontaneously in mid plane	29	31	33	32	69	76	79	94							
9	Regards only momentarily	50	59	54	46	46	21	13	6							
10	Regards starily	3	11	11	42	64	3	6	0							
11	Regards consistently	0	0	0	0	11	35	58	88							
12	Regards surroundings	59	67	78	57	25	29	15	28							
13	Regards examiner	35	58	54	96	58	57	61	61							
14	Regards hand	0	8	0	23	11	23	15								
15	Regards rattle in hand	10	24	14	35	45	79	93	100							
16	(Contact) hand clenches	60	65	48	46	0										
17	(Contact) arm becomes active	50	54	59	27	7										
18	(Contact) hand opens	65	58	89	83	79	93	100	100							
19	(Contact) hand opens immediately	43	31	61	75	80										
20	Near hand grasps rattle	0	0	0	6	25	70	87	94							
21	(In hand) holds actively	45	60	52	78	77										
22	(In hand) holds passively	90	68	87	61	38										
23	Arm increases activity	0	0	14	30	53	94	90	100							
24	Approaches	0	0	11	12	29	90	83	100							
25	Approaches after delay	0	0	0	4	20	24	29	10							
26	Approaches promptly	0	0	0	0	6	43	50	88							
27	Approaches with both hands	0	0	0	5	22	61	53	50							
28	Approaches with one hand	0	0	5	9	15	39	40	62							
29	Hands close on each other	0	0	0	5	14	18	7	0							
30	Hands to mouth	0	0	0	9	27	15	7	0							
31	Contacts rattle	0	0	7	4	15	56	61	94							
32	Grasps	0	0	0	0	0	47	61	94							
33	Grasps after delay	0	0	0	0	0	35	45	19							
34	Manipulates holding by bowl	0	0	0	0	0	0	20	46							
35	Retains ent. per. (placed in r. or l. hand)	45	63	42	75	54	—									
36	Retains entire period (placed in left hand)	37	33	37	47	37	35	31	65							
37	Opens and closes hand	45	36	27	33	35	17	18	9							
38	Brings rattle to mouth	30	28	22	39	59	64	73	78							
39	Waves or shakes rattle	0	0	0	0	16	33	38	32							
40	Brings free hand toward mid plane	10	12	5	44	50										
41	Free hand contacts rattle	10	8	5	22	29	56	85	78							
42	Free hand fingers rattle	5	0	0	17	11	17	42	22							
43	Grasps with free hand	0	0	0	0	3	42	40	50							
44	Transfers	0	0	0	0	0	3	25	40	50						
45	Drops	100	92	84	69	64	70	62	18							
46	Drops immediately	70	46	58	31	23	12	6	0							
47	If drops, responds to loss	29	25	13	25	60										
48	If drops, regards after losing	5	0	0	0	17	42	50	18							
49	If drops, strains toward lost rattle	0	0	0	0	11	36	52								
50	If drops, resecures rattle	0	0	0	0	5	20	43	50							
51	Rolls to side	3	0	7	4	42	62	68	60							
52	Frets	33	14	7	15	27	16	18	45							
53	Vocalizes	23	36	21	38	22	41	44	25							

Note: Placed in both hands up to 16 weeks, 15 cases only.

weeks, 46 per cent of the infants show a momentary regard, but at 28 weeks this occurs in only 6 per cent of the cases.

That the perceptual abilities of the infant are relatively immature throughout the first quarter of the first year of life is reflected in the fact that over two-thirds of the infants, up to 12 weeks of age inclusive, who showed regard for the rattle did so only when the rattle was in direct line of vision or after it was shaken. The percentages for delay of regard just given also suggest immaturity in perceptual organization. Of similar significance are the frequencies of regard for the surroundings, ranging from 5 per cent to 78 per cent for the age levels through 12 weeks. Regard for the examiner, sometimes at the expense of the rattle, shows a steady increase from 35 per cent at 4 weeks to 96 per cent at 12 weeks.

At 16 weeks, however, the rattle evidently takes on a new importance in the perceptual world of the infant. Or, to phrase the facts more behavioristically, the perceptive systems of the infant have integrated at a higher level. In more homely language, he now *stares* at the rattle. What does this staring denote? Probably not a passive receptivity but an active oculomotor reorganization which leads to a clarification of the object. Seeing has not yet become instantaneously automatic; visual perception in its nascent stages requires active, specific adaptation and staring involves inhibitory response which focalizes the area of such adaptation. A comparable restrictiveness, that is, a visually discriminative "interest" in the examiner, asserts itself at the 16 weeks age level.

But the figures for the behavior item *Stares at rattle* are especially arresting, for they rise from a low level of 3 per cent at 4 weeks to 64 per cent at 16 weeks with a precipitous decline to 3 per cent at 20 weeks and 0 per cent at 28 weeks. This sudden descent does not mean that the infant has a suddenly lost "interest" in the rattle; it may well mean that he has, through previous starings at similar objects, mastered the elementary optical constitution of the rattle and is now ready to become interested in it in a more advanced way. Accordingly, the frequency of the item *Consistent regard* (visual attentiveness) for the rattle mounts from 11 per cent at 16 weeks to 88 per cent at 28 weeks. And as for regard for the rattle when it is in his hand, whether placed there by the examiner or attained by grasp, this undergoes a significantly steady, gradual increase from 10 per cent at 4 weeks to 100 per cent at 28 weeks. At the latter age the infant has also achieved an elementary motor control of the rattle; and the two forms of control, visual and manual, are in close coordination.

Rapid visual pick-up increases in frequency and definiteness with age. This shows itself in increasing perceptiveness for the examiner's face as opposed to physical surroundings at 12 and 16 weeks. Prior to that time it is the surroundings which receive a greater share of the visual regard. Facility of regard in the mid plane, however, does not seem to depend entirely upon retinal maturity. It was noted that among infants of equal age some showed a greater freedom and scope of rotational head movements than did other infants in the same normative group. Those infants up to 12 weeks of age who were in general round-headed in type tended to perceive the rattle in the mid plane more readily than infants whose heads were longish. This observation is discussed at greater length in the summary of the dangling ring situation, which offers interesting points of comparison with rattle behavior. The tonic neck reflex so prominent in supine behavior up to 12 weeks of age suggests still further relationships between factors of head conformation, head activity, posture, and perception, laterality, and eyedness. The percentages for mid-plane regard of the rattle show a marked and consistent difference in favor of the round-heads in the following ratios: at 4 weeks 16:56; at 6 weeks, 16:56; at 8 weeks, 14:40; at 12 weeks, 16:80. At 16 weeks the groups were nearly identical, 100:94. It is even suggested that the long-heads do not *spontaneously* see the rattle at all in the mid plane until the advanced age of 16 weeks. The problem is being more carefully studied and for the present no statements can be made without qualifications.

Prehension. Grasp may take place either on visual or on tactile cues. Our normative data on the rattle enable us to make some comparison of both sets of cues. The development of visual perceptiveness as such has just been outlined, and it will be recalled that the handle of the rattle was persuasively pressed on or within the infant's hand if there was no spontaneous grasp.

Four kinds of motor reaction may take place on visual and tactile presentation of the rattle: (*a*) general body activity; (*b*) specific arm activity; (*c*) directed approach; (*d*) hand extension and closure, with and without completed grasp. These responses will now be briefly reviewed.

It is difficult to separate *a* and *b*, because *b* is a differentiation or accentuation which defines itself within a matrix of generalized response. What to ordinary observation seems to be a restricted reaction of the arm proves on cinema analysis to be intimately associated with a comprehensive postural response which involves the whole child. However, for descriptive purposes a rough distinction was made between the more general and the more specific forms of response. At 4 weeks of age no increase in general activity was noted on presentation of the rattle; if anything there was a tendency toward reduction of such activity if the rattle was perceived. There was, however, a slow increase from 6 weeks to 16 weeks.

In observing arm activity in the rattle position, it is very difficult to distinguish between movements which are fortuitously coincidental and those which are responsive to the specific stimulus. The form of these movements may be highly similar to that exhibited without the presence of the rattle. However, there was an unmistakable tendency for the sight of the rattle to initiate an increase in the rate and vigor of the "spontaneous" movements. Combining all forms of movement, a definite and decided increase in hand-arm activity asserted itself in 14 per cent of the cases at 8 weeks, 30 per cent at 12 weeks, 53 per cent at 16 weeks, 94 per cent at 20 weeks, and 100 per cent at 28 weeks. This very consistent trend covering a period of twenty weeks is correlated with the progressive organization of prehension on *visual* cue. Actual grasp on sight covers a much narrower age range, for it does not occur commonly until 20 weeks (47 per cent) and not generally until 28 weeks (94 per cent). Grasp on touch occurs much earlier, as will be noted presently.

When does increased hand-arm activity become directed approach? It is not always easy to determine, because there may be brief or sporadic movements of approach in a series of movements which superficially appear undirected. Moreover, except in cinema analysis, it is somewhat difficult to apply a stable criterion of distinction. Nevertheless, the figures for approach show a consistent trend which is developmentally significant. At 8 weeks 11 per cent of the infants made approach movements; at 16 weeks 29 per cent made such movements; at 20 weeks 90 per cent; at 28 weeks 100 per cent. The behavior at 16 weeks is transitional in character, because 53 per cent of the infants at that age were credited with increased hand-arm activity. This is almost twice the number of those who exhibited definite approach.

The mechanisms of early approach are by no means simple. Delay in approach occurred in from 20 to 30 per cent of the infants at 16, 20, and 24 weeks. Prompt approach is very rare at 16 weeks and occurred in only half the infants at 24 weeks; but at 28 weeks it reaches a frequency of 88 per cent. Bilateral approach is developmentally more primitive than unilateral and is especially characteristic of 20 weeks, when it occurred in 61 per cent of the cases. At this age likewise the hands closed on each other in 18 per cent of the infants. Such hand closure is very infrequent thereafter as well as prior to 16 weeks. However, unilateral approach was observed as early as 8 weeks, and rose steadily to a frequency of 62 per cent at 28 weeks. The approach movements are often completely abortive. They result in mere contact of the rattle and that only in from 7 to 15 per cent of the infants at 8, 12, and 16 weeks of age. Actual grasp rises precipitously from approximately 50 per cent at 20 weeks to 100 per cent at 28 weeks.

So much for prehension on visual cue aided or unaided by auditory stimulation. The behavior trends just outlined may now be compared with those in which tactile stimulation was used. At once it becomes apparent that tactile cues are genetically more fundamental and primitive. At 4 and 6 weeks visual stimulation failed to excite hand-arm activity, but when the rattle was *touched* to the hand, there was a responsive increase in such activity at these age levels and at 8 weeks as well. Closely associated with this arm reaction was a responsive clenching of the hand, and the two reactions tended to occur simultaneously. They were noted in from 50 to 60 per cent of all the infants at 4, 6, and 8 weeks. At 12 weeks hand clenching apparently was ascendant over arm activity and occurred in 46 per cent of the cases as opposed to 27 per cent (for arm activity). Still more striking is the fact that hand clenching reaches 0 frequency at the next age level (16 weeks) and the arm activity descends to 7 per cent. Since these observations were made on infants in the supine position enjoying unconstrained freedom of action, they indicate very forcibly the fact that the prehensory mechanism has proceeded far in the direction of individuation or partial differentiation within a general matrix of postural response. Of similar import is the fact that 80 per cent of the 16 weeks-old infants opened the hands immediately on contact by the rattle. These facts might be stated in terms of inhibition rather than individuation, but the upshot of the discussion would be the same.

Ability to open the hands is almost as essential to the act of prehension as the ability to close the hand. At the younger age levels the examiner finds the infant's hands usually closed before the rattle is touched to it but at 16 weeks the hands are open in 50 per cent of the cases. These figures again confirm the importance of this age level in the genesis of grasp. Immediate opening of the closed hand (when contacted with the rattle) is relatively infrequent at 4 and 6 weeks (43 and 31 per cent) but is characteristic of 12 and 16 weeks (75 and 80 per cent). At 8 weeks 61 per cent of the infants reacted immediately by opening the hands. Opening of the hand, whether prompt or delayed, occurs frequently at all ages, the percentages ranging from 65 per cent at 4 weeks to 100 per cent at 24 weeks.

It is interesting to note that in the supine situation spontaneous opening of the hand was associated with arm activity at the early age levels. In the rattle situation the reverse is true. Arm activity and active closure or fisting of the hand appear together. Opening of the hands, however, increases in frequency as arm activity decreases. In these relationships one again glimpses a process of differential individuation. Actual grasp of the rattle on tactile cue (contact) never, or rarely, takes place at the early age levels up to 12 weeks. At 16 weeks, however, one infant out of four grasps on tactile cue. At 20 weeks 70 per cent and at 28 weeks 94 per cent grasped on contact.

It is profitable to compare these percentages with those already given for grasping on visual cue. No child at 16 weeks grasped on visual cue and 47 per cent at 20 weeks grasped on sight, as compared with 70 per cent at 20 weeks who grasped on contact. Even at 24 weeks, grasping on contact occurs with greater frequency than grasping on sight. It is only at 28 weeks that the frequencies are equal. These figures illumine the developmental transitions which are taking place in the field of prehension in the age sector from 16 to 24 weeks.

Two forms of grasp are observed at the early age levels; namely, heel or palmar grasp and a more open palmar grasp with a passive, pseudo-thumb opposition. The difference between these two types of grasp lies in the position of the thumb. In the heel grasp, the thumb is usually fisted in the central palm, which results in pressing the rattle handle against the heel of the palm. In opening the hand, the thumb may be extended and come to lie in a position parallel to the fingers. In the heel grasp, the thumb is not involved; or, if involved, acts as one of the other digits. Passive thumb opposition occurs when the hand opens widely and the thumb not only extends but abducts to a slight degree. Accordingly, when the rattle is placed between the thumb and the fingers, the latter encircle the handle and the thumb rests at the side in pseudo-opposition. Heel grasp occurred in the great majority of infants at 4 weeks and with diminishing frequency at subsequent age levels. Passive thumb opposition showed some tendency to increase. At the age of 4 weeks, heel grasp was in marked ascendancy.

Once the infant has secured the rattle with or without its insertion into his hand, he manifests two distinguishable kinds of holding, namely, passive holding and active holding. These two methods again tend to vary in frequency with age; the former decreasing, the latter increasing. Passive holding may be regarded as highly characteristic of the 4 weeks level of maturity; active holding is almost as characteristic of 16 weeks. The touch of the rattle elicits regard only rarely at the earlier age levels and indeed even at 16 weeks in only 13 per cent of the cases.

Manipulation and Exploitation. Manipulation of the rattle in the hand will necessarily depend in part upon the infant's capacity to maintain a prehensory hold upon the rattle. This capacity apparently undergoes a very steady improvement with age. The percentages for the item *Drops the rattle sometime during the situation* decline from 100 per cent at 4 weeks with considerable regularity to a low level of 18 per cent at 28 weeks. Of special interest is the item *Drops immediately.* Here again there is a progressive developmental diminution with age from a maximum percentage of 70 at 4 weeks to 0 at 28 weeks. Indeed, even at 20 weeks only 12 per cent, and at 24 weeks only 6 per cent, of the infants dropped the rattle immediately. When the rattle was dropped, the examiner replaced it, if necessary by insertion in the infant's hand, and it will be recalled that in about half the cases up through 16 weeks the rattle was presented to both the occiput hand and the face hand as determined by the tonic neck reflex position. No marked differences of response other than visual were observed in relation to these two hand positions.

Reckoning the percentages on the basis of behavior observed in relation to either or both hands, we find that, in spite of the dropping tendency, 45 per cent of the infants even at 4 weeks retained the rattle in one hand throughout the brief period of observation. In the case of the older infants, 20 to 28 weeks of age, the rattle was presented to the left hand. Including these cases, we find that approximately one-third of the infants retained the rattle in the left hand during the entire period of observation from 4 weeks through 24 weeks, and two-thirds did so at the age of 28 weeks.

Assuming now some retention of the rattle, what kinds of manipulatory pattern assert themselves? One of the most elementary reactions is simple opening and closing of the hand without dropping the rattle. More or less rhythmic closure and opening of the hand occurred in 45 per cent of the infants at 4 weeks. This figure falls to 9 per cent at 28 weeks. The free hand may open and close in a similar manner, and when the free hand is brought upon the rattle the flexion of the digits simulates fingering. Fingering of some sort occurred in 5 per cent of the infants at 4 weeks, in 17 per cent at 12 and 20 weeks, and 11 per cent at 16 weeks, but rose to a maximum of 42 per cent at 24 weeks, falling to 22 per cent at 28 weeks. The significance of this fingering will be commented upon presently. It is quite probable that the fingering at 24 weeks has a different significance from that at the earlier age levels.

Very early the free hand shows some tendency to come toward the mid plane. At 4 weeks 10 per cent of the infants brought the free hand some distance toward the mid plane. At 16 weeks this was true of half the infants. Only 29 per cent, however, succeeded in actually contacting the rattle with the free hand at the age of 16 weeks. This percentage rises sharply to 56 per cent at 20 weeks, 85 per cent at 24 weeks, and 78 per cent at 28 weeks. This participation of the free hand results in diverse forms of manipulation and exploitation. It may result in mere contacting, in exploitive fingering, or in grasping, followed by actual transfer. Such grasping, with subsequent transfer, occurred in half the infants at the age of 28 weeks and in a quarter of the infants as early as 20 weeks. Very rarely (3 per cent) did grasping, followed by fortuitous transfer, occur at 16 weeks.

Mouthing is another early form of exploitation, closely associated with manipulation. At 4 weeks almost 30 per cent of the infants brought the rattle to the mouth. This number is doubled or more than doubled at 16 weeks and at the following age levels.

The very word rattle suggests waving, shaking, and brandishing. It is time to say a word in regard to these forms of behavior. They do not appear in the record, however, until the age of 16 weeks, when 16 per cent of the children are credited with waving. This percentage is doubled or slightly more than doubled at the subsequent age levels up to 28 weeks. To what extent can this shaking be regarded as a true exploitation of the rattle? The same question might be asked with regard to similar behavior items such as (a) hand opening and closing while holding the rattle; (b) contacting the rattle with the free hand; (c) fingering the rattle; and even (d) mouthing the rattle. If the observer naively dramatizes the situation, all these manifestations of behavior take on the aspect of true exploitiveness. But we have already hinted at the possibility that similar behavior patterns assert themselves without the intervention of the rattle as a stimulus object.

When the spontaneous activities of the infant in the supine situation, with and without the rattle, are compared, we find a high degree of parallelism in the behavior patterns with the exception of item d just mentioned. Cinema records show that at 4, 6, and 12 weeks even opening and closing of the hand occurred with relative frequency in the simple supine situation, when no object was in the hand.

Although the infant has no toy in the simple supine situation, he does have an opportunity to mouth his hand, and this tendency to mouth the hand may be compared with mouthing the rattle. Such a comparison shows that this hand-mouthing tendency without the rattle is quite similar to that with the rattle at 4, 6, and 8 weeks. At 12 weeks, however, the tendency to rattle mouthing is over twice as strong, and at 16 weeks over thrice as strong as the tendency to simple hand mouthing.

Although rattle behavior in so many ways resembles spontaneous supine behavior, it would be an error to suppose that the rattle means very little to the infant. Indeed, as early as 4 weeks 29 per cent of the infants respond in some way to the loss of the rattle (or the consequent sound) as soon as it drops from the hand. The response to loss of the rattle takes on various forms such as momentary startling, blinking, mild transient fussing, or even crying. The response tends to become better defined with age and at 16 weeks 60 per cent of the infants definitely responded in some way to the loss of the rattle. Only 17 per cent, however, made any visual pursuit of the lost rattle at this age and only 11 per cent strained posturally toward the rattle; only 5 per cent regained the rattle when lost.

These percentages undergo a definite increase at the subsequent age levels. At 24 weeks half the infants pursue the lost rattle visually or by motor straining. At 28 weeks half of them regain the dropped rattle. The ability to recover the lost rattle is conditioned to some extent by the capacity to roll to the side. We find that 60 per cent of the 28 weeks-old infants do roll to the side during the rattle situation whether the rattle is in hand or out of hand. However, recovery depends on still other factors, for while 42 per cent of the infants roll to the side at 16 weeks only 5 per cent actually regain the rattle.

This simple bit of adaptive behavior, therefore, depends upon the organization of other than purely motor abilities. It is difficult to make any objective statement concerning the affective aspects of rattle behavior. With the exception of the few infants who at certain ages may be startled by abrupt sounds of the rattle, the situation is one which is generally enjoyed. It is significant that vocalization was observed in a rather large proportion of cases during the rattle situation at all age levels from 4 to 28 weeks. Such vocalization, largely expressive of satisfaction, was heard on the average in one child out of three at each age level.

§18. TABLE TOP BEHAVIOR

(12 weeks–56 weeks)

The Situation

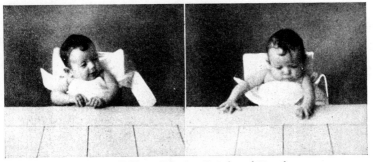

FIG. 18.—Table top behavior: 12 weeks and 16 weeks.

The infant was placed in the examining chair, securely fastened by the supportive band. The side rails were raised to the level of the infant's elbows. While the infant was sitting in the chair and looking in a forward direction, the examiner slowly brought the table top into a horizontal plane and placed it quietly and unobtrusively upon the side rails. If the infant's arms engaged the edge of the table top, they were disengaged and brought above the surface.

The examiner retreated to the rear of the crib; no further stimulus was applied.

Stimulus Factors

It is psychologically naive and adultomorphic to suppose that the infant reacts to the examining table *qua* table. For him the whole world is furniture and there are no discrete articles of furniture made for instrumental uses. Not until he is sophisticated by persistent convention does he quiescently sit before a table waiting well manneredly for an examiner to deposit upon its surface an important test object. The table top itself is an expansive test object, possibly more vital to the infant than the psychological materials secondarily placed upon it.

The table top offers to the infant a field for visual exploration and for tactile manipulation. It is not an indifferent surface. It is itself charged with primary stimulus factors which often prevail over those of the specific test objects. There is indeed a kind of stimulus rivalry between major table and minor object. The infant heeds first one, then the other; or he senses them both together; or he brings one into relation with the other, at first sketchily, perhaps confusedly, and only later consistently. These shifting emphases in the stimulus values of the table top are governed by developmental factors of maturity and experience. It is an interesting growth phenomenon to see how the table top in due season sinks to a secondary or subsidiary level in the infant's reactions.

In early infancy, therefore, the table must be considered as being full part and parcel of the total situation complex. Only toward the end of the first year of life does the infant begin to approximate the adult's perceptual reaction to the table as table. Prior to this time the table is more or less vaguely sensed as a surface with undefined boundaries, a surface which resists and resounds. But in its inner psychological essence we do not know when and how the infant actually perceives the table top. It is safer to suppose, even if it must be done hazily, that he perceives it with decidedly varying values as he matures, and that in some way these values arrange themselves into a developmental gradient.

While the infant is mastering the properties and the conventions of the table top, he also becomes aware of new properties, if not conventions, of the floor; that is, the platform on which he sits. The floor competes with the table top as a working surface. If he is working (that is, playing) with the cubes, for example, he brings them into exploitive relation with the platform or floor. There is thus set up a kind of ambivalence or even confusion between the table top and the floor.

This ambivalence serves to remind us of the vast number of physical orientations which each infant must acquire. He is not born with topographic instincts, any more than he is born with the capacity to speak words. The distinction between floor and table is a social amenity which concerns the field of cultural anthropology and also the field of developmental psychology. The infant, like his primitive ancestors, achieves the distinction slowly.

The infant's life begins within the womb; to its walls he must posturally adapt. After birth he must also "learn" to adapt to physical environs—to a bed, arms, lap, floor, room walls, chair, table. The adult takes the conventions of furniture for granted. Developmentally these conventions are extremely complex; one might say they are so technical that the infant can attain them only gradually. The method of his "learning" is an unwritten chapter of his psychology.

SITUATION: TABLE TOP (T)

T	Behavior items	4	6	8	12	16	20	24	28	32	36	40	44	48	52	56
1	Regards hands..........................				35	44	13	10	—	11	—					
2	Hand to mouth.........................				31	27	3	3	12							
3	Hands engage in mutual fingering.........				0	14	3	3								
4	Hands mutually contact..................				27	25	3									
5	Hand at table edge......................				33	34	27	29	27	19	14	3			4	
6	Hand pronate on table top..............					30	27	23	42	26	32	21	15	21	9	
7	Exploits table top......................				61	61	60	68	35	19	7	7				
8	Fingers table top.......................				58	32	20	23	—							
9	Scratches table top.....................				5	25	40	39	19	7	7					
10	Slaps table top.........................					4	3	32	62	48	57	45	19	21	16	16
11	Depends on mother.....................					0	0	15	15	4	7	22	25	29	12	
12	Adjusts poorly..........................				11	10	13	23	19	11	10	14	11	14	16	
	Per cent to whom toy was given..........					10	13	29	69	59	68	83	82	86	68	92

Reactions to the Table Top

At 12 weeks over half the infants were observed to finger the table top; at 28 weeks this simple fingering was no longer noted. When we say that the 12 weeks infant fingers the table top, we imply too much. This fingering is not accompanied by regard; similar digital flexion occurs independently of the table top but the resistance of the table doubtless makes of this a simple tactilemotor pattern of response. In a similar way the 12 and also the 16 weeks-old infant fingers, holds, and kneads the edge of the table top. Such manipulation of the edge is observed with diminishing frequency until 40 weeks of age. At 12 and at 16 weeks the hands of the infant may go to the mouth or engage at the mid line, or may mutually finger each other while he stares blankly ahead, possibly with no regard whatsoever for the table top. In a similar way over one-third of the infants at 12 and at 16 weeks stare preoccupiedly at their hands.

However, when scratching, fingering, kneading, and raking are descriptively lumped into the single category "exploitation," approximately two-thirds of all the infants from 12 through 24 weeks of age reacted to the table top in a manipulatory manner. At 28 weeks when well-defined pronate application of the hand to the table-top surface becomes prominent, the attack upon the table top without a toy or implement wears the aspect of definite exploitation in which sight, sound, and tactility all may figure. In the age range from 28 weeks to 40 weeks, from 62 per cent to 45 per cent of the infants slapped or banged the table top.

The table top presents a hard, grayish surface, marked with several lines as indicated in the illustration. These lines were rarely reacted to by the infant. The broad expanse of surface supplies a neutral background for optical configurations, a sounding board for banging and scratching, and a stage for manual exploitations. At the close of the first year some infants "discover" that the table has a nether aspect. They thrust their hands beneath the table and carry objects under it. This is another reminder of the psychological complexity of the infant's physical surroundings. They remain utterly simple and axiomatic to us until we glimpse the infant's point of view.

§19. CONSECUTIVE CUBES BEHAVIOR

(12 weeks–56 weeks)

The Situation

Stationed at the left rear corner of the crib, the examiner took the cubes from the container bag and transferred them to his smock pocket. Then he took a single cube and brought it circuitously below the farther margin of the table top. Holding it in the horizontal plane just above the table level, he slowly advanced the cube toward the infant. At the earlier age levels it was sometimes necessary to tap the cube against the table edge to elicit the infant's visual fixation. Using approximately two seconds to advance the cube from the far edge of the table top, the examiner placed the cube in the standard median position. He left the cube in this position for nine seconds if the child did not contact it, and then on the tenth second advanced the cube to the near median position, leaving it there for ten seconds if the child did not contact it. At the conclusion of the observation of the reactions to the first cube, the examiner placed the cube in the infant's left hand unless the infant had already spontaneously grasped the cube with the left hand. The examiner then presented the second cube in the

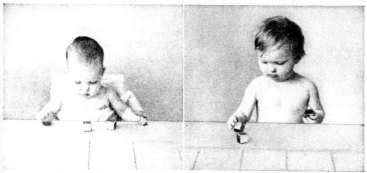

Fig. 19.—Consecutive cubes behavior: 20 weeks and 52 weeks.

manner already described. After appropriate observation, a cube was placed in either hand of the infant and the examiner presented a third cube.

Stimulus Factors

The cubes are made of firm, white wood, one inch in dimension, and painted a bright, non-lustrous red. In the consecutive cube situation only three cubes are required. In later situations ten cubes are used. Long experience has convinced us that these cubes are well suited to the purposes of behavior observation and they figure prominently in our examination procedures for all children from 12 weeks to 6 years of age. The cube is psychologically a good play object, but it is also a prototype of the building stone which since primitive days has played a prominent role in the psychology of man's work. The gradation of reactions of the infant to this time-honored vehicle of play and work, the building block or cube, reflects in outline the early infirmities and growth of human intelligence.

To what extent the cube is also reacted to as a potential food object can only be conjectured. It goes to the mouth frequently enough, but the mouth is an organ of perception as well as of mastication, and the subjective aspect of the stimulus must remain in obscurity. The stimulus values will vary with age and dentition. The firm texture of the cubes gives them enhanced value under the stress of tooth eruption.

In its physical properties the cube is well suited to the child's capabilities. The cube is not too large or too heavy to be easily prehended. It is, fortunately, too large to permit of swallowing, and yet it is small enough to enable the older infant to hold two cubes in one hand. It has a high degree of both stability and mobility. The edges and corners of the cube add to its tactile and visual values. The opposed surfaces of the cube help to define, for the observer, the child's manual and digital orientation. The red color of the cube establishes a definite contrast against the light gray table top. The stability of the cube is such that as many as ten cubes may be built into a vertical tower when the cubes are superimposed upon each other with approximate accuracy. The cubes make almost universal appeal. It is a highly exceptional infant who does not react positively to them whether presented singly or in massed formation.

In considering the behavior elicited by the consecutive cubes it should be remembered that this situation comes near the very beginning of the developmental examination. This fact may sometimes depress the reactions to the first cube; it is more likely to add the zest of novelty or even surprise. The presentation of two more cubes in succession tends strongly to add to the interest and to produce a warming-up effect. This procedure really gives the infant three opportunities to display his behavior patterns, and the examiner may take into account the whole period of the situation, as well as the distinctive reactions to the first, the second, and the third cube presentations. Each of these presentations virtually constitutes a separate situation because, from the standpoint of stimulus factors, it is interesting to inquire, What does the infant do when he has more than one cube at his disposal? Accordingly, the behavior items for consecutive cubes are tabulated for the individual presentations and also for the episode as a whole.

SITUATION: CONSECUTIVE CUBES (CC)

CC	Behavior items	4	6	8	12	16	20	24	28	32	36	40	44	48	52	56
1	Regards Examiner's withdrawing hand....				17	21	16	7	0	—	—	—	—	—	—	19
2	Shifts regard............................				78	94	52	55	51	75	44	73	68	85	80	81
3	Shifts regard to surroundings............				22	44	16	10	20	28	26	40	25	33	24	27
4	Shifts regard to Examiner...............				17	35	23	31	22	46	26	30	50	52	60	54
5	Shifts regard to hand...................				36	69	32	14	14	3	—	—	—	—	—	—
6	Approaches cube........................				22	33	71	86	100	100	100	100	100	100	100	100
7	Approaches after delay..................								41	76	56	60	56	57		
8	Approaches with one hand...............				17	15	30	30	46	74	82	92	92	96	68	72
9	Approaches with index finger............							3	4	4	7	20	15	15	13	8
10	Ap. cube on T.T. with cube in hand on pre.				3	0	0	0	41	43	60	65	52	55	73
11	Reaches for cube beyond reach..........				—	—	27	50	28	3	—					
12	Scratches table top (T.T.)..............				9	21	35	23	12	14	—					
13	Grasps without securing cube............					6	62	70	14	7	3	0				
14	Grasps cube............................				16	42	86	100	100	100	100	100	100	100	100	100
15	Grasps only one cube...................				11	33	24	12	14	0						
16	Grasps first and second cubes...........						63	77	82	89	96	87	100	95	96
17	Grasps first, second, and third cubes......				—	—	18	32	43	45	66	36	47	42	69
18	Grasps cube in right hand...............							26	36	44	41	50	51	59	77
19	Retains a cube in each hand.............				44	35	65	100	85	100	96	96	96	100	96
20	Holds one cube and grasps another.......					3	17	50	48	79	93	88	96	90	85
21	Grasps with thumb opposing fingers......						49	69	82	89	90	72	90	80	97
22	Inspects cube in hand..................				17	29	30	44	50	66	63	48	40	15	19
23	Manipulates cubes......................				30	57	72	92	92	100	73	80	90	97	100
24	Pushes or hits cube out of reach.........				—	—	44	53	25	—						
25	Pushes and pulls cubes on table top......				11	35	53	58	56	25	20	35	26	26	8
26	Bangs cube on table top.................				—	3	42	70	35	70	53	64	63	40	50
27	Cube to mouth..........................				5	13	42	62	88	89	85	90	80	44	40	31
28	Brings free hand to cube at mouth.......				—	13	20	52	40	37	33	15	0	9	—
29	Pokes cube.............................									0	23	15	11	8	8
30	Manip. cube above T.T. (ex. of transfer)..				—	—	—	28	39	48	57	42	51	61	77
31	Transfers cube..........................				—	9	24	63	75	85	73	92	60	57	65
32	Rotates cube............................					3	19	26	32	27	15	15	8	12
33	Twiddles cube...........................												20	16	8
34	Picks up one cube after another.........								—	27	41	32	62
35	Drops cube on table....................				85	63	71	76	90	89	88	86	87	81	80	96
36	Casts cube..............................												45	29	27
37	If drops cube, resecures it..............				5	8	39	71	72	87	70	80	95	93	80
38	Resecures cube from table...............				3	6	30	69	63	75	60	69	78	76	77
39	Brings cube to side rail.................										0	15	33	21	4
40	Drops cube over side rail................										0	12	19	16	—
41	Carries or pursues cube to platform.......				—	3	13	8	37	43	43	46	41	55	65
42	Drops and pursues cube to platform......				—	20	23	23	36	36	40	42	37	50	38
43	Brings cube to platform.................				—	—	—	0	4	22	23	36	33	55	58
44	Resecures cube from platform............				—	—	7	0	14	25	27	31	26	40	21
45	If drops, resecures cube from platform....				—	—	29	0	50	66	72	73	78	79	64
46	Combines two cubes.....................				7	3	3	12	48	68	77	88	67	90	92
47	Brings two cubes together...............				0	0	0	0	15	39	43	35	26	47	58
48	Pushes cube with cube in hand..........				0	0	0	0	22	14	17	27	22	13	8
49	Hits cube on table top with cube in hand.				0	0	0	0	22	43	40	52	22	32	36
50	Places cube in hand on cube on table top..				0	0	0	0	0	4	10	27	19	45	50
51	Builds tower of two cubes...............										0	7	11	24	31
52	Offers cube to Examiner or mother.......											0	8	16	35
53	Leans..................................				32	28	51	37	42	30	30	20	26	16	—
54	Postural activity.......................									11	57	65	65	67	53
55	Pivots.................................										23	34	44	32	27
56	Turns to side rail......................									11	33	62	58	58	31
57	Creeps.................................										6	7	7	16	—
58	Attempts to stand......................											11	24	12
59	Vocalizes..............................				26	15	35	38	33	42	30	33	80	52	60	38

SITUATION: FIRST CUBE (CC1)

CC1	Behavior items	4	6	8	12	16	20	24	28	32	36	40	44	48	52	56
1	Regards cube (s.m.p. or n.m.p.)........				78	100	97	100	100	100	100	100	100	100	100	100
2	Regards cube (n.m.p.).............				57	80										
3	Regards cube...............				48	81	90	97	96	100	100	100	100	100	100	100
4	Regards after delay................				43	25	27	13	0	4	0	0	8	4	8	0
5	Regards immediately.............				61	75	73	77	100	96	100	100	92	96	92	96
6	Regards momentarily............				48	79	33	10	4	—						
7	Regards recurrently.............				30	56	40	27	27	37	21	40	35	45	63	65
8	Regards intermittently..........				4	22	27	3								
9	Regards prolongedly............				26	37	27	27	12	0	0	0				
10	Regards passively.............				39	62	27	7	0							
11	Regards actively.............				35	38	73	93	100	100	100	100	100	100	100	100
12	Regards consistently..........					30	53	89	89	96	93	96	96	92	92	100
13	Regards predominantly.........				48	62	71	100								
14	Regards Examiner's presenting hand				48	17	17	3								
15	Regards hand..............				52	65	30	10	4							
16	Regards hand predominantly..........				48	48										
17	Shifts regard................				78	92	43	30	27	37	21	40	35	45	63	65
18	Shifts regard from cube to hand........				26	48	12	13	13	3	—	—	—	—	—	
19	Shifts regard to table top.............				22	48										
20	Arms increase activity...............				81	90	100	100	100	100	100	100	100	100	100	100
21	Directs approach.................				22	25	50	83	100	100	100	100	100	100	97	100
22	If approaches, approaches after delay....					30	34	12	—	—	7	7	8	11	13	12
23	Contacts.....................				22	40	61	90	100	100	100	100	100	100	100	100
24	Dislodges on contact............				0	6	33	45	42	19	14	3	0			
25	Grasps......................				0	8	33	77	96	100	100	100	100	100	100	100
26	(In hand) holds actively............				50	60	81	83	100	100	100	100	100	100	100	100
27	Manipulates on table top...........				0	10	35	53	42	30	21	20	12	7	26	15
28	Bangs on table top..............						3	30	31	32	43	33	42	41	26	23
29	Rubs cube on table top or platform......									7	11	30	8	11	13	7
30	Lifts cube...................				15	23	58	80	100	100	100	100	100	100	100	100
31	Brings cube to mouth.............				5	10	37	48	85	89	68	63	54	33	37	19
32	Manipulates and mouths............						—	—	54	57	45	53	38	24	15	—
33	Transfers....................					—	3	19	62	70	64	66	65	45	42	27
34	Manip. above table top without trans....									18	26	28	7	26	15	38
35	Drops immediately................				50	54	47	27	4							
36	Drops on table..................					60	47	43	62	37	29	13	27	26	32	46
37	Resecures from table top.............						13	40	60	27	90	23	74	100	75	59
38	Slaps table top.................							28	27	18	36	33	20	14	3	19

SITUATION: SECOND CUBE (CC2)

CC2	Behavior items	4	6	8	12	16	20	24	28	32	36	40	44	48	52	56
1	Regards....................					100	96	100	100	100	100	100	100	100	100	100
2	Regards intermittently.............					0	42	8	4							
3	Regards passively...............					85	31	12	4							
4	Regards actively................					15	69	88	96	100	100	100	100	100	100	100
5	Directs approach to second cube........					20	46	84	100	96	100	100	100	100	97	100
6	Approaches after delay................					10	15	24	8	15	25	27	36	19	18	12
7	Drops first as second is presented........					70	73	56	46	19	18	7	8	7	3	16
8	Retains first as second is presented......					30	27	44	54	81	82	93	92	93	97	—
9	Dislodges on contact.................					5	19	24	40	33	7	3	16	11	0	4
10	Ap. sec. cube with cube in hand on pre...									7	14	10	24	15	11	32
11	Grasps second cube...............						12	63	85	82	89	96	88	100	95	96
12	Manipulates cube on table top.........					10	35	57	54	45	32	27	38	30	21	20
13	Bangs cube on table top..............							10	35	15	25	30	36	19	18	24
14	Brings cube to mouth..............					5	15	44	42	67	50	66	24	11	24	12
15	Manipulates and mouths a cube........								22	25	37	42	19	3	8	
16	Transfers a cube.................						4	7	31	26	43	40	56	45	26	36
17	Man. cube above table top without trans..									14	37	33	26	18	43	52
18	Drops a cube on table top..............					60	65	65	65	56	61	60	64	59	45	72
19	Resecures a cube from table top........					5	0	12	68	37	66	43	50	100	89	78

SITUATION: THIRD CUBE (CC3)

CC3	Behavior items	4	6	8	12	16	20	24	28	32	36	40	44	48	52	56
1	Regards third cube...................					87	100	90	96	100	100	100	100	100	100	100
2	Regards passively...................					74	47	23	12	—						
3	Regards actively....................					13	53	67	84	100	100	100	100	100	100	100
4	Approaches after delay...............					7	5	14	4	26	25	7	17	19	34	32
5	Drops one cube as third is presented.....					7	53	57	28	45	39	67	24	45	18	20
6	Drops two cubes as third is presented....					33	37	33	52	15	29	10	8	11	8	20
7	Directs approach to third cube..........					14	25	48	88	89	79	93	100	85	90	100
8	Ap. third c. with c. in hand as third is pre.									37	43	57	63	48	55	68
9	Grasps third cube....................					6	5	31	36	45	54	66	50	56	42	72
10	Manipulates without grasping..........					—	—	8	45	25	37	16	30	45	29	28
11	Manipulates cube on table top.........					20	26	27	60	59	71	57	54	63	53	32
12	Bangs cube.........................								24	19	29	23	13	26	18	12
13	Pushes or hits cube.................									33	46	47	58	37	41	40
14	Hits cube on table top with cube in hand.									15	32	40	38	15	29	37
15	Places cube on cube.................									4	10	20	7	30		44
16	Brings cube to mouth.................					13	10	23	12	26	36	62	20	30	8	16
17	Man. cube above table top without trans.					—	—	—	—	10	11	16	23	17	21	32
18	Drops cube on table.................					47	70	70	76	79	64	70	56	63	61	92
19	Rescues cube from table top..........					0	0	24	49	72	81	76	66	83	75	52

Behavior Trends

Visual Regard. At 12 weeks less than one-quarter of the subjects fail to regard the single cube. At 16 weeks, *all* subjects regard the first cube. At 12 weeks, two-fifths of the infants show delay of regard; at 16, 20, and 24 weeks about one in four shows delay. Capacity for visual regard is present even at 8 weeks but to what degree we have not investigated. At 28 weeks and thereafter immediate and consistent regard for the first cube becomes almost universal. These statements sum up the general course of visual regard.

Some shifting of regard is observed in the first cube situation at all ages but is most marked at the highest and lowest age levels. Needless to say, the younger infant "shifts" his regard for other reasons than does the older. At 12 weeks eight out of ten, and at 16 weeks nine out of ten, infants shift regard from the cube to some competing focus like the table top, surroundings, own hand, or examiner. At these younger ages the shifts are twitch-like, and they go most frequently to the infant's own hand. At the advanced ages (52 and 56 weeks) these shifts are smoother and they appear more self-directed and less mechanical. They go preferentially to the examiner, and probably have a social as well as perceptual determination. But allowing for all of the deflections of visual regard at the extreme ages, there is a remarkable degree of sustained preoccupation for the first and the consecutive cubes. As early as 16 weeks the prevailing (that is, the preponderant) regard in two-thirds of the infants in the first cube situation is for the cube itself.

At 12 weeks four infants out of five, and at 16 weeks five infants out of five, give regard to the cube. This means that at 12 weeks the infant is already beyond the nascent stage of cube perception. At 16 weeks the infant regards the cube more promptly and more frequently returns to the cube after eyes have wandered away. Momentary regard, however, is much more characteristic of both age levels than is prolonged regard.

At 12 and 16 weeks, the infant's own hand is the most powerful rival as the focus of regard. In one-fourth of the children at 12 weeks, and in one-half at 16 weeks, the regard shifts from the cube to the hand for several possible reasons: the hand has motion, is at a more favorable optical distance, is larger, or is more significantly related to the apperceptual organization then dominant. For that matter, hand inspection may have a relatively specific, innate basis, comparable to the hand-to-mouth impulse.

Hand inspection is a universal growth phenomenon among normal infants. It is not, however, to be interpreted as a fixed, hard and fast reflex. In its external form, this pattern of reaction changes obviously with age and with the expansion of associated patterns. The inner undiscernible aspects of the reaction also undergo change. Hand inspection fades out of the picture rapidly and has almost completely disappeared at 28 weeks. It becomes more snatchy as it becomes vestigial. At 20 weeks one infant in three, and at 24 weeks one infant in ten, may selectively regard his own hand (some time during the first cube situation); but if he does so to a conspicuous degree thereafter it is an atypical and sometimes an unfavorable developmental symptom. Exaggerated and intrusive stereotypy of hand inspection is often seen in mental deficiency.

Similarly a selective regard for the examiner's hand occurs in almost half the infants at 12 weeks but has almost entirely dropped out at 24 weeks. It is a more primitive focus of visual interest than the infant's own hand and possibly more important in the early stages of his helplessness.

The distribution of regard in the cube situation does not lend itself to ready summary because the regard is complicated by rival cubes and at each succeeding age level by new drives of manipulation, based on progressive changes in the sensorimotor equipment. Consistent (sustained) regard for the first cube arrives slowly and does not become fully established until about 28 weeks. At 16 and at 20 weeks, approximately one child out of four displays an intermittent type of regard. This type of regard is almost entirely confined to these two age levels; it is too mature for 12 weeks, too immature for 24 weeks. A recurrent form of regard, however, is found at all age levels in from one- to two-fifths of the children up to 52 weeks; and in two-thirds at 52 weeks and at 56 weeks.

Because of its intimate dynamic and developmental association with the prehensory mechanism, the outward forms of regard show their most conspicuous changes from 12 to 24 weeks. It is significant that "active" regard, characterized by accompanying approach movements of arms and body, comes into sharp prominence at 20 weeks in three-fourths of the infants; whereas a prolonged "passive" regard is most characteristic of 16 weeks. Such a prolongation of ocular fixation suggests that for an object of this size the primary oculomotor system is at this period coming to a stage of relative perfection; and this is such a complex area of pattern differentiation that the most overt prehensory adjustments are for the time subordinated. The infant must grasp (apprehend) and hold the cube with his eyes before he does so with his hands. And apparently he gains as much satisfaction out of the ocular as out of the later manual performance. By the age of 24 weeks, passive regard is rarely seen, for he is already well on the path of prehension and manipulation.

While the infant holds the first cube, a second is presented. This introduces an interesting rival focus in the attentional field. How does this new focus affect the distribution of regard? All the infants (from 16 weeks on) pay regard to the second cube. At 16 weeks this regard is passive; at 20 weeks it is active; and it tends to be more intermittent for the second than for the first cube. This act of regard for the second cube influences the reaction to the cube in hand. At 16 and at 20 weeks seven out of ten children drop the first cube as the second is presented. This may be accounted for by the formative state of the eye-hand organization. Thereafter an increasing proportion of children, 80 per cent at 32 weeks and finally all, retain the first cube as the second is presented. This ability represents a widening of the scope of the total behavior pattern through greater integrative control or systematization. It is not merely an additive increment; it is an organizational one. At 32 weeks the infant may indeed be said to attend adequately to two cubes because he can continue his attention to the first (by maintenance of grasp) while he also pays regard to the second. At 16 weeks attention to the second cube tends to displace rather than to supplement attention to the first.

At the age of 16 weeks and also at the 44 to 56 weeks ages the infant tends to hold to each cube in hand when a third cube is presented. The similarity in this behavior item at these divergent ages is only superficial. At the intervening ages he drops one or both on the presentation of the third cube. At the later age levels he sometimes appropriates the third cube while still holding the cube in hand. This tendency to seize two cubes in one hand increases with age. His regard is thus influenced by his motor capacity.

The more refined differentiations in the distribution of regard will be suggested in the discussion of the exploitive aspects of cube behavior. These differentiations, although vaguely attributed to a function of exploitation, are genetically comparable to the more obvious patterns of regard which have been noted for the period from 12 to 24 weeks. In essence he is neither more nor less exploitive at the tenderer ages.

In summary: (a) Regard for the cube is at first a perceptual reaction in very loose association with the action system of prehension. (b) With the development of approach and grasp this association increases; visual apprehension and manual prehension become closely identified and occur almost as a single response. (c) Visual regard becomes somewhat freed so that visual fixation may take the lead, grasp following, and regard again shifts when prehension is achieved. The whole eye-hand field of behavior undergoes internal differentiations which multiply and refine but never lose connection with each other.

The developmental changes in visual regard strongly suggest that attention is simply a function or dynamic manifestation of patterned structure. We are not dealing with a mysterious energy factor or a directing drive but are witnessing in the phenomena of attention the end result of progressive differentiations in the total sensorimotor system. To be sure this involves associative and inhibitory mechanisms but these do not in any sense function independently; nor do they ever strictly initiate the responses. For they are themselves products of growth, historically built into the organ of unity of the infant, namely the total reaction pattern. It is for this reason that even the young infant may show excellent attention or "concentration." His concentration represents the active functioning of a pattern which is maturing; and if we knew the secrets of his inner life, we might find that he derives a genuine affective satisfaction out of early forms of eye-hand behavior which soon becomes automatic.

Prehensory Approach.   Hands and arms become active in the cube situation in nearly all infants at 12 weeks and at 16 weeks. This activity may or may not be coincident with regard for the cube, and it cannot always be determined whether the movements have an approach significance. In fact, in the prolonged regard somewhat characteristic of 16 weeks, these movements tend to subside, suggesting that defined visual perception is at this stage such a formative and complicated behavior process that the infant is not yet ready for a coordinated prehensory adjustment. Intermittent regard, characterized by short time shifts to and from the cube prior to approach, occurs in one child out of four at 16 weeks and at 20 weeks.

Reckoning the entire consecutive cube situation, about one child in five at 12 weeks, and one in three at 16 weeks, makes what is apparently a directed approach upon a cube. Actual contacting of the cube occurs in one out of five at 12 weeks; two out of five at 16 weeks; and three out of five at 20 weeks; and virtually five out of five at 24 weeks and thereafter. The steady ascent of this curve of contact indicates that "reaching" is a complicated act which depends upon the gradual developmental perfection of the neuromuscular mechanism. Even after successful grasping has become frequent or universal, approach is not always perfect; nearly half the children at 24 weeks and at 28 weeks displace the cube before seizure of it. Thereafter, however, such "inadequate contacting approach" becomes relatively rare or disappears. Unilaterality of approach increases with adequacy of approach. At 32 weeks three-fourths of the infants make a unilateral approach.

Grasp.   At 12 weeks grasp of the cube is in a highly nascent stage. There is no spontaneous grasp, and even when the examiner inserts the cube firmly into the infant's hand about one-half of the infants hold the cube momentarily and briefly; the other half hold it more actively and prolongedly. No 12 weeks infant regards the cube while he holds it, so we may consider the perception-prehension coordination quite nonexistent at that age.

Reckoning the entire cube situation, one child out of five at 16 weeks, two out of five at 20 weeks, four out of five at 24 weeks, and five out of five at 28 weeks spontaneously grasp a cube. Visual controls improve with this increasing frequency of grasp, but two-thirds of the infants at 24 weeks and 28 weeks make attempts to secure a cube which are unsuccessful. Such failures at later ages are rare because of improved visual judgment and motor precision.

At 28 weeks a large proportion of the children apply the thumb to a lateral aspect of the cube, but without full thumb opposition, which matures gradually during the next three months. During this same period the ability to grasp a second cube while retaining the first undergoes improvement. At 24 weeks only one infant out of five showed this ability; at 36 weeks, four out of five.

Manipulation and Exploitation.   It is difficult to separate these two terms. Regarded from the standpoint of mere mechanics, manipulation might well be considered in relation to prehension as an elaborating manifestation of sensorimotor equipment. For example, when an infant reaches a given stage of maturity he brushes a cube in hand back and forth on the table top. Is he simply exercising a nascent manipulatory capacity, or is he utilizing this capacity to secure visual, auditory, and tactile satisfactions which he repeats and varies in an exploitive manner? If his reactions were purely repetitive they might be interpreted from the standpoint of the mechanics of manipulation, but since they have a latent or actual exploitive value in addition, we may as well discuss manipulation and adaptive exploitation together. To what extent the impulses and objectives of exploitation genetically precede and exceed the mechanical capacities of manipulation is a problem of theoretical importance. It borders on problems of insight, volition, and originativeness. For the present summary it is safest to regard the range of exploitation as almost identical with the range of manipulation. This is in accordance with our mechanistic assumption that attention is primarily a function of pattern morphology.

The more elementary and primitive distributions of attention have already been discussed in connection with *regard*. We have noted that at 12 weeks the infant's own hand has an attentional value almost equal to that of the cube. At this age only half of the infants pay prevailing regard for the cube, but at 24 weeks all of the infants do so. At the latter age, effective though not perfected prehension is universally established among normal infants.

It is interesting to note that as soon as grasping is thus established numerous forms of manipulation are at once manifested. The infant is not content simply to prehend but forthwith he supplements prehension (or even substitutes it) with diverse activities. Twenty-eight weeks marks the age when numerous behavior items rise for the first time to normative frequency. The infant now transfers a cube from one hand to another (63 per cent); he resecures a dropped cube from the table (69 per cent); he bangs the cube on the table (70 per cent); he brings up his free hand to the cube at the mouth (53 per cent); he pushes or hits a cube out of reach (53 per cent); and tries to secure it when out of reach (50 per cent). Although these activities have been anticipated at 24 weeks, they are then less frequent and less defined; at the earlier age the act of prehension itself more completely dominated the behavior picture.

Diverse and vigorous as these 28 weeks activities are, there is among them no evidence of well-defined combining activity. At 32 weeks, however, about half of the infants pick up a cube and inspect it and bring two cubes into some kind of combination. This combining becomes more frequent, more defined, and more complex at subsequent age levels, though it often gives way to an exploitive manipulation restricted to a single cube, such as rotation with inspection (36 weeks), poking (40 weeks), twiddling (48 weeks).

There is a quantitative aspect to the development of this combining activity which has genetic interest. An ideal normative progression from approximate zero goes somewhat as follows: (0) He does not bring two cubes together except fortuitously (28 weeks). (1) He brings them together sketchily for a brief moment, repeating the sketchy approach intermittently (32 weeks). (2) He hits one cube on another in a more continuous, pursuant manner (44 weeks). (3) He places one cube definitely upon another with release (56 weeks). (4) He ranges multiple cubes in a horizontal row, say after 80 weeks. There is an extremely wide range of individual differences in the modes of exploitation, but certain activities like tower building are well-nigh universal among infants. The genetic antecedents of tower building are crudely suggested in the above summary but a close analysis of these antecedents will require a separate section.

In a spatial sense, the range of exploitive activities increases with age. This is due to the fact that the infant's postural as well as his manual coordinations are growing. He "learns" to rotate his trunk, to pivot his sitting stance, and to bend his trunk forward and sideways, but not at the expense of manipulation, for simultaneously he exploits the environment with his cube. At 44 weeks he turns to the side rail while he continues to manipulate the cube on the table top; at 48 weeks he relates his activity to the side rail, bringing the cube to the rail or casting it overboard (casting is a primitive form of release which precedes controlled placement of one cube on another); at 52 weeks he drops the cubes onto the platform, pursues them there, or recovers them and restores them to the table top. Here we have another excellent illustration of the manner in which growth proceeds. New patterns differentiate with maturity but they never completely individuate; rather, they articulate or merge with concurrent patterns, and while they are thus combining yet newer patterns are differentiating, and these in turn will be assimilated to the consolidating total action system.

The developmental changes in exploitive behavior are reflected in the general course of distribution of attention to the second and third cubes. All children even at 16 weeks give heed to the second cube, and nearly all to the third cube; but the regard is of a passive nature. At 20 weeks, significantly enough, the infant's regard for the second cube is intermittent, showing that the regard itself is moving into the range of adaptive exploitation. But he tends to drop the first cube as the second is presented. This tendency declines in strength and at 32 weeks and thereafter he retains the first cube on presentation of the second. At 36 weeks there is almost an equal chance that on presentation of the third cube he will drop neither, both, or only one of the cubes he has in hand. At 40 weeks he characteristically drops only one to secure the third; at 44 weeks he holds fast to those that he has, approaching the third cube with a cube in hand. At 56 weeks, as already noted, this approach is supplemented by definite release: he places one cube on another and thus begins the tower building which he will extend and elaborate throughout the preschool years.

By the end of the first year the exploitive cube behavior is so complex that it would take pages to rehearse in detail the different permutations of pattern displayed. This versatility need not be construed as an augmentation of a drive or of an instinct of exploitation. It is a genetic end product of the diversification and correlation of patterned action systems. These systems must be envisaged morphologically as well as dynamically. Acts of attention are kinetic manifestations of patterned structure. In this sense even exploitive behavior has a morphological aspect.

§20. Massed Cubes Behavior

(16 weeks–60 weeks)

The Situation

Fig. 20.—Massed cubes behavior: 16 weeks and 44 weeks.

Using a cardboard screen to conceal the maneuver, the examiner assembled nine cubes into a solid square and placed the tenth on the middle cube. With moderate dispatch, the examiner advanced both the screen and the cubes toward the infant, quickly withdrawing the screen when the massed cubes were in the standard median position. If the infant did not contact the cubes after a period of 10 seconds, the examiner advanced them to the near median position.

Stimulus Factors

The massed cube situation was devised as a variant of the consecutive cube situation. It was felt that the multiple cubes would disclose in various ways the infant's most elementary reactions to number, form, and arrangement. Since an architectural utilization of the cubes becomes a well-defined expression of later child play, it is of interest to inquire into the nascent and prenascent stages which precede orderly constructiveness and block building.

The cubes are presented in geometric square formation—three contiguous horizontal rows, with the central cube surmounted tower-wise by a capstone cube. With very moderate expenditure of energy the infant can decompose this formation into ten units. Does he react to the cubes as a mass? Does he give selective heed to the corner cubes or to the capstone cube? Does he show differential restraints in contacting the cubes? When they are in disarray, does the multiplicity of building materials stimulate to special forms of constructiveness? When, if ever, does he attempt to reconstitute the formation as he found it?

It is evident that a logical analysis of the possibilities raises many interesting questions concerning potential stimulus values. Some of these questions would yield to rather precise experimental study. With our own procedures the observations are not under uniform control. The course of behavior is naturally much influenced by the very first dislocation of the cubes which the infant himself produces. However, the nature of this dislocation and the infant's reaction to it are the very items which have genetic interest.

From the standpoint of purposive block building, the massed cubes situation is quite beyond the infant's capacities. The situation is one which might well be reserved for the third or fourth year of life, when the child's performance becomes obviously responsive, adaptive, and easily scorable. Nevertheless, these matured abilities rest upon preparatory patterns which may be observed throughout the first year of life.

The method of presenting the massed cubes carries with it elaborations which add considerably to the range of stimulus factors. The examiner conceals the assembly of the blocks with a pasteboard screen (size 8½ by 11 in.). This screen itself becomes a stimulus factor. Preoccupation with the screen may lead to delayed regard of the cubes. The infant may even reach out for the screen. Later he gives subsidiary regard for the screen, restrains his reaching, and waits with anticipation. The reactions to the screen display interesting differences in personality and insight.

The following summary will deal chiefly with reactions to the multiple cubes and will draw comparisons with the consecutive cubes situation.

Behavior Trends

Regard. At 16 weeks the infant gives immediate regard to the massed cubes. His hands and arms apparently become more active than in the single cube situation. He regards the cubes fixedly, *en masse;* but he also scans the formation. Although his perceptual behavior is distinguishable from that for the single cube, his regard yields with similar frequency to the "distraction" of the table top,

Situation: Massed Cubes (CM)

CM	Behavior items	4	6	8	12	16	20	24	28	32	36	40	44	48	52	56
1	Regards cardboard screen					42	64	85	93	82	93	87	59	83	63	70
2	Reaches for screen					—	23	65	64	68	75	73	45	48	45	41
3	Grasps screen						—	4	11	39	36	50	36	21	18	7
4	Regards cube (s.m.p.)					58	95	100								
5	Regards starily					47	18	12	4							
6	Regards intermittently					37	18	0								
7	Shifts regard					53	45	27	25	21	18	37	41	21	33	67
8	Shifts regard to surroundings					26	27	31	7	4	7	10	22	7	7	
9	Shifts regard to Examiner					31	27	8	28	18	14	20	41	14	23	41
10	Shifts regard to hand					42	14	4								
11	Shifts regard from cube to cube					10	41	62	82	79	86	83	74	83	63	63
12	Pursues visually to platform or floor						8	21	39	54	50	30	38	28	37	
13	Arms increase activity					63	95	100	100	100	100	100	100	100	100	100
14	Scratches table top					21	18	12	7	4	4	3				
15	Slaps table top					14	23	29	4	43	10	11	24	8		15
16	Contacts cube					47	86	100	100	100	100	100	100	100	100	100
17	Reaches for cube out of reach							8	39	32	25	13		10		
18	Dislodges on contact					47	77	69	36	18	11	17	11	7	15	—
19	Grasps a cube					5	45	77	96	100	100	100	100	100	98	100
20	Grasps two cubes at once						5	19	36	54	32	50	33	24	30	37
21	Holds one cube and grasps another						12	25	32	39	60	70	52	55		33
22	Hold. two cubes, drops one as grasps an.							18	29	25	40	30	17	8		7
23	Releases cube and immediately rescues it							4	14	18	14	17	22	14	20	7
24	Grasps one cube after another								4	7	7	10	19	38	25	45
25	Grasps one cube after an. using same hand								4	11	7	17	30	62	43	56
26	Hold. one cube, grasps one cube after an.										10	19	45	33	56	
27	Hold. two cu., gr. one af. an. us. same hand										7	11	24	15	4	
28	Grasps one cube after an. con. to table top									4	7	7	11	38	25	19
29	Holds two cubes						9	31	43	64	64	80	85	66	75	67
30	Holds two cubes in one hand								11	25	21	13	26	14	33	41
31	Drags cube						18	8	32	11	—	13	4			5
32	Pushes cube out of reach						19	36	21	14	—	4				
33	Scatters cubes					26	82	92	68	36	39	47	37	45	40	37
34	Hits cube to platform						14	27	32	43	32	33	26	35	30	19
35	Lifts a cube						36	69	96	100	100	100	100	100	98	100
36	Brings cube to mouth						14	38	50	36	61	50	41	24	20	4
37	Bangs cube on table top							15	32	39	32	23	19	24	28	11
38	Manipulates cube above table top						9	23	25	32	36	37	67	45	38	41
39	Transfers cube						5	15	14	14	29	20	22	10	13	11
40	Drops cube						36	50	79	79	96	83	82	100	88	89
41	(If drops) drops immediately						88	62	14	14	7	0				
42	Drops one cube as attends to another							31	21	8						
43	Drops cube in hand as ap. or grasps another							23	25	29	23	4				
44	Drops one cube and grasps another							15	46	54	57	70	63	83	63	74
45	Drops cube on table top						32	42	61	71	93	63	70	83	65	78
46	Drops cube to platform						5	8	29	29	43	47	30	48	38	52
47	Drops cube to floor											4	31	18	15	
48	Pursues cube to platform							14	29	36	57	37	38	25	37	
49	Transposes cubes								4	7	7	13	26	55	42	56
50	Casts cube											3	4	38	18	33
51	Combines two cubes								4	29	39	43	53	41	50	30
52	Hits or pu. cu. on ta. top with cu. in hand								4	25	39	37	41	14	23	4
53	Places cube on cube											3	4	17	28	19
54	Average number of cubes picked up:					0	1	2	3	3	3	3	4	5	5	7
55	Picks up one cube or more						45	77	96	100	100	100	100	100	95	100
56	Picks up two or more cubes						9	46	75	86	93	96	97	95	96	
57	Picks up three or more cubes						5	15	50	64	71	73	67	90	83	82
58	Picks up four or more cubes							8	29	43	43	57	56	76	65	74
59	Picks up five or more cubes								14	14	11	30	41	73	45	67
60	Picks up six or more cubes								7	11	11	13	30	52	40	56
61	Picks up seven or more cubes										4	10	19	28	33	48
62	Disarranges cubes					31	82	98	82	79	71	73	57	83	78	70
63	Leans					21	23	35	14						3	4
64	Postural activity									7	18	37	37	31	45	56
65	Vocalizes					26	14	42	18	11	25	27	41	45	15	19
66	Average No. cubes remain. on T.T.					10	9	8	6	7	6	6	6	6	6	—

surroundings, and his own hand. At 20 weeks, when the cubes are in disarray, two-fifths of the infants shifted regard from one cube to another. This shifting is better defined and more rapid at 24 weeks, and was noted in two-thirds of the infants at that age. The cubes now receive almost all of the regard. Regard for surroundings is relatively slight at all ages after 24 weeks; but regard for the examiner occurred in two-fifths of the infants both at 44 weeks and at 56 weeks. Needless to say the factors which determine these distractions of regard do not remain the same from age to age.

A selective perception of the capstone cube is at a nascent stage at about 48 weeks. By that age the infant has begun to inspect and to exploit the cubes in a discriminative manner. This suggests a more refined perceptual world than that which he enjoys at 16 weeks, when characteristically he stares at the pile of cubes and at his own hands and only rarely shifts his regard from one cube to another. Little do we know about this inner perceptual world but it may be safely inferred in part from the gains in manipulatory and exploitive behavior outlined below.

Manipulation and Exploitation.   At 16 weeks a little over one-fourth of the infants contact the massed cubes, suggesting that the perceptual equipment is well in advance of the prehensory. At 20 weeks, however, four-fifths of the infants contact the cubes with sufficient force to scatter them; two-fifths grasp a cube holding it momentarily. The grasp is chiefly on contact. At 24 weeks the grasp is initiated on visual cue. Though the approach is frequently ineffectual, seven out of ten children grasp a cube. The grasp, however, is still limited to one cube; therefore he does not secure a second cube while retaining the first. Even at 28 weeks only two-fifths of the infants held two cubes, one in either hand.

There is a great deal of scattering of the cubes at 28 weeks and a tendency to push them out of reach. The infant shifts his activity rapidly and freely from one cube to another; he frequently reaches for a remote, inaccessible cube. In quick succession he reacts to individual cubes, dropping one to pick up or to push the next. The multiplicity of cubes thus definitely influences the course of his activity, but if anything he gives less combining attention to two cubes than he does in the consecutive cubes situation.

At 32 weeks there is somewhat less scattering and more tendency to exploit two cubes at one time. The infant now holds two cubes simultaneously prehending them at the same time or dropping one to pick up another. There is less abandoned hitting than at 28 weeks. Two-fifths of the infants hit cubes to the platform and bang them on the table top. Here again the patterns of performance bear considerable resemblance to that of the consecutive cubes situation. The mere multiplicity of cubes has not operated to increase the range and incidence of combining activity.

At 36 weeks apparent combining is more prominent because the infant so definitely tends to hold one cube while he contacts, pushes, or bangs another. He is more pursuant in his regard, following the cube to the platform if it falls, and sustaining contact with it for longer periods. But again this is in no sense a by-product of the numerous array of cubes, because he displayed a similar combining behavior in the two and three cubes situations. In general his reactions are largely confined to a single cube which he mouths repeatedly, inspects on withdrawal from mouth, manipulates, and transfers. Mere multiplicity of cubes does not much alter his immediate patterns or propensities. Accordingly he is rather prone to slap the table top, even when he might well busy himself with the cubes.

At 40 weeks the periphery of his activity shows some expansion. He grabs for the screen as it is withdrawn by the examiner. He brings the platform into the range of his exploitation and carries on some activity with the cube in relation to the platform. He strongly tends to possess and to utilize two cubes. Holding one cube he characteristically grasps another. Holding two cubes he drops only one to pick up another.

At 44 weeks exploitational activity with one or two cubes is characteristic. This activity tends to be restricted in its scope and the multiple cubes are less scattered at this age than at any other, with the exception of 12 weeks. The manipulation is diversified and includes fingering, poking, transfer, transient waving, chewing, or rubbing against the teeth, occasional hitting of two cubes above the table top, and even a simple form of release with resecural. Vocalizations and shifting of regard to the examiner occur frequently. In general these behavior pictures are similar to those shown in the simpler consecutive cube situation, but the output of exploitational activity seems to be increased by the greater richness of the multiple cubes.

In the summary of cup and cubes behavior, it will be pointed out that 48 weeks marks the age when the infant "discovers" the cavitation of the upright cup. Similarly at 48 weeks he gives evidence of a maturing perception of "aboveness" and "belowness." We infer this from the fact that occasionally the infant will now selectively grasp and remove the capstone block from the rest. This simple bit of motor discriminativeness, so conspicuously absent at earlier age levels, denotes a significant developmental gain in the infant's perceptual world. Concurrently he is gaining a mastery in the art of release. He now picks up one cube after another from the table top, or he picks up the same cube twice or thrice, replacing it in different positions. Sometimes in this act of replacement his hand hovers momentarily but auspiciously above another cube. This behavior item has genetic promise because it leads presently to the elementary comprehension and building of towers.

The infant's physical world near the close of the first year is already slightly more externalized. He gives somewhat less attention to the cube in hand, mouthing is much less prominent. He is "learning" to release his hold of what he has in hand, a capacity of great importance in higher spheres of behavior. He exercises this capacity with a single cube and still more abundantly with multiple cubes at his disposal.

At 52 weeks and at 56 weeks the releasing capacity shows greater efficiency and elaboration. Even though he may be under a gross locomotive urge to pivot to the side, to kneel, to creep, or to stand, he yet pursues the several cubes in turn, picking up one after the other, poising or placing one over another, or otherwise exploiting them. In other words, the locomotive activity does not cancel his cube behavior trends, but simply complicates or elaborates the resultant pattern. His activity with the cubes is more sustained. His psychomotor orientation to the total situation is more inclusive. He seems to perceive the cubes as an aggregation as well as serially, and he brings both table top and platform more deliberately into his sphere of influence. At 56 weeks he may carry the cubes one by one by definite placement to the platform and in the same way restore them to the table top. At this age also he may extend one cube after another to the examiner. Such behavior in its serial repetitiveness is somewhat peculiar to the multiple cube situation and shows that the infant is now developmentally ready to take a new advantage of the environmental fact of multiplicity. At 52 and 56 weeks it is also more common for him to pick up two cubes at one grasp and to hold two in one hand.

Whatever the "number sense" of the one year old infant may be, he is now manifesting psychogenetic changes which have to do with the ultimate essence of number. With the cubes at least he is putting one and one, if not two and two, together. In their entirety the responses to the multiple cube situation have proved to be highly comparable to those in the more simple situation where cubes are presented consecutively. This itself is a fact of significance. But the distinctive behavior trends which the multiple cubes have disclosed are also of significance. As he matures the infant takes increasing and more ordered relations to multiple stimuli of a similar kind. Even the crude arithmetical averages of the number of cubes picked up per child per age level are indicative. The averages show a steady rise from 0.6 of a cube at 20 weeks to 7.1 cubes at 56 weeks.

§21. TOWER BUILDING BEHAVIOR

(44 weeks–60 weeks)

The Situation

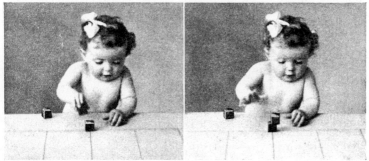

FIG. 21.—Tower building behavior: 52 weeks.

At the conclusion of the massed cube situation, the examiner removed all but four cubes. With moderately rapid maneuver he built a demonstration tower of two blocks near the farther margin of the table, securing the infant's visual attention to the demonstration. The examiner then placed the third cube in the near median position and proffered the fourth cube to the infant. The examiner attempted to secure responsive behavior by gesture, comment, and repeated building of the demonstration tower either in the far median position or in the standard median position.

Stimulus Factors

Tower building from the standpoint of child psychology represents a situation of considerable interest, both genetic and normative. The rearing of stone upon stone leads in primitive culture to the discovery and application of principles of engineering. It is instructive to note the nature of the difficulties which the infant exhibits at the threshold of his engineering problems. Tower building also has special interest from the standpoint of comparative psychology because the higher primates stack one object upon another both in play and in practical emergency.

Block building has significance not only as a performance test but as a key to the maturity of the child's perceptual organization. His geometric arrangement of cubes is not so much determined by manipulatory skill as by a regulative sense of form. Tower building, therefore, represents one of the most elementary problems of geometry, not incomparable to the task of drawing a vertical line spontaneously, after demonstration, or from a model.

The genetic antecedents of tower building have already been touched upon in the summary of the consecutive cubes and massed cubes situations. In these situations spontaneous tower building patterns had ample opportunity to assert themselves. The present summary is concerned with tower building under the influence of demonstration.

The demonstration tower was included in the normative examination of from 9 to 25 infants at the five age levels from 40 weeks to 56 weeks. It was found that variations in procedure had a palpable influence on the stimulus values of the situation. When the demonstration tower was built well out of reach of the infant, his interest in the tower and his responsive behavior were not so well defined. When the demonstration tower was accessible it often became the focus of activity. His incipient tower building might express itself by an attempt to place a cube on the examiner's tower. The older child is much more immune to such apparently innocent variations of procedure. When a function is in a state of nascency, the performance is more susceptible to slight differences in the relata. The infant is so far removed from a conceptual generalization of "tower" that his behavior is highly contingent on the arrangement of the stimulus factors. To unmake a tower of two blocks and then to recombine them is for the infant an easier task than to take two separate blocks and accomplish the same combination. The tower building situation needs to be explored with more controlled regard for these stimulus factors, but our present data show a sufficiently consistent trend to warrant brief summary of the responsiveness to demonstration.

SITUATION: TOWER BUILDING (Ct)

Ct	Behavior items	4	6	8	12	16	20	24	28	32	36	40	44	48	52	56
1	Ap. cube on table top with cube in hand..											45	44	75	76	86
2	Hits or pushes cube with cube..........											45	33	33	28	0
3	Places cube on cube....................											9	11	42	40	79
4	Releases cube on cube.................											0	11	25	16	43
5	Postural activity.....................											10	14	22	14	50

Behavior Trends

Response to Demonstration. At 40 weeks and at 44 weeks the infant regards the examiner's act of demonstration but apparently alters his subsequent activity slightly if at all. One cube is already on the table and another in his hand; the examiner gestures, commands, and points both to the base cube and to the tower, but in vain. Almost half the children merely approach the cube on the table top with the cube in hand but without adaptive combining. The model tower may also be approached; combining, if it takes place, resembles that which occurs in the simple consecutive cube situation. At best the infant picks a cube from the tower and pushes one cube with another.

At 48 weeks, however, as already noted in connection with the massed cubes, there are symptoms of a dawning sense of "above-ness" or of "verticality." He may pick off the top cube of the tower; he may hold one cube immediately above another, sometimes even with release. It is this poising of the hand and holding one cube above another which imparts an aspect of responsiveness to his behavior, but we must recall that he reacted similarly (in the massed and consecutive cube situations) without the aid of demonstration. Forty-eight weeks is the peak age for lifting the top cube from off the demonstration tower in the near median position. Such discriminative removal of the top cube, which itself signifies a rudimentary sense of twoness, developmentally precedes the deliberate bringing of one cube over another. Unmaking a tower is part of the network of ability required for rearing one. Genetically it may be said that it is impossible to build a tower unless one has first learned to unbuild a tower.

At 52 weeks this responsiveness is typically more adaptive. He may remove the top cube from the tower and then attempt to replace it. More often he combines the cube in hand with the single cube before him. This combining is varied and may include pushing or brushing, but at interruptive moments he holds one cube rather definitely above another, with or without release. If he releases it the cube usually falls amiss.

At 56 weeks he responds in much the same way except that the tower reaction is less momentary, less sporadic. It is already becoming persistent and repetitive and perhaps one child out of three actually succeeds in constructing a tower. Almost all the infants at this age at least attempt some kind of superimposing. At 60 weeks the pattern is more decisive.

The gradualness with which this ability is acquired indicates the presence of complicated maturational factors. In older children we have observed the same phenomena. The child of 18 months may build a well-balanced tower of four blocks but he must double his age before he builds a simple bridge of three. A pair of monozygotic twins may each, with identical facility, build a gateway of five blocks but will be equally nonplussed by the task of building a simple stairway of ten blocks. In another year they will "come by" this ability through processes of growth highly comparable with those by which they mastered their first tower of two.

§22. Cup Behavior

(12 weeks–36 weeks)

The Situation

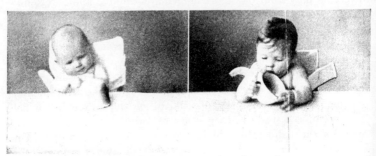

Fig. 22.—Cup behavior: 12 weeks and 28 weeks.

The examiner presented the inverted cup with the handle pointing toward the child, placing the cup in the standard median position and if necessary in the near median position, in accordance with general procedure.

Stimulus Factors

The cup is inverted when it is presented and it rests on its rim. Its size, its smooth, white surface with glistening high lights, and the handle of contrasting blue color impart to the cup a wide range of appeal for the infant. On the basis of our observations there can be no doubt that the cup has more provocative visual properties than the cube for infants 12 weeks old.

Although the cup is moderately heavy it moves with great ease when in the inverted position. This makes special prehensory difficulties and places some premium on bilateral manipulation. The circumference and curving sides of the cup also create special prehensory problems. Under these conditions adaptive utilization of the handle may be regarded as a primitive form of tool perception. Although the inverted cup situation has yielded interesting observations on this point, the reaction to the handle is complicated by other factors which embarrass the interpretation. The inverted placement of the cup, however, serves to reveal the mechanism of lifting and the trend toward turning the cup right side up.

To what extent the reactions of the infant to the cup are influenced by home experience in feeding it is difficult to say. Home practices vary a great deal with respect to the infant's independence in managing the cup. A few infants bring the cup to the mouth as though to drink, but in general they manipulate it as though it were an object for physical exploitation, unrestrained by any feeding conventions.

When the inverted cup is reversed and placed in normal position, its stimulus values and exploitational possibilities are increased. The blue enameled circular rim then stands out contrastively and presents a firm edge for grasping. The bowl of the cup permits and invites insertion of the fingers or the full hand. And if the cup is seized and lifted, the rounded edge of the rim provides an invitation for biting. Once lifted, the cup may be exploited in manifold permutations above the table top, or it may be brought onto the table top with a banging staccato and shoved about with a less noisy sliding movement; or the cup may lodge on its side where it may be made to rock with a clinking sound. All of these possibilities the exploitive infant pursues by happy chance or intent. The diversity of the possibilities is so great that it is difficult to reduce them all to a normative status, but this very diversity yields suggestive observations. Moreover a study of the stimulus values of the cup and of the spoon as separate objects serves to define the import of the distinctive patterns which arise when these two objects are presented in association.

SITUATION: CUP (Cp)

Cp	Behavior items	4	6	8	12	16	20	24	28	32	36	40	44	48	52	56
1	Regards immediately...................				81	89	97	100	100	100	100					
2	Regards momentarily..................				37	22	9	3	—	—	—					
3	Regards recurrently...................				44	68	28	21	4	18	15					
4	Regards prolongedly (n.m.p.)...........				56	69										
5	Regards prolongedly...................				37	57	47	3	—	—	—					
6	Regards predominantly................				73	93	94	100	100	100	100					
7	Regards consistently..................				0	5	38	66	100	100	100					
8	Shifts regard.........................				80	73	31	23	10	25	23					
9	Shifts regard to surroundings..........				40	33	6	3	—	4	15					
10	Shifts regard to hand.................				47	45	13	7	—	—	—					
11	Shifts regard from cup to hand.........				20	28	15	3								
12	Arm increases activity (s.p. or n.m.p.)...				75	79	78	93	100	100	100					
13	Brings hand to mouth (s.p. or n.m.p.).....				50	21										
14	Hands active on table top (s.p. or n.m.p.)				36	67										
15	Approaches (n.m.p.)...................				44	79										
16	Approaches...........................				6	25	72	91	100	100	100					
17	Approaches promptly (n.m.p.)..........				25	55										
18	Approaches promptly..................				6	13	44	81	96	100	100					
19	Approaches after delay (n.m.p.).........				25	23										
20	Approaches with both hands............				6	11	34	41	69	50	50					
21	Approaches handle first...............				0	5	25	38	56	64	58					
22	Contacts (n.m.p.).....................				44	67										
23	Contacts.............................				6	15	69	91	100	100	100					
24	Dislodges on contact (n.m.p.)..........				25	52										
25	Dislodges on contact..................					9	53	50	38	29	8					
26	Grasps...............................					13	52	85	100	100						
27	Grasps with both hands (n.m.p. or s.p.)...					5	22	53	52	36	42					
28	Grasps with both hands................						3	28	33	32	31					
29	Grasps with one hand..................						9	35	52	75	69					
30	Manipulates with hands encircling cup....						6	24	56	50	42					
31	Manipulates grasping by rim............						0	0	45	64	62					
32	Manipulates grasping by handle.........						6	31	59	92	81					
33	Pushes or hits........................					14	31	30	41	3	4					
34	Pushes or drags cup...................						19	24	33	50	31					
35	Bangs on table top....................					—	3	6	37	36	58					
36	Turns cup over on table top............						6	26	14	17	8					
37	Lifts cup.............................						6	45	82	100	100					
38	Lifts by handle.......................						6	35	59	79	81					
39	Brings to mouth.......................						3	24	63	60	66					
40	Manipulates above table top............						0	21	67	86	89					
41	Manipulates initially above table top.....					—	3	3	26	18	35					
42	Holds with both hands.................						3	35	63	46	46					
43	Transfers............................						—	—	19	43	42					
44	Turns cup right side up................						6	3	56	71	62					
45	Rotates..............................					—	3	—	3	21	31					
46	Drops................................						6	38	63	61	42					
47	Drops and resecures...................						—	7	15	39	19					
48	Fusses...............................				6	7	12	27	7	18	11					

Behavior Trends

Regard. The cup falls well within the range of perceptual abilities of the 12 weeks-old infant. Characteristically he gives immediate, prolonged, and recurrent regard. This regard, particularly in the near median position, is more ready, more prolonged, and better defined than that which he pays to the cube. Shifts of regard, however, are frequent and are chiefly directed to the infant's own hands. The examiner's hands elicit less attention than in the cube situation. Pronounced shifts of regard also occur at 16 weeks, but thereafter they are less frequent. These shifts are most often to the child's own hands. Even when he has just been regarding the cup staringly the ocular fixation may dart to his hand. At 16 weeks the cup regard is often of an absorbed, starey nature. At 20 weeks there is less shift of regard. With his improved head control the shifts which do occur are less confined to table top and hands, and include examiner or surroundings. The regard is now more sustained and more inspectional; it follows the cup when the cup moves from contacting. But not until 24 weeks do two-thirds of the infants pay the consistent regard which is universal at the later age levels. Selective regard for the handle, which appears at 20 weeks, is present in half of the infants at 24 weeks and becomes increasingly defined at subsequent ages.

Approach and Grasp. The prehensory response to the cup is significantly obscure at 12 weeks. Hands and arms are active in three-fourths of the children while the cup is regarded. Such activity may occur even without cup regard but is apparently increased by the presence of the cup, particularly when the cup is placed in the near median position. The arm activity is rather gross, jerky, and undirected, and in half of the infants the hand goes to the mouth. None the less it would be unwarrantable to call these movements random or fortuitous. They suggest a rudimentary form of prehensory approach which results in actual contact of the cup in almost half of the infants observed.

At 16 weeks the approach movements are more directed, more prompt, and more vigorous; two-thirds of the infants contact the cup in the near median position. However, there is still a greater tendency for the hands to come to the mouth instead of to the cup. This testifies to the immaturity of the approach mechanism; but there is visual pursuit when the infant dislodges the cup from position, an early token of eye-hand coordination.

The scope of the approach movements is restricted at 16 weeks. Contacting with displacement of the cup in the near median position occurs in half of the infants; whereas in the standard position only a few (one-tenth) establish such a contact. At 20 weeks, seven out of ten infants contact the cup in the standard position, and half the infants dislodge the cup in contacting, sometimes so forcibly as to send it out of reach. The approach is characteristically upon the sides of the cup, rarely to the handle.

At 24 weeks prompt approach with contact becomes highly characteristic, but actual grasp occurs in only half of the infants and frequently the cup is displaced in contacting. With one hand on the bowl the infant may move the cup about, but whether this represents abortive prehension or a form of manipulation is not clear. Grasping and lifting appear to be a real problem and fully one-fourth of the infants at this age fussed during the situation. One-half lifted the cup slightly above the table top chiefly with aid of the handle.

As in other situations, 28 weeks witnesses a marked increment in behavior capacities. Virtually all the infants approach promptly; eight out of ten grasp and lift the cup. The lifting is higher and accomplished with greater ease. The approach is characteristically bilateral (seven out of ten) but approximately six out of ten attain the handle, flex upon it, and lift the cup by the handle. Dropping of the cup occurs with similar frequency. Grasping sometimes occurs by clasping on the rim. It is characteristic to use both hands in holding the cup.

At 32 weeks it is highly characteristic to grasp at the outset with one hand, to make an approach upon the handle, to clasp it, and to lift the cup either with or without the aid of the other hand. There is no marked change at 36 weeks, but the handle is used more selectively and the thumb participates more fully. There is less manipulation before lifting.

Manipulation and Exploitation. Exploitation of the cup is limited by the powers of manipulation. At 12 weeks, the "interest" is visual; at 16 weeks it is still chiefly visual but the eyes follow in pursuit of the cup when it moves. The recurrence of regard at this age is a form of circular activity comparable to the repetitive manipulation of later ages.

At 16 weeks the manual contacts are rather brief and sketchy but at 20 weeks the hand clings more to the cup with greater consequent moving or dragging about of the cup, simulating manipulation. The cup dominates the attention.

Twenty weeks is just above the zero level for lifting, an ability which rises sharply and uniformly, reaching universality at 32 weeks. Lifting is itself a kind of exploitation which as such preoccupies the child. But as the lifting is mastered other forms of closely associated exploitation come into the behavior picture.

At 24 weeks the cup is usually dragged a bit before lifting. The infant cannot hold it aloft long or high; he manipulates it again on the table top but the range of activity is meager. He drags or rolls it over on the side and perhaps crudely thrusts the hand into the bowl. Mouthing is occasional.

At 28 weeks the manipulation becomes markedly diversified. Two or three different types of activity occur with more or less recurrence. Typically he moves the cup about briefly on the table top prior to grasp, then grasps it (often by the handle), lifts it to the mouth, mouths it, turns it over while at the mouth, chews the rim and handle, withdraws it, transfers, brandishes it above or on the table. In this process the inverted cup is frequently turned over and placed in right-side-up position. The activity is so vigorous and unrestrained that the cup frequently is sent beyond reach.

At 32 weeks the manipulations are more restrained. The cup is more frequently resecured after release. Rotational manipulation and transfer are more common. Holding hands upon the rim is very characteristic. Mouthing is about as frequent as at 28 weeks, but it is less pronounced and prolonged. It gives way to varied modes of manipulation both on and above the table top.

At 36 weeks these manipulatory modes are still present but with perceptible changes in form and accent. The rotation is more complete and may result in repeated turning of the cup end-for-end. Banging is very pronounced; fingering and intent inspection during manipulation are more evident. At this age the pattern of lifting and mouthing begins to approximate a true raising to the lips for drinking; the emptiness of the cup, however, obscures the full expression of this ability. Naturalistic observations of the behavior with a milk-filled cup show that 36 weeks marks the nascent stage of self-dependence. For brief periods during feeding the infant holds the cup without assistance.

§23. SPOON BEHAVIOR

(16 weeks–36 weeks)

The Situation

Holding the handle horizontally directed toward the infant, the examiner presented the spoon and placed it in the standard position after the manner of presentation described for the first cube.

Stimulus Factors

The spoon possesses distinctive perceptual and manipulatory characteristics. Under the conditions of the examination the spoon is reacted to as a play object with some possible reinforcement from feeding associations. The physical difference between the bowl and the handle of the spoon may reveal the presence or absence of discrimination in the child's manipulation. The placement of the length of the handle in the median plane may elicit orientational adjustment in approach and grasp. At the higher age levels

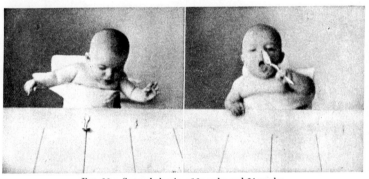

Fig. 23.—Spoon behavior: 16 weeks and 24 weeks.

the use of the spoon as a drum stick or lever may come into expression. It is effective for banging, mouthing, and chewing. Being a slender object it requires special adjustments in mouthing. The infant's unconcern or his difficulties in these adjustments serve to reveal limitations in the geometry of his perceptions.

Behavior Trends

Regard. Even at 16 weeks the spoon elicits prevailing or predominant regard throughout the situation. At 16 weeks eight children out of ten, at 20 weeks nine children out of ten, and thereafter virtually all children prevailingly regard the spoon. Immediate regard occurs with similar frequencies at these age levels. The percentages definitely suggest that the spoon is somewhat more potent than the single cube in arousing full regard at the younger age levels. Consistent regard, however, occurs in only one child out of ten at 16 weeks. Even at 20 weeks it occurs

SITUATION: SPOON (Sp)

Sp	Behavior items	4	6	8	12	16	20	24	28	32	36	40	44	48	52	56
1	Regards immediately....................					83	85	93	100	100	92					
2	Regards momentarily..................					30	33	7	4	—	11					
3	Regards recurrently...................					37	42	10	15	10	24					
4	Regards prolongedly...................					55	59	23	—	—	—					
5	Regards predominantly................					83	91	97	100	100	96					
6	Regards consistently..................					10	21	80	100	100	92					
7	Shifts regard.........................					53	55	21	22	10	38					
8	Shifts regard to examiner.............					20	6	3	12	7	12					
9	Shifts regard to hands................					27	24	10	4	—	—					
10	Arm increases activity................					83	91	97	100	100	100					
11	Approaches...........................					43	53	90	100	100	100					
12	Approaches with right hand...........					17	24	60	44	46	23					
13	Approaches with left hand............					17	30	20	45	18	46					
14	Approaches with both hands...........					10	—	10	11	36	31					
15	Approaches after delay................					23	30	3	4	—	—					
16	Approaches promptly..................					20	27	87	96	100	100					
17	Contacts spoon.......................					50	67	93	100	100	100					
18	Dislodges on contact..................					30	33	32	38	7	7					
19	Grasps...............................					10	30	77	100	100	96					
20	Grasps with right hand................					—	13	39	33	43	36					
21	(If grasps) grasps with right hand.......					—	43	50	33	43	36					
22	Grasps with left hand.................					11	18	32	48	25	50					
23	(If grasps) grasps with left hand........					100	60	41	48	25	50					
24	Grasps with both hands...............								7	18	11					
25	Grasps in palm.......................					3	9	43	37	25	35					
26	Grasps interdigitally..................					7	27	17	30	29	15					
27	Grasps with thumb opposing fingers......					—	3	23	33	21	46					
28	Manipulates without grasp.............					30	46	23	19	—	4					
29	Manip. on and above table top and mouths					—	9	7	48	29	38					
30	Brings first to mouth..................					—	9	29	22	46	35					
31	Lifts from table top...................					7	31	77	100	100	89					
32	Brings to mouth......................					—	21	57	92	75	58					
33	(If brings to mouth) brings to mouth first.						45	50	24	61	60					
34	Transfers.............................					—	3	26	70	68	58					
35	Rotates..............................					—	—	—	27	36	27					
36	Hits or bangs on table top.............					—	6	16	42	36	63					
37	Drops................................					10	18	36	55	36	27					
38	Drops and resecures..................					3	6	7	38	25	19					
39	Vocalizes.............................					22	12	16	42	25	27					

in only two children out of ten. At 24 weeks it rises sharply to a frequency of eight out of ten; at 28 weeks it is universal.

Three other modes of regard manifest themselves with relative frequency (from 30 per cent to 60 per cent) at 16 and 20 weeks, namely: momentary regard, recurrent regard, and prolonged regard. These forms of regard are infrequent at subsequent ages. Prolonged regard was not observed at all after 24 weeks. Shift of regard to the examiner occurred in one child out of five at 16 weeks. A shift to the child's own hand occurred in one out of four both at 16 and at 20 weeks. It is clear therefore that 24 weeks marks a rather definite turning point in the general nature of the regard.

At 24 weeks the regard becomes consistent in eight children out of ten. In general the spoon situation absorbs the infant's attention to the exclusion of regard for the examiner. Shifts of regard to the examiner are most frequent at 16 weeks but even then occur in only one child out of five.

The genetic advance in spoon regard may be outlined as follows: At 16 weeks the visual response is dominating and absorbing; the adaptive manual response is secondary. The infant fixates prolongedly with intent staring. At 20 weeks the starey quality has almost vanished. Fixation is still prolonged but is more facile, less absorbing. Adaptive manual response has become more prominent. At 24 weeks regard is still more facile and sustained. It is now more secondary to the total prehensory response. At 28 weeks regard is well established. The infant also regards the spoon definitely on withdrawing it from the mouth. Thereafter he gives more discriminative, inspectional regard to aspects of the spoon, in close correlation with his new and varied powers of manipulation. Selective regard and selective utilization of the handle are probably present at 36 weeks.

Prehension. At 16 weeks the hand-arm activity in relation to the spoon is somewhat ambiguous. This activity is apparently increased by the presence of the spoon, but it may occur without accompanying regard of the spoon. Half the infants contact the spoon in a manner that seems relatively fortuitous. Directed approach is not definite; the perceptual reaction itself is prominent.

At 20 weeks approach movements are better defined and more frequently directed toward the spoon without and with delay. The spoon is typically contacted from the side and hit to the side prior to grasp. Grasp occurs in three children out of ten.

At 24 weeks, the approach is more prompt and complete, the hand being placed over the spoon with eventual grasping and lifting. Very often the spoon is dragged, pushed, and pulled before and after seizure; whether this is because of immature grasping or manipulatory interest is not always clear. In grasping, the fingers are curled around the handle. This is very characteristic of the 24 weeks level. Grasping is the most characteristic achievement of this age but success is still dependent upon favorable accessibility after the spoon has been displaced by the initial contact. An inadequate contacting approach occurs in about one child out of three until the 32 weeks level.

At 28 weeks grasp is universal but it is interdigital in three out of ten infants, indicating that manual orientation with reference to the alignment of the spoon has not been achieved. Pushing the spoon out of reach prior to grasp also is frequent. Opening and closing of the fingers near or over the spoon are frequent and a primitive kind of release with resecural occurs in four out of ten children.

Anticipatory approach during presentation of the spoon is noted at 32 weeks. In one out of three cases this approach is bilateral. There is partial adjustment of the hand just prior to grasp and the infant is now able to secure and resecure the spoon with ease, regardless of its alignment on the table top.

At 36 weeks approach is typically unilateral, the left hand being used almost as frequently as the right. Grasping still usually takes place by curling the fingers around the handle but in one child out of three index-thumb opposition was noted. Grasp is more secure.

Manipulation and Exploitation. At 16 weeks manipulation is merely on the horizon. One-half of the infants contact the spoon; one in ten actually clasps the spoon. At 20 weeks three in ten grasp the spoon and there is apparent increase of activity after seizure, indicating a rudimentary exploitational response. This exploitation is confined to the table top. Typically the spoon is not raised. At 24 weeks it is lifted and carried to the mouth. The free hand usually comes up while the spoon is in the mouth. Mouthing is the most prominent activity but it is often preceded by crude knocking, pushing, and dragging on the table top. One child in three drops the spoon. The tendency is to hold the spoon firmly when the examiner attempts removal of the spoon. While the infant mouths the spoon he looks forward with a transfixed gaze somewhat suggestive of satisfaction.

At 28 weeks there is a definite increment in manipulatory exploitiveness. The activities are more varied both in type and in sequence and there is a tendency for certain types to be repeated. Whereas at 24 weeks one type of activity tended to dominate the behavior picture, at 28 weeks three or more types of activity become manifest. Mouthing is vigorous and often accompanied by bubble formation and also by vocalization. Though mouthing is predominant it gives way recurrently to inspectional withdrawal, manipulation, and transfer. Transfer is often repeated. It reaches a peak at 28 weeks.

At 32 weeks mouthing is somewhat less prominent, less prolonged, and less masticatory. The spoon is typically carried to
the mouth first but subsequent activity above the table top is most
characteristic. This activity includes withdrawal with inspection,
transfer with rotation, and some waving. Transfer is now accomplished with greater adeptness and precision. Rotational and partial
end-over-end manipulation comes into prominence. The free hand
participates more fully in manipulations.

It is significant that the affective aspect of mouthing is already
less evident. While the spoon is held at the mouth the infant is
under a compulsion to transfer and to remove and to rotate the
object. The oral pleasure gives way to this manipulatory exploitation. To be sure the spoon goes back to the mouth repeatedly
but each such return means that the mouthing has been inter-
rupted by a competing behavior trend. In all this mouthing it
is the bowl which goes to the mouth. The infant has ample opportunity to handle the spoon by the bowl and to mouth the handle,
but prevailingly he does not so elect. Can this discriminative
behavior be due simply to the physical characteristics of the
spoon?

At 36 weeks mouthing is still less prominent. Whereas at
32 weeks the spoon promptly goes to the mouth, at 36 weeks there
is usually a brief manipulation, characteristically transfer or
banging, on the table top just prior to mouthing. Recurrences to
mouthing are less frequent and the sequence of activity somewhat
less stereotyped, that is, less repetitive. A few infants even carry
the spoon below the table top and occasionally gross motor postural
changes occur during the exploitation. Exploitation above the
table top including rotational manipulation is less prominent.
Pushing and dragging are now rare. Banging is better defined and
highly characteristic. Even the free hand often slaps the table.
This sound production must be reckoned as part of the total
exploitation.

§24. Cup and Spoon Behavior

(32 weeks–56 weeks)

The Situation

Holding the upturned cup in his left hand, the spoon in his
right hand, the examiner simultaneously advanced both in parallel
lanes and placed them on the transverse standard line. After

appropriate observation, cup and spoon were removed from the infant's grasp and the examiner then placed the cup in the far median position, thrust the spoon perpendicularly into the cup bringing it against the sides with a to-and-fro motion producing a well-defined rattling sound. The examiner then re-presented both objects in the standard manner and observed the responsive behavior. Similarly a second demonstration and a third demonstration of the spoon rattle followed.

Stimulus Factors

When cup and spoon are presented simultaneously the stimulus values of the cup alone and the spoon alone are not simply compounded but the total situation undergoes a change. The cup is

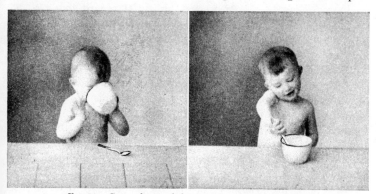

Fig. 24.—Cup and spoon behavior: 36 weeks and 48 weeks.

presented in normal rather than inverted position. Certain stimulus properties (if the term is permissible) of the single object continue to assert their power but in modified form. The typical reactions to the objects in combination cannot be logically deduced, much less predicted, from a knowledge of the reactions to the presentation of a single object. At 32 weeks and at 36 weeks the objects are presented singly as well as in combination; thereafter only in combination. The side-by-side situation sets up competitive tensions, possibilities of selective, alternating, and combinational response.

When the spoon rattle is demonstrated, social and auditory factors are strongly brought into the situation. The previous feeding experiences of the infant appear to have relatively small influence on his reactions. There is occasionally a slight initial hesitation or a brief mimetic drinking. It is of psychological interest that the infant exploits the cup and the spoon in much the same manner that he does nonconventionalized objects like the ring and string.

Two objects which singly have distinctive stimulus values for the infant naturally call forth new modes of regard and exploitation when these objects are presented in association. These peculiar modes of regard are revealed on initial presentation and also by the apportionment and sequences of attention during the course of activity.

Behavior Trends

Visual Regard. At 32 weeks the initial regard tends to be restricted to one object and after a variable interval shifts rather suddenly to the second object. At somewhat later age levels this shifting becomes less obvious, less naive, and the child attends to both objects more nearly at one confluent glance. At 32 weeks the regard is saccadic in the sense that the child fixates on one object and then by a twitch-like transition transfers this fixation to the second object. The regard may, of course, recur to the first object but it is significant that only six children out of ten (at 32 weeks) definitely attend to both cup and spoon during the situation. The other four children are preoccupied with a single object even though a second is available.

An alternating type of regard is still pronounced at 36 weeks. Typically one object, usually the cup, first secures the attention. This attention is sustained for a considerable interval and then shifts to the spoon. The spoon now absorbs the attention for a similarly sustained interval during which the cup is apparently ignored. But in due course the cup again receives sustained regard. This alternating apportionment of visual regard represents a stage of "attention," a dynamic pattern characteristic of the nascent period of combining. The preoccupation with one object to the exclusion of the other suggests that the combining stage has not yet been reached. But the very fact that this preoccupation presently shifts to the second object and eventually returns to the first indicates that the genetic basis for combining is already being laid down. The regard has a successional, quantum-like nature. Perhaps regard always retains this character even at the highest levels of synthetic combination but functions with such

SITUATION: CUP AND SPOON (Cp-Sp)

Cp-Sp	Behavior items	4	6	8	12	16	20	24	28	32	36	40	44	48	52	56
1	Regards cup and spoon									58	61	76	84	100	100	100
2	Regards cup and spoon alternately						—	—	—	59	60	21	23	—	—	—
3	Regards cup or spoon recurrently									4	11	21	38	27	37	65
4	Shifts regard to surroundings							—	—	—	4	4	23	12	10	4
5	Shifts regard to Examiner									4	—	14	23	23	22	54
6	Approaches cup first									59	50	55	42	31	24	4
7	Approaches spoon first									41	25	21	42	50	66	96
8	Ap. cup and spoon simultaneously						—	—	—	0	25	24	15	19	10	—
9	Grasps cup									81	96	97	96	80	86	89
10	Grasps spoon									97	86	97	100	100	97	100
11	Pushes and pulls cup or spoon									63	36	38	34	16	24	12
12	Bangs cup or spoon on table top									33	64	69	54	54	29	19
13	Hits or bangs cup on table top						—	—	—	15	40	54	38	38	7	12
14	Hits or bangs spoon on table top									22	32	31	27	33	30	19
15	Lifts cup									63	79	93	92	80	84	77
16	Brings cup or spoon to mouth									70	64	69	54	31	34	38
17	Brings cup to mouth									33	36	58	50	23	26	19
18	Brings spoon to mouth									55	47	27	19	12	12	26
19	Transfers cup or spoon											50	52	65	50	50
20	Transfers cup									8	18	35	46	27	10	4
21	Transfers spoon									30	40	35	38	23	22	50
22	Rotates cup									19	26	41	58	46	41	46
23	Releases cup						—	—	—	52	50	62	54	54	44	46
24	Releases spoon									63	43	66	62	77	51	54
25	Resecures cup									42	30	27	50	65	55	26
26	Resecures spoon									35	58	68	80	65	47	57
27	Releases and resecures cup or spoon									30	32	59	54	69	41	38
28	Releases and resecures cup									22	15	17	27	35	24	12
29	Releases and resecures spoon									22	25	45	50	50	24	31
30	Drops one reaching for other									33	29	24	15	23	12	15
31	Retains one, reaches for other						—	—	—	63	54	83	89	65	80	85
32	Retains one, secures other									48	54	79	89	65	80	85
33	Combines cup and spoon						—	—	—	59	57	83	89	92	95	100
34	Brings cup and spoon together									19	25	28	54	54	52	62
35	Brings spoon over cup									7	4	31	65	77	85	100
36	Places spoon in cup										4	24	50	65	85	100
37	Releases spoon in cup												4	27	24	38
	SPOON RATTLE DEMONSTRATED															
38	Combines cup and spoon									29	48	50	65	84	84	96
39	Com. cup and spoon only after demon.						—	—	—	21	22	35	15	16	10	—
40	Combining improves after demonstration											35	46	48	58	46
	BEFORE OR AFTER DEMONSTRATION															
41	Hits or rattles spoon in cup											15	19	40	45	62
42	Hits or rattles spoon in cup after demon.											14	27	42	65	65
43	Kneels or stands							—	—	—		3	12	8	30	8
44	Pivots						—	—	—		11	14	23	35	34	46
45	Frets									22	11	14	27	4	15	12
46	Vocalizes									29	32	31	54	23	34	42
47	Smiles									7	7	15	12	12	12	35

smoothness and speed that the alternating oscillations so evident in infancy are quite concealed.

Even at 40 weeks the alternating shifting of regard has become less conspicuous. The infant simultaneously manipulates both cup and spoon to a greater degree than at 36 weeks. The regard for the single object is more elaborate and inspectional in character. Combining is definitely established and the regard is correspondingly mature.

At 44 weeks the visual attention is rather equally divided between cup and spoon and they are doubtless becoming more intimately united in the perception of the infant. At 52 weeks he seems to regard them both at once.

The developmental progress of regard is reflected in the changes of attention from age to age, to the spoon rattle demonstration. At 32 weeks the infant smiles and often blinks at the din of the demonstration; he probably perceives the situation in the gross and not in mechanical detail. At 36 weeks also he smiles at the demonstration and he may make a face! At 40 weeks he smiles and looks at the examiner, but the subsequent activity is not much altered and he rarely places the spoon in the cup. If what he does is an index of what he sees, then we may conclude that however intent the regard, he does not actually perceive that the spoon is placed into the bowl of the cup until about the age of 48 weeks; and he sees it with increasing clearness at 52 weeks and at 56 weeks, when he repeatedly dips the spoon well into the cup.

The relationship between motor reaction and regard presents many problems of theoretical interest. There is probably no essential difference between the crude rovings of regard of the young infant and the swift, exploratory movements of regard of the older infant. Both forms of regard are adaptive oculomotor patterns. It may be, however, that the relative dominance of regard declines with advance in prehensory and exploitive abilities. Regard is then fashioned by manipulation, the eye constantly sees what the hand has just wrought; vision does not always go in advance like a scout to indicate what the hand shall do. It is for this reason that a genetic account of the development of regard becomes inextricably bound up with the details of manipulation and of exploitation.

Size and brightness are not all-determining in establishing regard even in the infant. To be sure, at 32, 36, and 40 weeks half or over half of the infants make an initial restricted approach upon the cup and one might attribute this to its greater optical mass. But the cup loses this preeminence, for at 52 weeks two-thirds, and at 56 weeks almost all, of the infants make a prior restricted approach upon the spoon with perhaps a swift glance at the cup. Why, it would be difficult to say.

It also becomes increasingly clear that regard is formed behavior. It is not a discrete faculty with a magic kind of independence which in some mysterious way emanates from the central or peripheral nervous system. It is not even a phase of pure receptivity. It is an outward manifestation of a response pattern which is dependent upon retinal stimulation but which is determined by the total and the specific reaction trends of the organism.

One speaks of regard and attention as though they were dynamic functions (and by implication, faculties). This is only for convenience or convention. It would be scientifically better to speak of "patterns" of regard and forms of attention to preserve the specific, morphological status of each and every act of attention. These acts are patterns of behavior as validly as an act of prehension.

Prehension. The cup and spoon situation produces few distinctive manifestations of prehension. The grasp in its mechanics naturally resembles that described for single objects. Toward the end of the year, however, there is evidence that the infant makes a discriminative seizure of the end of the spoon handle and dangles, dips, or deposits the spoon into the bowl of the cup. This seemingly simple bit of behavior is not suddenly achieved; genetically it is very complex and is dependent upon a neuromuscular refinement in the prehensory mechanism, to say nothing of the growth of adaptive perception necessary for the spatial identification of the end as opposed to the middle of an object. An elementary mastery of the principle of the lever is also involved. Indeed a minute examination of the prehensory improvements in the manipulation of the spoon would furnish a key to the earliest stages of the psychology of tool using.

A very primitive kind of tool utilization is suggested in the fact that the 32 weeks-old child selectively uses the handle to lift and turn the inverted cup right side up. In the cup and spoon situation at the same age the cup is in normal position and the handle does not so much come into play. Instead, the infant characteristically grasps the cup by the rim and curls his fingers about the handle of the spoon. Even this type of grasp is not directly effective and in almost two-thirds of the infants the cup is "pulled" or "pushed" about prior to seizure. Such dislocation of the object is probably a function of immature grasp rather than of manipulatory drive. At 36 weeks also he is quite likely to push the cup about a bit or to tip it on its side before he flexes his fingers on the rim or handle. At 40 weeks he still flexes on the rim but commonly pulls the cup toward himself and lifts it. At this age and at 44 weeks rotational manipulation of both cup and spoon is becoming well defined. It is now highly characteristic for the infant to retain one object while reaching for the other. He often retains grasp of both objects during the manipulation which follows.

Neat and facile placement of the spoon into the cup requires not only adaptive grasp but adaptive release, which is the obverse or inhibitory aspect of prehension. Such release is a positive and a difficult feat in infancy and it requires a complex developmental organization which is only roughly indicated by visible perform- ance. A dropping of the spoon is frequent from 32 weeks to 56 weeks and was observed in over half of the infants at all but one age level. Though the physics of this dropping remains uniform we may be sure that the behavior mechanism of the release changes from age to age; the extensor reaction system does not remain uniform; voluntary or adaptive factors come increasingly into the picture. The presence of these factors is strongly evinced in the late but steady emergence of an adaptive insertion of the spoon into the bowl of the cup, followed later by full placement.

We might call this "placement release" to distinguish it from a cruder form of dropping or losing. If we had all the developmental facts in hand we should find that we lacked a terminology to express the gradations from sheer "falling" to deliberate "letting fall." The existence of such gradations is revealed by two pretty curves of frequency: one for the item "dips (or places) the spoon in the cup"; the other for the item "releases spoon in cup." The first curve begins with zero at 32 weeks and ends with 100 per cent at 56 weeks. The steady rise of the percentages, 0, 4, 24, 50, 65, 85, 100 per cent, strongly confirms the developmental complexity of the spoon-into-cup reaction. The zero value at 32 weeks is somewhat ameliorated by a few children (one in 15) who bring the spoon over the cup without thrusting it into the cup, illustrating the important fact that a genetic zero is not absolute. *Dipping into the cup* is anticipated by *poising the spoon over the cup*.

The genetic or horizon zero for the item *releases spoon in cup* is located at about 40 weeks. At 44 weeks one child in 25 placed the spoon into the cup with definite release; at 56 weeks, approxi- mately two out of five children released the spoon in the cup. The fuller mastery of this placement release lies in the second year of life.

It remains to mention a third developmental trend which by inference probably has its nascent or horizon level at about 28 weeks. We refer to the interesting item *brings spoon over cup.* As just noted, no child at 32 weeks dips the spoon into the cup but at least one child in 15 at that age holds the spoon over the cup without thrusting it in. Similarly at 40 weeks 31 per cent of the infants held the spoon over the cup but only 24 per cent actually dipped the spoon into the cup.

This discussion began with the mechanism of release but leads by backward reference to associated mechanisms. It is seen from a comparative study of these three related curves of frequency how one reaction differentiates from another and yet remains genetically rooted in its antecedents. A genetic zero is always relative: dipping into the cup is anticipated by a preparatory poising of the spoon over the cup; dipping prepares for adaptive placement release. Each pattern is sufficient unto its genetic day but that day is brief. What was once a culminating achievement proves to be a preliminary one.

Manipulation and Exploitation. The close relationships between "attentional-regard," prehension, and exploitational activity have been repeatedly mentioned. This repetition is not idle if it helps to reinforce a recognition of the profound coherence of the infant's behavior. In all these activities there is a thoroughgoing dynamic repercussion and essential unity which makes it impossible if not illogical to look for sharp distinctions of cause and effect. We are dealing with the same kind of unity which pervades the relationship of heredity and environment. Confusion arises only if we make too much of an objective criterion of success in performance and ignore the developmental import of apparent failure. Infant behavior grows by a process of increasing approximation to changing goals, and we are in danger of underestimating the psychological importance of his immature patterns of response.

It is fair to say that the infant exploits his environment at all ages. Even before he can lay hold of that environment by active prehension he grapples it with his exploring eyes. His very growth projects him farther into varied contactings with the environment, with varied contactings which are determined by the complexity of his sensorimotor equipment at the moment. When his forearm is somatically and neurologically ready to rotate he shows a propensity to rotate an object held in hand. At the same time he usually is ready and prone to inspect the object as it rotates. Even though this reaction is based on a motor maturation it has psychological status as an act of exploitation. Accordingly nearly all new forms of behavior in the infant carry exploitational, experimental possibilities. To what extent and why these possibilities vary with individual infants need not be considered here. Individual objects may be exploited; two individual objects may be combined in the exploitation. The present summary deals chiefly with the manner in which the infant capitalizes the juxtaposition of cup and spoon and brings one into productive relationship with the other.

As already noted, the younger infants show a slight preference for the cup in their initial response, but by the end of the year the great majority make an initial selective response to the spoon. The spoon is promptly picked up and immediately brought into well-sustained relation to the cup, whereas at the younger ages the infant exploits first one object and then another. Between these two extremes lies a series of gradations of combining exploitation which has already been foreshadowed in the discussion of prehension and release. The developmental progression becomes most apparent when a series of cinema records of the advancing ages is viewed in close succession. If one disregarded the infant as the agent of the behavior and charted simply the routes of spoon and cup in their movements on the table top, one would get the impression that the cup exerted some magnetic power which at first fitfully but with increasing certainty and force attracted the spoon into itself. Although this would be a fantastic outlook upon the actual events, the charting itself would express the progressive changes of the nervous system which conditions these outward events. Fitfulness of contact reflects the early stages of a combining propensity. To what extent, if at all, fortuity figures it is difficult to say. We may be certain, however, that fortuitous contacts will not be followed up by truly adaptive combining unless the child has the requisite maturity which is evidenced in the propensity. Likewise his responsiveness to a combining spoon-rattling demonstration will be mainly determined by his developmental maturity.

There is very little spontaneous combining at 32 weeks (one child out of 15 brought the spoon over the cup in a relational manner, and one out of five hit the cup with the spoon), but one child out of three combined after demonstration. This age is, therefore, near the nascent level for combining behavior. At

36 weeks and at 40 weeks approximately one-half, and at 56 weeks nearly all the children combined after demonstration. Improvement in the amount or intensity of combining following demonstration was especially marked at one year; and actual responsive rattling occurred in six out of ten infants at the age of 56 weeks.

Spontaneous combining begins at 36 weeks. Not only does the banging of the individual cup and the individual spoon increase, but simultaneous approach upon cup and spoon rises to 25 per cent (from 0 per cent at 32 weeks). Cup and spoon are brought together above the table top (25 per cent at 32 weeks, rising to 62 per cent at 56 weeks). The spoon is hit against the cup before demonstration (29 per cent). This latter item reaches a maximum of 50 per cent at 44 weeks and declines to 19 per cent at 56 weeks, suggesting that placement and agitation of the spoon within the cup are becoming the dominant features of combining activity. Spontaneous agitation of the spoon in the bowl (hitting or rattling) rises steadily from 0 frequency at 36 weeks to 54 per cent at 56 weeks. Demonstration increases the incidence of hitting or rattling within the bowl at all ages from 40 weeks on, but it is not competent (because of the incompetency of the infant) to induce responsive agitation even at 36 weeks. Forty weeks may, therefore, be regarded as the nascent level for this particular kind of combining. Specific forms of combination can hardly be induced unless the child already has them in his repertoire of spontaneous behavior.

The following comment briefly indicates the diverse kinds of exploitation of individual objects. Mouthing of the spoon, most frequent at 32 weeks, declines to 26 per cent at 56 weeks. Release of the spoon on the table top, followed by resecural, is relatively frequent at all ages. Banging of the spoon reaches a low maximum of 38 per cent at 48 weeks. Transfer of the spoon reaches a maximum of 50 per cent at 56 weeks, but occurs at all ages with a frequency of 22 to 30 per cent. Transfer of the cup, on the contrary, is at its height at 44 weeks with a frequency of 46 per cent, and only 8 per cent at 32 weeks and 4 per cent at 56 weeks. Rotation of the cup (58 per cent), vocalization (54 per cent), and regard for surroundings (23 per cent) are also at a maximum at 40 weeks. The occurrence of transfer is evidently much influenced by the total situation. It may be noted that when the cup alone is presented at 32 weeks it is transferred in 43 per cent of the cases; but when presented in combination with the spoon, only in 8 per cent. A comparable discrepancy appears in transfer of the cup at 36 weeks, and transfer of the spoon at 32 weeks.

An accurate account of the developmental advance in combining behavior could be built up only by a minute analysis of characteristic sequences of activities over a given interval at successive ages. Such an analysis would show primitive and sketchy forms of combining at the younger levels leading to repeated and sustained combining at the older levels. Schematically this progression is somewhat as follows:

32 weeks: Attention goes to cup, shifts to spoon, shifts to cup. The cup is grasped and manipulated. Regard returns to the spoon. The cup is dropped, the spoon is grasped, mouthed, the cup is regarded again but the two objects are not brought into relation.

36 weeks: Marked alternations of regard for cup and spoon with rather equal division of attention. The regard weaves back and forth, sometimes rapidly. The infant holds both cup and spoon simultaneously, may bang one while holding the other, or momentarily bring them together above the table top. He does not bring the spoon to the cup as it rests on the table.

40 weeks: He gives conjoint attention to both objects, or marginal attention to one. The discrete alternating shifts of regard are disappearing. There is more confluent exploitation of both objects, and well-defined, recurrent combining is almost characteristic.

44 to 48 weeks: Definite combining now well established. It occurs more than once in the tide of activity. The infant brings the spoon over the cup, inserts it, or hits the rim or side of the cup with the spoon. Discrete and partially independent exploitation of the single object, however, persists and is proportionately in excess of actual combining. The combining may still be somewhat sporadic. Simultaneous manipulations may be more prominent than relational exploitations in which one object is the foil of the other.

52 to 56 weeks: Immediate, repetitive, and sustained combining. Prior, preferential grasp of the spoon and adaptive application of the spoon to the cup. Discrete exploitations and manipulations of the single object persist, but the total behavior picture shows a dominance of relational activity with the cup as a foil and the spoon as tool.

Developmentally, combining activity is closely articulated with patterns of individual or discrete activity. Two objects, *A* and *B*, lie adjacent. *A* elicits a discrete attentional-manipulatory response in its own right; so does *B*; so does *A* again. At a low stage of maturity these responses are independent events but at higher stages of maturity response *B* is influenced by stimulus *A* and tends to have a reference to *B*. It is not necessary to invoke a law of association or even of learning to explain this fact of reference. The phenomenon seems to depend more upon the scope of regard and the range of manipulation and these factors are determined by maturation. It is for this reason that a conspectus of the manifestations of combining reveals in general a steady, lawful, incremental advance, rather than a saltatory succession of dramatic insight episodes.

§25. CUP AND CUBES BEHAVIOR

(32 weeks–56 weeks)

The Situation

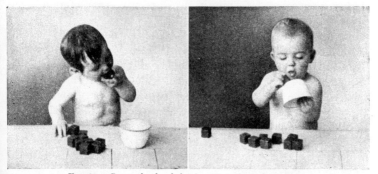

FIG. 25.—Cup and cubes behavior: 36 weeks and 48 weeks.

In the standard manner the examiner simultaneously presented the cup and the ten cubes used in the massed cube situation. These cubes were placed in an irregular cluster at the infant's right near the near median position and at the side of the cup.

Stimulus Factors

The distinctive stimulus values of the cup and cubes situation constitute a problem of more than speculative interest because we are able to analyze these values by comparisons with closely related situations. On the one hand we have the massed cubes situation which reveals the reactions to multiple cubes alone.

On the other hand we have the cup and spoon situation which narrows the stimulus and combining possibilities to two objects. A thorough-going comparison of the reactions in these three situations would throw considerable direct light on the perceptual capacities and perceptual organization of the infant. The differentiating details of response are somewhat concealed by similarities in numerous items of behavior for these three situations. But a close investigation of the total reactions and of the inflections of patterns within the total reaction discloses distinctive behavior characteristics of considerable genetic interest.

It is of course understood that all comments in regard to the perception of the infant contain interpretive hazard. However, the comparative analysis of differential responses in closely related situations, as above suggested, tends to place the infant's perceptual behavior upon an objective basis. We cannot actually reconstruct the inner aspect of the responses but we can deduce certain fundamental differences in this inner aspect which declare themselves infallibly in the distinctive characters of overt behavior.

The diversified possibilities of exploitive behavior in the cup and cubes situation may be listed as follows: (a) The cup by itself yields to manifold manipulations and dislocations. (b) Likewise a single cube by itself. (c) A single cube may be brought into relation to the cup or the cup may be brought into relation with the single cube in varied ways. (d) A single cube may be brought into relation with a single associated cube or with several associated cubes. (e) Exploitations may be confined to the cubes. (f) The exploitations of the multiple cubes may be referred in different ways to the cup.

This logical analysis of exploitational possibilities indicates an extremely wide range of permutations. In spite of the statistical magnitude of these possibilities, certain modalities and trends of behavior declare themselves consistently.

Behavior Trends

Regard. At all ages prior regard goes to the cubes, but the nature of this regard exhibits subtle and significant developmental changes from age to age. At 32 weeks the cup is perhaps nearest to a parity to the cubes in initial provocativeness. It is common for the regard to shift from the cubes to the cup and back to the cubes. Sometimes this shift is rapid and sharply defined. Prefer-

Situation: Cup and Cubes (Cp-C)

Cp-C	Behavior items	4	6	8	12	16	20	24	28	32	36	40	44	48	52	56
1	Regards cubes first									72	76	75	88	68	74	85
2	Attends predominantly to cubes									56	56	32	60	32	17	15
3	Attends alternately to cup and cubes									66	60	68	60	32	26	0
4	Attends simultaneously to cup and cubes									33	28	35	40	57	64	85
5	Shifts regard to Examiner									5	8	14	20	25	31	30
6	Approaches promptly									100	96	96	96	100	100	100
7	Approaches cubes first									61	68	71	84	57	77	82
8	Grasps cube									94	92	93	100	86	89	100
9	Grasps more than one cube									55	64	71	68	71	77	89
10	Average number cubes grasped									1	2	2	2	3	3	5
11	Grasps cup									66	60	64	56	79	82	82
12	Grasps cup only or cubes only									39	52	43	44	39	28	19
13	Confines some manipulation to cubes									61	64	61	68	68	69	67
14	Pushes or scatters cubes									28	44	43	28	14	31	4
15	Brings cube to mouth									39	40	18	36	25	15	11
16	Transfers cube									22	28	4	20	14	11	11
17	Casts cube									11	4	18	8	35	38	22
18	Releases and resecures cube									0	4	7	36	29	54	41
19	Drops cube, regrasps or grasps another									39	32	57	44	61	56	78
20	Picks up one cube after another									5	12	11	28	36	51	67
21	Casts or brings cube to platform									0	12	21	28	39	41	33
22	Confines some manipulation to cup									72	52	57	56	61	67	45
23	Lifts cup									22	40	50	52	64	74	70
24	Brings cup to mouth									28	12	21	20	14	29	19
25	Manipulates cup above table top									—	8	11	16	25	18	15
26	Transfers cup									—	4	7	4	18	10	7
27	Drops cup									44	44	46	40	39	51	37
28	Brings cup to platform									0	8	4	24	29	28	41
29	Drops cube, grasps cup									28	12	18	28	35	51	45
30	Grasps cube, cup in hand									33	20	28	12	43	46	48
31	Holds cup and cube, one in each hand									50	32	46	48	46	59	52
32	Holds two cubes, one in each hand									33	40	61	64	46	43	45
33	Combines cube and cube or cube and cup									33	32	57	68	72	72	82
34	Combines cube and cube									22	20	32	40	14	8	15
35	Combines cup and cube									22	16	39	40	71	70	74
36	Brings one object to another									28	28	50	60	68	69	78
37	Hits one object on another									28	28	46	36	25	20	26
38	Brings two objects together									5	12	21	16	14	10	15
39	Brings cube over cup									5	0	18	28	54	59	74
40	Places one or more cubes in cup									5	0	0	12	39	54	74
41	Releases cube in cup											0	12	32	51	63
42	Places two or more cubes in cup												4	18	38	63
43	Releases more than one cube in cup												4	18	33	52
44	Places three or more cubes in cup													11	15	56
45	Places four or more cubes in cup												—	0	13	48
46	Places five or more cubes in cup												—	—	0	45
47	Average number of cubes placed in cup												0	1	1	4
48	Removes cube from cup											14	16	35	41	56
49	Lifts cup containing cubes													11	40	59
50	Postural activity									0	12	18	20	39	51	19
51	Turns to side										8	18	12	32	40	11

ential attention is for the cubes, but there is close rivalry between cup and cubes. At 36 weeks the cubes secure predominant attention, but well-defined intervals of preoccupation with the cup also occur. This preoccupation largely displaces concern for the cubes for the time being. Combining is consequently scanty and sketchy.

At 40 weeks preferential attention for the cubes (or cup) is not so apparent because the regard for the second object is less secondary; the regard may be considered more synthetic because there is an increasing disposition toward combination of cube and cup. Roughly expressed, at 36 weeks the child heeds A (the cubes) and then B (the cup) and then again A; at 40 weeks he not only alternates between A and B but he applies A to B and B to A. At 44 weeks preferential regard for the cubes again comes into prominence. This phenomenon is only superficially inconsistent with an actual developmental increase of combining activity. The rather marked preoccupation with the cubes is due to the utilization of the combining possibilities which the cubes themselves possess. The cup is not, of course, altogether ignored but it is probable that the cup is not perceived as a possible receptacle for the cubes.

At 48 weeks, however, there is objective indication that the child now perceives at least dimly the bowl of the cup. As will be later detailed he brings the cube into more circumscribed relation to the cup. This delimitation of reaction may be taken as outward evidence of the more penetrating perception of the solid (or shall we say, hollow?) geometry of the cup. Accordingly, at 48 weeks there is further increase of attentive regard for the cup. The distribution of attention between cup and cubes is becoming more even and also more convergent. At 52 weeks this convergence expresses itself in definite and often recurrent insertion of at least a single cube into the cup. At 56 weeks there may be consecutive placement of several cubes into the cup with controlled release.

It is evident from this summary that the advanced stages in distribution of regard can be considered in more detail only through a discussion of manipulation and exploitation. A concluding comment should be made concerning the similarities and differences of attentional patterns at 44 weeks and at 56 weeks. At 44 weeks we noted a high degree of combining and serial exploitation of the cubes with somewhat secondary exploitation of the cup. At 56 weeks with more advanced patterns of prehension, release, and attention there is a comparable or superior combining exploitation of the cubes but now in productive relationship to the cup. This conjoint attentiveness to cup and cubes at 56 weeks reflects, in comparison with 44 weeks, the progressive structural complexity of specific and integrated patterns of response. The new subtleties of attentional regard are but outward symptoms of this hidden morphological complexity. Attention, as a function, has not increased but the total reaction system of the infant has undergone elaborated organization.

Manipulation and Exploitation. In the present summary the course of development of exploitational activity has been fore-shadowed in the outline of the changes in attentional regard. Regard and exploitation cannot of course be successfully separated. The efficiency and delicacy of exploitation are primarily conditioned by the maturity of the manipulatory equipment. But, as already suggested, the projectivity, the elaboration, and the adaptiveness of manipulation are also conditioned by the maturity of perceptual mechanisms, which are presumably cortical. In a neuroanatomical sense these perceptual patterns are in principle essentially comparable to those of manipulation and closely cor-related with them. Vision and the kinesthesis of manipulation contribute to the continuous organization of perceptual behavior.

At 32 weeks prior approach, followed by grasp, goes to the cubes. Activity with the cubes may include mouthing, transfer, pushing, hitting, dropping. Similar independent activity with the cup follows. Half the infants may hold the cup and cube simul-taneously, one in each hand, but the two objects are not brought into relation. There is instead a successive, oscillating distribution of activity. At 36 weeks this distribution is less evenly divided. There is more channeled preference for one object, though succes-sive regard from one to the other object also occurs. Active hitting or banging of the cubes and banging of the cup as well are common. One object may be hit against the other, cube against cup or cup against cube, or cube against cube. This latter activity is a primi-tive type of combining emerging from banging.

At 40 weeks, combining activity becomes more controlled, more frequent, and more sustained. The somewhat uncritical banging gives way to a more inhibited application of one object to the other. At 44 weeks the propensity to combine is most readily satisfied by the cubes. This marked preferential attention for the cubes has already been emphasized. Typically the infant holds a cube in either hand and brings these cubes together, or he holds a cube in one hand and combines this repeatedly with the cube on the table top. He is not yet fully sensitive to the receptacle values of the cup. He does not respond with cube placement even after demonstration by the examiner. However, he usually removes the cube from the cup after such demonstration. This reaction displays rather neatly the limitations of his combining and exploitive capacities. Developmentally, however, he will soon overcome this limitation because even at 44 weeks he may bring the cube over the cup or tap the cube against the rim of the cup.

Nevertheless, his combining propensities at 44 weeks are amply satisfied by the cubes alone. At 48 weeks there is a significant and sharp increase in the combination of cube with cup. There is a shift of regard to cup or rather the emergence of a new form of exploitation due to the perceptual realization of the physical properties of the cup. At 52 weeks this combining activity takes on a more controlled aspect owing probably to a refinement of the perceptual mechanisms and also to increased mastery of placement and release.

The infant is now able to remit hold of the object and by way of exercise of this new power, he repeatedly lifts one cube, releases it, or casts it aside. Normally, however, his activity never becomes stereotyped because presently at 56 weeks this prehension-placement-release pattern takes on a serial exploitational character. He does not sporadically or repetitively pick up and drop a single cube but takes up first one and then another and still another in a more or less rhythmic sequence. Having placed as many as four cubes serially into the cup he removes them and then replaces them. Here we have an excellent example of the manner in which a simple pattern undergoes elaboration. We have yet another example in the fact that the 56 weeks-old infant is not content even after he has placed four cubes into the cup, for he seizes the cup forthwith and holds it aloft with the contained cubes. He then restores the cup to the table top, removes the cubes, and reduplicates with inevitable variations his newly mastered exploitation. In this process of elaboration and progressive individuation we have an image of the developmental mechanics of the higher adaptive mental processes. We may well believe that in the highest intellectual spheres of adult invention, a comparable mechanism of developmental patterning asserts itself. Events do not happen quite *de novo* but as variations and elaborations of a proliferating complex.

Supplementary Comment

There are three situations which are so similar that they invite brief comment in connection with the present summary:

(a) the massed cubes, (b) the cup and spoon, (c) the cup and cubes. Comparison of a and c will suggest the special potencies of the cup: comparison of b and c may suggest the differences in stimulus value between two objects in contrast with multiple objects. Although the situations do not keep these variables under rigid control, they reveal distinguishable influences on the trends of behavior.

When the incidence of behavior items for a (massed cubes) and c (cup and cubes) is compared, it appears that in general the forms of cube manipulation and of exploitation are much alike for both situations up through 44 weeks. Grasping, dropping one cube to secure another, holding two cubes, follow the same trends. Even in the presence of the cup, the cubes get predominant attention at 44 weeks and two cubes are combined in a similar manner in both situations at this age. The cup, however, has the effect of bringing forth combining activity somewhat earlier than massed cubes alone. At 48 weeks the cup affects the reactions more strikingly. There is a marked increment of combining of cube with cup (71 per cent) in contrast with 14 per cent of cube and cube combining, when multiple cubes alone are at the infant's disposal. A general inference from these percentages may be hazarded: Objects differing in shape and size are combined with greater frequency and definiteness than objects identical in shape and size when the perceptual discrimination has reached a requisite level of maturity. In the case of cube and cube *versus* cup and cubes, this level lies near 44 weeks. At that age 41 per cent combine cube with cube when cubes alone are available; 40 per cent combine cubes and 40 per cent combine cup and cubes when both these objects are available. But at 48 weeks, as just noted, seven out of ten children combine cup and cubes and only one child out of seven combines cubes. This sharp increment indicates a new psychological potency in the cup.

When we compare cup and cubes and cup and spoon, we find one or two lines of contrast. The cubes in the cup and cubes situation attract the first approach throughout all the age levels; but in the cup and spoon situation, the cup receives prior attention at 32, 36, and 40 weeks. Cup and spoon are individually subjected to more exploitive manipulation than the cubes; there are less mouthing and transfer of the cubes than of the spoon. At 40 and at 44 weeks, cup and spoon are combined with approximately the same frequency as cup and cube; but the spoon is dipped into the cup at 44 weeks, whereas the cube is not dropped or released into the cup until 52 weeks.

§26. PELLET BEHAVIOR

(12 weeks–56 weeks)

The Situation

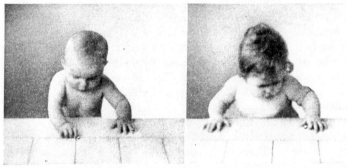

FIG. 26.—Pellet behavior: 36 and 44 weeks.

Grasping the pellet between the index finger and the thumb and holding the convexity down, the examiner advanced the pellet in the horizontal plane and placed it in the standard median position. If after ten seconds the infant had not seized the pellet, the examiner advanced it to the near median position.

Stimulus Factors

The pellet has proved to be a peculiarly potent and revealing device for eliciting gradations of behavior pattern in infants. In a dimensional sense it represents the smallest stimulus object used in the developmental examination. In spite of, possibly because of, its small size it tends to provoke relatively sustained reaction when the child has the requisite perceptual capacity.

At the older age levels the pellet not infrequently goes to the mouth with such avidity as to suggest that the pellet is regarded as food. In these cases the motivating value of the pellet is increased, but in general its stimulating power does not seem to depend upon secondary factors.

The selection of the pellet as a test object in the original developmental schedule arose out of our desire to establish a normative cleavage between the 6 months level and the 12 months age level. The pellet response did indeed prove to be a useful criterion of 9 months maturity. Some of the most interesting behavior responses take place in the age zone between 32 weeks and 44 weeks. An extended study, however, has shown that the pellet can be used as a visual stimulus object for infants as young as 8 weeks and that it elicits distinguishable gradations of response at lunar month intervals from 12 weeks through 56 weeks. These gradations in prehensory pattern have proved in general to be so consistent that we have come to regard the pellet situation as having a superior degree of inherent experimental control.

Here, as elsewhere, there are variable factors of personality, current mood, immediately antecedent experience, and possibly also constitutional variations in neuromotor type. In spite of all of these variations the development of patterns of approach and of appropriation, and to a lesser extent of disposal, pursues a lawful course which is summarized in some detail below.

Behavior Trends

Regard. Table top situations were not presented to infants below the age of 12 weeks. We have, however, seen one normative 8 weeks-old infant pay unmistakable regard to the pellet under the conditions of the normative examination. This infant was briefly made an exception because of his advanced postural control. About one child out of four in the normative group of 12 weeks infants pays some kind of regard for the pellet. This regard is usually delayed, momentary, and passive. Nearly all of the infants, however, give regard to the examiner's incoming hand, the remaining regard going to the table top, to the surroundings, or to the infant's own hand. The examiner's hand is such an attractive focus of attention that it sometimes displaces regard for the pellet. Pellet regard, therefore is nascent and insecurely established at the age of 12 weeks. Frequently the examiner must give directive assistance by tapping to elicit the regard which is obtained. Sometimes the examiner resorts to repeated trials to elicit objective signs of ocular fixation upon the pellet.

Even at 16 weeks it is at times difficult to confirm visual fixation. This indefinite regard may be momentary or starey in either the standard or near median position. Exactly one-half of the infants fail to perceive the pellet under the conditions of the examination. The incoming hand of the examiner receives definite regard and, interestingly enough, 30 per cent of the infants at 16

SITUATION: PELLET (P)

P	Behavior items	4	6	8	12	16	20	24	28	32	36	40	44	48	52	56
1	Regards (s.m.p. or n.m.p.)				28	50	91	94	97	100	100	100	100	100	100	100
2	Regards with definite fixation				15	34	80	89	97	100	100	100	100	100	100	100
3	"Regards" (confirmed)				5	27	74	83	94	96	100	100	100	100	100	100
4	Regards after delay				21	20	44	33	24	12	11	3	3			
5	(If regards) regards after delay				75	45	48	35	25	12	11	3	3			
6	Regards immediately				0	20	41	58	64	82	86	92	94	100	96	100
7	Regards momentarily				20	31	59	39	6							
8	Regards recurrently				15	11	27	25	15	0	9	11	18	14	11	15
9	Regards prolongedly				10	13	27	33	18	11	0	3				
10	Regards consistently							22	73	94	94	95	97	97	100	100
11	Regards passively				15	29	65	11	3							
12	Regards surroundings				45	36	12	11	9	3	6	5	3	0	9	
13	Regards Examiner				50	25	12	19	3	18	3	5	29	33	21	11
14	Regards Examiner's hand				80	68	38	47	15	15	9	5	24	11		
15	Regards table top				55	40	24	8	3	3						
16	Regards hand				40	56	18	14	9	3	0	0	3			
17	Fingers table top near pellet					6	39	24	11	3	3					
18	Approaches				10	9	27	83	91	100	100	100	100	100	98	100
19	Approaches promptly					4	3	45	73	85	86	86	94	92	96	89
20	Approaches with one hand				0	9	11	53	67	85	91	95	94	100	98	93
21	Places hand over pellet							28	64	38	29	19	4	19	9	
22	Approaches with index finger extended						3	5	18	29	32	60	44	14	17	12
23	Dislodges on contact					0	7	24	33	36	27	20	8	6	3	2
24	Contacts pellet				5	27	27	58	91	100	100	100	100	100	98	100
25	Hand flexes on pellet						0	19	64	76	97	100	100	100	98	100
26	Hand flexes, thumb participates						0	5	21	53	80	84	94	97	98	96
27	Flexes fingers on or near pellet					0	8	33	76	91	72	62	32	25	23	12
28	Flexes fingers on or near pellet, thumb par.					0	8	33	64	59	32	19				
29	Flexes fingers on or near pel., thumb op. fin.							0	12	37	26	16	15	—	4	—
30	Thumb and index finger meet							5	9	35	72	81	91	97	98	96
31	Flexes fingers, thumb and index meet							5	9	29	37	33	29	25	19	8
32	Flexes thumb and index finger independ.							0	3	12	37	57	59	72	79	92
33	Fl. fin., th. meets in. and sec. fin. or sec. fin.							0	0	6	17	16	24	14	15	8
34	Hand flexes without grasp					0	8	16	58	82	60	54	35	19	15	4
35	Manipulates pellet on table top					12	21	45	61	44	52	57	24	14	11	11
36	Pokes pellet							6	3	11	35	6	6	8	8	
37	Grasps pellet					0	0	0	30	59	72	100	94	100	98	100
38	Grasps promptly									25	38	38	70	77	96	
39	Grasps with fingers								27	56	52	51	32	25	19	8
40	Grasps with finger flexion, thumb not par..								21	21	14	16				
41	Grasps with finger and thumb flexion								6	15	14	8	9	0	4	
42	Grasps, thumb participates								15	41	66	81	85	97	96	100
43	Grasps between thumb and index finger								9	24	52	76	71	81	91	96
44	Grasps, thumb-index meeting, fingers flexing									21	29	30	29	25	19	8
45	Grasps with inde. thumb-index finger flexion								9	6	29	51	53	70	79	92
46	Plucks pellet										3	3	18	25	28	19
47	Brings to mouth								3	6	20	16	47	42	38	59
48	Manipulates pellet above table top										9	22	38	42	28	33
49	Brings pellet to platform										17	11	24	11	9	7
50	Drops								21	47	46	30	44	36	35	37
51	(If grasped) drops								70	80	63	30	46	36	35	37
52	(If drops) drops immediately								100	57	20	26	6	8		
53	(If drops) resecures from table top								29	23	60	66	62	100	83	82
54	Retains pellet									12	32	38	68	70	68	82
55	Releases and resecures pellet											11	24	28	26	30
56	Vocalizes				15	9	6	14	6	11	10	7	7	10	7	4
57	Frets				5	9	31	28	15	22	3	3	4	7	4	
58	Postural activity											14	24	25	26	37

weeks—as compared with only 10 per cent at 12 weeks—regard also the examiner's outgoing hand. This visual pick-up of hand withdrawal represents a growth increment in the perceptual field.

One-half of the 16 weeks infants were credited with regard for the pellet. This regard is usually passive and only rarely is it prevailing or even recurrent. The infant's own hands are a dominant source of distraction but regard also goes to the examiner, to the surroundings, and to the table top. Only occasionally does regard shift from the hand to the pellet. Although the regard is sufficiently mobile to pursue both incoming and outgoing hand, the manifestations of recurrent and consistent pellet regard are relatively meager. The pellet clearly reveals the formativeness and primitiveness of perceptual patterns at this level of maturity.

By 20 weeks a definite increment asserts itself in the perceptual field. Three-fourths of the children perceive the pellet in the standard median position and give definite regard which can be readily confirmed by altering the position of the pellet on the table top. In four out of ten children the regard is immediate. Characteristically it is passive, the hands and arms remaining relatively quiescent. This is in significant contrast to the active regard evoked by a larger object like the cup. Regard for the pellet is characteristically momentary, but it is less fitful and sketchy than at 16 weeks and can be more easily elicited by the examiner.

At 24 weeks nearly all of the children give definite regard to the pellet. In six out of ten this regard is immediate. In eight out of ten it is active rather than passive. The relative quiescence of arm and hand movements at 16 weeks during momentary regard may mean that the perceptual mechanisms then were so immature that their restricted exercise was more important in the economy of development than the establishment of correlated prehensory approach movements. Since these movements are more accentuated at 24 weeks, it may be inferred that the perceptions themselves are more advanced. It is probable that the visual organizations are generally in advance of the prehensory. The hand waits on the eye, even though the eye may in time become a surrogate of the hand.

At 24 weeks momentary regard is still frequent (39 per cent), but is giving place to more prolonged, recurrent, and sustained forms of regard. Regard still wanders readily from the pellet, but perceptual susceptibility is greater; for, by a tap of the finger, the examiner can readily redirect the regard to the pellet. The labile and formative nature of the perceptual trends at this age is shown by the fact that shifts of regard were noted in four out of every ten infants. At 28 weeks such shifts of regard are much less frequent and three-fourths of the children give sustained and consistent regard throughout the situation. Two-thirds of the children give immediate regard. Immediacy of regard becomes virtually universal at 40 weeks and thereafter. Consistent regard becomes well-nigh universal at 32 weeks and remains so during subsequent age levels.

Speaking in broad summary it may be said that the first half of the first year of life is concerned with steadily building up and almost completing the perceptual equipment for the visual regard of small objects like the pellet. During the second semester the associated mechanisms of approach, of grasp and appropriation are built up in a comparable manner and are near perfection by the end of the year. Throughout the first semester the infants contact the pellet only through the eyes but at 28 weeks nearly all contact it with the hand as well. At 28 weeks eye and hand functions have come into closer correlation. But the finer mechanisms of grasp in swift obedience to visual control are so refined that another half year of maturation is necessary to bring about this perfection.

A. Prehensory Approach. The pellet situation neatly reveals the progressive advances in promptness and precision of approach, which constitute the first phase of the total act of prehension. Approach is a slightly broader term than reaching. It includes all manual and arm movements stimulated by any object which on visual (or tactile) perception becomes the goal of immediate appropriation. The object may be within or beyond reach. It may be the moon or it may be the pellet. Thus definite approach movements are closely associated with head straining and with postural adjustments. Seemingly nonadaptive hand and arm movements which occur even at 8 weeks in the presence of an exciting object may be considered approach movements if these movements are accentuated or increased by the presence of the visually perceived object. In its broad sense, approach must be considered a form of goal-seeking orientation which merges into reaching, as reaching merges into grasp, and as grasp merges into manipulation. Because of this genetic and dynamic continuity, one can scarcely draw a sharp line between approach and grasp.

At 12 weeks the infant may flex his fingers, or abduct and adduct his hand on the table top after the pellet is presented.

But since only about one infant in four perceives the pellet, most of this arm-hand activity cannot be construed as approach. When the intensity and duration of the activity bear a demonstrable relation to the visual perception, we may regard it as rudimentary or incipient approach. At 16 weeks these movements may undergo reduction during moments of visual fixation upon the pellet, possibly to favor development of perception itself. But such an inhibitory effect upon the manual and arm movements must also be considered as a phase in the development of approach and appropriation.

At 20 weeks active approach movements are more conspicuous and frequent. One child in four actually contacts the pellet, albeit fortuitously, during periods of increased activity. Passive regard, however, is highly characteristic of the 20 weeks age level. As already suggested, the sensory aspect of perception is in the formative stage and dominates the total pattern of adjustment. The hand-arm movements are somewhat secondary and only crudely associated with the visual perception. At 24 weeks this association is so far advanced that approach takes on a directed, striving, and unilateral character. Very few of the infants actually contact the pellet but the hand, which previously rarely attained the pellet, is now coming within the penumbra of its goal. At 24 weeks the approach movements are crudely executed without any fine adjustment or anticipatory flexion of the fingers. The fingers are in partial extension, the pronate hand functioning like a paw and sweeping in from a lateral direction.

At 28 weeks there is a significant improvement in this crude, paw-like orientation. Indeed the orientation is becoming true reaching, and approach adjustments are made even before the pellet is placed in position. Moreover, the infant is now able to place his hand squarely over the pellet and to flex his fingers upon it. To be sure, he drops the pellet, even if he secures it, from lack of refined grasp. But approach has been achieved and completed at a rudimentary level.

Nature does not, however, permit the infant to linger on this low plateau of achievement. Approach undergoes progressive delimitation throughout the remaining cycle of the year. Gross manual orientation is refined through a specialization of the radial digits. Uncritical manual placement gives way to digital aiming. The pronate attitude of the hand gives way to a tilting of the palm and this leads to abbreviation of time, condensation of mechanism, fluency of movement, and a focalization of approach. In a metaphorical way one may visualize the genetic gradations in the image of a diminishing spiral which symbolizes increasing directness and deftness of movement. This progressive focalization is recapitulated in the following developmental "stages." A stage, it will be recalled, is a degree of progression.

Stage 1. The hand is in its most remote relation to the pellet. There is perception but no reaching. The hand is either quiescent or in relatively uncoordinated activity. This is the zero level of approach.

Stage 2. The hand circumducts on a horizontal plane and comes near the margin of the pellet. Contact, however, is fitful and almost fortuitous.

Stage 3. The hand locates near the vicinity of the pellet. Flexion of the digits may occur in the vicinity of the pellet. Contact, though more frequent, is still more or less uncertain.

Stage 4. The orientation is more adequate. The hand comes over the pellet. Approach is overhead as well as lateral.

Stage 5. The gross manual approximation has given way to a digital approximation. The index finger is placed on the pellet; orientation depends on tactile as well as visual cues. This placement of the index upon the pellet becomes more refined and accurate with age.

Stage 6. The tactile cues diminish in importance and in their stead visual (and kinesthetic) factors operate with such precision that the index finger neatly overshoots the pellet and comes to a poised position beyond the pellet prior to a plucking prehension. Concurrently the wrist through forearm rotation assumes a tilted attitude and the remaining digits are suppressed in either extension or flexion and the act of prehension is consummated in a deft, synchronized closure of index finger and thumb. Grasp is implicit in the approach.

When all of these orientations are reviewed in perspective it becomes clear that the maturational factors at the basis of pellet prehension work in a highly lawful manner to build up a precisely sensitive instrument for fine prehension. The gradations are so continuous and merge so consistently (and on the whole so uniformly) for different children from one stage into another that the whole process declares itself to be one of organic growth rather than of training,—a process in which primitive forms of reaction are partially retained through progressive incorporations in which the subtler mechanisms become grafted upon the grosser. It is a process of balanced consolidation and differentiation. Accordingly almost every age level appears to be a transitional one in which alternative types of prehension are used by the growing infant. But normally he does not retain the cruder forms of prehension even though for a time they are more effective than the genetically newer forms.

B. *Grasp.* We have already referred to the genetic and dynamic continuity between approach and grasp. Indeed in drawing up the present summary we had first planned to make our discussion of approach brief and to concentrate the details in the section on grasp. But the detail has crept into the discussion of approach and the summary of grasp is thereby correspondingly shortened.

Approach proves, after all, to be anticipatory grasp and the final mechanism of grasp is foreshadowed in the pattern of approach which the child displays in the first phase of the act of prehension. At the age of 12 weeks only one child out of 20 makes "approach movements" sufficiently vigorous and pertinent to result in contacting the pellet. Such contacting is far removed from grasp. At 12 and 20 weeks the number of contacts is significantly increased and some of these contacts may have a threshold value in the genesis of grasp because they at least represent partial successes which have been occasioned by an advance upon the pellet. Subtle differences in the patterns of contact of the 16 weeks-old infant and of the 20 weeks-old infant can be established by careful cinema analysis.

At 24 weeks approach movements are more unilateral; both hands make approach but one hand distinctly leads. Fifty-eight per cent of the infants actually contact the pellet, but these contacts are crudely executed. The hand locates pronately in the vicinity of the pellet, but the fingers flex without further orientation so that the effective grasp is only occasionally achieved. Flexion may take place without actual contact; contact may take place without flexion. The pellet is displaced but not grasped. At 28 weeks the hand descends over the pellet; hand closure upon the pellet occurs in about two-thirds of the children. As a result of this hand closure, the pellet may be momentarily grasped, but it is not held. Typically the infant drops the pellet; his grasp is so inept that the pellet falls. Frequently he seems to brush, drag, or hit the pellet on the table top. These activities are probably not true exploitation but are functions of his inadequate contact and crude hand closure. The thumb at this age does not participate in the grasp efforts.

This then is the threshold level for a palmar type of grasp in which the fingers flex simultaneously, raking or dragging the pellet against the palm. Sometimes at a yet earlier age, there occurs a more primitive palmar grasp, in which the heel of the palm, by a sweeping movement synchronous with simultaneous flexion, results in appropriation of the pellet within the hollow of the hand. This might well be characterized as a primitive palmar scoop, genetically older than the raking flexion.

At 32 weeks the thumb participates more definitely in this raking flexion. The approach upon the pellet is still pronate, the mechanism is one of simultaneous flexion of the digits synchronously with adduction of the thumb. The radial half of the hand is more concerned than the ulnar, but the directional control is imperfect and very frequently the prehensory attempts are unsuccessful. An ineffectual contacting approach is highly characteristic. The patterns show transitional and formative characteristics. Grasp is usually effected by a modified raking prehension in which oppositional activity of the thumb occurs without contributing any practical results.

The 36 weeks age level likewise is transitional, but now the transition is from a raking to a picking type of prehension. The restriction of activity to the three radial digits is more defined. An increased mobility and independence of the thumb are evident and tend toward a forceps type of approach upon the pellet. But the thumb mechanisms are still so immature and so imperfect that the grasp takes on a variable scissors form. Typically the thumb sweeps in as the remaining digits are flexed and the pellet is caught between the volar surface of the thumb and the mesial aspect of the index or second finger. There are many variations of this scissors pattern depending upon the position of the pellet and the maturity of the coordination of the thumb and radial digits. The scissors type of grasp is displayed characteristically at the 36 weeks level but it by no means occurs uniformly in its classical purity. In general, successful grasp at 36 weeks may be described as a raking flexion with thumb cooperation. Thumb opposition is more defined than at 32 weeks and the digits are usually in extension during the approach upon the pellet.

The specialization of the radial digits comes into clear expression at 40 weeks. Typically the infant extends the index finger on approach, places it on the pellet, and picks the pellet by synchronous flexion of the index finger and thumb; the remaining fingers flex soon if they are not already flexed. Sometimes he uses the scissors grasp. This is the nascent period for index finger extension, a behavior trait which shows itself in many other situations at this and the next succeeding age level. In his exploitations and explorations, the infant pokes at varied foci in his environment. Frequently his index finger lingers upon the pellet in a manner which expresses this same poking proclivity. This lingering may also express his dependence upon tactile cues. He makes what may be called a contacting approach upon the pellet and prehends it on the basis of this tactile contact.

At 44 weeks the index finger extension is still better defined; raking flexion is infrequent and visual guidance displaces tactile. The index finger does not linger so long, and its placement upon the pellet is more accurate. Hand closure without grasp, which recurs with great frequency at intervals from 28 weeks through 40 weeks, is now relatively infrequent and will have disappeared almost completely at the end of the year. Although the scissors grasp may be resorted to frequently, it is on the wane. Forty-four weeks marks the beginning of true picking of the pellet by opposition of the volar surfaces of the index finger and thumb with increased suppression of the remaining digits in the act of seizure.

At 48 weeks the picking type of grasp is yet better defined. It is more prompt and skillful; the hand is more tilted in approach; and the visual control is more precise, as shown by the promptness of secural. Inhibition of the ulnar digits is correspondingly more advanced. This focalization of the act of prehension comes to culmination at 52 weeks and at 56 weeks of age. The visual control, as already indicated, is so well established that the index finger is neatly aimed to overshoot the farther margin of the pellet or it approaches tangentially in a manner which makes for promptness and nicety. The infant frequently executes his prehension with such dispatch that the pellet may be in his mouth before we have time even to begin a description of the behavior pattern. The cinema records, as analyzed by Castner and by Halverson, reveal a remarkable perfection of mechanism which suggests that by the end of the first year of life the infant has come near to an adult level of neuromuscular adeptness.

Disposal. During most of the first year of life the pellet appears to present a problem of prehension and the exploitational activity is relatively small in amount. Not until the age of 32 weeks do over 50 per cent of the children secure the pellet. Both at this age and at 28 weeks, the pellet is frequently contacted in a manner which objectively simulates pushing, dragging, or hitting. These terms suggest that the child is an active agent exploiting the pellet in a purposive manner. Such connotations are heavily laden with interpretation and are not justified by evidence. Most of this activity with the pellet on the table top arises out of the physical limitations of the pellet's size and of the neuromuscular insufficiency of the child. At these age levels he frequently drops the pellet if he should grasp it. This dropping is not to be interpreted as exploitive activity, although at the 52 weeks level such exploitational dropping may occur. At 32 weeks he does not resecure the pellet if he drops it. At 40 weeks about one child out of three definitely pokes the pellet on the table top. But even this term must be used with caution because the application of the tip of the index finger to the pellet may be more safely interpreted as a necessary part of the new type of prehension which is taking place. The infant is not necessarily poking the pellet for the sake of poking. Sometimes, however, the poking becomes an active tracing exploitation which displaces grasp.

At nearly all ages the infant is usually more absorbed in the act of prehension as prehension and his follow-up activity after secural is relatively meager until about the age of 44 weeks and thereafter. At 44 weeks active exploitation, including deliberate releasing for resecural and mouthing, increases in frequency. The pellet may be held up for inspection. It may be transferred. It may be rolled and twiddled, although even here there must be caution with regard to interpretation. Exploitation at these ages is further limited by the facility and directness with which the child carries the pellet to the mouth. The hand-to-mouth tendency in some children is much stronger than in others and is probably based upon food motivation. Some children at the age of 52 weeks manipulate the pellet as though it were an object to be played with and not to be eaten. At 56 weeks over half of the children carry the pellet to the mouth, many of them with great dispatch. The interpretive hazards attached to the concept of exploitation have already been suggested. It must be borne in mind that for many weeks before the time when the infant is able to grasp the pellet, he shows a consistent degree of interest in it. This interest may have no relation to potential manipulative exploitation.

All things considered, it is a very impressive fact that the pellet has such a nearly universal appeal from the age of 20 weeks onward. It is no small task to make a theoretical explanation of this fact. Does the appeal rest on some peculiar configurational potency inherent in small objects per se? Time and time again in the course of our examinations of infants we find the infants definitely, even though momentarily, distracted by tiny scratches on the table top, by a small mark on the bottom of the cup, by a shred of cotton, etc. Recently we observed a profoundly defective child two and a half years of age who scarcely gave heed to the chair, to the table, or to the cabinet of toys in her immediate surroundings. A pellet was placed upon the table and, in spite of her pathological instability of attention, she gave transient heed to this pellet though she had disregarded all other objects in the room.

Attentiveness to the pellet, therefore, may be due to a peculiar form of discreteness which gives it a paradoxically disproportionate stimulus value. The great absorption and perseverance which infants display in their prehensory attacks upon the pellet also suggest that the dynamic factors cannot be construed in terms of playful or exploitive interest. It is more as though the child were driven by a zeal to exercise and to perfect his mechanisms of prehension. Whether a small object like the pellet has a peculiarly affective value is of course a matter of pure speculation. The selective interest which infants display in pursuing tiny crumbs of bread or cake or individual granules of sugar on the high-chair tray are familiar. Here again we may ask, Is the primary interest perceptual, psychomotor, or gastronomic? It may of course on different occasions be any one of these.

The whole problem has a comparative aspect which might repay investigation. Food seeking requires an interest in small objects, and it may well be that in early stages of racial evolution sensitiveness to small sources of food had survival value. May this evolutionary factor add zest to small objects which come within the range of the infant's vision? Such considerations, however, are so speculative and inadequate that we prefer to interpret the patterns of pellet behavior as an expression of the growth needs and growth characteristics of the infant. He is interested in small things as soon as his organic equipment permits him to sense them, and he strives to acquire them because he cannot achieve full mastery of his environment or attain the potential organization of his nervous system unless he perseveringly strives, as do all infants, toward even such a small and insignificant object as the 7 mm. pellet.

§27. PELLET AND BOTTLE BEHAVIOR

(32 weeks–56 weeks)

The Situation

FIG. 27.—Pellet and bottle behavior: 44 weeks and 48 weeks.

With the bottle in the left hand, the pellet in the right, the examiner brought both objects into the infant's plane of vision above the transverse standard line. The examiner dropped the pellet into the bottle while the infant was looking and then proffered the bottle to the infant or placed it in the near median position. After appropriate observation, the examiner placed the bottle in the lane to the left of the standard median position and the pellet beside it at the right. If the infant did not spontaneously combine pellet and bottle, the examiner attempted to induce insertion by command and pointing close to the neck of the bottle.

Stimulus Factors

The stimulus values of the pellet are elsewhere described. The pellet alone was used as an observation device as early as 12 weeks. The pellet and bottle together were first presented at the 32 weeks age level. The bottle is two and a half inches in height and one and three-eighths inches in diameter, the neck is seven-eighths inches wide. It is made of strong glass. Its hard, smooth texture and glistening surface make appeal to hand, mouth, and eye. The transparency of the glass readily permits the infant to see the pellet within the bottle. The pellet remains a visible, but not a directly accessible, object. How does he overcome a transparent barrier?

The rivalry in stimulus values of the pellet and the bottle is tested in several ways. At first the infant sees only the bottle as the examiner holds it before him. While the infant looks on, the pellet is dropped within the bottle. In a later situation the pellet and bottle are placed side by side about four inches apart. If the infant does not spontaneously insert the pellet in the bottle, the stimulus of the examiner's command and gesture is added. Once within the bottle, the pellet creates a new problem if the infant feels impelled to separate the pellet from the bottle. This mechanical problem of securing the pellet, which is so simple for the child of 18 months, is far from simple for the infant less than one year of age. The movement of the pellet when the containing bottle is agitated creates a novel situation for the infant and may excite him to exploitive behavior. This interest in the movement of the pellet occasionally displaces his interest in securing the pellet, but the latter interest usually dominates.

In combination the pellet and bottle have proved instructive observation materials which maintain an exploitive interest for the child throughout the preschool years. The relationships of container and contained are diverse, and present many problems to the infant. They figure in the cup and spoon, cup and cube, formboard, and other normative situations. These relationships reveal their complexity in pellet and bottle behavior.

Behavior Trends

Regard. All the normative children from 32 to 56 weeks of age regard the bottle. It is probable that at some time in the situation most of the children also give at least momentary visual heed to the pellet, but at 32 weeks the preoccupation with the bottle may be so strong as to exclude perception of the pellet. There is an interesting reciprocal relationship between attentiveness to the bottle as opposed to attentiveness to the pellet. Our percentages show a regular decline in predominance of interest for the bottle from 32 to 56 weeks, and a corresponding increase in predominance of attention to the pellet between these same ages. On a graph the curves cross; 44 weeks is a transitional period. At that age slightly over half of the children give predominant attention to the bottle,

SITUATION: PELLET AND BOTTLE (P-Bo)

P-Bo	Behavior items	4	6	8	12	16	20	24	28	32	36	40	44	48	52	56
	PELLET IN BOTTLE															
1	Regards pellet as dropped in bottle......									31	33	80	82	83	75	23
2	Regards pellet in bottle................									12	26	37	67	69	78	96
3	Attends predominantly to bottle........									90	88	65	53	24	22	16
4	Attends predominantly to pellet.........									10	12	24	36	53	78	84
5	Attends simul. to pellet and bottle......										0	11	11	23	0	0
6	Manipulates bottle on table top.........									44	56	57	33	41	32	12
7	Bangs or hits bottle on table top........									31	30	30	22	38	19	4
8	Brings bottle to mouth.................									69	67	60	45	45	35	19
9	Manipulates bottle above table top......									50	85	83	82	97	92	96
10	Rotates bottle........................									19	33	30	37	31	25	8
11	Turns bottle upside down..............									12	19	37	22	41	49	19
12	Turns bottle over.....................									19	30	10	22	21	36	54
13	Waves or shakes bottle.................										7	23	22	37	37	27
14	Pokes at pellet.......................									12	15	27	33	52	50	54
15	Pokes finger in bottle.................										11	7	19	17	25	31
16	Pellet falls out of bottle...............									56	59	77	82	83	95	77
17	Apparently adapts manip. so pellet drops out........................										0	14	21	42	48	56	78
	PELLET DROPPED FROM BOTTLE															
18	Manipulates bottle as before...........									77	81	65	22	29	22	5
19	Attends to bottle only.................									66	56	43	31	20	18	0
20	Perceives disappear. of pellet from bottle										25	30	45	63	68	75
21	Regards pellet after dropped from bottle.									44	44	69	82	83	79	90
22	Pursues pellet........................									11	31	35	68	75	73	90
23	Grasps pellet.........................										19	30	45	54	68	70
24	Manipulates pellet above table top......											13	0	38	41	55
25	Combines pellet and bottle.............											9	8	37	41	55
26	Brings pellet to bottle.................											9	0	20	37	50
27	Places pellet in bottle.................													12	26	40
28	Turns to side, pivots or creeps.........										4	7	19	28	12	15
	PELLET BESIDE BOTTLE															
29	Holds pellet over bottle...............												6	35	63	63
30	Releases pellet over top of bottle........												6	35	47	54

even while the pellet is in the bottle; at 48 weeks, an equal number of children give predominant heed to the pellet. This rise and fall in the individual curves for these two competing objects reflects fundamental growth changes in perception and exploitation. Otherwise the trends would not be so consistently shown.

At 32 and at 36 weeks only one child in three definitely regards the pellet as it is dropped into the bottle. At 40 weeks, however, this regard becomes well defined and remains so in most children throughout the remaining age levels. The infant also begins to peer into the neck of the bottle, itself a new behavior item. Indeed, at 40 weeks, almost half of the children perceptibly lower their eyes to follow the pellet in its descent. At 44 weeks and thereafter, about three-fourths of the children lower their eyes in this adaptive manner. The number of children who give regard to the pellet in the bottle increases steadily from 12 per cent at 32 weeks to 96 per cent at 56 weeks, rising normatively to 67 per cent at 44 weeks of age.

When the pellet falls out of the bottle, either by accident or by adaptive manipulation, its disappearance is not heeded by two children out of three even at the age of 40 weeks. At 48 weeks, on the other hand, approximately two children out of three do perceive the disappearance of the pellet. In other words, at 32 weeks and at 36 weeks the bottle continues to absorb the attention, and activity with the bottle continues as though the pellet had not dropped out. Even at 40 weeks the activity continues unchanged in two out of three children. After 44 weeks, however, the course of activity with the bottle definitely alters with the expulsion of the pellet, activity shifting to the pellet. The pellet is pursued or it is grasped.

In these behavior items we have confirmatory evidence of the fact that 44 weeks is a transitional period in which the perceptual organization permits somewhat equal attentiveness to pellet and bottle. At later ages there is a progressive focalization upon the pellet. These perceptual trends, however, can not be considered in isolation because they are closely bound up with changes in exploitive activity and are a function of the child's response to the total situation rather than of his receptivity as such. But when one considers the numerous variable contingencies in the pellet and bottle situation it is remarkable that the trends from age to age are as defined as they are. These trends are equally evident in a biographic cinema record such as that which is delineated in the *Atlas of Infant Behavior.*

It is difficult to discuss the perception of infancy in any general terms. We have already noted that even the 12 weeks-old infant may give momentary regard to the pellet. We do not bring this perceptual capacity into question when we note that the 32 weeks-old infant may entirely disregard the pellet in the pellet and bottle situation. In competition with the glistening bulk of the bottle the pellet, which against a neutral background mobilizes the whole reaction system of the infant, now sinks into obscurity.

When the pellet and bottle are placed side by side, the perceptual reactions are similar to those already outlined, but there are differences which arise from the altered juxtaposition. Observation of a limited number of cases suggests that initial regard is for the bottle at 40 weeks, but at 44 weeks the initial regard is for the pellet.

Prehension and Manipulation. Nearly all of the normative infants (from 32 to 56 weeks of age) approach the bottle without delay after the pellet is dropped in. The infants may extend the arms before the bottle is within reach, apparently expressing anticipation and eagerness. At 40 weeks and beyond, the index finger is often extended and directed toward the pellet in the bottle, suggesting selective interest in the pellet as well as increased independence of the poking digit. Virtually all the children pick up the bottle at 32 weeks; it is grasped by encircling fingers and with partial thumb opposition. At this age the child grasps the bottle somewhat crudely with one or both hands, and after momentary inspection carries it to the mouth. He may withdraw the bottle with brief inspection and return it to the mouth. Manipulation is very limited and usually restricted to a slight degree of turning.

At the higher age levels, prehension of the bottle becomes digital and thumb opposition is better defined. At 32 and at 36 weeks, bimanual grasp and manipulation are common. At 40 weeks both hands are frequently applied to the bottle, but with a shifting of manipulatory activity from one hand to the other with partial or complete transfer. At the higher age levels, unilateral manipulation is characteristic because a growing interest in combining activity prompts the infant to apply the pellet to the bottle, or, it may be, the bottle to the pellet. Descriptively this last sentence is permissible; but it may contain unwarranted interpretation. The *because* is gratuitous; it is also reasonable to suggest that unilaterality brings about new forms of discriminative combining activity. Neither is brought about by the other alone; both grow together.

During the 40's when there is a distribution of interest between the pellet and the bottle, first one object is grasped and then the other. At 52 weeks the pellet may receive almost exclusive attention. But at 52 weeks, when the pellet is beside the bottle, there may also be simultaneous approach upon and simultaneous seizure of both objects. Although this interesting change in pattern has not been studied in detail, it marks a significant advance over the cruder bimanual approach upon the bottle, without regard for the pellet. This simultaneous seizure of pellet and bottle at 52 weeks is followed by immediate combining. Again the causal relationships are obscure. Does attention to two associated objects have to wait upon the neuromuscular maturation of the ability to simultaneously seize these two objects?

There is clearly a developmental increase in the versatility and degree of rotational manipulations of the bottle. These rotational manipulations may at first result in accidental spilling of the pellet, but at 52 weeks and at 56 weeks about half the children show an adaptive turning of the bottle upside down to expel the pellet. Waving, brandishing, and shaking of the bottle are almost absent at 32 weeks, and at 36 weeks of age. This type of manipulatory exploitation was noted in 37 per cent of the children both at 48 and at 52 weeks of age. Interest in mouthing is more casual at 44 weeks. Gross motor activity, including pivoting and even creeping, occurs in one child out of four at 48 weeks. At 32, 36, and 40 weeks, exploitational activity is chiefly confined to the bottle, which is manipulated on the table top with greatest frequency at these ages. Banging may occur at every age except 56 weeks.

Spontaneous combining activity in the pellet beside the bottle situation was present in only one child out of five at 44 weeks. The percentages (based on a reduced number of cases) for this item rose from 0 per cent at 40 weeks to 74 per cent at 52 weeks and to 67 per cent at 56 weeks. The combining consisted in approaching the bottle with the pellet or the pellet with the bottle. The combining increased in precision and adaptiveness. At 44 weeks only 9 per cent of the children held the pellet over the bottle; at 52 and at 56 weeks, 63 per cent of the children held the pellet over the bottle. It is significant, however, that a smaller number (47 per cent at 52 weeks and 54 per cent at 56 weeks) attempted to release the pellet, usually with success, at these ages. The number of children at 44 weeks who approached the bottle with the pellet was definitely increased when the examiner made the command with accompanying gesture.

Whereas only 8 per cent combined spontaneously at 44 weeks, 37 per cent combined responsively by holding the pellet over the bottle. Of these one in three released the pellet in the bottle. If we merge the cases of spontaneous combining and responsive combining, we find that slightly over half (53 per cent) of the children attempted or accomplished release of the pellet in the bottle at 48 weeks. Usually the child holds the bottle in one hand while he inserts with the other. At 52 weeks he sometimes leaves the bottle standing on the table top while he responsively brings the pellet to the neck of the bottle. This is a more advanced reaction.

Release of the pellet shows a significant increase of deftness and prehension with maturity. This ability is only imperfectly developed by the first birthday and undergoes subsequent improvement. When the child is two, three, or four years of age, we may place as many as ten pellets beside the bottle and witness a nice placement of each pellet in the bottle. Sometimes the older child picks up three or four, or even more, and successfully transfers them with prompt release into the bottle. With age, the tendency toward "ritualization" becomes manifest; spontaneously the child pours all the pellets from the bottle only to reinsert them, without suggestion or command by the examiner. Ritualization is a reinstatement of the situation, a method of defining and perhaps improving new abilities; but it is itself a general ability, an intrinsic product of growth.

In following the course of pellet and bottle behavior, it is difficult to differentiate between cause and effect and between maturation in the broad sense and learning in the specific sense; between chance and intention; between indifferent manipulation and experimental exploitation. Expulsion of the pellet from the bottle is at first (at 32 and 36 weeks) so fortuitous that it may not even be noted by the infant when it happens; but at 56 weeks a highly adaptive turning of the bottle to expel the pellet is present. Flashes of insight seem to occur but only when the infant is sensitized thereto by his maturity. The momentary insight, however, is not so far reaching that he achieves once and for all a mastery of the act of adaptively turning the bottle. There is a progressive improvement in this adaptiveness which is determined by the gradual maturing of his neuromuscular equipment; likewise, his spontaneous "insight" and his responsiveness to demonstration have to wait for such maturing.

The developmental trends of pellet and bottle behavior may be outlined in seven stages. For simplicity, the stages are made to correspond (approximately) with successive lunar month intervals.

Stage 1 (32 weeks). Predominant interest in the bottle, shown by mouthing and limited manipulation.

Stage 2 (36 weeks). Increased manipulation of the bottle but disregard of the pellet even on spilling.

Stage 3 (40 weeks). Heedfulness of the pellet as examiner drops it into the bottle. Predominant interest in the bottle with monentary or secondary regard for the pellet in the pellet and bottle situations.

Stage 4 (44 weeks). Selective interest in the pellet as shown by fugitive poking of it in the bottle and by primary interest in the pellet when it is beside the bottle.

Stage 5 (48 weeks). Elaborated interest in the pellet shown by a poking pursuit of the pellet in the bottle. Greater readiness to insert the pellet on command.

Stage 6 (52 weeks). Adaptive manipulation of the bottle to expel the pellet.

Stage 7 (56 weeks). Spontaneous insertion of the pellet in bottle.

§28. BELL BEHAVIOR

The Situation

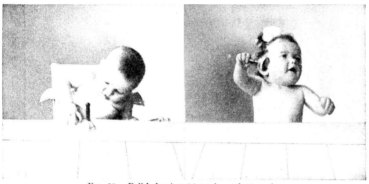

FIG. 28.—Bell behavior: 16 weeks and 52 weeks.

The examiner presented the bell in the standard manner, placing it in the standard median position and when necessary in the near median position. After appropriate observation the examiner demonstrated bell ringing. He seized the bell with overhead grasp, waved it up and down three or four times and then placed it in the near median position. After an appropriate interval of observation, he repeated the demonstration a second and a third time.

Stimulus Factors

In physical make-up the bell is a relatively simple object, but it is sufficiently diversified in its stimulus factors to call forth significant, progressive differentiations in the infant's reactions. These differentiations proceed by subtle gradations, but become striking in the long perspective of ten lunar months, from 16 to 56 weeks.

To adult analysis the bell consists of a combination of a cylindrical handle, a conical bowl, and a swinging lever (the clapper).

The infant makes no such analysis, but he discovers and defines these components of the bell in his own way. Optically the bell presents a contrast in the blackness of the handle and the bright silveriness of the bowl. This is a stimulus factor to which the infant responds surprisingly early. The perpendicularity and low center of gravity of the bell make distinctive physical problems for prehension and manipulation. The rim and the cavity of the bowl and the pendant clapper constitute specific foci for selective and for more or less sustained regard and, later, for active exploitation. The sound-producing properties whether self induced or demonstrated by the examiner widen the stimulus values of the bell and increase its usefulness as a clue to advancing patterns of behavior.

Behavior Trends

Regard. At 16 weeks regard is typically immediate, intent, starey, and prolonged. It is likely to fixate first on the handle, then shifts to the bowl and then back to the handle, imparting a simple inspectional aspect to the behavior. The regard may shift to surroundings or examiner, but it recurs to the bell, which is the preferential object of attention. These varied characteristics of regard show trends which are rather pronounced in the period up to 28 weeks. The occasional initial delay of regard drops out almost completely in this interval; likewise the prolonged staring and fluctuating forms of regard. Prompt, consistent, and sustained regard is almost universal after 28 weeks. Occasional regard for the examiner may occur at all age levels, but becomes more defined and probably more personalized after 48 weeks. At 56 weeks two-fifths of the infants extended the bell to the examiner.

A few infants look into the bowl of the bell at 28 weeks; a few poke into the bowl at 32 weeks. Thereafter the exploitation becomes increasingly discriminative and there is a corresponding refinement and projection in the attentional regard. Genetically this increase in subtlety of regard is continuous with the cruder forms of visual discrimination noted at 16 weeks. It is impossible to follow the nimble niceties of regard at the higher age levels; we may, however safely infer these maturing perfections from the changes in exploitational behavior which will be presently summarized.

A. Prehensory Approach. Almost one-fourth of the 16 weeks and over one-half of the 20 weeks-old infants make obvious approach movements toward the bell. At 24 weeks nearly all, and thereafter all, infants make a prompt, defined approach. Nearly

SITUATION: BELL (B)

B	Behavior items	4	6	8	12	16	20	24	28	32	36	40	44	48	52	56
1	Regards (s.m.p. or n.m.p.)					100	100	100	100	100	100	100	100	100	100	100
2	Regards					95	100	100	100	100	100	100	100	100	100	100
3	Regards immediately					86	96	97	100	100	100	100	97	100	100	97
4	Regards momentarily					5	20	—								
5	Regards recurrently					50	24	3	17	4	14	3	4	7	18	16
6	Regards starily					59	12	7								
7	Regards predominantly					73	72	90	100	96	100	100	100	100	100	100
8	Regards consistently					—	40	77	100	100	100	100	100	100	100	100
9	Regards prolongedly before approach					95	44	14								
10	Inspects before approach					54	52	10	3	—	—	—	—	—	—	—
11	Regards handle predominantly					50	24	3	7	8						
12	Regards handle first					64	40	3								
13	Shifts regard					59	40	10	20	12	18	27	19	14	40	72
14	Shifts regard to surroundings					18	24	3	17	4	7	3	4	3	3	8
15	Shifts regard to Examiner					9	20	3	7	12	7	20	12	10	23	44
16	Arms increase activity					45	64	97	100	100	100	100	100	100	100	100
17	Approaches bell					23	60	90	100	100	100	100	100	100	100	100
18	Approaches after delay					23	24									
19	Approaches promptly					—	36	90	100	100	100	100	100	97	97	96
20	Approaches with both hands					—	12	28	28	27	14	27	12	3	10	4
21	Approaches with one hand					23	44	62	72	65	75	74	84	93	81	96
22	Approaches with right hand					9	12	45	31	46	50	57	65	62	61	52
23	Approaches with left hand					14	32	17	41	19	25	17	19	31	20	29
24	Contacts					23	64	90	100	100	100	100	100	100	100	100
25	Inverts hand on approach							7	66	62	61	40	42	24	33	44
26	Dislodges on contact					23	40	35	38	12	7	13	8	—		
27	Manipulates without grasping					23	40	35	45	20	18	23	8	—		
28	Grasps					—	40	83	100	100	100	100	100	—	100	100
29	Grasps after delay					12	14	10	—	4	—	—		3	3	4
30	Grasps promptly						28	69	90	100	96	100	100	97	97	96
31	Grasps with right hand only						4	45	28	54	54	53	58	59	64	52
32	Grasps with left hand only						28	24	48	23	21	23	8	24	13	24
33	Grasps with left or right hand							7	17	15	14	23	27	14	10	16
34	Grasps in palm						40	48	31	8	7	13	4	10	5	12
35	Grasps interdigitally							10	17	4						
36	Grasps with thumb opposition						—	17	31	35	39	40	58	59	67	52
37	Grasps with thumb and first two fingers									7	17	15	24	15	36	48
38	Grasps top of handle								8	11	20	54	31	36	48	
39	Holds with both hands						8	35	41	19	29	10	8	7	5	4
40	Manip., holding between thumb and fingers						10	7	12	18	20	35	21	38	20	
41	Manip., holding with fingers around handle						55	59	38	32	27	19	14	18	24	
42	Manipulates, holding bowl rim					8	14	24	4	4	7	12	7	8	—	
43	Manip., holding with fingers around bowl					12	24	31	27	32	40	42	24	15	8	
44	Manipulates, holding by clapper									4	7	12	10	20	8	
45	Manipulates bell on table top					23	48	45	41	40	15	23	16	0	5	16
46	Drags on table top					—	4	14								
47	Pushes and pulls					8	17	6	28	11	10	12	0	5		4
48	Lifts					36	76	100	100	100	100	100	100	100	100	100
49	Manipulates above table top					16	35	76	100	96	100	100	100	97	100	100
50	Bangs on table top					8	21	38	42	32	43	27	35	30	4	
51	Brings to mouth						24	62	90	81	79	70	58	52	41	4
52	Mouths bell handle					16	38	59	42	36	30	35	24	15	4	
53	Transfers					12	17	55	73	82	83	89	69	62	44	
54	Transfers frequently							24	35	43	53	46	38	21	20	
55	Turns bell end for end							21	52	62	54	87	81	79	69	68
56	Waves					4	10	34	47	50	76	92	83	94	88	
57	Rings					—	3	21	38	46	60	62	73	82	52	
58	Pokes								12	4	20	19	7	13	28	
59	Regards clapper							14	35	22	70	54	76	68	76	
60	Pokes clapper					—	4	7	0	12	21	43	50	65	66	72
61	Pulls clapper											12	10	23	16	
62	Brings bell to platform					—	4	3	3	4	7	10	15	24	10	8
63	Brings bell to side panel							7	8	7	10	19	21	10	4	
64	Proffers bell to Examiner (or mother)										10	8	8	8	40	
65	Drops					20	42	45	27	21	43	38	24	28	28	
66	(If grasps) drops bell					50	50	42	27	21	43	38	24	28	28	
67	Pursues bell (if drops)					45	55	91	50	80	88	88	100	88	100	
68	(If drops) resecures bell					40	45	91	50	80	88	88	100	88	100	
69	Releases and resecures bell					8	17	31	12	14	27	27	21	15	16	
70	Waves bell after demonstration								32	50	47	81	88	94	88	79
71	Rings bell after demonstration								10	41	37	60	49	53	88	57
72	Waves or rings bell only after demonstration								10	0	0	20	32	15	33	29
73	Waves or rings bell both be. and af. demon.								22	50	47	60	49	73	61	50
74	Postural activity					5	8	3			8	43	58	38	48	40
75	Pulls to side										4	7	15	10	15	
76	Pivots												31	31	18	20
77	Frets					23	24	35	14	12	25	7	4	7	10	4
78	Vocalizes					14	20	14	10	15	32	43	27	24	23	32

half of the 16 weeks infants showed some form of hand-arm activity but barely one-fourth contact the bell and these do so with delay. At 20, 24, and 28 weeks slightly over one-third of the infants make an inadequate contacting approach; that is, they dislodge the bell without effecting immediate grasp. Similar ineptness continues infrequently to the forty-fourth week. Bilateral approach is present variably in from 3 to 28 per cent of the cases at all age levels. Unilateral approach increases fairly steadily from 23 per cent at 16 weeks to 96 per cent at 56 weeks. On first presentation left-hand approach was more frequent than right-hand approach at 16, 20, and also 28 weeks of age; but at all other ages right-hand approach was from two to three times more prevalent. On successive presentations, however, from 7 to 27 per cent of the normative infants 24 weeks or more of age grasped with the left *or* the right hand. Both hands may participate in initial approach, one taking the lead.

B. Grasp. No 16 weeks infant actually grasps the bell. At 20 weeks 40 per cent, at 24 weeks 83 per cent, and thereafter 100 per cent grasp the bell. At 28 weeks promptness of grasp becomes well-nigh universal, rising sharply in frequency from 28 per cent at 20 weeks to 69 per cent at 24 weeks. The distributions for right- and left-hand grasp are comparable to those noted in relation to approach. The form of grasp alters with age. At 20, 24, and 28 weeks it is ordinarily palmar in type and less frequently interdigital. At 20 and 24 weeks the manual attitude is characteristically pronate and seizure is often at the bowl. At 28, 32, and 36 weeks adaptive supination appears just prior to and also after grasping. Thumb opposition becomes increasingly well defined after 32 weeks. Associated with this increase of mobility of the forearm and of the thumb is an increase of deftness in initial grasp of the handle and a selective utilization of the upper end of the handle by a pincer-like adjustment of the thumb and first and second fingers. From 24 weeks onward the bell is most typically grasped by the handle, though it is often held at the bowl as well until 44 weeks. After 44 weeks there is a steady decline in holding at the bowl.

Manipulation and Exploitation. At 20 weeks the bell remains prevailingly on the table top during manipulation; 36 per cent at 20 weeks lift the bell above the table top as contrasted with 76 per cent at 24 weeks and 100 per cent at 28 weeks. Thereafter most of the activity with the bell is above the table top. At 48 weeks one-fourth of the children carried the bell below the table top, but this manipulation is relatively rare at all other ages. Similarly at 44 weeks and 48 weeks almost one-fifth of the children carry the bell to the side panel; this manipulation does not occur at all prior to 28 weeks and only rarely at the remaining ages. From 20 to 43 per cent drop (or release) the bell during manipulation at all ages. Release followed by immediate resecural occurs with rare or occasional frequency from 20 to 56 weeks. Manipulation without grasp occurs occasionally or oftener at all ages prior to 44 weeks; only rarely at 48 weeks, and not at all thereafter. Pushing and pulling with grasp were reported in 28 per cent at 32 weeks and less frequently at other ages.

Transfer of the bell from one hand to another takes place at all ages rising steadily from a frequency of 12 per cent at 20 weeks to 89 per cent at 44 weeks, diminishing to 66 per cent, 61 per cent, and 44 per cent at the remaining age levels. The method of executing the transfer, the promptness, frequency, and predominance of transfer in the total behavior episode show significant developmental changes from age to age.

Turning the bell end for end is a form of manipulation distinguishable from transfer but closely related both dynamically and genetically. It arises out of a combination of transfer and rotation. This reaction is first noted in one-fifth of the children at 24 weeks and rises to a frequency peak of 87 per cent at 40 weeks, with a gradual decline to 68 per cent at 56 weeks. Often the child scrutinizes the bell closely as he turns it, thus revealing an exploitive tendency almost inseparable from manipulation. Waving or brandishing the bell is another form of exploitive manipulation which rises steadily from a low frequency of 4 per cent at 20 weeks to a high frequency of 92 per cent at 44 weeks and 94 per cent at 52 weeks.

Carrying the bell to the mouth, whether for tactile satisfaction or for active chewing of the handle, may be regarded as exploitational behavior. Mouthing rises precipitously from 24 per cent at 20 weeks to 90 per cent at 28 weeks, declining moderately to 41 per cent at 52 weeks and to 4 per cent at 56 weeks. Chewing of the handle was less frequently noted but varied similarly for the different age levels. Banging of some kind occurs at every age, least frequently at 20, 24, and 56 weeks. At the remaining ages approximately one-third of the children banged.

What does the free hand do when the grasping hand retains the bell? Here we have another indication of exploitational activity. The free hand is brought up to the bell in 35 per cent of the cases at 24 weeks, in 41 per cent at 28 weeks, and less frequently at other ages, to participate in the holding or to indulge in gross fingering. Frequently this chain of events results in "automatic" transfer as already noted. But there comes a time, or rather out of this matrix there comes a pattern, in which the one hand definitely holds the bell up for inspection while the free hand comes up to finger or poke in an exploitive manner. Transfer which is itself a form of manipulation is thus suppressed for a higher order of manipulation.

Inspectional peering into the bowl occurs occasionally at 28 weeks and rises to frequencies of 70, 76, and again 76 per cent at 40, 48, and 56 weeks. Peering precedes poking and occurs more often. No poking was observed at 28 weeks; 12 per cent poked at 32 weeks. This percentage rises steadily to a maximum of 72 per cent at 56 weeks. Early poking tends to be vague and fugitive, using one or more of the radial digits including the thumb. But this poking becomes defined and prolonged at more mature ages, and the index finger comes increasingly into play. The tip of the index is thrust momentarily or lingeringly against the clapper. At 44 weeks 12 per cent and at 52 weeks 23 per cent of the infants plucked and pulled the clapper between index finger and thumb.

Induced Behavior. The frequency of waving or brandishing of the bell has already been noted in the discussion of manipulation. Somewhat ambiguously at first but with indisputable definiteness later, this waving becomes a defined, "purposive" ringing. It is not always possible to make a tenable distinction between waving and true ringing. The latter is reported in only 10 per cent of the cases at 28 weeks, but in 60 per cent at 40 weeks, in 88 per cent at 52 weeks, and in 57 per cent at 56 weeks. The high incidence at 52 weeks is significant though it must be noted that the duration, the repetitiveness, and the emotional accompaniments of the ringing vary with individuality as well as with age. Often this ringing is entirely self-initiated.

The responsiveness of the infant to the first, second, and third demonstration of ringing by the examiner can not always be objectively determined, but the broad developmental trends are well indicated in the percentages. Forty weeks may be regarded as a critical or transitional period with respect to this somewhat general factor of "responsiveness" or "imitativeness." At that age 60 per cent of infants ring *both* before and after demonstration; 20 per cent ring only after demonstration. At 44, 52, and 56 weeks almost one-third of the children ring only after demonstration. The negative figures are still more significant: 68 per cent at 28 weeks, 50 per cent at 32 weeks, and 53 per cent at 36 weeks did *not* react responsively after the demonstrations of bell ringing. These percentages decline to 18 per cent, 11 per cent, and 6 per cent at 44, 48, and 52 weeks. At 56 weeks 29 per cent were non-responsive but doubtless because of stronger competing impulses rather than because of lack of capacity.

The amount of social attention to the examiner during and after demonstration varies with personality make-up as well as with age. During the 40's and at 52 weeks the child is increasingly susceptible to the bell ringing demonstration. The susceptibility often is greater on the first than on the second and third demonstrations. It is a complicated pattern complex in somewhat unstable equilibrium with visual, auditory, motor, and social components which must all be attuned to each other to produce maximum results. Such instability of pattern is a normal growth characteristic. It is in a sense a protective factor, for otherwise the infant would learn too much and learn too well. No single pattern or group of similar patterns can usurp the field of behavior. While the infant is furiously ringing the bell in response to demonstration he suddenly stops to poke into it with inquisitive index. This poking was not part of the demonstration but it is part of the child. Throughout infancy innumerable formative patterns of behavior assert themselves with a degree of autonomy as well as in growing relationship to the attained organization of the individual.

§29. RING AND STRING BEHAVIOR

(28 weeks–56 weeks)

The Situation

Seizing the ring between index finger and thumb of the left hand at a point opposite the string attachment, and plucking the distal end of the string with the right, the examiner held both tautly in the horizontal plane and advanced them to the standard position at the table top. He laid the ring beyond the standard median position and the string in oblique alignment just within the scope of the infant's right reach. Two or three presentations were made in this manner to elicit characteristic behavior. If after the third presentation the string was not secured, it was re-presented and laid in vertical alignment along the median line with the end slightly in advance of the standard median position. When not secured, the ring was moved to the standard position for observation of grasp and manipulation.

Stimulus Factors

The same ring which the examiner dangled before the supine infant is now presented to the sedentary infant and is placed horizontally upon the table top. Physically, of course, the ring and string have not altered, but the infant is more mature and the

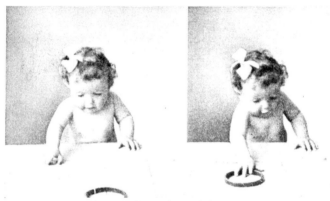

FIG. 29.—Ring and string behavior: 52 weeks.

stimulus potentialities of the ring and string are greatly changed by their new orientation and background. Although the perceptual factors in the situation are apparently simple, a minute analysis of the behavior patterns evoked discloses many complicated considerations. The perceptual behavior is determined not alone by the geometric attributes of the red circle and white oblique straight line against a neutral gray background; motivational factors enter which determine the selectivity of the child's regard and of his manipulatory exploitations.

Does the red circle elicit prior and dominating regard? Is the long white string ever perceptually more potent? Is there a rivalry or fluctuation in the stimulating values of ring and string? Is there a maturity difference in perceptual response to the oblique alignment versus the median alignment of the string? Is the regard centrifugal, proceeding from ring to string; or is it centripetal, proceeding from the string to the ring? Does the regard focalize on the end of the string? Do developmental changes occur with respect to the oscillations of regard from ring to string? Are ring and string fused in a single perceptual response? A partial answer to these questions can be found in a minute analysis of the patterns of adaptive behavior. Developmental trends can be observed in the initial adjustments to the situation, in the distributions of visual attention, and in the exploitive activities with the ring and string.

The string as a stimulus object has distinctive peculiarities arising out of its great mobility and flexibility. It creates special problems of prehension and multiplies the possibilities of manipulation. It will be interesting to note that the infant is sometimes intrigued by these possibilities to the temporary disregard of the ring.

The ring and string are presented three times in succession and this procedure serves to define the preferential foci of regard and the improvement of insight.

Behavior Trends

Regard. Throughout all the age levels studied (28 to 56 weeks) the ring generally makes a more instant appeal to the infant. From 65 to 89 per cent of all children regard the ring before making an approach upon the string. Only very rarely does an infant fail to regard the ring. But the string is often disregarded or attention to it is entirely subordinated to the ring. At 32 weeks and at 36 weeks, however, one-third of the children give prior, sole regard for the string before making an approach upon it. Commonly at all ages (from one-half to two-thirds of the children) the regard shifts successively from ring to string to ring before approaching the string. The character of this shifting reflects many subtle changes with increased maturity. Both the ocular and manual responses become more confluent and encompassing.

From 70 per cent to 85 per cent of the infants (in the age range from 36 weeks to 56 weeks) regard the ring alone as it approaches on pulling. The remainder of the infants regard both the ring and string or the string alone. At 36 weeks one child in five paid exclusive regard to the string both as he reached for it and as he pulled it in. At 44 weeks, however, all the infants pay regard to the

SITUATION: RING AND STRING (R-S)

R-S	Behavior items	4	6	8	12	16	20	24	28	32	36	40	44	48	52	56
1	Regards ring.........................								100	94	85	97	94	94	100	95
2	Regards ring first....................								89	68	65	69	77	81	79	84
3	Regards string.......................								71	90	88	83	74	61	76	74
4	Regards string first (regard before appr.)..								11	32	35	28	23	19	17	21
5	Shifts re. from ring to str. or ring-str.-ring								54	58	53	64	55	52	55	58
6	Approaches ring......................								54	28	26	8	6	6	5	8
7	Approaches ring first.................								50	28	26	5	6	—	5	8
8	Approaches string....................								50	81	92	97	94	97	100	100
9	Approaches string first................								43	69	83	95	94	97	100	92
10	Contacts string before ring............								46	75	92	95	97	95	100	100
11	Grasps string........................								18	53	83	92	91	92	100	92
12	Hand closes on string ineffectively.......								21	41	32	27	24	—	8	8
13	(If hand closes on string) grasps ineffect...								55	71	53	46	36	25	11	8
14	Grasps string immediately.............								0	16	32	65	67	89	90	83
15	Pulls or drags string in...............								29	53	83	95	94	95	97	96
16	Regards str. only as reaches and pulls str..								4	16	23	5	15	8	3	17
17	Regards ring as approaches and pulls string								18	34	60	87	82	78	74	50
18	Regards ring only as appr. and pulls string.								4	3	34	46	52	44	42	25
19	Regards ring only as ring approaches....								7	25	80	81	85	75	69	42
20	Manipulates string before securing ring ..								0	22	6	5	15	8	0	0
21	Pulls ring off table top before secural.....								0	9	9	11	15	25	5	8
22	Dangles or bounces ring before secural....								0	9	6	8	3	25	16	17
23	Secures ring using string								29	47	86	95	97	92	97	92
24	Hits or bangs ring on table top...........								17	27	14	16	35	9	24	17
25	Brings ring to mouth..................								46	58	39	30	32	24	13	20
26	Transfers ring........................								46	42	43	43	16	18	16	17
27	Turns ring...........................								17	23	18	35	23	6	11	0
28	Brings ring to platform................								13	15	7	38	42	33	26	50
29	Brings ring to side panel..............								0	4	0	5	10	24	21	13
30	Manipulates string after contact with ring.								33	58	79	73	84	73	66	71
31	Holds ring in one hand; string in other....								0	12	36	19	29	12	29	29
32	Dangles ring by string.................								0	8	29	49	48	58	58	58
33	Dangles ring by string after con. with ring.								0	0	25	43	45	36	50	58
34	Drops ring completely.................								33	31	36	33	39	55	45	50
35	Resecures ring.......................								25	15	21	27	29	39	21	17
36	Turns or pivots......................								0	0	0	15	37	34	47	33
37	Postural activity.....................								0	0	12	19	40	47	53	58

ring alone while pulling the string. At 28 weeks 18 per cent, at 32 weeks 34 per cent, at 36 weeks 60 per cent regard the ring both as they reach out and as they pull in the string.

These trends closely analyzed suggest that 36 weeks is the transition age when the string is losing its autonomy and is becoming assimilated into a more unified perceptual response. At 56 weeks the focalization of regard on the ring is less conspicuous, possibly because the infant is now adept and a glance suffices to initiate response. Indeed even young infants may avert their eyes and yet successfully seize the string. At 36 weeks almost one child in three seems to give sole regard to the string before approach upon it. One child out of four regards the string alone as he reaches and as he pulls the string.

Such preoccupation for the string during the act of prehension drops out almost completely at 40 weeks. Why? Because the child now seems to give merely a preadjustment glance at the string, fixates on the ring, and gives regard to the ring (87 per cent) as he reaches and pulls. This represents a perceptual subordination of the string to the ring based upon more advanced insight or comprehension. At 44 weeks this subordination is still better defined. But development refuses to remain simple and at 48 weeks it appears that the string is again receiving somewhat more regard. Why? Because the child is now more disposed to pull the ring from the table top and to dangle it by means of the string before seizing the ring? He has attained a new appreciation of the string and pays it a modified regard. He uses the string instrumentally in a new dimension and for a new purpose.

Prehension. At 28 weeks the child is at a kind of threshold in the organization of his prehensory abilities. He approaches either the ring or the string with almost equal frequency. He makes unsuccessful attempts to secure the string and only one child in five actually grasps the string at 28 weeks of age. Placement of the string in the median position favors effectual grasp and enables the child to secure the ring. This difference in the orientation of the string suggests that the oblique presentation tends to make the prehensory problem of the string comparable to that of the pellet. When the string is in the oblique position the infant of 28 weeks characteristically makes unsuccessful attempts to secure the string by raking flexion, or he stretches his arms out toward the ring. Only 46 per cent of the infants contact the string; only one child in five actually grasps the string.

One-half of the infants make prior or sole approach to the ring. This direct approach to the ring, whether made initially or after delay, declines rapidly and occurs in less than one-tenth of the infants after the age of 36 weeks. On the other hand, direct approach to the string at some time during the situation mounts rapidly in frequency and becomes almost universal after 36 weeks. Prior or sole approach to the string occurs in from 70 per cent to 100 per cent of the infants from 32 to 56 weeks of age. At 32 weeks, three-fourths of the infants are able to contact the string and one-half of the normative group actually grasp it. Thereafter from 83 per cent to 100 per cent accomplish grasp. The string always presents difficulties of prehension to a few children at all age levels. From 32 weeks on the frequency curve for unsuccessful grasp attempts showed a steady decline from 70 per cent to 8 per cent. At 32 weeks two out of five children scratch or rake at the string in these attempts.

At 32 weeks and at 36 weeks the infant may hit, push, or flick the string about before securing it. This behavior is not exploitive but is due to the difficulties of prehension. Ineffective grasp occurred at some time in from two-fifths to one-quarter of the infants from 32 weeks to 44 weeks of age. At 40 weeks, however, 65 per cent of the infants immediately grasp the string and 92 per cent grasp it immediately or after delay. This age, therefore, marks the virtual attainment of prehensory mastery of the string.

At 36 weeks only 32 per cent grasp the string immediately, but 86 per cent grasp or otherwise secure the ring with fair promptness. At 40 weeks twice as many make an immediate grasp, often with great deftness. Approximation of thumb and index, by a scissors or plucking form of prehension, is common. At 48 weeks nine out of ten children grasp immediately. Precise, pincer-like prehension of a superior type is becoming universal. With improvement of prehension there is less regard for the string at the moment when it is being secured. At 52 weeks and at 56 weeks the initial prehension is typically prompt and effective as though it were a well-established ability. There is also increased precision in selection of the end of the string prior to pulling. This is an expression of better "judgment"; it influences prehension but might well have been considered in the discussion of regard.

Manipulation and Exploitation. Only one child out of five, as already indicated, spontaneously secures the ring at the age of 28 weeks if the string is placed in oblique alignment. The examiner, however, makes secural possible by placing the string in the median position or he puts the ring in the child's hand. On seizure, the infant characteristically carries it to his mouth. He may remove the ring for brief inspection; he may drop the ring and pick it up again. Transfer occurs in almost half of the infants. During manipulation the string receives meager, secondary, or sketchy attention. One child in three manipulates the string.

With increasing maturity the string will be exploited for its own sake as a more or less independent object, also as a tool for manipulation of the ring. Dangling is manipulation *ad distans.* The ring and string situation is peculiarly interesting because it reveals the gradualness of the growth of tool-using insight.

At 32 weeks mouthing reaches a peak value of 58 per cent and declines regularly to 20 per cent at 56 weeks. Transfer, dropping, resecural, banging, and brandishing also occur at 32 weeks with frequencies similar to those found at 28 weeks, but there is a definite increase of attentiveness to the string. Fifty-eight per cent of the children approach, finger, mouth, or otherwise exploit the string after contacting the ring. This exploitation is apparently oblivious of the relation of the string to the ring.

At 36 weeks mouthing is less prominent. There is increased attention to the string and eight out of ten children contact and exploit the string after contacting the ring, or exploit the two in close alternation or simultaneously. More frequently than at other ages (36 per cent) the infant holds the ring in one hand and the string in the other. This nearly parallel exploitation of both ring and string is a kind of transitional pattern which follows successive exploitation first of one and then of the other, and which precedes instrumental exploitation of one *by* the other. Indeed we might schematize the exploitational gradient in four adjectives: from *single* to *successive*, to *parallel*, to *instrumental*.

The manipulation at 40 weeks reflects the trend toward instrumental behavior, for one-half of the infants at least briefly dangled the ring by the string. This dangling becomes less sketchy, less repetitive, more sustained, and (we may say) more deliberate with age. It tends increasingly to occur after prior contacting of the ring and from 48 to 56 weeks was present in six out of ten infants. At 40 weeks the infant displays a widening repertoire of exploitations: he intently inspects the ring as he moves it, often turning it over and over (35 per cent); he still transfers it (43 per cent); waves it; drops it with resecural; and even brings it into relation with the platform. He moves rapidly from one form of activity to another but tends to resume rather repetitively an activity previously engaged in. Personality differences of course come into play but, making due allowance for these, one can discern the forerunners of activities (or patterns) which will become more clearly configured and are adaptively pursued at later age levels.

For example, at 44 weeks dangling is better defined and tends to occur somewhat earlier in the course of activities. There is a more obvious tendency now to repeat a sequence of two or three activities. This tendency to repeat sequences continues somewhat reduced into 48 weeks.

Dangling is a well-defined pattern at 48 weeks. It does not occur even by accident at 28 weeks and is very rare at 32 weeks. At 36 weeks and at 44 weeks, however, one-third of the infants hold the string in one hand and the ring in the other. This is a genetic prelude to dangling. At 48 weeks dangling is so native to the infant's ability and interest that one child out of four dangles or bounces the ring by the string *before* even grasping the ring. A similar number pull the ring off from the table top before grasping the ring. This reaction is different in its psychology from the adaptive tug of the string which serves to make the ring accessible to grasp. When the infant pulls the ring off the table top and dangles it, he is making, or has already made, a discovery: he manipulates the ring "telesthetically"; he uses a tool. In a few significant instances at 48 weeks, the infant moreover replaces the ring on the table top and pulls it off again with one fell swoop. He has also been observed to reverse the fitness of things by dangling the string with the ring.

Is dangling a trivial pattern of behavior? Through such trivial but progressive elaborations the structure of the child's mind is formed. Each differentiation in the genetic elaboration is essential; in its nascency it takes on the aspect of initiative and discovery; in retrospect it proves to be an organic prerequisite of a higher pattern of behavior. In its mechanical essence, dangling is virtually mature by the end of the first year of life. The adult may not dangle a ring with the same zest as the infant, but he dangles it, neurologically speaking, in a manner highly comparable to that displayed by the infant in *his* late forties.

At 48 weeks the infant shows his further versatility by suppressing the impulse to dangle; or, to put the matter more objectively, the infant is more versatile at 48 weeks because he has a newly reinforced capacity to release hold of both ring and string. Over half of the infants at that age released or dropped the ring and resecured it. Many manifested this pattern repetitively. Further versatility rises out of new locomotor capacities; one-third of the infants rotated the trunk or pivoted the whole body and brought the ring to the side or rear panels of the crib. This postural variation is introduced still more frequently at 52 weeks. With the increase in locomotor drive, there is less intensive and less diverse manipulatory exploitation of the ring and string.

By 56 weeks the boundaries of the exploitation area are expanded. The infant is both physically and socially more mobile toward his environment. When he is not engrossed with the intriguing properties of the ring and string, he is likely to refer his activity to onlooking examiner or parent. There is a marked and significant increase of activity which brings the ring into relation with the platform. He is plumbing a new sphere of exploration below the table top.

§30. RING, STRING, AND BELL BEHAVIOR

(32 weeks–56 weeks)

The Situation

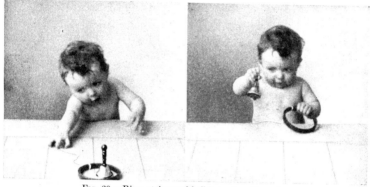

FIG. 30.—Ring, string and bell behavior: 44 weeks.

This time holding the ring between medius and index finger of the left hand and holding the bell between index finger and thumb of the same hand, the examiner presented with one maneuver the ring, string, and bell. He then rang the bell briefly and replaced it within the ring.

Stimulus Factors

Here, as elsewhere, not only must the immediate situation be taken into account, but also the immediately preceding one. Earlier in the examination the infant has had an opportunity to exploit the bell, which perhaps has been removed even while he was in full tide of enjoying it. He has also just had the opportunity to secure the ring and to exploit it, or the attached string. The present situation is therefore a combination of two previous situations. It is probable that these prior experiences with these objects have enhanced rather than reduced their stimulus values. New rivalries, if not confusions, are set up by the new juxtaposition of the materials. In the ring and string situation, the *string alone* is an instrumental object. In the ring, string, and bell situation, the *ring and string together* become the instrumental object. Will the presence of the bell excite a higher degree of adaptive utilization of the string? Will the secural of the bell dominate the course of the subsequent behavior? Will the ring cease to be an object of independent exploitation? If the ring is exploited, will it be an independent exploitation or will the exploitation be altered by the presence of the bell?

This situation has some of the elements of the formboard situation. The old relationship of container and contained re-appears in new guise, for the ring makes a well-defind circular rampart within which the bell may be introduced by the infant as it was introduced by the examiner. Or will the container be placed over the contained? For the infant, such relationships are more novel and fluid than they are for the adult. In the form-board situation, the infant sometimes superimposes the board upon the blocks; likewise in the present situation, he frequently super-imposes the ring over the bell. If one reckons the string and the ring and the bell as separate objects, this particular situation should release significant forms of combining and tool-using behavior.

SITUATION: RING, STRING AND BELL (R-S-B)

R-S-B	Behavior items	4	6	8	12	16	20	24	28	32	36	40	44	48	52	56
1	Approaches string first..............									67	67	77	90	86	75	64
2	Approaches ring or bell..............									33	33	23	13	17	28	44
3	Grasps string......................									56	70	94	93	94	86	84
4	Fails to grasp string immediately.......									50	19	32	23	20	0	0
5	Pulls ring or bell within reach.........									44	74	97	93	92	86	84
6	Pulls ring off table top..............									6	19	14	30	14	17	20
7	Holds ring in one hand, bell in the other.									0	10	38	27	27	26	28
8	Holds one object and reaches for other..									14	20	25	37	18	11	8
9	Drops bell or ring..................									43	40	44	50	69	46	44
10	Manipulates ring first................									57	50	56	37	15	11	4
11	Manipulates bell first................									29	30	31	40	64	57	72
12	Manipulates bell.....................									14	30	44	50	64	57	64
13	Manipulates bell independently........									43	60	50	40	77	69	80
14	Manipulates ring independently........									57	55	56	40	33	23	24
15	Manipulates ring and bell simultaneously									29	55	62	67	64	60	80
16	Brings bell, ring, or string to mouth....									71	35	16	10	6	11	4
17	Brings bell to mouth.................									57	30	9	10	6	9	—
18	Transfers bell, ring, or string..........									14	15	19	37	24	3	4
19	Waves or rings bell..................									14	30	38	37	57	40	56
20	Brings bell or ring to platform........									14	5	19	20	24	32	16
21	Combines ring and bell..............									5	9	20	37	41	40	72
22	Places bell in ring or ring over bell.....									0	15	3	13	33	26	56

Behavior Trends

The summary of behavior trends will deal chiefly with the influence of the bell on the behavior patterns characteristically elicited by the uncomplicated ring and string. Special attention will therefore be given to the adaptive and exploitive aspects of behavior with brief comments concerning prehension.

Prehension. Two-thirds or more of the children approach the string first. But at the age of 56 weeks as many as 44 per cent of the children made a direct approach upon the ring or the bell. This is probably due to the fact that the child is more able, at the later age, by postural straining to reach to the ring without the utilization of the string. None the less, 84 per cent of the children of that age grasp the string. At 32 weeks only 56 per cent of the children grasp the string. Nearly all of them fail to grasp it immediately. Ineffective grasping of the string is rather characteristic of the 32 weeks age level, for at the next succeeding age level only one child out of five fails to grasp the string immediately. Only 44 per cent at the age of 32 weeks pull the ring or bell within reach. Thereafter three-fourths or more of the children do this with increasing deftness and economy. The developmental trend in adaptive behavior is in general indicated by a more precise adjustment of the amount of tug at the string to the distance necessary for secural of the bell. This trend is unmistakable even though it is apparently contradicted by a tendency, especially strong at 44 weeks, to pull the ring completely off the table top for exploitational reasons which will be presently considered.

Exploitation. Seven age levels are considered, 44 weeks being at the mid point. At this age it proves that the bell on one hand and the ring and string on the other stand an equal chance of being the object of first choice. Half or over half of the infants up to 44 weeks of age display prior or sole activity with the ring. After 44 weeks prior or sole activity is with the bell, rising from a frequency of 29 per cent at 32 weeks to 64 per cent at 48 weeks and 72 per cent at 56 weeks. But even at the ages when the ring is the object of initial preference, the bell receives rather more attention; it is mouthed more often than the ring. The frequency with which ring waving occurs remains approximately uniform but bell waving increases markedly with age.

Since both bell and ring are almost equally accessible at all ages this trend in the percentages reflects a steady rise in the lure potency of the bell. The effect of the bell is also shown in a reduction of the amount of exploitation of the string. Relatively there is more activity with the string in the simple ring and string situation. Bell activity reduces but does not displace dangling. Thus, although we may say that the bell prevails in its competition with the ring and string, the infant is not delimited by this choice; he tends even in a brief period to exploit all the resources of the environment. He exploits ring and string separately and in combination as before or he brings them both into productive relation.

Activity involving the ring and the bell simultaneously rises from 29 per cent at 32 weeks to 55 per cent at 36 weeks and 80 per cent at 56 weeks. At 40 weeks 38 per cent of the infants held the ring in one hand and the bell in the other, and at 44 weeks an equal number held one object while reaching for a second. Prior to 44 weeks over half of the infants confined some of their activity to the ring, while after this age it was more characteristic to confine some of the activity to the bell.

From 44 weeks on there is a tendency to bring the ring and bell into more definite combination. One object is brought near to the other, sketchily or vigorously as in banging. The infant may simply hit the bell against the ring (or vice versa) but he may also thrust the bell within the circle of the ring while it lies on the table or while he holds it above the table top. Combining becomes more discriminating and culminates, in over half of the infants at 56 weeks, in a well-defined insertion of the bell within the ring or a crowning placement of the ring over the bell. Sometimes this placement is speedily repeated and again repeated. And occasionally the infant may even tug again at the string, thus autonomously reinstating the entire situation for the exhibition of his most mature combining behavior pattern—that is to say, most mature for 56 weeks. So consistent were the gains in exploitational activities after the age of 32 weeks that we can predict with confidence that the lunar months beyond 56 weeks bring with them similar elaborations of exploitational behavior, elaborations which follow general genetic laws.

§31. PAPER AND CRAYON BEHAVIOR

(36 weeks–56 weeks)

The Situation

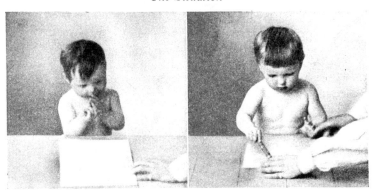

FIG. 31.—Paper and crayon behavior: 36 weeks and 56 weeks.

Holding the farthermost edge of a sheet of paper (8½ by 11 in.) in the left hand, and holding the crayon in the right hand, the examiner placed both objects simultaneously on the table top in parallel alignment with the median line. The near edge of the paper was placed at and along the near edge of the table top. The crayon was placed with its point near the center of the paper, and directed away from the infant. After observation of the infant's spontaneous behavior, the examiner initiated a demonstration of scribbling. A new sheet of paper was placed with its farther margin at and parallel to the farther margin of the table top. The examiner took the crayon in his right hand and applied it obliquely to the paper, making back-and-forth strokes near its farther margin. He then immediately represented this sheet of paper and the crayon to the child as before. This scribble demonstration was repeated a second and a third time.

Stimulus Factors

Two objects are placed before the infant without ceremony: paper and crayon. Both are equally accessible. The paper is green; the crayon, red. The paper is expansive and flexible; the crayon is compact and rigid. Perhaps it also may look good to eat, we do not know; but it frequently goes to the mouth. These contrasts in size, color, shape, and physical characteristics make the whole situation more complex than it seems on the surface. This very complexity makes more significant the indubitable behavior trends which declare themselves.

If paper and crayon are more or less ambivalent as stimulus factors at 36 weeks, they soon cease to be so. The division of the situation into two parts—spontaneous and demonstrational—permits many comparisons of free and induced behavior. There is the further possibility of detecting differences in response on the first, second, and third trials.

The procedure of the paper and crayon situation attempts to make a sharp distinction between spontaneous and induced reactions. In the interpretation of the child's behavior, this distinction is not always easily made, but the close contiguity of the two phases of the situation serves to show the primary dependence of the induced behavior upon the spontaneous capacity. Although the behavior with the paper and crayon may sometimes seem lawless and unordered, a critical analysis of the numerous behavior characteristics will show significant predilections in the modes of response. For example, in combining exploitation the infant might well bring the paper to bear upon the crayon, and occasionally he does so. But in the overwhelming majority of cases it is the crayon which is spontaneously brought into relation with the paper. In the infant's utilization of the crayon, we have an opportunity to glimpse the psychogenesis of his early knowledge of physics. The moving, pointed, cylindrical crayon embodies basic elements of lever and tool. The very manner in which the child picks up the crayon, tilts it, and applies it as a stylus to the paper reflects a subtle progression toward implemental insight. From the standpoint of stimulus factors the instrumental import of the crayon should not be overlooked.

Nor should the complexity of the act of demonstration be underestimated. It has social aspects; the examiner attempts by a quick maneuver to secure the infant's attention. Does the infant look at the examiner? Does he look at the paper? Does he look at the crayon? Does he look at the examiner's hand? Does he look at the roving marks made on the paper? These questions disclose that the simple demonstration instates a complex perceptual field which permits of many kinds of attention response. The younger infant makes both perceptually and motorwise a gross reaction to the situation. As he matures his regard becomes increasingly analytic and the stimulus factors change accordingly.

When he himself takes the crayon in hand and uses it productively upon the paper, the stimulus situation becomes still more complex, for now he has made his own mark. When does he heed the marks that he makes? When does he bring them into direct comparison with those of the demonstrator? Such questions might be multiplied but these are enough to indicate the richness of the paper and crayon situation for purposes of clinical and normative observation.

SITUATION: PAPER AND CRAYON (Pa-Cr)

Pa-Cr	Behavior items	4	6	8	12	16	20	24	28	32	36	40	44	48	52	56
	CRAYON BESIDE PAPER															
1	Approaches crayon first										52	85	92	81	85	96
2	Approaches paper first										43	19	8	8	15	4
3	Manipulates crayon exclusively										43	54	46	35	26	17
4	Manipulates crayon										48	27	17	38	36	41
5	Brings crayon to mouth										67	50	42	31	26	15
6	Transfers crayon										33	38	42	15	18	33
7	Combines paper and crayon spon										5	19	33	42	54	74
8	Hits crayon on paper										0	19	25	15	31	32
9	Marks on paper with crayon										5	15	25	38	46	74
10	Makes staccato marks										0	11	27	18	38	39
11	Makes staccato marks only										0	11	23	14	33	0
12	Makes linear marks										5	4	4	14	10	74
13	Makes linear marks only										5	4	0	11	5	35
14	Makes short linear marks										0	4	4	7	8	57
15	Makes both staccato and linear marks										0	0	4	4	5	39
16	Average number of marks										0	0	1	2	2	5
17	Average number of staccato marks										0	0	1	1	2	2
18	Average number of linear marks										0	0	0	0	0	3
	SCRIBBLE DEMONSTRATED															
19	Regards scribble demonstration										72	89	92	91	80	85
20	Manipulates paper during demonstration										45	38	29	14	13	—
21	Manipulates paper										45	56	46	18	30	35
22	Hits crayon on table top										9	22	15	29	3	4
23	Brings crayon to mouth										73	59	42	36	23	12
24	Combines crayon and paper										5	30	54	64	83	92
25	Combines paper and crayon repeatedly										0	8	15	14	43	58
26	Hits crayon on or at paper										5	26	31	46	38	15
27	Marks on one or more sheets										14	37	50	50	62	96
28	Marks on two or more sheets										9	19	31	36	54	87
29	Marks on three or more sheets										0	4	15	25	33	57
30	Draws crayon over paper										0	0	23	29	54	62
31	Makes lin. marks on one or more sheets										5	11	19	32	43	91
32	Linear marks on two or more sheets										0	4	8	21	31	74
33	Linear marks on three sheets										0	0	4	11	15	52
34	Makes linear marks only										0	7	8	18	30	74
35	Adaptive respon. apparently increases										14	26	42	43	50	57
36	Aver. num. of staccato marks to a page										0	1	1	2	2	1
37	Aver. num. of linear marks to a page										0	0	1	2	3	6

Behavior Trends

Regard. At 36 weeks interest goes almost equally to the paper and to the crayon. Prior approach is to the paper in 43 per cent of the infants but thereafter the proportion rapidly declines. From 40 to 56 weeks over 80 per cent of the infants make prior approach to the crayon. In view of this marked trend in favor of the crayon, the ambivalence at 36 weeks is interesting. It suggests that the two objects are perceptually responded to almost independently. Indeed even at 40 weeks half of the infants prior to demonstration are entirely preoccupied with the crayon. But thereafter the crayon is increasingly brought into combination with the paper and it is evident that the child does not simply see first one and then the other, but perceives them in some kind of togetherness. The details of his perceptual selectivity can in some measure be inferred from the nature of his manipulations and exploitations.

Changes in this selectivity can also be inferred from the manner in which he gives heed to the scribbling demonstration of the examiner. At 36 weeks 72 per cent of the infants give attention to the demonstration but often only momentarily, and almost half of the infants manipulate the paper during demonstration, which fact itself denotes that perceptual regard or interest for the total act of demonstration is quite rudimentary. There is in general an increase of attention both to the act of demonstration and to its product. Yet later the infant shows a dawning interest in the marks which he himself makes. The developmental elaboration of this form of interest is an interesting phenomenon more characteristic of the second year of life. Even at 52 weeks the infant shows only slight and fleeting attention to his own marks.

During the demonstration the 36 weeks-old infant seems to attend chiefly to the crayon or to the moving hand; or his attention may shift to the paper. He may reach out for the paper or crayon in a manner which suggests that he is seeking an object but is not in any sense heeding the demonstration as such. At 40 weeks, also, he may reach out for and manipulate the paper during one of the demonstrations but sometimes he regards, or at least seems to regard, the scribble on the second or third demonstration. Very rarely does he attend to his own marks.

The simple item *Manipulates paper during demonstration* shows a consistent decline which indicates a significant trend in the organization of attentional behavior. At 36 weeks about half of the infants (45 per cent) grasp for the paper during the demonstration scribble. Twenty weeks later not a single infant made such a grasp. Whether one describes this developmental change in terms of changing interest or of inhibition, it denotes an important gain in the selectivity of regard. At 56 weeks the infant perceives in detail and in interpretive context a situation which previously he reacted to in grosser and more general terms. One cannot put these facts into causal relations. Does he now make marks by "intention" because he is able to clearly attend to the marks of the demonstrator? Or does he give his clear attention to the demonstrator's marks because he is now able to make similar marks by his own intention?

Attentional-regard appears to be a function of the motor organization of the total reaction system. The same growth processes which bring the infant to the brink of scribbling at the close of the first year project themselves into the second, the third, and the fourth years. Growing by subtle increments and individuations the maturational complex lays the basis for progressive achievements which lead from crude to precise imitative stroking, from vertical to horizontal lines, and later to circle, cross, and square. In a systematic study of the genetic sequences both of spontaneous and of induced drawing, we find a striking validation of Sir Thomas Browne's dictum: "Nature geometrizeth and observeth order in all things."

Spontaneous Manipulation and Exploitation. For convenience of reference this summary will offer separate discussions of the spontaneous and induced aspects of paper and crayon behavior. Spontaneous behavior comes first in development and also in the observed situation. It should be considered first.

At 36 weeks the initial response may be to the paper. The infant fingers it, picks it up, grabs it grossly, or slaps it. Rarely is the activity confined to the paper. Characteristically he picks up the crayon and puts it immediately into his mouth. He may mouth without further manipulation. Any marking of the paper which may occur is apparently adventitious. Even at 40 weeks he may give exclusive attention to the crayon (54 per cent). He may manipulate it with regard before putting it to the mouth, he may transfer it (38 per cent), or he may hit the crayon on the table top, and by the same drumming movement he may make staccato marks on the paper. But spontaneous combining is barely incipient and these marks too are by-products rather than end products.

Well-defined spontaneous combining of paper and crayon is not present even at 44 weeks. About one child in three combines by drumming, dragging, or dangling the crayon, which leaves faint meandering marks. This element of restraint making for delicacy of response should perhaps be regarded as a developmental increment rather than a personality characteristic. It may occur in association with vigorous hitting. It has already been noted in the cup and spoon situation.

At the three age levels, 48 through 56 weeks, spontaneous combining becomes increasingly well defined and rises in frequency from 42 per cent to 74 per cent. There is a corresponding trend toward prolongation and repetition of combining. The very intensity, number, and length of the strokes which the infant makes show some tendency to increase with age. Linear marks as contrasted with staccato show a significant increase at 56 weeks, rising from a frequency of 10 per cent to 74 per cent. Whereas at 52 weeks one child in three made staccato marks only, there were no such instances at 56 weeks. On the contrary one child in three made linear marks only at 56 weeks. This tendency toward linearity in spontaneous combining lies at the basis of the increasing responsiveness to the scribble demonstrations in the period from 48 weeks to 56 weeks. Considering the vigor and dominance of staccato marks at the earlier age levels, it is an impressive fact that after demonstration three-fourths of the 56 weeks-old infants made linear marks *only*.

Manipulation and Exploitation after Demonstration. There is a reciprocity between spontaneous and induced behavior but the essential dependence of the latter on the former has already been made apparent. At 36 weeks the infant attends to the demonstration only momentarily. He probably neither heeds the marks made by the examiner nor senses the import of applying the crayon to the paper. Indeed to what degree he actually comprehends the scribbling demonstration even at the age of one year will not become entirely clear. But at 36 weeks the demonstration has little if any effect on his subsequent behavior. Excluding purely accidental instances, he never makes any mark upon the paper. Even at 40 weeks few marks are made accidentally or otherwise. The infant indulges in a wide range of activities, exploiting the paper by waving, crumpling, transferring, tearing; or he may manipulate and mouth the crayon. Combining only after demonstration occurs in one child out of five. At 44, 48, and 52 weeks such combining occurs in one child out of three. At 56 weeks again in one child out of five. The significance of these trends will be presently commented upon.

At 44 weeks the inducing effects of demonstration are more noticeable and there is a decided increase over 40 weeks both in staccato and in linear marks. At 48 weeks two-thirds of the infants combine crayon and paper sometime during the entire situation (one-third after demonstration only). But this combining tends to be fleeting and casual. It is not sustained. Although there is some evidence of improved performance, the infant does not mimetically duplicate the back-and-forth scribble motions. But with successive demonstration, the staccato marks sometimes become heavier and there is an increase in the number of linear marks. Even at 48 weeks many infants (29 per cent) still hit the crayon on the table top. Significantly enough at 52 weeks all but 3 per cent of the infants confine the crayon to the paper.

At 52 weeks both spontaneous and responsive combining become more frequent and decisive. However, the infant may still show a secondary interest in the paper and he seems to heed and to reproduce the general movement of the demonstrator's hand rather than the scribble itself. The responsiveness to one of the demonstrations is at least unambiguous even though the infant's scribble is accomplished by a rather aimless brushing or scrubbing motion. Half of the infants at 52 weeks and three-fourths of the infants at 56 weeks combine paper and crayon both before and after demonstration. This indicates that the nascent age for scribbling may be placed at one year, but it is now clear that even such a nascent stage has its prenascent preparations.

At 52 weeks the infant is more susceptible to the demonstration. There is more evidently a learning or particularizing factor in his response. The character of his marks tends to show a change from the first through the third demonstration. Drumming and tapping strokes now give way in some measure to side-to-side strokes. A larger number of marks is made after demonstration than before, which is a decided reversal of the behavior at 48 weeks. At 56 weeks, the reaction to the demonstrator (and often it is the first demonstration) becomes yet more responsive. The infant prehends and employs the crayon more as though it were an instrument to be applied to the paper. He may transfer it to the preferred hand. Even spontaneously he tilts the crayon to bring it to bear on the paper; he drags or brushes it across the surface.

After demonstration, combinations are made repetitively and the marks may approximate those of the examiner. Lateral stroking predominates over staccato stroking though either and both may occur. Especially in response to demonstration, the marks now become linear in nine children out of ten, and in two-thirds of these instances, the marks are long. Frequently these linear marks assume an unmistakably directed character. This dawning mastery over linearity heralds drawing. The 56 weeks-old infant is at the nether threshold of drawing.

§32. PERFORMANCE BOX BEHAVIOR

(40 weeks–56 weeks)

The Situation

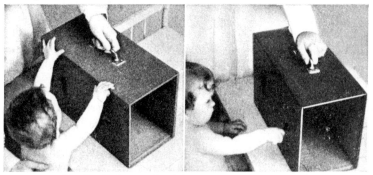

FIG. 32.—Performance box behavior: 40 weeks and 48 weeks.

Holding the performance box by the handle, the examiner placed the box with its lower edge parallel to the transverse standard line. After appropriate observation of the reactions to the box, the examiner took the rod in the left hand and proffered it in oblique alignment to the infant. Spontaneous behavior with the rod was then observed. While the infant was holding the rod the examiner pointed with the right index finger to the center hole of the performance box saying, "Put it in there." The examiner made a tapping gesture toward the hole. If the infant retained the rod without inserting it, the examiner removed the rod and himself inserted it deliberately into the round hole of the performance box. The rod fell with audible report within the box. The examiner removed the rod and proffered it to the infant as before. Three consecutive demonstrations were made in this manner.

Stimulus Factors

The performance box grew out of several needs and circumstances. We had become impressed with the inveterate propensity of many infants over nine months of age to pry and probe with the index finger into holes and cavities. These infants were interested in the exploration of the interiors of boxes and in the insertion and extraction of things. It was also noted that they were as interested in vertical surfaces as in horizontal ones.

While the preschool developmental test materials were taking shape, we had become accustomed to placing them in a filing case as a container. With the addition of a handle, this container became a portable kit. By leaving one end open and by sawing out three holes on one of the vertical surfaces, the kit was then transformed into a performance box, which was used in both formal and informal ways to elicit reactions from young children. The performance box is a type of formboard more primitive than the conventional, horizontal kind which will be described in the next section.

Unless we except the table top, the performance box is the most massive stimulus object used for purposes of normative observation. Because of its size, it might well have been used to explore in a simple way some of the perceptual responses of the very young infants. Using standardized procedures, it would be possible to present the performance box to infants from 12 weeks to 2 or more years of age with full assurance that the reactions would reveal instructive genetic gradations. As already indicated, however, our interest was in the more advanced stages of motor adaptiveness, and the performance box observations were begun at 40 weeks, the poking age. Stimulus factors will be briefly discussed with special reference to their implications in the field of formboard behavior.

When the performance box is slowly brought into the scope of the child's vision, it may have an aspect of strangeness; in a few exceptional instances its formidable dimensions actually excited temporary apprehension. In most infants, however, the initial response, if we may use interpretive terms, is in the nature of wonderment and surprise. With many infants, the size and position of the box immediately release postural responses. The hands thrust themselves simultaneously forward and come to rest on the upper edge of the box. The infant pulls himself up as he might in his crib or play pen.

Here is an excellent proof that the stimulus value of an object is a function of the current action trends and capacities of the infant. If because of maturity or temperament he is posturally sensitized, he reacts gross motorwise. He rises to the occasion and his exploitations take on a definitely athletic character, so vigorous that the examiner himself may have to use athletic measures to keep the situation under control. But when the gross motor impulses are partially satisfied, a refinement of response asserts itself. The infant then peers into the open end of the box or he resumes his seated position and begins to explore the holes with his hands and fingers. Some infants are preoccupied by all or one of the three holes. The differences in position, shape, and size of the holes permit observations of preferences in perception and exploitation. Since the small, round hole is in the middle, a stimulus priority over the angular holes can come into evidence.

After the performance box has been kept in the transverse position at right angles to the median diameter of the table top, its position may be changed by a rotation of 30° or 40° away from the prehensory hand of the child. This shift in orientation, though not part of the standard procedure, interestingly reveals the importance of postural factors in adaptive behavior. Infants who did not succeed in inserting the rod when the box was in full transverse alignment, may promptly succeed when it is in oblique alignment.

The rod greatly elaborates the stimulus potentialities of the performance box situation. The rod may be exploited alone; it may be brought in diverse ways against the box. Spontaneously inserted, or inserted by the examiner for demonstration, the sound of wood against wood apparently adds greatly to the stimulus of the situation. Whether or not there is a sense of mystery in the disappearance of the rod within the box, the situation frequently awakens the investigatory impulses of the infant. His behavior will be discussed chiefly in terms of his motor and perceptual adaptiveness, but it may be said that the performance box has many informal uses for supplementary clinical observations of personality characteristics. In older children, motor adaptiveness may be observed by offering a square block instead of the rod for insertion into the upright rectangular opening.

SITUATION: PERFORMANCE BOX (PfB)

PfB	Behavior items	4	6	8	12	16	20	24	28	32	36	40	44	48	52	56
	PERFORMANCE BOX ALONE															
1	Places hands on box.................											77	92	61	62	71
2	Prior manipulation of box..............											54	54	22	34	30
3	Manipulates box exclusively............											19	38	13	19	13
4	Reaches to top of box.................											62	67	48	28	70
5	Manipulates box near holes.............											69	50	78	69	79
6	Prior manipulation of holes.............											42	38	70	56	65
7	Manipulates holes exclusively...........											19	20	26	41	30
8	Pokes in holes.......................											31	42	74	66	65
9	Manipulates both box and holes.........											58	42	52	34	57
	ROD PRESENTED															
10	Manipulates rod......................											52	42	30	19	36
11	Transfers rod........................											32	27	15	5	16
12	Brings rod to box surface or holes.......											64	65	74	81	88
13	Brings rod to box surface..............											44	46	26	16	16
14	Brings rod to right or left hole..........											0	15	33	43	64
15	Brings rod to middle hole..............											4	15	19	35	60
16	Rubs rod against box..................											20	35	15	19	4
17	Inserts rod in hole....................											0	19	56	60	72
18	Inserts rod in middle hole..............											0	0	0	33	40
19	Inserts rod, never releases.............											0	19	56	38	40
20	Releases rod in hole...................											0	0	0	21	32
	INSERTION DEMONSTRATED															
21	Pursues rod as Examiner inserts.........											19	23	35	22	43
22	Manipulates box.;....................											50	62	65	40	43
23	Pokes holes..........................											42	42	50	40	43
24	Manipulates and mouths rod............											54	50	42	28	33
25	Drops rod without relation to box.......											23	31	8	12	35
26	Brings rod to box.....................											65	73	92	97	95
27	Brings rod to box surface only..........											42	54	54	33	10
28	Brings rod to box and releases..........											0	27	35	67	74
29	Brings rod to vicinity of holes only.......											12	19	35	51	29
30	Brings rod to box on repeated demonstra.											33	35	67	79	75
31	Hits rod on box......................											27	19	0	0	8
32	Rubs rod against box surface...........											19	31	42	30	5
33	Inserts rod in hole....................											0	38	58	76	86
34	Inserts rod without ever releasing.......											0	38	46	38	24
35	Inserts rod in middle hole..............											0	8	35	66	76
36	Releases rod in hole...................											0	0	12	39	62
37	Releases rod in middle hole.............											0	0	4	26	52
38	Releases rod into box.................											0	0	12	30	52
39	Activity with right or left hole..........											4	15	30	57	67
40	Activity with middle hole..............											0	15	42	58	86
41	Evidence of induced behavior...........											27	42	38	58	67
42	Postural activity.....................											8	23	30	26	48

Behavior Trends

The situation is presented in three phases and it will best serve
the purposes of summary to treat each phase separately in the
order of the procedure, namely: (*A*) Reactions to the performance
box alone; (*B*) Behavior after presentation of the rod; (*C*) Behavior after demonstration of rod insertion. Five age levels are
considered. At 40 weeks the infant typically gives prior and
predominant heed to the box, with secondary, shifting attention

to the holes. At 56 weeks there is a prior, predominating and almost exclusive preoccupation with the holes. It will be the purpose of the following summary to trace the stages by which this developmental transformation of behavior is achieved.

A. *Reactions to the Performance Box Alone.* At 40 weeks the infant is initially interested in the massive aspects of the box. He promptly reaches out, usually with both hands, which he places on the top of the box. Later he gives rather transient heed to one or more of the three holes, and he may bring his fingers in the vicinity of a hole, but only one child in three definitely pokes into a hole. At 44 weeks there is typically a more equal division of attention between box and holes, though nine children out of ten contact the box with both hands, usually immediately after presentation. Two children out of five confine their subsequent activity to the box, one out of five to the holes. At all age levels a few children limited their manipulatory activity either to the box or to the holes but the rule is a distribution of activity with increasing exploitation of the holes.

Even at 44 weeks it is rather characteristic for the infant to visually regard the holes before or during his reaching for the box. At 48 weeks, however, his prior approach is for the holes themselves, most frequently the middle and right holes. These he explores by a prompt and probing extension of the index finger, but, having done so, it is then almost equally characteristic for him to exploit the box *en masse* by pushing and pulling, or by raising himself with hands placed on the upper edge. The prior manipulation of the holes shows a very neat genetic peak at this age, 70 per cent flanked by 38 per cent at 44 weeks and 56 per cent at 52 weeks.

At 52 weeks the manipulatory preoccupation with the holes becomes very marked. Characteristically the initial attention goes to one of the holes with a prompt thrust of the right index finger (the thumb is only rarely used). The attention is now more sustained and the shift of manipulatory activity to the box itself is relatively slight in its accent. This is a developmental reversal, for three months earlier the distribution of attention was opposite in character. Accordingly two children out of five now confine their manipulation to the holes (compare 44 weeks, when a similar proportion restricted their activity to the box). At 56 weeks the selective interest in holes asserts itself even when there is a strong drive to postural activity. There is evidence of a preferential interest in the middle, circular hole after presentation of the rod. At this age, too, the infant may bring his eye up to the hole to peek through it—an interesting new acquisition which came from where?

B. *Behavior after Presentation of the Rod.* The rod is placed in the infant's hand and his spontaneous behavior is then observed. The possession of the rod introduces new possibilities of behavior, but close examination will reveal that these possibilities are not unique; they follow the action patterns already noted in the unimplemented hand. Indeed the index finger is a hinged rod which the infant conveniently carries in his own anatomy, and what he presently does with the wooden rod is well anticipated by what he has already done spontaneously with his most extensible digit.

Two-thirds or more of the infants spontaneously combine the rod and the box in some way at each age level. At 40 weeks the normative infant at once accepts the rod and brings it against the frontal surface of the performance box, often in a broadside manner. He is quite heedless of the holes, or, more accurately, he does not bring the rod into relation with the holes even though he may glance at them. He may mouth the rod, transfer it, and otherwise manipulate it. In half of the infants, much of the activity was restricted to the rod. Such restrictive rod activity is less frequent and less pronounced at subsequent age levels.

At 44 weeks the rod behavior presents transitional characteristics, similar to those already noted, when the infant used only his hands in his reactions to the performance box. He may manipulate the rod by itself and drop it without relation to any exploitation of the box. Commonly he brings the rod flatly against the box in a crudely adaptive manner. Rubbing the rod back and forth transversely and diagonally is rather characteristic. Occasionally the end of the rod is applied to the vicinity of the holes, and rarely it is caught against a margin of the hole in a manner which resembles or foreshadows the poking of a later age. His forefinger has been caught in the same holes in a similar manner.

At 48 weeks there is a decisive developmental increment in this pattern, and poking or inserting the rod rises sharply to 56 per cent (from 19 per cent at 44 weeks). Although the infant has by no means mastered the simple reorientation of a right-angulated adjustment, the rod is not brought so flatly against the box. The larger lateral holes are quite evidently discriminated and the rod is definitely even though awkwardly thrust into the opening. The teleology of this thrust we do not know. It is characteristic for the infant at 48 weeks *not* to release the rod while it is in the hole. The act of poking itself seems to be the dominant behavior value for the infant and variations of pattern are not so diverse as at the next age, when the technique of poking is already more established.

At 52 weeks the mechanics both of orientation and of insertion is nearer perfection. One infant out of three applied the rod to the middle hole, which was relatively avoided at 48 weeks. Release of the rod occurs only occasionally, both at 52 and at 56 weeks.

At 56 weeks the perceptual and motor capacities show further perfection. Three-fifths of the infants display manipulatory interest in the smaller and more difficult middle hole; two-fifths spontaneously insert the rod in this hole; one-third release the rod. It is interesting to note that of the three performance tasks presented by the three holes, the infant does not evade the technically most difficult.

C. Behavior after Demonstration of Rod Insertion. When behavior improves after demonstration, we are likely to ascribe it to the stimulus of the demonstration; it is, however, impossible to appraise the amount of specific adaptation which takes place as a direct result of the demonstrations themselves. The demonstrations serve to channelize activity already under way; they may have a directive rather than a genuine modeling effect upon the performance. It is for some such reason that postdemonstration behavior is often so closely akin to the spontaneous.

At 40 weeks the repeated demonstrations scarcely have any observable effect upon the child's behavior. One-fourth of the children hit the rod on the box. No infant inserted a rod in the hole at any time during the situation. The infants apparently give due visual heed to at least one of the demonstrations, and then blithely pursue their erstwhile activities. There is virtually no increase in the number of combinings of rod and box at this age, although at all the later ages the percentages show such an increase after the demonstrations. There is a slight increase in the poking of the holes by the finger, particularly after the examiner inserts the rod. It is as though the demonstration served to sharpen the recognition of the holes. The poking follows immediately and may be by the finger of the free hand, or by a finger of the prehensory hand. It is significant that the child will poke with his finger even while he is holding the rod; he has a better mastery of his own digit than of an extraneous tool.

At 44 weeks he has a better command of the rod in relation to the holes. There is an increase in the incidence of insertions as a result of the demonstrations, but now and at 40 weeks he often manipulates the box or the holes independently of the rod. Broadly speaking we may say that at 40 weeks demonstration may influence his perception of the holes; at 44 weeks it influences his application of the rod with reference to the holes.

At 48 weeks there is a still more lively alertness to the relationship of rod and hole. One child out of three pursues with his own finger the disappearing rod as the examiner releases the rod in the box. The demonstrations, however, have no striking effect upon performance. We have already noted the "natural" rise in the percentage of insertions during the spontaneous period prior to rod presentation. This percentage remains almost unchanged after demonstration. However, there is a tendency toward an increase in the number and in the precision of the responsive applications of the rod to the box. There is more insertion into the middle hole. Indeed, no child at 48 weeks spontaneously inserted in the middle hole, while one in three so inserted after demonstration. Behavior was usually at its optimum after the third demonstration. All of these facts suggest that the demonstrations now have some effect upon the course and the specific adaptiveness of activity. However, the child is by no means a paragon of imitativeness; he still rubs the rod across the box in a vigorous and disruptive manner (reported in 42 per cent of the cases) which declares inner necessities that defy the external model.

At 52 weeks responsiveness appears to increase. Perhaps it is not responsiveness in the abstract which increases, but there is an access of new ability, particularly that of release. Practically all infants now bring the rod combiningly into relation with the box after demonstration. Insertions or attempted insertions, including those in the middle hole, increase. There is a tendency toward repetitive insertion. Release of the rod occurs much more frequently (two-thirds of the infants now manifest release), but often the release is ill timed and the half-inserted rod falls back onto the table top. Orientation in approach also shows improvement; one child in four at 52 weeks releases the rod in the middle hole. The general item *Releases the rod in hole* shows a significant gain at 48, 52, and 56 weeks. Prior to demonstration, the percentage frequencies at these ages were 0, 21, and 32. After demonstration, the percentages rose to 12, 39, and 62.

Release in the middle hole shows a developmental increase from
0 per cent at 44 weeks to 4 per cent at 48 weeks, 26 per cent at
52 weeks, and 52 per cent at 56 weeks. The capacity of adaptive
release grows slowly. It is not reported at all at 40 weeks; but at
52 weeks two-thirds, and at 56 weeks three-fourths, of the infants
are credited with the ability to bring the rod to the box with
subsequent release. However, even at 44 weeks no infant released
the rod so that it fell into the box; at 56 weeks 52 per cent so released. This proportion would have been increased had the performance box been placed in a slightly oblique position. The
orientational difficulties of rod insertion indicate neuromuscular
and possibly also perceptual limitations, which in turn limit the
effects of practice and demonstration.

§33. FORMBOARD BEHAVIOR

(20 weeks–56 weeks)

The Situation

Fig. 33.—Formboard behavior: 24 weeks and 40 weeks.

Holding the board in the horizontal plane with the circular
opening at the right of the infant, the examiner placed the board
on the table top in the near median zone. After appropriate observation of the reactions to the board, the examiner presented the
round block in the standard manner, advancing it edge-wise
toward the infant. Spontaneous behavior with the board and
block was observed. The examiner then removed the block from
the infant's grasp and without delay or ceremony slipped the block
into the round hole. Again spontaneous behavior in relation to

the inserted block was noted. If in his efforts to insert the block, the formboard tended to slide out of position, the examiner anchored it with his own hands.

Stimulus Factors

Our formboard calls for a brief historical note. Formboards have become one of the most popular of all devices in testing the performance of both children and adults. A complete collection of such formboards would fill a sizable museum. Formboards trace back at least to Dr. Itard, the French physician, who used a simple geometric board in his famous educational venture in training the wild boy of Aveyron. His device was two feet square and on this surface he pasted three pieces of brightly colored paper, a red circle, a blue triangle, and a black square. Pieces of cardboard of the same forms and colors were provided to match with these.

Our infant formboard, therefore, proves to have some correspondence with the board used by Itard. Itard's formboard was the modern prototype of an unending succession of geometric formboards. Our point of departure was the Seguin formboard. Seguin constructed several types of formboards, some of which are still used at the Seguin training school. He believed that the geometric blocks were a valuable aid in the treatment of idiocy by what he called the physiological method. He devised formboards of varied models and made sets of them for several American institutions which he visited from time to time.

The Vineland version of the Seguin formboard, consisting of ten geometric insets, was planned by Dr. Naomi Norsworthy. In her original version the similarities of circle, hexagon, and octagon made difficulties which Goddard removed by substituting a cross for the hexagon and a five-pointed star for the octagon. This Itard-Seguin-Norsworthy-Goddard formboard has proved a very useful tool in the clinical study of both normal and defective children.

When we began our investigation of preschool children we thought it desirable to devise a simplified formboard adapted to their immature capacities. In the interests of continuity in developmental research we decided to construct this formboard along the lines of the Vineland model and made the dimensions of the blocks identical. (The board is rectangular in shape [6½ by 14 in.] with three open holes approximately 3 in. in diameter.) These holes in order are circular, triangular, and square, and into each hole a corresponding block, white in color, may be inserted. Unlike the Vineland model there is no backing to the formboard, and the surface of the table top appears through the openings. These modifications in construction make the formboard more flexible and widen the range of stimulus factors for the infant.

For purposes of developmental study we have found it profitable to present the formboard situation as early as the age of 20 weeks. In a sense, it seems almost presumptuous to present such a geometric problem to an infant so young. It should be borne in mind, however, that we are interested in the formboard not as a performance test per se but as a stimulus object which may be systematically used to explore the stages which precede successful adaptations to the geometric requirements of the performance problem.

For the same genetic reasons we present this situation in three progressive stages at each age level. Formboard behavior in the sophisticated sense does not begin until a child can on sight adaptively place the three geometric forms in their appropriate positions. Ordinarily this does not occur in the normal infant until about the age of two years, but this successful adjustment is preceded by an impressive series of progressive adaptations, all of which seem to be developmentally necessary for the later level of performance.

The three stages of presentation just mentioned are as follows: (A) Presentation of the formboard alone; (B) Presentation of the round block; (C) Demonstrational insertion of the round block by the examiner. This method of presentation multiplies the stimulus factors and gives wide opportunity for their analytic study.

When the board alone is presented it is possible to make note of both massive and discriminatory reactions. Does the infant react to the board as a whole or does he react to the individual holes, and what manipulatory orientations does he make to an object so large? Genetically, it is important to recall the fact that a 6½ by 14 in. board is a sizable object even for the adult. Comparatively, for the infant whose height is less than double the length of the formboard, this object is large and also relatively heavy. In fact, the round block alone proves to be somewhat too heavy for the 20 weeks-old infant to hold. For such reasons we were, of course, tempted to reduce the size of the formboard, to temper its weight, and to make its dimensions suitable to the dimensions of the infant himself. However, as already suggested, it seemed more desirable in the interests of external continuity of the data to examine these very difficulties and to keep the situation experimentally in series with observations made by means of the Vineland formboard.

The formboard tends to lie flat on the table top. The propensities of the infant to rotate and to lift the board and to change its orientations are made evident by presenting the board alone. Does the board have priority over the block? And when and how does the infant attain the characteristic behavior pattern of bringing the block into a matching relationship to the board? These questions are of more than trivial import when we recognize that they concern the development of form perception and the recognition of spatial conventions. A spatial convention is a physical relationship which has the sanction of social custom. Even at the advanced age of two years, as well as earlier, under the conditions of the normative examination, we occasionally find that the child addresses himself to the board and brings the board into relationship with the blocks rather than vice versa. In other words, when the circular, triangular, and square blocks lie before him, he seizes the board at either end and attempts to superimpose the board precisely over the blocks—an interesting and not unoriginal disregard for conventional procedure.

Because with the younger child the stimulus values of block and board are equally divided, it becomes necessary at certain stages of the examination for the examiner to place his own hand on the board in order to give opportunity for the relational behavior with the block. Ordinarily, however, the infant is given full scope to exploit the block and board without restriction. In the second phase of the situation the block alone is presented and the spontaneous behavior observed. The block is then taken by the examiner and without formal demonstration the examiner places it in the hole. At once the whole stimulus pattern changes because the infant is now confronted with a new perceptual situation and with difficult problems of grasp and of extraction.

Developmentally we may ask, When does the infant react to the situation in terms of container and contained? What reaction patterns are necessary for the act of voluntary extraction? How does the infant solve this elementary engineering problem, which in one way or another involves the principle of fulcrum and lever? And what is the genetic relation between the capacity of extraction and the capacity of insertion? Does one developmentally precede the other or do these patterns mature independently without dynamic relationship to each other? When does the infant pay regard to the holes? Does he give preference to any one of the three holes in his regard and his applications of the block? Although the subjective aspects must remain in obscurity, these questions can be answered in part by observing the developmental sequence of reactions to the formboard situation. Some of these questions have arisen in different context in other situations like the pellet and bottle and the performance box. It would be possible to pursue the comparisons with these situations, but we confine ourselves now to a summary of the three-hole formboard behavior, dividing the discussion into three parts conforming with the three stages of presentation.

Behavior Trends

Presentation of the Formboard Alone. Although the formboard is a massive object, it is interesting to note that as many as 17 per cent of 20 weeks-old infants do not manually contact the board. Thereafter contact is virtually universal. All 20 weeks-old infants, however, regard the board. There may be discernible shifting of the eyes scanning the edges of the board but only occasionally is there a suggestion of regard for the holes. Perception of the holes is in a nascent stage and does not become well defined until the age of 24 weeks. This increment in perceptual behavior is interesting and significant. Two-thirds of the 20 weeks-old infants show "undirected" hand-arm activity in the presence of the board. Such activity was rarely or never observed at 32 weeks and thereafter. The term "undirected" is of doubtful value if it suggests that the infant was not adjusting to the situation in making these digressional movements. Indeed three-fourths of the infants made an apparently definite approach upon the board. Such approach is practically universal at later ages. At 20 weeks the contact results in a crude pushing and less frequently in a pulling or dragging kind of "manipulation." Half of the children manipulate without grasp. Lifting and pulling the formboard off the table top were very exceptional.

At 24 weeks two-thirds of the children manipulate without grasp and half of them placed a hand in the holes. This insertion of the hand in the hole is rather characteristic of 24 weeks, al-

SITUATION: FORMBOARD (F)

F	Behavior items	4	6	8	12	16	20	24	28	32	36	40	44	48	52	56
	FORMBOARD ALONE															
1	Contacts						83	97	100	100	100	100	100	100	100	100
2	Undirected hand-arm activity						65	48	32	9	0	0	0	0	0	0
3	Approaches						74	94	100	100	97	100	94	93	97	100
4	Manipulates without grasp						48	65	52	56	47	41	41	26	33	10
5	Places hands in holes (implied)						17	52	45	47	32	35	25	29	33	25
6	Moves about on table top						57	68	71	75	65	41	50	48	31	35
7	Pushes						39	55	42	34	24	15	31	32	23	20
8	Pulls or drags						22	26	45	53	38	24	16	10	5	10
9	Lifts						4	13	32	50	71	74	72	74	82	50
10	Pulls off table top						13	7	19	38	21	6	13	10	5	5
11	Brings to platform						0	0	10	9	6	27	19	13	5	0
12	Brings to side rail						0	0	0	0	0	0	0	13	0	0
13	Releases						0	3	10	22	24	38	31	32	23	50
14	Turns over						0	0	0	0	6	6	13	13	28	35
15	Fusses						9	35	10	6	3	12	6	7	15	0
	BLOCK PRESENTED															
16	Contacts round block						57	89	87	81	100	100	100	100	100	100
17	Examiner places block in hand						50	21	10	0	0	0	0	0	0	0
18	Holds block only momentarily						50	18	0	0	0	0	0	0	0	0
19	Holds block actively						20	64	94	88	97	91	91	94	90	100
20	Block to mouth						9	57	68	50	62	50	36	32	18	15
21	Block to mouth immediately						9	50	45	34	36	24	12	0	0	0
22	Transfers block						7	7	35	31	30	41	33	18	10	19
23	Turns block						0	7	23	16	40	38	40	44	25	23
24	Drops block						72	54	58	53	58	68	73	74	83	92
25	Drops block on table top						43	50	29	38	27	35	21	29	8	12
26	Releases block on formboard						29	18	29	19	33	41	42	56	68	77
27	Resecures released block						0	7	16	16	9	24	21	21	25	54
28	Manipulates formboard						21	18	16	25	42	18	36	29	33	23
29	Brings block to formboard						28	18	42	34	49	62	73	76	88	89
30	Hits block on formboard						0	4	13	19	18	21	36	21	5	8
31	Brings block in relation to holes						7	4	7	6	18	21	36	41	60	85
32	Applies block in vicinity of hole						0	4	7	6	9	12	27	18	35	35
33	Releases block in vicinity of hole						0	4	0	0	0	3	9	12	33	27
34	Incipient insertion of block						0	0	0	3	3	3	15	34	40	62
35	Inserts block in hole						0	0	0	3	0	0	9	21	18	38
	BLOCK IN HOLE															
36	Contacts block in hole						60	71	87	97	100	100	97	100	100	92
37	Attempts secural of block						40	57	68	94	100	100	97	100	100	92
38	(If attempts secural) unsuccessful						100	67	62	41	26	3	12	3	0	4
39	(If attempts) gives evidence of difficulty						100	91	81	76	77	66	67	59	28	12
40	Scratches at block in hole						0	19	23	35	45	23	24	25	3	4
41	Pushes at block in hole						20	19	52	55	65	60	61	56	31	24
42	Turns block about in hole						0	14	29	42	39	26	21	13	5	4
43	Pulls at block in hole						40	24	26	52	55	54	58	47	38	28
44	Removes block from hole						0	14	29	61	74	97	88	97	100	84
45	Removes block immediately						0	0	13	23	23	34	30	41	72	76
46	Pushes block out from hole						0	5	23	32	42	54	51	50	31	28
47	Pulls block out from hole						0	5	7	35	42	37	42	34	38	20
48	Pulls or picks out block from hole						0	5	7	35	42	37	46	50	62	64
49	Picks out or grasps block						0	0	0	0	0	0	6	16	26	52
50	Grasps block after removal						0	0	10	35	55	77	73	81	87	68
51	Mouths block						0	0	3	16	29	23	18	19	5	4
52	Carries block to side rail or platform						0	0	0	3	3	29	40	9	5	12
53	Manipulates formboard						0	14	29	23	23	46	18	22	23	20
54	Brings block to formboard						0	0	0	10	30	60	52	59	64	52
55	Hits block on formboard						0	0	0	0	13	29	21	13	5	8
56	Releases block on formboard or table top						0	0	7	26	35	54	51	75	79	68
57	Releases block on formboard						0	0	0	0	19	29	27	50	59	48
58	Brings block to vicinity of holes						0	0	0	0	3	17	30	19	21	24
59	Brings block to formboard holes						0	0	0	3	9	17	40	50	59	60
60	Incipient insertion of block in hole						0	0	0	3	3	3	18	41	62	48
61	Inserts block in hole						0	0	0	0	0	3	6	28	54	44
62	Postural activity						0	0	0	0	0	11	28	29	48	50
63	Frets						20	29	32	32	23	3	15	22	5	16

though the reaction occurs frequently at all subsequent age levels. The 24 weeks-old infant often scratches the table top while his fingers are within the hole. The psychological meaning of this reaction can only be conjectured. We do not know whether in some illusory sense he is trying to seize the hole. It is true, however, that with advancing age the recognition of the hole as something which cannot be handled declares itself and the child's behavior indicates an established distinction between the hole and the block.

At 28 weeks this differentiation is in progress. A characteristic form of behavior consists in a slapping or fingering of the form-board, alternating with a similar contact upon the holes. But the holes are more definitely scrutinized and there is a suggestion that the child addresses himself to the round hole more than to the two other holes. The increasing activity with the holes indicates that the perceptual as well as manipulatory components of his behavior have undergone further organization. His manual activity with the board is vigorous. He tends to push it away from himself instead of to the side, as at 24 weeks. Lifting is more frequent and occasionally release occurs after lifting (10 per cent). Although these differences in manipulation are somewhat difficult to describe, they testify to very definite advances in the prehensory control and in the repertoire of his movements.

Superficially, all of the behavior appears random but when closely analyzed it is evident that the type of manipulation is changing in a progressive manner. This is borne out by the progressive trend of the percentages. For example, pushing reaches a peak frequency (55 per cent) at 24 weeks, whereas pulling or dragging reaches its peak frequency (53 per cent) at 32 weeks, declining with regularity thereafter. Lifting likewise shows a remarkably steady increase from 4 per cent at 20 weeks to 90 per cent at 56 weeks with a normative frequency of 50 per cent at 32 weeks. Because of these trends, which concern the mechanics of behavior, the pulling of the formboard off the table top attains its peak frequency of 38 per cent at 32 weeks. Releasing likewise is a manipulatory behavior item which shows a regular increase from 0 per cent at 20 weeks to 80 per cent at 56 weeks.

Thirty-two weeks proves to be a transitional period in which manipulatory interest in the holes is increasing. Typically at 28 weeks the child's activity consists predominantly in pushing and pulling the formboard about on the table top, while at 32 weeks there is also a recurrent visual regard for the holes, a regard which becomes more defined at 36 weeks. The actual behavior at 32, 36, and 40 weeks consists in a gross manipulatory activity, including lifting from the table top, carrying the board to the side of the crib or to the platform, and mouthing the edge. At 44 weeks the infant may let the board fall or may bang it on the table top.

Similar activity occurs at 48 weeks and occasionally the board is dropped over the side rail.

At 52 and at 56 weeks these varying manipulations take on a more controlled and deliberated aspect. The infant may rotate the board trundle-wise on the table top or hold it vertically on edge for a brief period, as though he were attentive to spatial relationships and had matured beyond less critical forms of manipulation. Peering through one of the holes or thrusting the hand through the hole comes into the behavior picture.

Presentation of the Round Block. The 20 weeks-old infant is scarcely able to seize the round block when it is proffered. In half of the cases the examiner placed the block in the child's hand. Only one child out of five held the block actively and half of the infants held it only momentarily. It falls from sheer weight, unsupported by the feeble grasp. Characteristically, the 20 weeks-old infant does not pursue the block when it is dropped.

At 24 weeks a definite increment is visible, for now most of the infants make a direct approach upon the block and two-thirds of them hold the block actively for a more or less extended period. The block usually goes immediately to the mouth and is chewed. After a brief period of mouthing or manipulation it drops to the table top. Both hands usually participate in the prehension. After 24 weeks, immediate approach, independent seizure, and sustained holding of the block are the rule with but few exceptions.

At 28 weeks some manipulatory activity characteristically occurs after mouthing. This manipulation consists in turning and transfer with and without inspection. Although mouthing occurs even more frequently (68 per cent) than at 24 weeks, it does not occur so completely to the exclusion of other forms of activity.

The activities at 32 weeks are similar to those at 28 but there are more evidences of incipient combining behavior. Although activity may be confined first to the board and then to the block, the infant may also occasionally hold at one time both board and block and may shift his regard from one to the other.

At 36 weeks this conjoined regardfulness for both board and block is still better defined. Half of the infants bring the block to the formboard and one-third of them now release the block on the formboard. Although this behavior is subject to errors of interpretation it seems to denote an increasing, even though somewhat ill-defined, reference of the block to the board. One child out of five brings the block into some relation to the round hole.

Although this behavior is in no sense to be regarded as block insertion, it foreshadows a trend toward such an ultimate reaction. The item *Brings the block into relation with the hole* accordingly shows a regular ascent from 18 per cent at 36 weeks to 85 per cent at 56 weeks.

Forty weeks shows an accentuation of these trends and almost two-thirds of the infants bring the block to the formboard in some manner without release, or by placement with release, or by banging or dropping, but all this relational activity is still rudimentary and there is little spontaneous, specific adaptation of the block to the region of the hole.

Even at 44 weeks the combining activity is relatively crude. Hitting the block on the formboard reaches a peak of 36 per cent. However, three-fourths of the infants bring the block to the formboard in some manner and one child out of four briefly applies the block in the vicinity of the hole in a sketchy manner; one child out of seven (15 per cent) makes a partial, momentary insertion. This percentage rises steadily to 62 per cent at 56 weeks. Because of the consistency of this trend we may well believe that the few instances of partial insertion observed at 44 weeks were not entirely fortuitous. Rather, they were prophetic indicators of a patterned propensity which is steadily strengthening. Propensities are patterned; they are not generalized impulses.

At 48 weeks this propensity is already so strong that one child out of five spontaneously inserts the round block in the round hole. At 56 weeks approximately two out of five children make such a spontaneous insertion. At this age also release of the block on the formboard rises to a normative frequency of 56 per cent, which increases to 77 per cent at 56 weeks. At this latter age there can be no doubt about the definite combining character of the block and board activity. Succesful insertions at 52 and 56 weeks rise from 18 to 38 per cent. There is a marked increase of incipient and partial insertions (from 15 per cent at 44 weeks to 62 per cent at 52 weeks). The spontaneous activity is better defined and is more persevering and repetitive. These increments of ability are not readily formulated, but comparatively viewed in the cinema and in the protocols they are clearly discernible.

Demonstrational Insertion of the Round Block by the Examiner. We shall not hazard any interpretation of the perceptual response of the 20 weeks-old infant to the inserted block. He apparently regards the block as it rests in the hole and he is able to contact the block in a manner which crudely simulates pulling or pushing. However, he is quite incapable of exerting any traction and it would probably be very journalistic to describe his reaction as an attempt to remove the block. The reaction, however, may be considered an attempt to secure the block even if the attempts are always unsuccessful. This is not altogether to his discredit, since unsuccessful attempts at secural occur in approximately two-thirds of the children at 24 and 28 weeks of age and may on occasion occur at the advanced age of 56 weeks. Indeed, attempts which show evidence of difficulty occur with a frequency of 59 per cent at the age of 48 weeks and only drop to a low level of 12 per cent at 56 weeks. These consistent trends suggest that the removal of the block constitutes a practical mechanical problem of real difficulty for the infant even though he must be credited with some manipulatory desire to remove one object from its relationship with another.

In spite of the developmental awkwaraness and crudity of the manipulation, 14 per cent of the infants at 24 weeks of age are able to accomplish removal of the block from the hole. This percentage shows a steady increase through the subsequent ages to a maximum of 100 per cent at 52 weeks. The consistency of this trend indicates that lawful developmental factors are at work in organizing the increasing mechanical effectiveness of the infant. This suggestion is further confirmed by the steady rise of the percentages for the item *Removes the block immediately*. Prompt removal of the block was not observed in any 24 weeks-old infant and in only 13 per cent at 28 weeks, but this proportion rises to a maximum of 76 per cent at 56 weeks.

No figures are available for the element of persistence but this also undergoes some increase with age. At 24 weeks a small proportion of the infants scratch, push, pull, or turn the block in some manner, but they do not show any persistence in these reactions. However, the 24 weeks-old infant addresses himself to the problem of extraction for a brief period and may even fuss in a manner that suggests that he feels thwarted in his attempt.

The 28 weeks-old infant shows a somewhat lengthened persistence, but his efforts at secural and removal are relatively brief. Pushing at the block in the hole represents his characteristic method of procedure.

At 32 weeks 61 per cent of the infants successfully remove the block from the hole. This constitutes a marked increment over 28 weeks, when the proportion of successful removals was only 29 per cent. How shall we account for these striking increments of achievement? The 32 weeks-old infant is, of course, stronger than his juniors but the successes are more ascribable to his superior technique. He shows not only more persistence but also a better perception of the relationship of the block and the board and a better direction of control of his hand activity. Even when the 28 weeks-old infant succeeded in dislodging the block partially from the hole, he did not exploit his advantage. The 32 weeks-old infant is more ready to follow up partial successes with a completing effort. He even brings his thumbs into requisition. It is quite possible that his greater success must be attributed to the same factors which led to an increase of prehensory successes in the pellet situation.

At this point we may summarize briefly the methods of traction used to remove the block. From 32 weeks on the infant resorts first to one method and, if not successful, to others. He is not likely to confine himself to one method of attack. Ranged in the order of developmental maturity, his methods of attack may be listed as follows: (a) scratching at the block; (b) outward traction away from himself, or pushing; (c) inward traction toward himself, or pulling; this traction may be through pressure of the palm or thumbs or fingers; (d) picks out the block by lifting and prying; (e) grasps the block by spanning the hand over it.

The pushing method of removal occurs most frequently at 40 weeks (54 per cent). Pulling traction occurs with relative frequency at a wide range of ages from 32 weeks to 52 weeks. Picking out or grasping the block by spanning rarely occurs at 44 weeks but mounts to a frequency of 52 per cent at 56 weeks. Although the infant's behavior reveals the complexity of the act of extraction, he rises at 56 weeks almost to an adult level of technique, if not of facility. Partly because of the size of his hand, the infantile grasp is relatively pronate, whereas the larger adult hand would prehend the block by a digital approach upon its margins.

It remains to summarize the subsequent manipulation after the block has been attained by the infant. This manipulation in general resembles the spontaneous activities described in connection with the presentation of the round block. Although the demonstration of insertion and the act of extraction increase the number of insertions of the round block into the hole, there are no marked differences in the patterns of activity. Fifty-five per cent of the 36 weeks-old infants grasp the block after removal but only 35 per cent release the block on the formboard or the table top. No combining takes place even after an additional demonstration of insertion, and mouthing is prominent. Likewise at 40 weeks, the trend of the reactions shows little influence from the demonstration and much of the subsequent manipulation of the block is also apparently uninfluenced by the presence of the formboard.

At 44 weeks, however, there is a well-defined tendency to apply the block to the formboard in a relational manner. The infant may carry the block to his mouth or to the platform or to the side rail rather frequently, but one child in three brings the block into one of the holes or into its vicinity.

At 48 weeks the demonstrational insertion seems to have a distinct effect because there is more reference of the block to the formboard than during the second phase of the situation without the benefit of demonstration. The demonstration apparently serves to direct the activity toward the region of the hole and there is also a striking increment in the frequency of release. Half of the children now release the block on the formboard.

At 52 weeks immediate removal is highly characteristic and incipient insertion of the block in the hole is almost equally characteristic. The insertion, however, is not necessarily immediate but often follows after an interesting refractory period of delay. At 56 weeks there was a slight decline in the number of infants who, partly because of postural activity, successfully inserted the block in the hole. Nevertheless, the adaptation of the 56 weeks-old infant to the rotation of the formboard was superior to that of the 52 weeks-old infants.

Normatively we conclude that the age of one year marks the threshold of insertion of the round block into the round hole after demonstration. Supplemental observations indicate that genetically there is a preferential perception for the round configuration and that a comparable adjustment to the square and triangular forms is characteristic of later stages of development, which lie between one and two years. In such developmental sequences nature "geometrizeth," in a literal as well as a figurative sense.

§34. BALL PLAY BEHAVIOR

(40 weeks–56 weeks)

The Situation

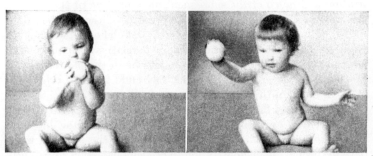

FIG. 34.—Ball behavior: 40 weeks and 56 weeks.

The examiner removed the table top and with playful social approach initiated the game of ball play. The infant was placed with his back near the head end of the crib in sitting position, legs spread somewhat apart. Then the examiner took position at the foot end of the crib and rolled the ball slowly toward the infant, suiting words and gestures to the game. If the child secured the ball, the examiner encouraged him to return it, stretching out a receiving hand across the end of the crib and beckoned the infant to roll the ball in that direction. If the infant persisted in holding the ball, the examiner gently removed it or caused it to roll out of the infant's hand in a manner suggesting responsive release. The game was then reinitiated two or three times.

SITUATION: BALL PLAY (Ba)

Ba	Behavior items	4	6	8	12	16	20	24	28	32	36	40	44	48	52	56
1	Regards Examiner or Examiner's hand.....											58	58	92	84	86
2	Regards Ex. or Ex's. hand, fur. re. delayed											53	8	4	3	5
3	Retains ball............................											53	38	29	23	14
4	Releases ball without defined ref. to Ex....											*47*	13	33	35	23
5	Pushes or hits ball on platform...........											*31*	*33*	20	10	14
6	Responds................................											21	50	79	81	77
7	Places ball in Examiner's hand............											5	*25*	*25*	16	9
8	Throws or rolls ball......................											21	46	71	74	77
9	Throws or rolls ball to Examiner..........											5	25	58	61	68
10	Throws ball.............................											0	8	46	58	64
11	Definite repetitive ball play..............											0	4	13	29	59

Stimulus Factors

The stimulus factors in the ball play situation are numerous. The situation occurs near the end of the examination. Rapport between the child and the examiner is by this time well established. The table top is removed and the infant has wide scope for both postural and social reactions. The situation is an informal one and is vivified by the ball, the most universally intriguing of all toys.

In analyzing the stimulus factors, we therefore have to reckon with the social context of the situation. The situation is not extremely different from the pellet and bottle, the cup and spoon, and performance box situations, in all of which there is a demonstrational episode. The social reciprocity between child and examiner is peculiarly close in the ball play situation. The play is initiated by the examiner. The child secures the ball as it is rolled to him and we observe to what extent he, himself, initiates a response.

The examiner may easily make the error of expecting the game to be too complete. After all, our psychological purpose is not to institute a game but to determine the manner and degree in which the child participates in a situation which combines insight and social factors. The five age levels from 40 weeks through 56 weeks were studied. Although the situation might have been profitably used at the earlier age levels, 40 weeks represents a transitional period which lies near the threshold of responsive capacity, when the game is played with a relative stranger.

Behavior Trends

At 40 weeks the child may regard the overtures of the examiner and the rolling of the ball somewhat soberly. It is rather characteristic for the child to look at the examiner's hand without making a subsequent response of referring the ball back to the examiner. He is very likely to retain the ball or to release it in an ill-defined manner which does not indicate clear responsiveness. He may lift the ball, mouth it, wave it, or transfer it; or he may simply hold it and the examiner may be under the necessity of extracting the ball from the infant's hands in order to reinstitute the game. Occasionally the ball may be brushed, hit, or pushed about on the platform without grasping, but this again is a localized kind of manipulation which is not definitely referred to the examiner.

In its formal essence this behavior is highly comparable to the reactions which the infant displays before the mirror and we shall note that his mirror play at 40 weeks is likewise at a transitional level from the standpoint of reciprocal responsiveness. But from a developmental standpoint one should not overlook the rudiments of reciprocal reaction even at 40 weeks. The child's perception is not completely confined to the ball. He has a selective interest in the examiner's hand and he probably is beginning in a vague way to sense the propulsion of the ball at the moment of release. He does not, of course, analyze or verbalize these relationships and yet his appreciation of them is a prerequisite for his later performance. With only a slight access of maturity he will be able to perceive and execute the cooperative elements in the situation. Not till then will he exhibit a pattern of actual participation. Repeated rolling of the ball by the examiner is observed by the infant with a receptive attitude, but at 40 weeks this stimulating factor yields meager immediate results because the infant's make-up is too callow.

At 44 weeks responsive behavior is somewhat less incipient but it is still very rudimentary. No real ball play can be elicited. The infant places the ball on the platform and hits or brushes it so that it rolls; frequently he vocalizes. He may look regardfully in the direction of the examiner and show a pleasurable reaction, indicating that on an emotional level at least he is entering into the game with enjoyment. One child out of four at the 44 weeks age level extends the ball toward the examiner's hand. If any and all reactions are reckoned, as many as half of the infants show a measure of responsive behavior. Although this behavior shows a palpable advance over 40 weeks, it is quite transitional in character, when 48 weeks is considered; for at 48 weeks definitely responsive behavior occurs in about three-fourths of the infants.

Typically the 48 weeks infant at some time during the situation throws or rolls the ball in such a way that it takes a course toward the examiner. His ability to release is better defined and more strongly established, but it shows itself somewhat sketchily. His reactions often are delayed and he may extend the ball to the examiner instead of rolling it. The ball play is in no sense continuous and has by no means taken on a battledore and shuttlecock character.

At 52 weeks, however, a cooperative kind of ball play comes into full evidence. Three infants out of five definitely throw or roll the ball to the examiner and about one in three repeats the rolling in a responsive manner. The infant is somewhat less dependent upon the gestures and commands of the examiner. The responsiveness is less sketchy and more continuous then that noted at 48 weeks. Although no distinctive abilities have appeared, the responsive release is more skillful and the total pattern of behavior is distinguishable from that at 48 weeks.

At 56 weeks the cooperative characteristics of the ball play are still better defined, the responses of the child are more vigorous, and more specialized. The play is more animated and there is a true reciprocity in the relationship set up between the examiner and child. Moreover, the ball play may be initiated immediately in two children out of five.

The act of throwing also is better defined. Throwing as a motor skill is genetically related to release. It is a kinetic kind of release which takes on a large variety of patterns. Some children lift the ball in a tossing manner, others allow it to roll out of the supinate palm, others hurl it. The hurling is at this age often accomplished by a downward thrust so that the ball bounces, but we do not gain the impression that the infant is deliberately attempting to make it bounce. The mechanics of throwing represents an interesting problem in the field of developmental kinesiology.

It is apparent, however, from the foregoing summary that the nature of the child's reactions in ball play is not solely dependent upon the ability to throw or to bowl the ball. His performance depends as much upon perceptual and social abilities, which must be correlated as they mature. Superficially it is difficult to distinguish the patterns of ball play at 48, 52, and 56 weeks, but genetic analysis indicates clearly that the behavior is subject to formative trends which will continue and which will make his ball play still more responsive and elaborate in the lunar months to come.

§35. MIRROR BEHAVIOR

(40 weeks–56 weeks)

The Situation

At the conclusion of the ball play, the examiner placed the infant squarely in front of the curtain which concealed the mirror at the end of the crib. While the infant was looking toward the curtain, the examiner raised the curtain with a moderately decisive maneuver, lending support to the child if he tended to lose his sitting balance. In this situation the infant was given full postural freedom and permitted to stand if he desired.

Stimulus Factors

The mirror presents a situation in which the problem of stimulus factors becomes bewilderingly complex. The infant himself may be bewildered, and surely the psychologist is, if he attempts to appraise all the perceptual possibilities involved.

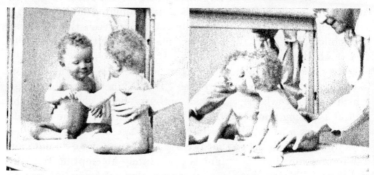

Fig. 35.—Mirror behavior: 44 weeks and 52 weeks.

From a purely extraneous standpoint, the situation is simple and controlled. The infant is seated squarely in front of a curtain which conceals a fixed mirror. The mirror fills the whole end panel of the crib. The curtain is rolled up with dispatch and the infant then beholds—what?

The perceptual responses which may occur at the five age levels from 40 to 56 weeks are numerous enough if one hazards to list them. The infant may see with apparent mystification the swift ascent of the curtain; he may follow the examiner's withdrawing hand; he may catch the mirror image of the examiner; he may catch his own image in part or whole; he may manipulate the mirror as mirror or may in various ways seek contact with his self-image. How social, how narcistic, how impersonal, how confused, how illusory, how investigatory, or how naive his responses are, we cannot really determine and the risks of interpretation are numerous because emotional as well as maturity factors greatly affect each individual reaction. The situation, however, has much interest for the examiner as well as for the child. It comes at the end of the examination and creates at least a pseudo-social stimulus which frequently releases emotional and vocal expression. Such expressions contribute to an understanding of the personality make-up of the infant.

The novelty of the experience inevitably varies among any group of children. Mirrors at home are usually above the child's visual level and many mothers make no effort to bring the child before a mirror. Exceptionally one finds a parent who has a superstition that mirrors are unlucky and prefers that the mirror menace be postponed to later years.

SITUATION: MIRROR (M)

M	Behavior items	4	6	8	12	16	20	24	28	32	36	40	44	48	52	56
1	Sober..................................											43	29	26	13	27
2	Smiles.................................											61	71	57	52	73
3	Vocalizes..............................											43	43	30	57	55
4	Waves arms............................											22	38	17	13	9
5	Brings hands to mirror..................											61	81	74	57	55
6	Pats mirror............................											17	19	13	17	41
7	Approaches image socially...............											13	43	30	65	64
8	Brings face to mirror...................											13	33	17	39	55
9	Plays peeka-boo with image..............											0	0	4	17	23
10	Postural activity......................											17	29	48	61	64
11	Stands................................											9	14	22	30	45

Behavior Trends

With due regard for pitfalls of interpretation, we may risk a brief summary of the trends of behavior. These trends show an increase in the sociality of the response. It is doubtful whether the infant identifies himself in any way with the image. Even at the age of 5 years a pair of twin girls made misinterpretations of their mirror images. Each considered the image not a self-image, but called it by the name of the cotwin. We had also noted that in infancy these same twins showed a strange indifference to their mirror images. Was this indifference bred by constant familiarity with the ever present cotwin? For the singleton (as opposed to the true twin) the mirror image is in the nature of a spurious cotwin. But it is not necessary to multiply the difficulties of construing the mirror situation by introducing twins!

The trend toward sociality in the mirror responses from 40 to 56 weeks is suggested by changes in emotional accompaniment and by the general patterns of the behavior. At 40 weeks, always subject to individual differences, the responses tend to be some-what delayed and even restrained and sober. Soberness was noted in two-fifths of the infants, whereas it is much less frequent at later age levels. At 56 weeks, on the contrary, social, outgoing response to the image is characteristically prompt and prominent. The infant seems to be completely deceived and he acts as though he were in full social commerce with another child.

At 40 weeks, however, interest in the mirrored image of the examiner is rather conspicuous. In time the infant also regards the image of his own face and he also smiles, but his response is comparatively sketchy; he gives particular heed to the moving images of parts of his body. The situation is not so personalized as it appears to be at later ages.

At 44 weeks, too, he will reach towards the image of his hand, but he gazes also at his whole figure which delights him. Three-fourths of the children smiled as they looked. Waving of the arms was most frequently observed at this age. The infant may regard his own image, look up at the examiner, and then back at his own image.

At 48 weeks he may look at the examiner's image and then up at the examiner, with some suggestion of perplexity or inquiry. He leans forward to the mirror, reaches toward it, and pats or waves, but the social nature of his response is not clearly defined, and many of his reactions still suggest a perceptual as opposed to a personal exploitation.

At any rate, the social aspects appear more vivid at 52 weeks. There is less shift of regard and more preoccupation with the self-image, even though postural and locomotor activity is becoming prominent. One-third of the children pull themselves to a standing position, and one child literally tried to walk through the mirror. Some would crawl and grope behind the mirror if the crib permitted it. Two-thirds of the children now make well-defined social approaches such as the following: brings face to mirror, mouths mirror, kisses, laughs and talks at image, offers object to image, and makes faces. These approaches are not only four times more frequent, but much more animated than at 40 weeks.

At 56 weeks they are still better defined, and a kind of peeka-boo game is self-initiated by one child out of four. Active patting of the mirror also attains its maximum frequency. Over half the infants now bring the face against the mirror while mere waving of the arms is very infrequent. Vocalization occurs in over half of the infants both at 52 weeks and at 56 weeks. Whether the peeka-boo game in which the infant apparently plays with his own image is a form of insight or of social reciprocity it would be difficult to demonstrate. All insight is psychologically a sort of look-and-see process by which we initiate a reaction, but only after we have first caught it on a reflective surface. When the reflective surface is bright, the insight is sharp and clear; when the surface is dull, insight resembles groping. There are developmental gradations in the alertness with which the infant pursues and interprets the moving image of his mirrored self.

§36. LANGUAGE BEHAVIOR

(4 weeks–56 weeks)

Introductory Note

In spite of voluminous literature on the subject of children's speech, the ontogenesis of language in the first year of life has had relatively little systematic attention. A strictly objective study of language behavior presents many difficulties and has numerous limitations. In the present investigations we have not undertaken to surmount these difficulties. Our data have been necessarily based on incidental observations and reports gained through individual interviews. Because of inevitable variabilities, the percentages derived by these methods must be regarded purely as suggestive and usually as understatements. The figures, however, reveal trends which, in connection with the associated data, are sufficiently significant to be summarized with comment.

This comment will perhaps serve to indicate that in spite of complexities and special methodological difficulties, language does not present unique developmental phenomena. The genetic problems of language may be approached by objective, normative procedures, comparable to those which we have used in the analytic study of prehension and other tangible patterns of behavior.

In the present discussion, we shall use the term "language" in its broadest sense as including any means of expressing or communicating feeling and thought. Language, therefore, includes not only articulate and vocal utterances but any gestures or attitudes which have a characteristic, expressional significance. By using the term *language* as an adjective in association with the broad term *behavior*, we widen still further the scope of the category and make it embrace all forms of auditory and visual responsiveness which are developmentally related to the total observable field of language as expression. This will tend to make certain areas of language behavior merge into areas of perceptual and social behavior, but this is genetically to be expected. It is undesirable to think of speech or language as the end product of some instinctive function which undergoes elaboration. On the contrary, language has an extensive matrix within which fixed modes of expressing meaning take form through specific adaptation to affective conditions and social needs. Although this widening of the domain of language behavior increases the number of data which demand consideration, it is possible that such a widening of approach may clarify the developmental mechanisms at work and may divest language of some of its claims as a unique function.

The Situations

During the ordinary course of the examination, the examiner dictated his observations to a stenographer behind a one-way vision screen. This procedure in itself introduced language into the total situations. As already noted, such spoken narrative generally served to make the child feel more at home.

The examiner occasionally also directed a few words toward the child somewhat informally as an incident to the presentation of the materials, not assuming that the child paid heed to the words except perhaps as a token of friendliness. In infancy even uncomprehended words serve a purpose of social communication. We did not, however, regard it as good examination procedure to talk frequently and abundantly to the infant. The infant gathers reassurance from the examiner's face and from the total atmosphere of the examination perhaps even more than from the voice.

In addition to the informal and incidental speech just mentioned, which varied naturally with the age and personality of the infant, a few formal language situations were instated. At a favorable transitional moment, while the infant was holding some object like the ball, a definite verbal command was once, twice, or thrice directed toward him. The examiner said: "Give it to me," holding out a receptive hand. If the response was ambiguous or negative, a similar command was repeated on another similar occasion. The cube, the ball, and the tri-colored rings were used most frequently for this situation, which was limited to ages from 40 through 56 weeks.

At 48, 52 and 56 weeks, a cup was placed before the infant at the farther right-hand corner, a box at the left-hand corner, and a shoe transversely across the median line. All three objects were ranged along the farther margin of the table top. Taking a position at the foot of the crib, the examiner said in order, "Where is the box? Where is the cup? Where is the shoe?" The question was repeated and "comprehension" was determined by the child's discriminative ocular fixation. The objects were interchanged to check on the consistency of response.

At the age levels from 4 to 24 weeks, hearing responses were observed by means of the bell ringing situation. The examiner took the small bell in one hand and a silenced (clapperless) bell of identical appearance in the other hand and then brought both bells as inconspicuously as possible within four inches of the corresponding ear of the supine infant. Both bells were then briefly and mildly shaken. The child's head turning and other reactions were noted. The bells were exchanged to repeat and to check on the observations.

During the course of the examination and particularly in the supine situation at the younger age levels, spontaneous vocalizations and smiling were noted and recorded. Facial brightening in social approach and in the postural situations was also noted.

Stimulus Factors

A consideration of stimulus factors plunges us at once into the heart of the psychological issues of the language problem. A critical definition of these factors would raise crucial questions concerning the genesis of language. Genetically it is impossible to confine any analysis of factors to the field of verbalization, for verbalization is preceded by syllabification, vocalization, and respiration, to say nothing of the whole complex of autonomic systems, which determine the affective life, which in turn determines the earliest language phenomena. For example, it is impossible to exclude crying from consideration. Although crying is a very primitive function and one which is in a measure shared with lower animals, the human cry very early undergoes differentiations which bring the act within the category of language. Rather early, too, the cry transforms itself into a wail with phonetic inflections and modulations which bring this primitive act still closer to the realm of speech. The most fundamental stimulus factors, as far as they may be given separate analytic status, are affective and concern the current physiological state of being. The infant cries and laughs as an outcome of these bodily conditions which are rooted in his physiological mechanisms both above and below the diaphragm.

These mechanisms of laughing and crying basically involve digestion and alimentation. Such language responses are mediated by the oldest portions of the nervous system, the sympathetic and autonomic. The overt language responses are simple in the sense that they express pleasure and pain with movements that are relatively stereotyped. But the mere enumeration of the diverse situations which will provoke smiling in an infant would disclose a prodigious complexity of stimulus factors ranging from tickling and patty-cake to playful surprise and social tenderness.

Affective factors probably always play a primary role as stimulus factors. The affective states at first may be relatively massive and undefined but with age these states take on a social reference so that the stimulus factors seem to move into the external social world. If the infant remained at a primitive vegetative level, his expressional behavior would be confined to crying, snarling, smiling, laughing categories. But as he matures, his sensorimotor apparatus undergoes elaboration which introduces new stimulus factors. His growing capacities in postural and perceptual fields make him increasingly sensitive to bodily attitude and gesticulations in his social environment; even if he is born a deaf-mute, he comes into a significant degree of social communication with this environment. He communicates through gesture and he understands the gestures of others. Gesture, which is a form of posture, lies at the root of all language. Normally, however, the visual-motor signs of gesture occur in close association with auditory-motor signs which operate as stimulus factors in the genesis of language.

Just as the infant deploys his eyes and hands in progressively changing patterns of reaction, so also he deploys the maturing motor systems which involve his larynx and the associated musculature of the mouth. From the standpoint of developmental neurology, there is no mysterious difference in the aural and oral reaction patterns, on the one hand, and the visual-manual patterns, on the other hand. Just as in the manipulation of the cubes the infant perceives what he does, so in the babblings of spontaneous vocalization he comes to hear what he does. This hearing becomes a powerful stimulus factor which may even operate on the principle of the echo and lead to repetitive activity. He thus identifies what he hears. But the endogenous stimulus factors in this vocal play are very deep seated. For example, even when he is in the throes of a vigorous crying squall, he may abruptly stop his crying to engage in a pleasurable exercise of some newly acquired form of vocalization. Thus a sputtering vocalization can amusingly interrupt a primitive flow of fussing.

The relationship of nutritional oral patterns to vocalization constitutes an interesting genetic problem. It is possible that reactions associated with feeding are somewhat identified or confused with language reactions and that in their early stages mouthing, biting, and babbling are developmentally not unrelated. Auditory stimulus factors are probably not sharply differentiated from tactile satisfactions and other forms of internal, organic perception. The exact nature of the young infant's auditory experience is, of course, concealed to us but there is evidence that he acquires auditory localization only very gradually. With such localization, a sound becomes associated with objects and with agents in his external environment. Even before the end of the first year he seems to definitely imitate these sounds. In essence, this act of imitation is like the responsiveness which he manifests to sounds of his own production.

But as we have seen in the discussion of other behavior situations, imitation does not operate as a circumscribed all-or-none function. Responsiveness to observed demonstrations undergoes gradual elaboration with age. In the visual-manual field the infant acquires imitative insight very slowly, and only after progressive approximations does he finally reduplicate models. He exhibits the same limitations in the field of language, and his vocalizations remain in keeping with the imitative capacities that he manifests in nonlanguage behavior situations. To be sure there are individual differences in talent and articulational adeptness, but we are now stressing the general growth similarities.

Consider for example the account of the development of responsiveness to demonstration in the paper and crayon situation. This account with relatively slight alterations could be safely transposed to outline the generic lines of development which apply to the acquisition of infantile language. As stimulus factors, sounds, words, and even social relations are genetically comparable to *things*, and the infant attains mastery of these insubstantial realities in the same way in which he achieves adjustment to cubes and crayon. Since the elaboration of language is dependent upon basic behavior capacities, the stimulus factors in language change progressively with the maturity of the infant. The capacities of comprehension probably are closely correlated with the general level of maturity. Since language, however, is so deeply rooted even at its more sophisticated levels in the affective life of the infant, it is probable that personality factors assert themselves more strongly here than in almost any other field of behavior. It must therefore be assumed that the personality make-up and the current mood of the infant greatly influence the language output at any given time.

Such personality and mood differences asserted themselves in the normative examinations. The language behavior of the infants varied within wider limits than other forms of behavior, particularly at the older age levels. Far from being inhibited, infants at the younger age levels were often stimulated by conditions of the normative examination. Such infants would babble for periods or intermittently throughout the examination. Older infants, silent in the beginning, often became vocal toward the end of the examination. It was also found that certain situations like the mirror and the cup and spoon situations provoked vocalization with special frequency.

The Developmental Patterning of Language Behavior

Language behavior in its development reflects several ascending levels of maturity: primitive vocalization, phonetic syllabification, perceptive and expressive identification of gestures and of vocal signs with situations and objects, articulate naming of these situations and objects, self-initiated manipulatory use of names or words. So complex is the genesis of language that in the first year of life words remain in a presophisticated stage.

In the most primitive vocal stage expression is accomplished chiefly through the respiratory mechanisms. But even in the neonatal weeks the larynx comes into rudimentary function as a molder and modulator of sounds. The very young infant produces feeble vocalizations of an *ah*, *eh*, or *uh* character. These vocalizations become more vigorous and decisive with the maturation of the neuromotor structures so that almost one-half of the 4 and

Situation: Bell Ringing (Br)

Br	Behavior items	4	6	8	12	16	20	24	28	32	36	40	44	48	52	56
1	Postural activity ceases	45	39	29	23	20	37	25								
2	Postural activity diminishes	71	71	61	45	43	37	25								
3	Starts or blinks	7	18	21	14	9	17	11								
4	Regards Examiner	7	14	43	41	34	17	18								
5	Turns head	10	7	25	9	39	67	89								
6	Turns head to bell	7	7	18	9	27	47	79								

Situation: Give It to Me (G)

G	Behavior items	4	6	8	12	16	20	24	28	32	36	40	44	48	52	56
1	Does not respond											50	21	24	11	15
2	Regards Examiner or Examiner's hand											43	0	19	4	20
3	Extends object to Examiner											50	79	76	85	45
4	Releases object											29	53	71	77	75
5	Places object in Examiner's hand											29	21	38	19	10
6	Releases object in Examiner's hand											7	17	43	63	30
7	Releases object but not to Examiner											0	0	0	7	25

Situation: Cup-Shoe-Box (C-S-B)

C-S-B	Behavior items	4	6	8	12	16	20	24	28	32	36	40	44	48	52	56
1	Responds to "shoe"													14	37	57
2	Disregards "box"													90	70	71

Situation: Vocalization (v)

v	Behavior items	4	6	8	12	16	20	24	28	32	36	40	44	48	52	56
1	Face brightens	40	68	—	—	—										
2	Chuckles	0	0	36	42	24										
3	Smiles	22	65	96	100	100										
4	Laughs	0	0	7	31	88										
5	No vocalization heard	45	31	21	15	28										
6	Vocalizes small throaty noises	84	72	3	4	4										
7	Vocalizes ah-uh-eh	40	96	82	96	67										
8	Coos	0	3	42	88	76										
9	Blows bubbles	0	0	3	42	44										
10	Gurgles	0	0	10	42	56										
11	Vocalizes da					0	7	7	18	59	64	63	62	69	67	59
12	Vocalizes ma or mu					5	11	26	43	47	51	60	52	60	64	64
13	Two syl., 2nd rep. first, ma-ma, ba-ba, etc.					14	11	7	25	66	70	80	83	86	79	91
14	Makes "d" sound					0	7	22	21	66	64	69	62	88	67	73
15	Makes "m" sound					5	11	26	43	47	58	63	55	60	64	64
16	Makes "ē" sound (at end of word)						0	4	7	16	12	14	35	46	48	64
17	Makes "b" sound					9	4	15	14	22	24	32	41	32	57	64
18	Says no "word"					100	100	100	93	88	79	66	31	23	12	5
19	Says one "word" or more							0	7	12	21	34	69	77	88	95
20	Says two "words" or more							0	4	0	3	3	28	34	67	86
21	Says three "words" or more											0	10	26	40	68
22	Says four "words" or more											0	7	9	26	36

6 weeks-old normative infants were actually overheard to make small throaty sounds. At 8 weeks 42 per cent of the infants were observed or reported to coo. This cooing is a more elaborated and sustained form of vocalization, in which the vowels become more robust and consonants begin to figure. Such cooing is prominent at 12 weeks and at 16 weeks. Three-fourths or more of the infants at these ages were credited with cooing sounds. Gurgling, blowing bubbles, and chuckling are developmentally somewhat more advanced than cooing, and they occur with normative or near normative frequency at 12 weeks and at 16 weeks. Chuckling is more common at 12 weeks (42 per cent) than at 16 weeks (24 per cent). Chuckling may be roughly defined as a rudimentary or nascent laugh. Discerning mothers distinguish it from true laughing. Well-defined laughter occurs in nearly all children at the age of 16 weeks and was reported in one out of three children at 12 weeks. It is noteworthy that the chuckle was relatively characteristic at 12 weeks but not at 16 weeks, and that laughing became highly characteristic at the latter age, reaching a frequency of 88 per cent.

Not reckoning crying and laughter, vocalizations were heard in the course of observation in well over a majority of the infants at all age levels, with perhaps the least frequency at 4 weeks. At that age no vocalizations were noted in 45 per cent of the infants; but at 12 weeks they were noted in 85 per cent of the cases observed and at 16 weeks mothers report that the infant "talks to himself."

The most primitive phonetic utterances are small throaty sounds which are very characteristic of 4 and 6 weeks-old infants. Utterance is almost too strong a word, for the sounds are soft and submerged. They drop out soon and are rare even at 8 weeks. They are replaced by a soft aspirant *ah*, *uh*, or *eh*. The voice is low pitched and typically the syllable is short and uttered only once, but sometimes it is repeated several times and even drawled. That even an 8 weeks-old infant can drawl testifies to the burgeoning character of language behavior!

At 12 weeks the infant has already acquired a considerable repertoire of vocalizations. He blows with his lips, he makes gurgling *guh-grr* sounds with his soft palate and the base of the tongue. The newly acquired mobility of the posterior tongue (acquired through developmental individuation) introduces new patterns and problems in his feeding as well as in his phonetics.

In the early phonetic stages the vowels are favored and consonantal values are not so well defined, but consonantal sounds come in with amazing rapidity and his larynx originates sounds which he will not even be called upon to use in later life. The diversity of vocalization is considerable and it is suggested that by 28 weeks or earlier an infant may be capable of making all of the sounds of the vernacular.

The amount of time devoted to vocalizing activity varies, of course, with age, with maturity, and with personality factors. We have reported elsewhere a complete 24 hour record of the vocalizations of an infant six months of age.* The language behavior chart for this 24 hour day showed 104 separate moments of vocalization varying from a one-letter sound to a single syllable repeated 32 times. Seventy-five different sounds and combinations of sounds were observed.

Our normative data indicate that the syllables *ma* and *mu* occurred in almost half the infants at the age of 28 weeks. This is probably an understatement. The syllable *da* was reported in only 18 per cent of the cases at 28 weeks, but in approximately 60 per cent or more of the cases at 32 weeks and at subsequent age levels. A well-defined *e* sound was reported in almost half the infants at 48 weeks and at 52 weeks and in two-thirds of the infants at 56 weeks. Fifty-seven per cent at 52 weeks and 62 per cent at 56 weeks were credited with a *b* sound. These figures, although doubtless understatements, suggest at least the sounds which have prominence in the intimate observation of the mothers. It is not without significance that virtually no mother reported the utterance of a word by the infant during the age periods prior to 32 weeks.

One word, exclusive of *dada* or *mama*, was reported or observed in from 70 to 95 per cent of the infants from 44 weeks to 56 weeks. Sixty-seven per cent of the children at 52 weeks and 86 per cent at 56 weeks uttered two words, 68 per cent at 56 weeks uttered three words, and only 36 per cent at 56 weeks uttered four words. Incidentally it may be noted that these averages fall below the vocabularies reported in the literature. Waddle found that the year-old vocabulary was from three to 24 words with an average of nearly nine words, but his calculation was heavily weighted with cases from professional and higher socio-economic levels. Miss

* GESELL, ARNOLD, *The Mental Growth of the Preschool Child*, New York: Macmillan, 1925, 447 pp.

Shinn's famous niece had used actually only five words at the age of 1 year, but Miss Shinn was of the opinion that this niece comprehended 84 words, all securely associated with ideas, and that she knew words for 51 people and things and 28 action words.

At this point it may be well to indicate briefly the course of development in the comprehension aspects of language. Since comprehension is dependent upon perception, the first formative stages must be sought at early ages. Comprehension is indeed a form of perception.

The anticipatory reactions of the supine infant in feeding and other child care situations fall genetically in the lower categories of comprehension. He betrays expectancies in the presence of certain sights (activities and attitudes) or certain sounds. When these expectancies express themselves in adaptive movements, the infant has already begun (in his way) to comprehend. He reaches full comprehension when his capacity to adapt is perfected or complete.

A simple bell ringing test was made while the normative subjects were in the supine position. A muted and a functioning bell were simultaneously rung near the ears. This test showed that nearly half of the 4 weeks-old infants (45 per cent) ceased postural activity on the sounding of the bell. Nearly three-fourths of them (71 per cent) showed a reduction of activity both at 4 weeks and at 6 weeks. At early ages mere listening to a simple repeated sound requires suppression of general body activity. When auditory perception is more fully differentiated, auditory responsiveness occurs without reduction of accompanying bodily activity. We therefore find that at the age of 24 weeks only one child out of four exhibited cessation or diminution of postural activity on the ringing of the bell and yet these infants doubtless heard the bell. At 8 weeks one child in five responded with a blank or a mildly startled reaction. At 8 and 12 weeks two children out of five definitely fixated on the examiner when the bell was rung. The limitations of head turning in the first quarter of the first year have already been noted. At 16 weeks two-fifths of the children, at 20 weeks two-thirds, and at 24 weeks nine-tenths of the children responded with some head turning movement in the bell situation. At 20 weeks about one-half and at 24 weeks 80 per cent turned adaptively to the bell which was rung. These figures give a crude indication of the limitations of auditory localization in the first half of the first year of life. The infant has many difficult problems of auditory orientation which he must solve as a prerequisite for linguistic comprehension. In the discussion of stimulus factors we have already indicated that he must also achieve a differentiation between the sound of his own voice and that of other persons.

Comprehension of the postural attitudes, movements, and gesticulations of other persons is also prerequisite to word comprehension. Rudimentary recognition and comprehension begin early. The perceptual identification of the mother's face which hovers over him, the increasing perceptiveness of the variations in facial expression of the maternal countenance, the perception of body attitudes of leaning and aversion, and the numerous attitudes of approach and withdrawal, lay the basis for the infant's affective and cognitive social behavior. This behavior precedes linguistic comprehension and is never completely dissociated from the latter.

As already indicated, the complex world of social attitudes expressed by motor signs is comprehended even by the deaf-mute infant. The hearing infant, however, perceives this world of gestures in close association with vocal accompaniments. Long before he can have any articulate perception of words he hears their repeated utterance in situations of feeding, bathing, social approval and disapproval, and so forth. Concurrently he is exercising his own phonetic repertoire and the sounds which he makes come to have some crude parallelism with the sounds that he hears. The sounds that he makes furnish the basis for the identification of sounds which arise in the external world, just as the movements which he makes furnish the basis for the movements which he may sometime duplicate by deliberate imitation. But he comprehends movements before he comprehends words and we may suppose that in their nascent stages the word-sounds are closely bound up with a system of motor predispositions or anticipations. The words do not have a distinct and mobile status in his mental life. They are moored in his postural and manipulatory reaction system. Accordingly he comprehends many words before he masters their utterance and, even after he learns to speak them, it may be years before the words attain a high degree of detached autonomy in his thinking.

Because the infant in the first year of life lives so completely in a world of visual-motor comprehension, it is possible to conduct virtually all of the normative examination without uttering a word. The examiner uses words and sentences to impart a social aura to the whole procedure, for the sounding of the words, even though meaningless, serves to socialize the situation for both infant and adult. But the words themselves are needless.

At 40 weeks of age and later, a few verbal commands were included in the examination to throw light on the infant's comprehension. When the child was holding a cube or a ball, the examiner held out a receptive hand and said, "Give it to me" repeatedly. At 40 weeks half of the children did not respond to this situation, or they simply regarded the examiner or the examiner's hand. At 56 weeks only 15 per cent failed to respond, but probably not because of lack of comprehension. At 40 weeks half of the infants regarded the examiner or the examiner's hand; an equal number extended the object to the examiner. At 52 weeks 85 per cent of the infants extended the object to the examiner. Again at 56 weeks only 45 per cent extended the object, but a strengthened retention of the object also indicated deepened comprehension or wariness.

At 40 weeks less than one-third of the children proffered and released the object when the examiner took hold of it. This percentage rose to 53 at 44 weeks and to 75 at 56 weeks. Although these responses are affected by personality factors, the trend in percentages is partly due to the mechanical difficulties of release itself. At 48 weeks 62 per cent of the infants placed the object in the examiner's open hand. At 52 weeks an equal number released the object in the examiner's hand. These figures indicate primarily a responsiveness to a gesture in a social situation. To what extent the command as command was influential in determining the response we can only conjecture. Words in a certain sense were superfluous for most of these children. But there gradually comes a time when the words are not superfluous. The oft-repeated hearing of "Give it to me" in comparable situations leads finally to a comprehension of the sentence and, in due season, of each individual word. Throughout the first year of life, however, the infant lingers at the sentence and phrase stage and has very slight mastery of individual words as tools.

An additional normative situation throws some light on the infant's word responsiveness. A cup, a shoe, and a box, widely spaced, were placed along the further margin of the table top. The examiner repeatedly asked, "Where is the cup?" "Where is the shoe?" "Where is the box?" Only 14 per cent of the infants at 48 weeks reacted responsively by looking in the proper direction when the word *shoe* was pronounced. This percentage rises to

37 at 52 weeks and 57 at 56 weeks. The word *box* was disregarded by 90 per cent at 48 weeks and by approximately 70 per cent at 52 weeks and at 56 weeks. This simple word comprehension test furnishes indicative data. In a normative sense specific comprehension of the spoken word *shoe* is characteristic of the 56 weeks-old child. He is not responsive to the word *box* even when *cup* and *shoe* are the only alternatives in a multiple choice situation.

The one-year-old infant reacts to a wide range of words but these words are cues to situations; they have very meager psychological independence. This is true in a measure even of the words which the child himself articulates. Their very articulation is dependent upon a total situation and often cannot be elicited by the adult's repetition of the word. A child may wave "bye-bye" or say "bye-bye" to his father, but at a certain stage of development he may not be able to demonstrate either ability in relation to some other person; the ability is highly specific.

The words which an infant articulates are determined (1) by his phonetic capacity, (2) by the emotional and social values of the situation, (3) and by the socialized premium which is placed upon the utterance through circumstances or family conspiracy. For this reason the most common "words" are *dada* and *mama*. *Kiki* (kitty) is another word which has been found with frequency as early as 36 weeks. The capacity to make the *k* sound explains the appearance of the "word" *car* as early as 40 weeks.

We have listed all of the words, exclusive of *mama* and *dada*— unless these words have been definitely specified as being equivalent to mother and father—and find that the diversity of words increases steadily from 28 weeks of age to 52 weeks of age. Listing all of the words reported for the entire normative group, three different words were found at 32 weeks, six at 40 weeks, 17 at 44 weeks, 42 at 48 weeks, and 109 at 52 weeks. It should be mentioned that the larger number of infants examined at 52 weeks tended to swell the number assigned to that age.

Classifying the words found at 52 weeks, they fall with ascending frequency into the following groups: (1) things to eat, (2) qualities of objects, (3) activities or relationships, (4) inanimate objects, (5) persons, (6) exclamations to attract attention, (7) relating to self, (8) animals, (9) interjections, and (10) social intercourse.

In summary, five stages in the development of spoken language may be distinguished as follows: (1) primitive vocalization, (2) double-syllable vocalization, (3) the vocal sign, (4) the designatory name, (5) the instrumental name. If the infant remained arrested at the lowest level of vocalization he would be virtually inarticulate. His needs, great and small, unimportant and dire, would be expressed in cries and grunts. However, his crying soon becomes modulated by syllabic variations and overtones which lead to numerous differentiations. The cry may even become a jargonized wail and the jargon in this wail constitutes a matrix out of which still more precise articulations or babblings will emerge. The babblings are very diverse, almost superabundant; some prove transient.

In the second stage of development, certain phonetic values become better defined as patterns are reinforced by the method of doubled articulation. The individual throaty sound is now replaced by a double phrase like *dada, baba, mama.*

In the third stage the vocalization becomes a true vocal sign expressive of the child's attitude or of an elementary association which he makes with a complex social situation. By this vocal sign, even though it may be a monosyllable or a disyllable, he expresses in his only partially articulate way a whole sentence or even paragraph. The vocal sign is an indicator of a total situation or a state of being.

At a later stage the vocal sign becomes more specific and slightly more under control. It becomes a designation which the infant definitely applies to a central object or to a salient aspect of a situation. To be sure, the infant may generalize the name and may apply the designation to a large range of objects or persons, but beneath this diversity there is a common social or emotional value which makes his utterance a true designation. The utterance, however, does not have much independent status and the infant does not utilize it freely at will. It is an utterance which arises when the psychological situation is appropriately set.

In the fifth stage, however, this designation becomes a name in the instrumental sense. The word becomes sufficiently detached from the total situation so that it has to some extent a self-subsisting psychological status. The child comes at last into partial command of the word as a tool. The qualification *partial* is necessary because careful studies have shown that a sophisticated, conceptual mastery of words is an attainment which is scarcely reached within the early years of childhood.

When the language behavior of the infant is considered in its natural settings, it proves to be an extremely complicated process, but not entirely unique. There are developmental modalities in language behavior which are similar to those displayed in the manipulation of the physical world. Many interpretations of infantile language miss the mark because they are colored by adult concepts of mature speech. Gentically, articulate language cannot be understood except through a careful study of non-verbalized behavior. Words are rooted in such behavior.

§37. SOCIAL AND DOMESTIC BEHAVIOR

(4 weeks–56 weeks)

Under this heading we propose to consider very briefly the behavior characteristics of the infant as expressed in (a) his reactions to persons, (b) his responsiveness to gesture and speech, and (c) learnings and habituations which arise out of his home life. These subjects are vast in their implications and we do not assume that the procedures of the normative investigation were sufficient to do them justice. Indeed, we made no specific and direct attack upon the social and personality aspects of the infant's psychology, partly because these aspects are so ubiquitous that they are present in some degree in all behavior situations. The development of social and personality factors in the individual can be investigated only by biogenetic methods, and in later publications it is hoped to present biogenetic data based on consecutive studies of the same child. For the present we limit ourselves to suggestive normative data derived from an objective study of behavior patterns.

It might be contended that social and personality characteristics cannot be adequately explored by normative methods, that these characteristics are too closely identified with emotional and individual motivational factors to yield to the same treatment that we apply to impersonal phenomena like posture and prehension. The contention is sound to a degree, for we shall never truly know the inner, personal life of the infant until we can get out of our own subjectivity into his. We can do this now through speculation, but with no scientific validation. The hazards of such speculation are numerous. We cannot even answer conclusively the primary question, Is the infant's affective life essentially like our own?

SITUATION: SOCIAL BEHAVIOR (so)

so	Behavior items	4	6	8	12	16	20	24	28	32	36	40	44	48	52	56
1	Responds to smiling and talking	8	62	63	—	—										
2	Visually pursues moving person	12	69	74	—	—										
3	Knows mother	3	21	39	81	92										
4	Sobers at strangers	0	3	4	35	56										
5	Turns head on sound of voice	0	3	26	42	50	100									
6	Accepts strangers	100	100	100	100	80	61	52	59	41	39	39	26	18	18	14
7	Withdraws from strangers	0	0	0	0	19	8	24	16	47	42	19	48	44	30	9
8	Adjusts to words					0	8	12	16	47	68	75	94	82	89	73
9	Responds to "bye-bye"					0	3	3	3	13	35	53	65	38	59	27
10	Adjusts to commands					0	0	0	3	22	23	31	55	56	73	50
11	Responds to inhibitory words					0	0	0	3	25	23	28	45	44	52	23
12	Responds to "So big"					0	0	0	0	6	7	8	26	18	34	—
13	Elicits attention					0	0	0	0	9	16	14	26	27	53	50
14	Plays pat-a-cake					0	0	3	6	19	23	25	42	27	50	9
15	Plays peeka-boo					0	6	6	0	9	13	11	13	9	25	9

SITUATION: PERSONAL BEHAVIOR (per)

per	Behavior items	4	6	8	12	16	20	24	28	32	36	40	44	48	52	56
1	Regards hand	0	3	15	73	80										
2	Brings hands together	0	0	7	42	72										
3	Hands active in mutual fingering	0	0	4	23	52										
4	Pulls at dress	8	7	22	73	64										
5	Pulls dress over face	4	0	4	31	52										
6	Kicks off blankets	35	59	85	—	—										
7	Kicks in bath	4	24	45	69	80										
8	Likes sitting	0	0	3	50	57										
9	Sits propped with pillows	0	0	4	42	63										
10	Resents supine	0	0	3	15	36										
11	Anticipates feeding on sight of food	0	0	7	42	68										

SITUATION: PLAY OPPORTUNITIES (pl)

pl	Behavior items	4	6	8	12	16	20	24	28	32	36	40	44	48	52	56
1	Is held	13	32	38	47	20										
2	Plays in crib	100	80	53	60	50	40	21	35	35	21	26	15	10	23	8
3	Plays in carriage	0	28	46	38	50	67	84	48	48	39	35	27	24	31	12
4	Plays in crib or carriage	100	96	88	91	90	80	63	69	78	55	61	42	31	12	16
5	Plays in high chair	0	0	0	0	6	13	16	52	22	28	30	31	38	27	4
6	Plays in high chair or swing	0	0	0	13	6	20	16	61	26	31	30	31	45	3	4
7	Plays in pen	0	0	0	0	0	0	0	4	0	10	13	35	31	31	37
8	Plays on floor	0	0	0	0	0	0	16	4	26	23	26	35	31	42	75
9	Plays on floor or in pen	0	0	0	0	0	0	16	9	26	34	39	62	52	62	57
10	Plays in Taylortot or kiddy car	0	0	0	0	0	0	0	4	2	13	31	31	8	4	
11	Plays on floor or in pen or kiddy car	0	0	0	0	0	0	16	9	30	36	52	88	79	65	91
12	Plays with paper					0	25	26	8	11	15	8	8	—	9	—
13	Plays with spoon					0	18	7	15	44	31	23	23	18	18	0
14	Plays with clothespin					0	4	15	12	39	15	0	23	9	5	1
15	Has rattle	0	3	11	29	66	93	100	58	50	62	23	23	9	18	
16	Has doll or toy animal	0	0	0	0	10	36	70	58	72	62	69	62	64	55	70
17	Has one toy	0	3	11	31	75	100	100								
18	Has only one toy	0	3	11	27	63	29	0								
19	Has two or more toys	0	0	0	4	13	71	100								
20	Has three or more toys	0	0	0	0	0	46	74								

SITUATION: FEEDING HABITS (f)

f	Behavior items	4	6	8	12	16	20	24	28	32	36	40	44	48	52	56
1	Has night feeding......................	91	90	94	89	80	67	69	65	49	57	41	33	17	18	9
2	Has no night feeding....................	7	7	7	11	20	31	18	23	48	43	55	60	83	79	86
3	Has two night feedings or more..........	65	38	40	35	29	19	16	23	4	0	3	7	3	0	5
4	Is nursed...............................	65	62	50	42	41	53	41	50	41	32	28	30	11	5	0
5	Is nursed only..........................	48	38	29	27	27	38	31	35	30	29	10	19	10	5	0
6	Has bottle feeding......................	52	62	71	73	73	62	72	65	70	64	79	70	73	60	74
7	Is bottle fed, not nursed................	36	38	50	58	59	47	59	54	59	61	63	59	73	60	73
8	Has bottle feeding and is nursed.........	16	24	21	15	14	15	10	11	11	4	17	11	0	0	0
9	Fed with spoon.........................	0	4	8	12	35	59	64	75	80	96	97	97	98	89	98
10	Fed with cup...........................	0	0	0	0	0	0	4	12	18	23	28	37	50	61	68
11	Has cod-liver oil.......................	32	45	68	81	71	72	66	54	63	54	35	34	43	35	41
12	Has orange juice........................	26	45	75	92	74	66	74	57	70	71	59	52	67	48	77
13	Has cereal..............................	0	0	0	4	19	34	59	65	88	89	83	89	93	75	91

SITUATION: TOILET HABITS (to)

to	Behavior items	4	6	8	12	16	20	24	28	32	36	40	44	48	52	56
1	Has no regular toilet training............	100	100	100	97	87	65	52	53	41	39	17	14	10	4	13
2	Has regular toilet training..............	0	0	0	3	12	35	48	47	59	71	83	86	90	96	90
3	Never soils diapers.....................	0	0	0	3	3	4	7	8	7	17	18	21	20	23	30

WAKING HOURS DURING 24 HOUR PERIOD

Age..................	4	6	8	12	16	20	24	28	32	36	40	44	48	52	56
Number of cases........	30	28	28	26	49	31	31	30	33	35	34	32	36	46	27
Boys and girls: Average.............	*Hours* 4.20	5.73	6.12	6.85	7.31	7.63	8.41	8.43	8.64	8.88	9.24	9.63	9.99	9.98	10.46
Sigma...............	1.72	1.94	1.14	1.78	1.60	1.38	1.25	1.54	1.59	1.45	1.43	1.09	1.38	1.59	1.74

AVERAGE NUMBER OF HOURS IN LONGEST WAKING PERIOD

Boys and girls.........	*Hours* 1.93	2.66	2.59	2.91	3.14	3.30	3.90	3.59	3.95	3.94	4.23	4.92	4.94	5.39	5.76

SLEEPING PERIODS IN 24 HOURS

Boys and girls: Average.............	6.56	6.14	6.46	5.81	5.53	4.97	4.65	4.87	4.09	4.17	3.88	3.38	3.22	3.02	2.78
Sigma...............	1.14	1.16	1.52	2.02	1.19	1.03	1.03	.80	.94	.97	1.08	.96	1.13	.88	.63

As far as this question must be answered in order to define a premise, it is probably safest to choose a judicious affirmative. When the issue is made to rest on a purely scientific basis, perhaps it is wiser to suspend the answer altogether until more data and better techniques are available. Meanwhile it is possible to make some approach upon the phenomena of social and of personal behavior with the same objective observation and analysis which have been brought to bear on other forms of behavior. Personal and social behavior expresses itself in characteristic patterns and capacities which are subject to laws of growth. And even though one does not attempt to set up a definition of personality or a criterion of sociality, one can find developmental evidences of personal-social behavior in almost all situations.

Let us first look for some of these evidences in the postural situations, a field of behavior which superficially lies quite remote from social behavior and yet cannot be divorced from it. Over two-thirds of the infants from 4 to 16 weeks of age paid some regard to the examiner during the supine situation. No one can assess the social content of this regard. It is an important fact, however, that selective regard for the examiner's figure and for his face is characteristic of the early perceptual responses of the infant. It is possible to trace certain incrementations and changes in these perceptual responses, which must be highly correlated with the maturing of the infant's social make-up.

At 4 weeks of age, the infant's facial expression is for the most part vacant and detached, but under the conditions of the examination it was found that large distant objects like the window and the lights were not fixated as frequently as the examiner's face, even though the infant's countenance was itself suggestive of indifference. Under social stimulation, however, there may be slight increase of mouthing movements, and head fixation in the mid line may be very momentarily prolonged even in the 4 weeks-old infant. The examiner makes a social approach by bending over the infant, nodding, and "talking" to him. At 6 weeks, the face of the infant is less impassive, and by social approach the examiner elicited facial brightening in over half of the infants. At this age it is always possible to secure regard; even "smiling" was sometimes observed.

At 8 weeks, the facial expression is decidedly more alert, smiling is practically universal, and the examiner receives intent and prolonged regard. Responsiveness to the examiner's social approach is characteristically brief and delayed, but occurs with patterned definiteness. The infant of 8 weeks seems already to have attained a definite personal status in the domestic circle. His social reactiveness expresses itself immediately or, more often, after an initial period of sobering during which there is, for 15 seconds or more, a reduction of activity, followed by increased activity. This increased activity includes leg movements, arm thrusts, increased vocalizations (sometimes melodious cooing), and increased respiration. The regard shows a certain partiality for the examiner's face. The infant's eyes follow the moving examiner and the infant may even extend the head back to keep the examiner in view. When the examiner disappears, a brief reaction suggestive of searching (if not of disappointment!) ensues, but the infant rarely rediscovers the examiner at once.

At 12 weeks social responses are more prolonged, more intent, and more readily elicited. The examiner does not need to come into the direct field of vision to secure regard. The infant perceives him in the periphery. Responsive smiling is frequently immediate. Characteristically there is a prompt increase in facial as well as general activity. This activity includes mouthing, accelerated respiration, increased activity of the head and upper back. The general excitement may also result in increased kicking of the legs. Smiles occur in rapid succession. The infant's regard seems to be more sober during the inspection of objects than during inspection of the examiner. Whereas the 8 weeks-old infant easily lost sight of the examiner, the 12 weeks-old infant readily rediscovers him. The whole behavior picture, therefore, is marked by definite incrementations in the intensity, amount, immediacy, and possibly also the depth of the reactions.

Even though we have no precise unit for the measurement of such incrementations, they indicate that a growth process is molding the patterns of social behavior in a manner comparable to the morphogenesis of less personal forms of behavior. We cannot describe the affective accompaniments of the perception of persons, yet it seems very evident that these accompaniments are different from those which prevail in more impersonal perceptual situations. Persons are perceived in a different manner from things. A difference is suggested by the percentages for the two contrasting items *Knows mother* and *Anticipates feeding on sight of food*. At 12 and at 16 weeks, the recognition responses for the mother occur with frequencies of 81 per cent and 92 per cent, respectively, as opposed to 42 per cent and 68 per cent, respectively, for the food.

When the infant is somewhat more advanced, familiars are perceived differently from strangers. The discrimination between the parent and the stranger probably depends primarily upon both visual and emotional factors. It is very difficult on the basis of our present knowledge to distinguish the developmental from the purely temperamental aspects. By nature some infants are more sensitive to strangers than others.

At 12 weeks and at 16 weeks, eight or nine infants out of ten are said to "know" their mothers. As early as 12 weeks one-third, and as early as 16 weeks over one-half, of the infants were reported to sober on the sight of strangers. This sobering is interpreted as a discriminative response which does not necessarily mean withdrawal or apprehension. As a matter of fact, 80 per cent of the infants at 16 weeks, and from 50 to 60 per cent of the infants at 20, 24, and 28 weeks, accept strangers with alacrity or friendliness. At these ages there are relatively few children who positively withdraw from strangers. But at 32 and 36 weeks, and again at 44 and at 48 weeks, from 42 to 48 per cent of the children were reported to exhibit definite withdrawing responses, including more drastic sobering in the presence of strangers. It is a common observation that the infant will perform nursery tricks for the mother which he will not perform for a stranger who uses similar technique and persuasion to induce the behavior. This suggests the presence of discriminative factors.

In general it appears that the infant is relatively self-contained and unapprehensive in the presence of strangers up to the age of 40 weeks, subject of course to significant individual variations. Our observations of the deportment of children in the examining room and in the photographic dome indicate that approximately one-fourth of the children showed some dependence upon the mother during the period of the examination at 44, 48, and 52 weeks of age. They tolerated only partial separation and preferred to have the mother at least in the margin of regard. In diminishing order the following degrees of independence may be differentiated: (1) the infant who nonchalantly tolerates separation; (2) the infant who tolerates separation but needs or prefers the occasional reassurance of a brief sight of his mother; (3) the infant who needs recurrent and more prolonged sight of his mother; (4) the infant who demands that the mother be constantly in his range of vision; (5) the infant who needs to feel the contact of her supporting hands.

These differences are of course subject to temperamental factors and fluctuating conditions. They are, however, also influenced in a broad way by maturity factors. Such differences in dependence and independence reflect themselves in the play habits and play opportunities of the infants.

Outstanding normative trends in play behavior may now be briefly noted. From 13 to 47 per cent of the infants from 4 to 12 weeks of age were picked up and played with at home while held in the mother's arms. Playing in the crib was reported as universal at 4 weeks with decreases to 10 per cent at 48 weeks and to 8 per cent at 56 weeks. At 8 weeks, the spontaneous activity in the crib results in kicking off the blankets in 85 per cent of the children. Playing in the carriage was reported with greatest frequency at 20 weeks and at 24 weeks (67 per cent and 84 per cent). Play in the high chair was not mentioned with any frequency until the age of 28 weeks (52 per cent). Some infants (about one in ten at this age) were placed in a domestic swing instead of a high chair. From 44 weeks on about one-third of the infants were reported to play in the pen. Floor play became most prominent at 56 weeks (75 per cent). One-third of the children used a kiddy car or a similar toy at 44 weeks and at 48 weeks. If we combine the kiddy car, pen, and floor play, we find that this item reaches a normative frequency at 40 weeks with an increasing trend thereafter.

Seventy-one per cent or more of the children were reported to have two or more toys at all ages from 20 weeks onward. Seventy-five per cent could boast a rattle at 16 weeks, 93 per cent at 20 weeks, and 100 per cent at 24 weeks. This ancient toy was prominent until the age of 40 weeks, when (by mothers' reports) less than one-third of the children continued to play with the rattle. Playing with paper was most characteristic of 20 and 24 weeks. Play with the spoon and with a clothespin was most characteristic at 32 weeks. Dolls and animal toys did not come strongly into the picture until 24 weeks of age, when 70 per cent of the normative infants were in possession of such a toy.

These selected percentages afford some picture of the general trends in regard to play opportunities and play activities. It would be futile to attempt to make a thorough-going distinction between self-initiated play and social play, because under the natural conditions of domestic life the individual and induced aspects are in a state of constant fluctuation and alternation. Merely to receive a toy from the parent becomes a social experience as soon as the infant even in a vague manner identifies the mother as the source of the satisfactions which he gets from the toy.

Toy deprivation also reacts to build up percepts of the social world. Eliciting the attention of others is a fairly objective and significant bit of social behavior, particularly when the method is vocal. For example, a child may cough, look at his mother, and cough again until she looks at him. Behavior of this type was reported in one-fourth of the normative infants at 44 and at 48 weeks and in one-half at 52 and at 56 weeks. Such behavior is more primitive than pointing to an object, saying "See," or walking to the mother and tugging at her dress to attract attention.

Many things of social import may happen when the infant has been playing preoccupiedly with his toy: he may lose it; the parent may restore it to him; the parent may intervene to assist him in its manipulation, or may set up some informal game of give and take; or the toy may be snatched from him. Many things, quite trivial when considered individually, happen; but they happen so often from day to day and in such varying contexts that the infant finds in them ample materials and points of departure for building up a growing system of "social" percepts. The developmental mechanism for such percepts is essentially comparable to that which governs the perceptual organization of his physical environment.

In many respects the most important situations which affect the social reactions of the infant are those which occur day in and day out in connection with bathing, cleansing, feeding, elimination, sleep. These situations were beyond the scope of the normative study, but by means of interview it was possible to gather data which reveal developmental trends in the routine of the infant's behavior day. The changes in routine carry many implications concerning the social as well as physical maturity of the infant.

One consistent growth change related to the lengthening of the wakeful periods and the correlated lessening of the number of waking-sleeping periods. There are interesting differences between boy and girl infants which will not be considered here. The average number of hours awake during 24 hours rises steadily from 4.36 hours at 4 weeks to 10.46 hours at 56 weeks. The average number of hours in the longest waking period likewise rises from 1.93 hours at 4 weeks to 5.76 hours at 56 weeks. The number of sleeping periods in 24 hours fell from an average of 6.56 at 4 weeks to 2.78 at 56 weeks.

The feeding habits of the infant disclose similar developmental changes. At 4 weeks nine children out of ten had a night feeding; at 56 weeks approximately one child out of ten had such a feeding. The figures decline with much regularity. At 28 weeks two-thirds of the children had a night feeding; at 44 weeks only one-third of the children had such a feeding. The number of night feedings is ordinarily only one or two. At 4 weeks two-thirds of the children had two night feedings and at 28 weeks only one-quarter of the children had two night feedings. From 32 through 56 weeks the number who had two night feedings varied from 0 to 7 per cent. The practice of a single night feeding, however, is found at all age levels. It occurs in from 7 to 11 per cent of the children from 4 through 12 weeks of age; thereafter the proportion rises from 20 to 86 per cent.

Breast feeding occurred at all ages except 56 weeks with a frequency of 65 per cent at 4 weeks, declining to 41 per cent at 32 weeks and to 5 per cent at 52 weeks. At 4 weeks nearly half of the infants were breast fed only. From 6 to 36 weeks from one-quarter to one-third of the children were entirely breast fed. The number of children who were fed only by bottle rose from 36 per cent at 4 weeks to 73 per cent at 56 weeks.

As the infants grow older the feeding situation involves an increasing array of social factors. The use of the spoon and cup creates mixed patterns of dependence and independence. The spoon first comes into the behavior picture at the age of 6 weeks, when 4 per cent of the children were fed with the spoon; at 12 weeks 12 per cent were so fed, and at 16 weeks 35 per cent. From 20 weeks through 56 weeks, this percentage rose from 59 to 98 per cent. The cup does not come into the behavior scene in the normative group until the age of 24 weeks (4 per cent). At 28 weeks one-eighth, at 44 weeks one-third, at 48 weeks one-half of the infants, and at 56 weeks two-thirds of the infants were fed with the cup. Cod-liver oil and orange juice were fed at all ages. Cod-liver oil figured with highest frequency at 20 weeks (72 per cent), and orange juice with highest frequency at 12 weeks (92 per cent). Cereal was first fed at 12 weeks (4 per cent) and became a characteristic feature of the diet at 24 weeks and later (from 59 per cent to 93 per cent).

Regular training in toilet habits was reported as early as 12 weeks (3 per cent). At 32 weeks 59 per cent, at 56 weeks 90 per cent of the infants were reported to have regular toilet training. At the latter age about one-half of the infants had attained bowel control.

The foregoing figures are offered without comment. In specific detail and in incidence, the patterns of domestic behavior vary widely with temperamental and socializing factors. Infants do not respond equally to the age-old forces of domestication. Moreover, the premium which is placed on self-help varies greatly in different homes. The normative percentages, however, suggest anew that the patterns of domestic behavior are also governed by developmental factors which determine the infant's capacity to profit by experience and to achieve independence.

The degree and elaborateness of the infant's sociality are primarily a function of the perceptual maturity of the infant. The nature of these maturity factors has already been indicated in previous discussions of various normative situations including language. Almost half of the infants at 32 weeks definitely adjust to words, and at the age of 36 weeks two-thirds or more of the infants so adjust. This item, although based on mothers' reports, is a reliable indicator of the social status of the child. It is not assumed that the infant "understands" any given word, but he does react responsively to the word as a cue in a social situation. Adjustment to commands is not reported with normative frequency until the age of 44 weeks (55 per cent). At 52 weeks, 73 per cent of the children adjust to commands. Responses to inhibitory words like "No! No!" rise to near normative frequency at 44 weeks (45 per cent) and to 52 per cent at 52 weeks. The normative percentages with regard to nursery games supply further indication of the social and learning capacities of the child. At 40 weeks 53 per cent respond with appropriate gesture to "Bye-bye"; at 44 weeks 26 per cent, and at 52 weeks 34 per cent, respond to the nursery game "How big is the baby?" Pat-a-cake was reported in 42 per cent at 44 weeks, in 50 per cent at 52 weeks. Peeka-boo rises to its highest percentage, 25 per cent, at 52 weeks.

Although these percentages are merely suggestive, they indicate that the social docility of the child comes into marked prominence at about the age of 40 weeks, when the child displays increasing susceptibility to words, to gestures, to demonstrations. This susceptibility has been analyzed in considerable detail in connection with the paper and crayon, performance box, ball play, and mirror situations. These situations have much social content and the reader may well refer to their discussion for an outline of factors which fundamentally determine the patterning of social behavior. Although the mirror situation does not cast any positive light on the nature of perception of other persons, it does indicate concretely the developmental factors which are at work and which limit such perception. The ball play situation instructively reminds us that the infant's social behavior is delimited by his sensorimotor abilities in the same way that his manipulative behavior is so limited.

The specific adaptive responses to a situation may be inferior to the underlying social attitude of the infant. Social orientation on an affective plane may be slightly in advance of his overt social acts. For example, his responsive behavior in the ball play situation at 44 weeks is very rudimentary. No real ball play can be elicited, and yet the infant looks regardfully in the direction of the examiner and shows pleasurable reactions which indicate that on an emotional level at least the infant is joining in the game with enjoyment. Full motor participation will complete the cycle of his adjustment. Such is the general mechanism of his social development throughout the first year of life.

We do not gain the impression that this social development is radically dependent upon the emergence of a series of differentiated instincts. Pervasive general propensities, more or less unique for each infant, are present from birth. The infant seems to be governed by these propensities, which do not greatly alter in character as he grows older but which are so basic that they constantly press him into the social environment. In a developmental sense one may say without exaggeration that the infant is a social individual at 4 weeks as well as at 40 weeks, even though from an adult point of view he has so much more social stature at the latter age. Not only through toys and socialized nursery games, but through feeding, bathing, dressing, cleansing, toilet, and the countless, ceaseless ministrations of domestic life, he constantly incorporates through growth processes a vast, intricate web of anticipations. These anticipations, negative and positive, both constitute and determine the patterning of his social behavior.

CHAPTER FOUR

THE ONTOGENETIC PATTERNING OF BEHAVIOR

The Early Growth Cycle and the Correlation of Behavior Forms

§38. THE EARLY LIFE CYCLE

INFANT behavior grows with such swiftness and profusion that it is almost impossible to bring the multifarious phenomena into a single view. To elucidate the richness and the nature of early mental growth, it has been necessary to give consideration to the specific detail of individual patterns. But these patterns in all their multiplicity assume correlations and sequences which are themselves patterned. To envisage this general patterning of correlated patterns, we must retreat from the foreground of detail and let our attention travel down into the full vista of the early life cycle.

The vanishing point of this vista is the germinal stage in the growth of the individual. The *germinal stage* begins with conception and continues about a week. In this period, the fertilized ovum, or zygote, transforms into a blastula, a minute globular sac, with an embryonic area.

The *embryonic stage*, about six weeks in duration, begins with the appearance of a defined embryo in this area. The embryonic cells multiply and differentiate into groups which transform into the fundamental organs and structures of the fetus.

The *fetal stage* extends from approximately 7 weeks to 40 weeks. With birth the fetus becomes a neonate.

The *neonatal stage* lasts about 4 weeks. The remainder of the first year of postnatal life may be conveniently subdivided into four trimesters, or quarters. The almanac for this total prenatal and postnatal span of 23 lunar months follows. An inspection of this almanac will suggest that the younger the organism the greater the developmental value of a given unit of time. In a broad way this holds alike for physical and for mental growth.

Age	Developmental Periods

Prenatal weeks
0   *Germinal* (zygote and blastula)
1   *Embryonic* (embryo at 4 weeks, approximate length 2.5 mm.)
7   *Fetal* (fetus at 7 weeks, approximate length 19 mm.)
40 BIRTH
Postnatal weeks
0   *Neonatal* (newborn infant measures approximately 52 cm.)
4   *First Quarter* (4 weeks infant measures approximately 55 cm.)
16 *Second Quarter* (16 weeks infant measures 63 cm.)
28 *Third Quarter* (28 weeks infant measures 68 cm.)
40 *Fourth Quarter* (40 weeks infant measures 72 cm.)
52 *First Birthday* (52 weeks infant measures 76 cm.)

The foregoing frame of reference may be used to bring the whole scope of behavior development into a unitary focus. For rapid summary we shall consider four distinguishable areas or spheres of behavior, namely: (1) Posture and Locomotion; (2) Prehension and Manipulation; (3) Perceptual and Adaptive Behavior; (4) Social and Language Behavior.

If we are to bring the developmental events into compact view, we must sacrifice precision of detail for emphasis of trend. The ontogenetic trend of the behavior will be sketchily traced through the succession of age zones beginning with the embryonic period.* Incidental comments will be added to stress the continuity of behavior growth and to show the past and future implications of immature stages.

§39. The Growth of Posture and Locomotion

Prenatal and Neonatal Period. At the end of the first lunar month after fertilization when the embryo is about 2.5 mm. in length, the heart is already beating, and muscle tissue has begun to form. In the early organization of the axial and limb musculature we look for the first evidence of postural behavior. In two

* We have especially drawn on the following references in the discussion of prenatal and circumnatal aspects of behavior:
COGHILL, G. E., The early development of behavior in Amblystoma and in man. *Archives of Neurology and Psychiatry*, vol. 21, pp. 989–1009, 1929.
CARMICHAEL, LEONARD, Origin and prenatal growth of behavior, Chap. II, *A Handbook of Child Psychology* (2nd ed., Carl Murchison, editor), Worcester, Mass.: Clark University Press, 1933.
PRATT, KARL C.: *The neonate*, Chap. III, *A Handbook of Child Psychology.*
See also: GESELL, A., *Infancy and Human Growth*, Chap. XV, (pp. 299–333).
———, The mental growth of prematurely born infants. *Journal of Pediatrics*, vol. 2, no. 6, pp. 676–680, 1933.

more weeks, in an embryo 20 mm. long, this musculature may be sufficiently advanced to produce slow back-and-forth movements of arms and legs.

At the second lunar month, when the embryo has become a fetus and attained a length of about 30 mm., spontaneous worm-like movements of the arms, legs, and trunk have been observed. To what extent these movements are determined by neural activation is not known. Soon after this, the vestibular apparatus is anatomically well developed and mediates labyrinth reflexes which should be counted among the early manifestations of postural behavior. The fetus lives in a fluid medium and Minkowski suggests that it has use for an equilibrium function.

Between 10 weeks and 20 weeks many movements of a postural character occur: the trunk curves and straightens; legs and arms flex, extend, and rotate; the head moves from side to side, and up and down. Under the conditions of observation, these movements often assume a diffuse and uncoordinated character; but Coghill properly stresses the fact that the movements also show true coordination. For example, as early as the tenth week stimulation of one limb caused a response of *both* limbs. Even earlier, both legs may move in association with mouth movements. Both legs also participate in the eyelid reflex.

At the third lunar month shoulders move with flexure of the trunk, neck, and limbs. Such simultaneity of action in various components denotes coordination and strongly suggests an underlying general pattern of neuromuscular organization, which involves the entire body and its appendages.

At the fourth and fifth lunar months stimulation of one foot results in flexion of the corresponding leg and extension of the contralateral leg. Turning the head to one side frequently causes movement of the arm on that side. Moreover, when this postural attitude is once initiated, it tends to maintain itself tonically, perhaps due to the proprioceptor sensibility of the neck. Here we glimpse more than an adumbration of the tonic neck reflex. We see its first ontogenetic lineaments.

Closely related is the diagonal reflex. Stimulation of one foot evokes a reaction in the opposite hand. This is in the nature of a "trot" reflex, which brings it emphatically enough into the category of locomotion. It might also be called a "swimming" reflex, for the fetus lives a liquid life. But ontogenetically it is more aptly a trot reflex, for it undoubtedly represents the fetal framework for the mechanisms of escape, crawling, and creeping, to say nothing of walking, toddling, and running. From a mechanical or engineering standpoint, alternating lateral—contralateral reaction is one of the most fundamental features of man's make-up. The foundations for such reactions are laid early. They are laid before the prenatal period is half over.

Rhythmic timing of movements of the extremities probably is not established until the latter half of the fetal period. Yet lashing movements have been observed as early as the twenty-fourth postconception week. Arm thrashing of a windmill type is a prominent neonatal response.

The plantar "reflex" deserves brief mention because mechanically, and in a measure morphogenetically, it concerns standing and stepping components essential to walking. The response to plantar stimulation is so variable that the reflex concept should not be applied too strictly. When the sole of the fetal foot at the age of 10 weeks is stimulated, the response is extension of the leg and dorsal flexion of the foot. At a slightly later age the foot also rotates and the toes flex plantar-wise; at a yet later age the great toe extends. At birth there is marked extension of the great toe with extension and fanning of the other toes, a Babinski type of response which disappears at the age of walking.

The postural activity of the fetus is, of course, much restricted by physical confinements. His very attitudes are in a measure molded by the conformation of the uterine walls, and the postural attitudes of the newborn infant are accordingly reminiscent of the womb. The extremities of the neonate are markedly flexed and this, together with a persisting rounding of the back, causes him to roll to his side when placed supine. The rolling is quite involuntary. His rounded back was well adapted to the uterus but makes a poor presenting surface for a flat bed. Accordingly, he rolls from gravity rather than innervation. Likewise, the marked flexion of the legs elevates the pelvis when he lies prone. Orthopedically he still is better adapted for a concave bed. In full sleep, however, the trunk straightens; he lies on the flat of his back and his arms assume a symmetrical averted position, semiflexed and outwardly rotated.

The typical postural attitude of the quiescent neonate, even at one week, is that of the tonic neck reflex, in which the head and, in part, the trunk rotate to one side, the arm of the opposite side flexing sharply, bringing the hand near the occiput. One gains the impression that even this postural reaction is an expanded version of a bodily attitude which was well suited to the confinements of the uterus. It is quite conceivable that the fetus makes many active as well as passive postural adjustments to his surroundings. Quickening movements are not necessarily mere leg movements but may be interpreted as active postural reactions under partial proprioceptor control. It is therefore not surprising that the tonic neck reflex pattern of the neonate is foreshadowed in the early fetal period. Nor is it surprising that this fundamental reflex is conspicuous until the sixteenth postnatal week. Indeed it never disappears, for it remains an implicit or active component of numerous forms of gesture, locomotion, and bodily control.

The First Quarter (4 *to* 12 *weeks*).   The supine position is the accustomed position throughout this period. Both in sleeping and in waking hours it is the posture of preference and necessity. The infant cannot, even if he would, reinstate the curled-up attitude of his uterine existence. Nor can he, even if he would, escape the confinements of his crib. At 12 weeks he may roll the pelvis; as a rule, he cannot roll his entire body even to the side; he may kick his legs with sufficient energy to propel him a bit headward; but beyond this he has no capacity for locomotion.

Even when he is placed in the prone position he makes no advance by the crawl-like flexion of his legs. He rests haplessly on knees, abdomen, chest, and head. At 12 weeks he rears his head and sustains a part of his foreward weight on his forearms.

When he is held horizontally in ventral suspension, he extends his head and for a moment does not allow it to droop. But if he is held in a sitting position, his head sags, or at best is held only bobbingly erect. His back is markedly rounded and relatively flaccid as he sits, supported. Held in the standing position, his head at 12 weeks sets forward but may remain steadily erect. His legs support no weight and offer but slight resistance to the platform (4 to 8 weeks); his toes flex.

The outstanding, indeed the dominating, postural characteristic of this period is the tonic neck reflex attitude. The infant maintains this attitude more or less completely throughout his waking life. For twelve weeks his head remains prevailingly rotated to one side, and his hands are predominantly closed. But he is no automaton. During the first trimester the tonic neck reflex attitude becomes progressively less rigid and less stereotyped. It fluctuates and adapts to changing stimuli, internal and external. With the beginning of the second trimester, it almost dissolves out of the behavior picture, because the new versatility of head and arms masks or replaces the earlier patterns. The tonic neck reflex posture, using the term somewhat loosely, denotes a general configuration of head, trunk, and arm attitude. This attitude expresses a necessary morphogenetic stage in the primary organization of closely identified elements in perceptual, postural, and locomotor behavior.

The Second Quarter (16 to 24 weeks). Sixteen weeks marks many transitions. The infant in the second quarter becomes a propped-up as well as a supine individual. His head shows only slight or initial lag when he is pulled to the sitting position. He now holds his head set forward, steady, and erect. He relishes the new orientation to his physical and social world. His eyes widen, his pulse and breath quicken at the moment of translation from horizontal to a more or less precarious perpendicular. His trunk assumes more tonus and uprightness; his supported body holds relatively erect (at 20 and 24 weeks). As he leans forward he erects his head, and at 24 weeks he can even sit a moment unsupported in this leaning attitude, using his own hand as a stabilizer. Though rather immobile in this leaning stance, he turns his head freely when seated in a chair.

When placed prone he rears his head well aloft and lifts the upper chest from the platform, sustaining part of his weight on the forearms; but prone locomotion is still well in the future, even though he can lift his plantigrade hand at 16 weeks.

In the supported standing position he reveals new powers. He holds his head steadily erect (16 weeks), extends his legs recurrently, and momentarily sustains a large fraction of his weight. He enjoys placement in the standing position.

In the supine position he shows important postural gains. He can roll to the side (16 weeks). He lifts his head from the platform. His head rotates freely from side to side and favors the mid rather than the side position. His hands, which formerly were sundered from each other by his postural limitations, now contact and engage in the median plane and his arms thrust out in vertical as well as lateral directions. These increments of mobility in the posturing of head, trunk, and arms signify much for the general organization of his behavior patterns and bring him closer to independent balance and locomotion.

The Third Quarter (28 to 36 weeks). In this period the supine position is still further outgrown and the infant attains the ability to sit alone for several minutes. He erects himself unaided when leaning forward (36 weeks). He thus reaches the halfway station on his developmental journey toward the upright position.

He is more tolerant of the prone position. When placed prone he erects his head completely. He sustains an increased proportion of weight on his arms and lifts the chest farther from the platform.

In the standing position he now supports his entire weight (32) and rises to his toes (36 weeks).

When supine, he can grasp his toes, he can roll to prone and gain the sitting position independently or with only slight assistance.

From the standpoint of postural self-dependence, this is a transitional period. For the most part he still needs props, safeguards, and help; but he is improving his equilibrium and will manifest a considerable degree of motor independence in the next period.

The Fourth Quarter (40 to 52 weeks). This period is distinguished by the assumption of erect posture. This important human trait came late in the history of the race. Ontogenetically it comes with relative precocity but it requires preparatory stages which reach back even into the uterine period.

The supine attitude is in the fourth quarter so far outgrown that it is almost obnoxious to the wide-awake infant. But for a time it is not altogether clear whether he is destined to become a quadrupedal or a bipedal creature.

Sitting is well mastered. He can maintain balance even when he turns to the side, and can sustain balance for prolonged periods. He rarely falls while sitting. He can pivot, adapting his sitting orientation to acquire an accessible object. He can reorient his posture, changing from sitting to prone and vice versa.

In the prone position he usually assumes a creeping stance, supporting his torso on hands and knees. Not infrequently he assumes a full plantigrade stance, resting on soles as well as palms. Although knees were not evolved to serve for prone progression, they are so used and sometimes with amazing alacrity.

However, they were evolved to facilitate shifts of posture and ontogentically the more significant use of the knees is as fulcrums for the assumption of the upright attitude. Gravity and a hoary ancestry conspire against the attainment of this attitude; but during the infantile 40's, the knees are brought into heavy requisition. With or without assistance the infant pulls himself to a standing position. He stands holding the rail on which he pulls; a little later (56 weeks) he stands independently. He cruises or walks using such support, and again a little later he walks independently. The adult hands which had to aid his balance at 40 weeks are now withdrawn. He is nearer man's estate than he was at birth, when a reflexogenous kind of supine posture was the limit of his postural capacity.

§40. PREHENSION AND MANIPULATION

Prenatal and Neonatal Period. Prehension as such has no place in the economy of embryo and fetus; but the first chapters in the ontogenetic history of prehension none the less lie in the prenatal period. Even postnatally the act of prehension is a product of slow growth; it does not appear in its perfected form until the very end of the first year of life. It is the result of a long and finally subtle coordination of postural, perceptual, and grasping mechanisms. These mechanisms are refined through progressive individuations and systematizations of specific patterns. The patterns arise out of a total system to which they remain subsidiary. For this reason even the primitive arm and trunk responses of embryo and fetus are significant in the ontogenetic patterning of prehension.

Limb buds appear in the embryo as early as 3 weeks; but not until about the fortieth postnatal week are the limbs serviceable for locomotion. The anterior limbs must be organized for purposes of prehension and manipulation, but their phyletic relationship to the ancient uses of swimming and of quadrupedal progression are constantly suggested in the early patterns of reaction. In interpreting these early patterns it is not always possible to say whether they are prelocomotor or preprehensory in their developmental significance. The fetus and infant do not recapitulate these behavior patterns in a ritualistic manner; but, since locomotion and prehension are both attained through a process of progressive individuation, the primitive reactions of fetus and infant are not to be regarded as relics of the past but as necessary morphogenetic stages. These stages are never fully transcended but supply a contribution and a potentiality in the growing repertoire of the organism.

Prehension emerges out of posture. Prehension essentially is a focalization of posture for purposes of appropriation. Fetal arm movements occur in close relationship with reactions of the axial musculature. As early as the tenth prenatal week symmetric movements of arms, legs, and shoulders occur in a generalized way after a jarring stimulus. At the eleventh week arm adduction and rotation occur on touching the palm. The shoulders typically participate in these movements; there is relatively little independent activity at the digital, wrist, and elbow joints. Even in the neonate (a week or two old) the arm behaves somewhat like a flipper. Its movements are stereotyped and restricted. Characteristically there is no movement at the elbow without movement at the shoulder, and often there is movement at the shoulder without at the elbow. The distal segments are so immature that the hand remains fisted. The knuckles of this fisted hand often find the mouth. Sucking then ensues. The neonate appropriates by mouth; but not by hand. Directed manual prehension does not occur until the elbow and distal segments acquire, through maturation, more mobility and until the eyes coordinate with the hands in the act of appropriation.

Here again the ontogenetic significance of the tonic neck reflex confronts us. Does not this postural attitude prepare the way for hand inspection which is such an important stage on the pathway toward prehension? Whether considered mechanistically or teleologically, the prevalence of the tonic neck reflex attitude during the first four postnatal months favors (or denotes!) the coordination of eye and hand. The infant lies with face directed toward an extended arm. His gaze at first has no relation to the hand or to the arm; but he is becoming predisposed to look at least in the general direction of any activity he may initiate. His arm brushes time and again across his field of vision. His retinal receptors are sufficiently sensitized to take vague note of the movement. Later, at 10 or 12 weeks, he takes defined, even transfixed, note of forearm or hand. It is a most important ontogenetic step in that coordination of eye and hand which leads to prehension. It would not augur well should he persist in merely mouthing his hand rather than looking at it.

Although developmental organization procedes in general from fundamental to accessory muscles and from proximal to distal segments, there are exceptions or pseudo-exceptions to the rule. For example, as early as the twelfth prenatal week conjoint spontaneous movements of the fingers and trembling of the thumb have been observed. Flexion of the fingers and a grasping reflex of the toes have been elicited at about this age. To what extent such response is due to cutaneous or to deep muscle stimulation is not known.

At about 26 weeks the fetus manifests an energetic grasp in response to pressure applied to the palm. When the pressure is only lightly applied to the skin, the response is more variable and inconstant. The newborn infant has, therefore, been prepared *in utero* for his prodigious capacity to take grasp-hold of a rod and to suspend his own weight for several or many seconds.

A tonic type of grasp is highly characteristic of the neonate. His hands are predominantly fisted and it takes prying force to uncurl his tight fingers. Contact of the back of his fingers does not result in hand opening though it may result in increased activity. He can grasp reflexly; he cannot yet prehend.

The First Quarter (4 to 12 weeks). During this period the infant lies supine in both his sleeping hours and waking intervals. If by prehension we mean the visual detection of an object, a consequent approach upon it, culminating in a grasp, then the infant at these ages lacks all power of prehension. But he performs in snatches and in partial synergy many acts which belong to the later coordinated patterns of prehension. He clenches his hand if an object like the rattle is placed within the palm. He holds it passively or actively, sometimes for a prolonged interval, though usually without visual fixation. Eye and hand in the prehensory sense are meagerly coordinated. Often, particularly at 4 to 8 weeks, he drops the object speedily, his hands opening and closing willynilly. However, when an object is once in hand at 12 weeks, he clenches it repeatedly as though reacting to the dermal stimulus. When an object is brought to the palm or lightly against the back of his flexed fingers, he often responds by opening the hand (at 12 weeks). This is genetically a significant reaction, for, although it does not result in seizure, it is an anticipatory adjustment to grasp. At 20 weeks this adjustment is so closely associated with approach that even a slight tactile cue induces movement toward the stimulus and successful grasp.

In the first trimester the infant does not, at any age, characteristically regard an object (even a rattle) while it is held in his own hand. He may fasten on an object with his eyes; he may fasten it in his grip; but he does not automatically and simultaneously fasten with both hand and eyes. He is at the brink of this achievement, for at 12 weeks he gives sustained regard to his empty hand. It is the grosser components of prehension and particularly those of approach which are undergoing developmental change. His shoulders are becoming more mobile, his elbows more flexible.

This results in diagonal and near vertical pumping movements of the arms, movements which have little obvious import for prehension but which are ontogentically and mechanically necessary for later acts of closing-in and reaching. The hands are drawing together and even at 12 weeks they may sometimes contact at the mid line, but they cling close to the chest. True prehension requires a perfection in these orientational adjustments of trunk, shoulder, upper arm, forearm. Hand and digits are merely accessory instruments for grasping and even they are governed by the synergic control of the larger segments of the prehensory limb. Approach is genetically the oldest and remains the most important aspect of prehension. The basis for visually directed approach is ontogenetically patterned during the first twelve weeks.

The Second Quarter (16 *to* 24 *weeks*).   In this period elementary prehension is achieved. The fourth lunar month clearly marks the transition. The 16 weeks infant increases his arm activity on mere sight of the rattle. He gives much more visual attention to the rattle while he holds it and he brings his free hand toward the mid-plane. These behavior patterns forerun definite approach movements on visual cue. At 20 weeks, both in supine and in sitting situations, the infant makes a back-hand fling or a corralling approach upon a visually fixated object. Typically he approaches the dangling ring with both hands, and manages to grasp it. He contacts a cube on the table. Actual grasp of objects on the table, like the cube and bell, is not characteristic until 24 weeks. Tactile cue and favorable proximity are rather necessary for grasp at 20 weeks, but at 24 weeks a visual cue suffices. The infant promptly approaches the cube on sight, lifts it, mouths it, and even gives heed to and grasps a second cube. His approach movements are somewhat atactic; he raises his hand, thrusts, lowers, and slides it more or less by shifts; the movements are not so fluently blended as at 28 weeks. Sometimes they are ineffectual. The hand is directed to come pronately, palmar-wise over the cube. Often the cube is touched without immediate grasp and the free hand frequently comes in to participate.

The Third Quarter (28 *to* 36 *weeks*).   Twenty-eight weeks marks the transition to more advanced modes of prehension and refinements of grasp. Approach becomes more unilateral, more direct, less pronate, the hand tilts slightly just prior to grasp and the thumb begins to participate more firmly in the grip on objects. The infant is so adept that he retains one cube as a second is presented, makes approach upon a third, and picks up two or three cubes in the massed cube situation. He transfers an object from one hand to another and retransfers with relative ease if the object is not too small.

The improvements in the technique of prehension at 28 weeks are developmentally very significant but they need further refinement to become adequate for the tasks of fine prehension. The 28 weeks-old infant often grasps a spoon interdigitally, he places his hand rather crudely over a pellet, flexes on it, and usually fails to secure it. He is similarly inept in grasping a string. At 32 weeks he grasps the pellet successfully with increasing use of the thumb. At 36 weeks he brings thumb and index finger together scissors-wise so effectually that not only the beginning but the attainment of elementary thumb opposition may be credited to the third trimester.

The Fourth Quarter (40 to 52 weeks). This period marks the attainment of prehension patterns which closely resemble those of the adult. It is a striking fact that once the infant has reached the level of grasping on sight (24 weeks) it takes him only about a half year to bring his performance near the adult level. He must be under strong impulsions to reach that level, for, although he will sometimes take recourse to primitive methods of grasp and approach to secure a coveted object, it is more characteristic for him to perseveringly employ a developmental innovation in advanced method even at the expense of failure. Immediate efficiency does not seem to be a rule of developmental economy.

For this reason we find the effective scissors grasp gradually replaced by a forceps procedure in which the radial digits are more precisely poised and the ulnar digits increasingly repressed. These refinements are not confined to digits and wrist but involve the trunk and shoulders as well. This testifies to the underlying unity of ontogenetic patterning. Although at early stages the shoulder played a leading role in the execution of prehension, it does not sink out of the mechanism when less primitive components come into prominence.

§41. PERCEPTUAL AND ADAPTIVE BEHAVIOR

Prenatal and Neonatal Period. The sensory life of the prenate is no longer a completely closed book. Numerous observations of prematurely born infants under conditions of both natural and experimental stimulation have demonstrated a wide range of forms and degrees of receptivity. It has been suggested that the motility of the fetus is itself a mode of self-stimulation whereby sensory as well as motor development is served. The interaction of receptivity and response is probably very intimate in fetal life, particularly in the sphere of proprioceptive activity, where even slight movement may stimulate the neuromuscular spindles embedded in the striped musculature and its tendon insertions. Such receptor spindles are extensively found as early as the sixteenth prenatal week. The demonstration of deep tendon reflexes (response of a muscle on percussion) as early as the eleventh week suggests that the proprioceptors play an active role in the prenatal ontogenesis of behavior. The relative darkness, silence, and isolation of the uterus enhance the importance of that role.

Studies of the reflexogenous areas of the skin in both man and animals suggest that cutaneous sensibility is at first especially marked in the oral region and tends to spread somewhat progressively from the head posteriorly. Stroking evokes response earlier than punctiform pressure. Light stimulation may evoke positive and intense stimuli, negative or withdrawing responses. Sensitivity to temperature changes is probably present during the latter half of the gestation period. Sensitivity to pain is more in doubt. Hunger contractions of the stomach, if not hunger pangs, occur. Sensitivity to suffocation may exist although one trend of speculation has insisted that the fetus lives in an hedonic Eden, rudely terminated by the cataclysmic trauma of birth.

Taste buds are present well before the middle of gestation but gustatory experiences must be very limited indeed until after birth. The premature infant, however, is able to distinguish sweet from salt and sour, and shows smell reactions and evidences of a chemical sense. The neural and accessory receptor structures for hearing are well developed before birth but the fetus is probably deaf to ordinary sounds—deaf but not necessarily immune to unusually loud or jarring noise. The visual receptors are not fully developed at birth but again the premature infant proves to be mature enough to distinguish between light and darkness and to react with the pupillary reflex.

In spite of his lack of visual experience, the prenate probably has a rudimentary sense of tactile localization. We have seen a prematurely born infant with a mildly infected eye bring his tiny fist unerringly to the focus of irritation. Such accuracy of aim signifies a form of localization.

The newborn infant is sensitive to variations in light intensities. He reacts to a bright light with iris and eyelids. If the stimulus is very intense this response involves the whole body with a startle reflex. Convergence reflexes are prompt but immature. After the second week he follows an object with eye and with head pursuit. Head pursuit decreases with age, eyes operating more independently. The newborn infant also reacts to loud sounds with a startle reflex. To lesser sounds he may react with eye closure, with changes of respiration and pulse, and extensor reactions of arms, legs, hands, toes, and fingers. Taste reactions are most discriminative for sweet and salt; the reactions are expressed by facial expression, distinctive sucking responses, and by circulation and respiration changes. Sensitiveness to pain stimuli increases definitely in the first week after birth.

The sensory life of the prenate has always been a favorite field for speculation. So little is directly knowable that speculation breeds readily. We cannot even be certain whether, how much, and in what manner the fetus sleeps. If he sleeps, does he waken himself or is he awakened? It is possible that all vegetative functions have an overt rather than submerged status in his psychology. It is probable that kinesthesia and the closely related static senses are a most important aspect of his sensory experience. Postural behavior is a profoundly pervasive feature of his life. This behavior may well be regulated by his proprioceptors long before outside stimuli come to bear upon the cutaneous and retinal receptors. In the postnatal cycle these proprioceptors, so well developed in the prenatal period, continue to assert their influence, but they play a less exclusive role.

The neonate approximately one week of age rarely wakes of his own accord. His major occupations are sleeping, eating, and some fussing. They are not sharply separated and may occur in partial combination. When his eyes are open he usually stares impassively without fixation, without inspection. Sometimes only one eye is open. He moves his eyes coordinately but lapses into strabismus. He does not regard a rattle when presented in the mid-line or when placed in his hand. When a dangling ring is brought into his field of vision he regards it usually after delay and follows it with eye pursuit for a short arc. Hearing responses are not always clear cut. On hearing a bell he may react with a blink or a general start, and if he is active or fussing he promptly becomes quiescent. He may resume crying when the bell ringing ceases.

From an ontogenetic standpoint "perceptivity" and "adaptivity" are closely related concepts. Genetically it is impossible to identify the beginning of "intelligence" unless we trace symptoms of increasing discriminativeness and selectiveness in sensorimotor responses, particularly in the field of visual regard. Perception, apperception, judgment, insight are similar functions and by combining the categories of perceptual and adaptive behavior, the ontogenetic equivalents and prerequisites of "intelligence" become more apparent.

The First Quarter (4 *to* 12 *weeks*).   The 4 weeks infant stares vacantly and detachedly at large masses like windows, ceilings, and adults. The range of his vision—perhaps to his best developmental interests—is narrowly limited by the side position of his head; but within this range he will sometimes pick up visually a small object like a dangling ring. Rarely does he regard an object in the mid-plane; but under social stimulation he may hold his head momentarily in the mid position to gaze transiently at his mother's face. In the next two months he will develop a similar selectivity of regard for the adult hand which comes into his slowly widening range of vision. To say that he is perceptually interested in motion is not clarifying; because it is things which move and through their movements he organizes his perceptual patterns of these things. Three "things" which constitute major nuclear points for organization in the first quarter are the animated adult face, adult hands, and the infant's own hand. Perceptual patterns are groupings of anticipations, and these multiply not only through the cumulative repetitiveness of his environment, but also through the maturationally determined elaborations of his sensorimotor equipment. Through primary growth processes his head becomes more mobile, his eyes make wider and steadier excursions, his arms and hands also gradually become more versatile through basic postural changes, which have already been summarized. These changes play a primary role in the ontogenesis of perceptual behavior. Granting a given receptor mechanism, the development of perceptual behavior depends on the progressive organization of adaptive modes of response. These modes of response show increasing specification, and this specification comes to wear an aspect of judgment and of insight and perspicacity. But from an ontogenetic standpoint the primitive perceptual achievements of the neonate also wear such an aspect.

At 6 weeks the infant still displays in his starey gaze a predilection, though no doubt a more discriminating one, for large objects. But at 8 weeks, thanks to a more diversified neuromusculature, reinforced perhaps by rotundity of skull conformation, he makes rapid, numerous, almost constant shifts of gaze. The staring kind of fixation is now secondary. Such fixation is supplemented by true inspection of the environment. He may even turn his head back to pursue the retreating figure of his mother and show a moment of searching when she vanishes. At 12 weeks he may even shift his regard up and down from the ring to the hand from which the ring dangles.

From the standpoint of behavior ontogenesis, such inspectional behavior represents a remarkable achievement of profound developmental significance. It has no startling prominence in the normative schedules; it makes no dramatic entrance into actual life; it comes with silent surety. It is genetically in direct lineage with more impressive manifestations of perceptual behavior which come late in infancy and which are associated in our own minds with the functioning of intelligence.

This inspectional shifting of the eyes undergoes many refinements and elaborations with growth. Through it are built up familiarities with spatial forms, distances, and qualities. The eyes must "learn" to pursue in horizontal, vertical, and curved directions; they must "learn" to scan the outlines of objects, to halt at corners, to detect depressions, elevations, irregularities. Such subtleties are now beyond the ken of the 8 weeks infant. But in another 8 weeks he will be able to discern a tiny 7 mm. pellet placed before him; and at 40 weeks he will give heed to a small bit of lint and he will be visually, as well as emotionally, sensitive to slight shadings in the facial expression of his mother. The same ontogenetic processes which mold the visual world of the infant doubtless continue to operate throughout childhood and adult years. Tactile and kinesthetic experience contributes richly to this perceptual world, but intrinsic sequences determine the general order in which the infant will become sensitive to the shape and sizes of things. At the end of the first year he will display a significant prior perceptiveness of circularity as opposed to squareness.

The Second Quarter (16 *to* 24 *weeks*).   At 16 and 20 weeks head control is becoming versatile and the nimbleness and range of visual perception are thereby widened; but even at 16 weeks the infant is still given to protracted moments of starey fixation and of passive regard. He retains a perceptual predilection for his own hand. However, he can see a pellet. It is characteristic of him to pay only momentary regard to a cube; but he looks at it recurrently. This recurrency of regard is a significant developmental item which shows the close relationship between sensory, perceptual, and intelligence factors; for recurrence of regard denotes a kind of memory and a projection of attention which is fundamental to adaptive mental processes at a higher level. At 24 weeks, his perception or his attention is so sustained that he regards a cube consistently (that is, with only minor diversions) throughout the situation. But perception still makes demands on him, for he drops the first cube when the second is presented. Not until the third quarter does he retain the first cube while he addresses himself to the second.

The Third Quarter (28 to 36 weeks).   The head became versatile in the previous trimester, the hand becomes versatile in this one. This hand versatility has already been mentioned in connection with the growth of prehension. Here it is important to emphasize that such increased dexterity carries with it many behavior values of perceptual import. The hand is less paw-like, the wrist hinges, the forearm rotates. The tactile sensitivity of the palm and proximal phalanges probably increases, and the proprioceptors of the many joints and muscles of the hand come into fuller play. Cause and effect are so reciprocal that it is useless to ask whether motility or sensibility comes first. But the hand becomes more of an antenna, an organ of palpation as well as of manipulation. It is used more discriminatingly both in approach and in handling. The 28 weeks-old infant, for example, inverts the hand for making approach to the bell; he also uses the handle in lifting the cup; when an object is in hand he tends to transfer it and to rotate it. He is much preoccupied by an object in hand. He even regards a pellet consistently even though he fails to grasp it. Eye and hand now function in very close interaction, each reinforcing the other, each guiding the other.

As it was typical for the 12 weeks infant to inspect surroundings, it is typical for the 28 weeks infant to inspect an object in hand. Both activities involve shifts of visual regard and a correlation of visual and kinesthetic experience. From an adultomorphic point of view, we probably underrate the complexity of the younger infant's perceptual achievements; but it is true that the manipulation of an object with a mobile forearm and a flexible wrist adds greatly to the diversification of experience. The 28 weeks-old infant seizes a cube, senses surface and edges with his grasp, lifts the cube to the mouth, feels its qualities per mouth, withdraws the cube, looks at it on withdrawal as he rotates it, restores it to his mouth, withdraws it and again inspects with rotation, transfers it to the other hand, bangs it, contacts it with the free hand, restores the cube to the mouth, etc. All of this is perceptual behavior; it transpires in a few seconds; it illustrates the ontogenetic method by which perceptions multiply and pattern. Sense organ physiology of the elementary textbook variety tends to oversimplify perception. Perceptual behavior is extraordinarily complicated and it takes time to mature.

This active, manipulatory type of behavior is adaptive as well as perceptual, for it constantly reveals to the infant the physical relationships of things. Banging, for example, entails vision, hearing, tactility, kinesthetics. In its more primitive form "banging" seems to be undiscriminating and crude. But with age it becomes more restrained, less repetitive, and somewhat more exploratory. Perception is not simply reception, but is fused with exploitiveness, which brings it into the realm of adaptive behavior.

The Fourth Quarter (40 *to* 52 *weeks*).   In the second quarter the head, in the third, the hand, and in the fourth, the fingers show an increase of versatility of movement. This is a natural correlate of the proximal-distal trend in the development of perception and of adaptive manipulation. The two important radial digits, forefinger and thumb, acquire a high degree of independence which leads to refinement and precision of response. The extended, prying index finger is outward evidence of the ontogenetic elaboration which is taking place. The 40 weeks infant pokes the pellet, the 44 weeks infant pokes the clapper of the bell, the 48 weeks infant pokes his finger into the small hole of the performance box. Such behavior signifies a progressive perceptual penetration into the third dimension of things.

Since this behavior is so inquisitive in both a visual and a tactile motor sense, it leads to the discovery and the control of relations between things. The infant is less restrictively preoccupied with a single object. He reacts to two. He manifests a new awareness of a something else, a sense of twoness, of container and contained, of top and bottom, of side-by-side, and even of cause and effect. He does not entertain these relationships in the form of concepts or ideas; but on a practical sensorimotor level he perceives and even reinstates the relationships. He also becomes knowingly perceptive of what others do, and in increasing measure, he reduplicates their models of behavior in his own behavior. Indeed, he comes so near to our own methods of practical thinking that now we accord him attributes of intelligence and insight.

But he does not come into possession of these attributes through the emergence of some generalized dynamic function. The method of ontogenesis remains what it was in the fetal and neonatal periods, a continuation of a progressive patterning of innumerable specific modes of response.

The trend and the configuration of this patterning can be best illustrated by behavior items which lend themselves to arrangement on a maturity gradient. At 40 weeks he combines cube and cube or cup and cube; at 44 weeks he hits the cube on the table with one in hand; at 48 weeks he brings a cube over the cup; and at 52 weeks he releases the cube in the cup. Here is the paradigm for endless permutations of combining activity, always closely limited, however, by the attained stage of perceptual organization and of neuromotor equipment.

A few miscellaneous items will recall more concretely the range and variety of his adaptive, combining behavior in the last quarter of the first year. He rings the bell after demonstration (40 weeks); he grasps the string immediately to pull the ring (40 weeks); he dangles the ring by the string (48 weeks); he brings the crayon to bear upon paper (44 weeks); his scribbling response improves with demonstration (52 weeks); he inserts the rod in the performance box spontaneously (48 weeks); he places the round block in the formboard (52 weeks).

All of these adaptive behavior traits could be formulated with emphasis on their perceptual components; and conversely, the development of perceptual behavior could be construed in terms of its adaptivity. We have already noted how performance is influenced by the prehensory mechanisms and how these in turn are dependent on postural development. All these interrelations arise out of the essential unity of ontogenetic patterning.

§42. SOCIAL AND LANGUAGE BEHAVIOR

Prenatal and Neonatal Period. From a biological point of view it is easy to exaggerate the changes which are wrought by the event of birth. The developmental continuities which unite the prenatal and postnatal periods should always be stressed. In the realm of social and language behavior, however, we can only demonstrate antecedents for behavior patterns which belong uniquely to the postnatal period. It is possible that the prenate acquires a few habituations or conditioned responses which have a remote social origin in the life of the mother; and if he is prematurely born he may to a meager, subtle degree respond to social stimulation during the period of his prematurity. But beyond such exceptions the formation of social behavior belongs peculiarly to postnatal infancy.

The newborn infant (1 week) already has the neuromusculature to make facial grimaces and in moments of sneezing and yawning his countenance shows considerable mobility. He is, however, socially deaf and blind to the approach of another person who bends over him and gives him every social provocation to respond. But he is not completely numb, for he seems to soothe when he is picked up and held. This tactile responsiveness must be set down as an early genetic item in the social column. During the neonatal month the infant forms numerous anticipations which arise out of personal care and which therefore have social import. Even at 4 weeks the infant still exhibits characteristics reminiscent of his immaturity at birth. Sneezing, yawning, and startling and spontaneous clonus of the jaws occur with a frequency not observed at later ages.

The First Quarter (4 *to* 12 *weeks*). At 4 weeks he fixates rather readily on a face that confronts him. His own facial activity may subdue or slightly brighten, but the transient perceptual intentness is his chief reaction. At 6 weeks, too, facial expression tends to subdue; regard is more prolonged and the head shows a tendency to shift briefly to the mid position under social stimulation.

At 8 weeks the infant is already a personal individual, even though a rudimentary one, in the family circle. His facial expression is more alert, more animated, more adaptive to other persons, whether these persons stand near or move about. The searching perseveration of the infant when a person suddenly vanishes from his view has already been commented on as a perceptual phenomenon. It is of course also a social phenomenon and that it should assert itself so precociously in relation to the human face is highly significant. Under social stimulation the 8 weeks infant also displays increased general activity, accelerated respiration, and even melodious cooing. Social behavior shows no lag in postnatal ontogenesis. Indeed it shows a certain developmental precocity. It appears that nearly all of his behavior arises in a social matrix.

At 12 weeks social regard is still better defined. Smiles occur in rapid succession, followed by more prolonged, higher pitched vocalization, expiratory *ahs, ehs, uhs,* and even *ums,* gurgling, and chuckling. Such behavior characteristics abundantly testify to the sociality of the infant even in the first quarter of the first year.

The Second Quarter (16 to 24 weeks). During this period the cumulative effects of the infant's daily routine assert themselves in the organization of his social behavior. He comes to "know" his mother in a very elaborate though inarticulate way by virtue of the innumerable expectancies implanted through feeding, bathing, dressing, and toilet, nursery play, and expressions of affection.

In this summary it would serve no purpose to interpret his behavior in terms of drives or generalized dynamic functions. We prefer to stress the structured substance of the infant's social behavior equipment, and this consists of concrete expectancies, patterned predispositions which arise out of the physical and the personal events of his domestic life. The ontogenesis of perceptual behavior and of social behavior is essentially similar. The two fields can be separated only in analysis, for there are socialized ingredients in the infant's perception of his bottle, his mother's hand, his cup, and spoon, and clothes. As the infant's perceptual abilities and experience increase so his social apperception deepens and becomes discriminative.

At 16 weeks the infant sobers at the sight of a stranger. In the next quarter (32 weeks) he may actively withdraw from a stranger. At 16 weeks he turns his head to the voice, an important developmental gain which yields him much socially in a well-constituted home.

During the second quarter the infant completes most of the technical foundation for verbal articulation. In his spontaneous vocalizations he produces the vowels, consonants, and many of the syllables and diphthongs he will later use in speech. He produces many more which, lacking social sanction, will never be crystallized into words.

Although this early phonetic utterance constitutes in a sensorimotor way a complex wealth of behavior patterning, it is only the instrumental or technical aspect of language. More fundamental from the standpoint of ontogenetic patterning is the substructure of behavior mores and of social understanding. Comprehension of postural attitudes, movements, and gesticulations and an intricate web of motorized predispositions, arising out of the situations of everyday life—these are prerequisite to all social exchange, including the use and recognition of spoken words. This comprehension is affective as well as cognitive and lies at the basis of social relations. Social behavior patterning therefore begins with birth and continues unabated throughout infancy. The growth of social and language behavior proceeds by cumulation as well as by differentiation and integration.

The Third Quarter (*28 to 36 weeks*).   In this quarter the spoken word is nearing a defined status in the life of the infant. He himself duplicates a syllable and vocalizes combinations like *dada* at 32 weeks; at 36 weeks he listens to a word and makes some adjustment to it. In the next quarter he will give still more discriminating heed to words, will adjust to a simple learned command at 44 weeks and to inhibitory words at the age of one year.

In the third quarter he widens the range of his acquaintance with persons and shows differentiated social responses to them. He demonstrates increasing discrimination in his social evaluations and unless he is of very hardy temperament he is likely to withdraw from strangers at 32 and at 36 weeks. Through sheer habituation as well as maturity, he steadily increases his "knowledge" of how human beings behave and this is incorporated into the patterns of his own social reactions. He could not be asocial, even if he would.

In a comparative sense, however, the third quarter of life is distinguished by a certain self-containedness. The infant takes great delight in the exercise of his own abilities, without referring this activity to the onlooker. He exploits even a single object for long periods in a highly extrovert manner. If he senses no insecurity or strangeness (and his capacity to do this is a very important social trait) he can be contented with himself and his own devices for long periods.

This self-containedness is a developmental symptom and perhaps a safeguard. For this is the period when zealous adults impute to him a kind or degree of sociality which he lacks, and go to great extreme to teach him highly socialized nursery tricks. If he had a general social instinct of docility he would learn a great many of these household accomplishments; but nature has protected him. This is the period in which through ceaseless prehension and manipulation he acquires his groundwork of physics; his acquaintance with the most elementary properties of things. He does not yet to any great degree bring even two or three things into relationship with each other; but single objects he appropriates and exploits with much concentration. But in the next period, combinations of objects, increasing sensitiveness to a personal environment, and a deepening appreciation of the relations between things and human agents, tend to take him out of his self-containedness and make of him a more social being.

The Fourth Quarter (40 to 52 weeks). Forty weeks marks the rise of a stronger and in some ways a new social susceptibility to words, to gestures, and to demonstrations. The intentness with which the 40 and 44 weeks infant pays regard to what another person does contrasts significantly with the relative heedlessness and nonperceptiveness of the 32 weeks infant. Frequently the 40 weeks infant will not combine cup and spoon, for example, except after a demonstration; and throughout the fourth quarter the combining responses tend definitely to improve after demonstration. Evidence of induced and imitative behavior is especially marked at 52 and at 56 weeks.

The increasing susceptibility to social impress does not lead to parasitism for there is an obverse side to the infant's social reaction. In much the same way that he comes to perceive relationships between pellet and bottle he gradually comes to perceive that others are socially susceptible to him, that is to *his* words, gestures, and demonstrations. Here is a good rule which works both ways.

The ontogenesis of the patterning of social behavior cannot be understood unless this reciprocal nature of social relationships is recognized. This reciprocity not only intensifies social interaction, but it preserves a working balance between the individual and the group. The infant not only pat-a-cakes out of acquiescence to the group but also to gratify a certain not altogether fictitious sense of dominance over the group.

The infant shows a significant tendency to repeat performances laughed at. He pleases himself thereby as much as his audience. Through such situations he builds up the patterns of his individuality and enjoys a growing sense of personality.

Toward the close of the first year he begins to use vocal signs and words in situations highly charged with social values. If necessary he may even cough or clear his throat to elicit attention! But he also uses more primitive forms of communication and of control, gestures, crying, and numerous kinds of negative behavior. The kind of language he utilizes depends first of all upon maturity factors. Much, however, depends upon the kind of rearing he has had and the type of temperament he has inherited. Here normative criteria are almost impossible to formulate. Some infants show surprising stolidity and imperturbability; others an equal degree of sensitiveness and a tendency to neurotic utilization. A few, even in infancy, show an extraordinary perceptiveness of the emotions of others, and a superior capacity to influence and to adjust to those emotions adaptively as part of the game of living.

The responses of the infant in the "Give it to me" situation show in outline significant stages of development in the sphere of social behavior. During the third quarter the child holds rather fast to a toy in hand. He is self-contained. Although he may permit its removal he does not usually extend it to the requesting hand. At 40 weeks there is an even chance that he will extend the toy; at 44 weeks there is a similar chance, and at 48 weeks a strong chance that he will place the object in the requesting hand. At 52 weeks he will release it in the hand.

He is now socially compliant. But at 56 weeks a new reaction asserts itself. He is less naive in his surrender and he hesitates or refuses to give up the toy because he now fears that release may mean loss of the toy. Thus he becomes less docile, less socially suggestible, more resistant; at a higher level he is again more self-contained. Checks and balances are necessary to preserve the individuality of the infant and we see these operating in the way in which he ignores and sometimes healthily defies social pressure. Society itself has no regulations which work so advantageously for the individual as his own growth mechanisms.

Chapter Five

MENTAL GROWTH AND MATURATION

The Role of Maturation in the Patterning of Behavior

IN THE foregoing chapters the chief aim has been to set forth the facts of behavior growth in an orderly manner. The treatment has been analytic and descriptive, and only incidentally interpretive. We have not hesitated, however, to point out that the progressions in the patterning of behavior raise insistent questions concerning the endogenous mechanisms of mental growth. It seems desirable to discuss these questions in a general manner, with special regard to their theoretical implications.

Maturation is a term which serves to define the implications. The term has come increasingly into use, probably as an offset to the extravagant claims which have been made for processes of conditioning and of habit formation. In spite of its partial vagueness the concept of maturation should prove a useful aid both to experimental investigations and to theoretical interpretation. The present chapter attempts to indicate the role of maturation in the early patterning of human behavior and will consider the related concepts of heredity, environment, learning, growth, and development.

If we manage to envisage maturation as an active physiological process, we overcome the rather stilted antithesis of the nature *versus* nurture problem. Galton tells us that in his day the very term heredity was strange. With the advent of Mendelism the term took on popularity and became oversimplified. Individual unit characters of inheritance were too specifically identified with discrete chromosome particles, and heredity came to be regarded too mechanically as a fixed mode of transmission. Geneticists now emphasize the fact that these particles are chemicals which interact with each other and with many other factors to produce the organism. And if we but knew the biochemistry and biophysics of the interactions we should be making much less earnest use of such words as heredity, environment, and maturation.

§43. Concepts of Development and Environment

The heredity and environment of an organism can be completely separated only in analytic thinking, for in actual nature such separation would lead to instant death of the organism, even though the philosopher making the analysis might himself survive. Life depends upon "extraneous" factors like ultra-violet rays— rays which would become lethal if not filtered by the earth's thin layer of ozone. Life is dependent upon combined or fixed water of crystallization, often on free water, and on carbonic acid. L. J. Henderson (24)* has dwelt both scientifically and philosophically on the peculiar fitness of the inorganic world for life. There is a "fitness of environment" which is quite as impressive as the fitness of organisms. Development can not be understood unless both forms of fitness are coordinately recognized. "Just because life must exist in the universe, just because the living thing must be made of matter in space and actuated by energy in time, it is conditioned. In so far as this is a physical and chemical world, life must manifest itself through more or less complicated, more or less durable physico-chemical systems."

Development is a process in which the mutual fitness of organism and environment is brought to progressive realization. This process may be thought of mystically; but scientifically it is a series of biochemical, morphogenetic events: a process of continuous differentiation, "coordinated in time and place, leading to specific ends." It is unnecessary to draw an absolute distinction between physical and mental developments. They occur in close association and may be considered basically unitary. Both express themselves in changes of form and of patterning, which may be investigated from a morphological standpoint.

Likewise it is unnecessary, and even undesirable, to insist upon a distinction between growth and development. We shall use these terms interchangeably and make them equally applicable to mind and body. In proper context the word *growth* may be used to designate augmentation or increase instead of differentiation of structure and of function. This, however, represents a purely analytic abstraction because all organic growth actually involves changes in configuration and organization. Growth always produces alterative as well as magnitude changes.

*The figures in parentheses refer by number to the references listed in the bibliography at the end of this chapter, sec. 57, p. 323.

294 MENTAL GROWTH AND MATURATION §43

Mental growth (or development), therefore, is a progressive differentiation and integration of the action systems and behavior patterns of the total organism. Without implying any dualism, it is suggested that mental growth, like physical growth, is a process of morphological organization.

The term maturation also is equally applicable to mental and physical phenomena. Maturation is the intrinsic component of development (or of growth) which determines the primary morphogenesis and the endogenous variabilities of the life cycle. Although the word growth is sometimes loosely used as synonymous with maturation, the former is the more comprehensive term including all the developmental differentiations of the organism in response to external as well as internal environments.

Learning, in a psychological sense, may be regarded as that aspect of growth (or of development) which is a functional perfecting of behavior adaptation to specific situations present or past. Thus defined, there is a distinction between maturation and learning which may be applied in the study of problems of child development. Experimentally it is difficult to demonstrate the distinction because growth itself is a highly unitary process which depolarizes the two opposing categories of heredity and environment. Growth is not an easily dissected function in which elements of inheritance are readily distinguished from factors of environment or of training. The constitution and conditions of the organism are intimately interdependent. The organismic pattern of one moment, responsive to both internal and external environment, influences the pattern of succeeding moments. In a measure previous environmental effects are perpetuated by incorporation with constitution. Growth continuously contributes to its own conditions. It is subject to the regulatory influence of the very products of growth. Present growth hinges on past growth.

Accordingly there is a very reciprocal interrelationship between heredity and environment. The intimacy of this relationship may not, however, prevent us from ascribing a priority and possibly even some preponderance to hereditary factors in the patterning of human behavior. Although it is a truism, it should be emphasized that no environment as such has the capacity of growth. *Environmental factors support, inflect, and modify, but do not generate the progressions of development.* Growth as an impulsion and as a cycle of events is uniquely a character of the living organism and neither physical nor social environment contains

any architectonic arrangements even analogous to the mechanism
of growth.

§44. THE GROWTH CYCLE AND GENES

And where does this growth cycle of events have its source?
We shall briefly consider some of the biological facts which underlie
the development of the human embryo, since the role and the
manner of maturation in the shaping of the individual are foreshadowed in the earliest genetic stages.

It seems that the first ground plan of the body is due to the
mother alone. In certain animals in which the cytoplasm carries
coloring matter, the first steps in the development of the egg, prior
to fertilization, have been minutely followed. The nucleus, consisting of chromosomes, which in turn consist of genes, enlarges by
taking fluid from the cytoplasm. The membrane of the swollen
nucleus (or germinal vesicle) dissolves and fluid passes into
the cytoplasm. These physical and chemical interactions between
nucleus and cytoplasm constitute a fundamental process of
development. They take place at every subsequent cell division,
in the millions of individual cells which comprise the organism (31).

But in the single cell stage, the entire interior of the ovum is
observed to transform, to rearrange itself, to take on a definite
structure. Three zones corresponding to the outer body, the ali-
mentary canal, and the skeletal and other parts of the organism
define themselves, "the first visible diversities produced in development." It is a remarkable fact that the foundation plan of the
individual is thus laid down under the influence of the mother's
genes only. This reflects the indigenous nature of the original
growth potency, which has already been emphasized. Do the genes
ever lose a control in the patterning of the organism?

With fertilization, half the genes from the mother (one from
each pair in the chromosomes of the ovum) are lost and replaced
by corresponding genes from the father. Egg (the maternal gamete)
and sperm (the paternal gamete) combine to form the zygote which
becomes, or indeed already is, the individual. This individual
grows by cell division and cell differentiation, passing through a
continuum of phases which together constitute the life cycle;
the germinal, embryonic, fetal, and neonatal phases, followed by
infancy, childhood, adolescence, maturity, and senescence. In
this inescapable succession of life stages we have the broadest
expression of maturational factors. It must be remembered that

the genes find lodgment not only in the reproductive cells but in all the somatic cells. Into each cell of each tissue and of every bodily organ go appropriate subdivisions of both paternal and maternal genes. These ancestral genes are found in every neurone. They produce, as well, the hormones which secondarily regulate the development at all ages, prenatal and postnatal. It is these genes which are the focal sources of directive and constructive energy. They interact with the cytoplasm, which is always influenced by intracellular and extracellular environment; but the primary physiological factor in this interaction traces to the gene. To this degree the genes always figure in the physiology of development from the moment before conception to death. Moreover, Morgan has suggested that every gene affects the entire organism (38). Surely they must contribute substantially to the determination of individual differences, not excluding behavior differences among children and men.

Are these genes more than a hypothetical formula? They are realities. They are too small to be actually seen by the ultramicroscope; but by experimental methods as many as 50 have been identified in one chromosome of the fruit fly. Maps even have been drawn up showing the relative positions of such genes in the chromosome. Estimating the number of genes through the mutations produced by x-rays in thousands of flies, the total number in one cell is said to be not less than 14,380. The size of a single gene measures about one-quintillionth of a cubic centimeter, or the equivalent in volume of fifteen protein molecules.

In these myriad genes we have an ample basis for the operation of maturational processes throughout the whole life span of the individual including infancy. The genes should not be thought of as little eugenic packets which determine hereditary characteristics prior to birth. They should be thought of as the biochemical agencies which constantly participate in the complex physiology of both prenatal and postnatal development.

§45. THE EXPERIMENTAL ANALYSIS OF DEVELOPMENT

The knowledge of the nature of this complex physiology is increasing at a significant rate. Three monumental volumes on chemical embryology have appeared (39) and there is a stupendous literature in experimental embryology which deals especially with the mechanisms of growth regulation—investigations of symmetry, size, form; the effects of light, heat, cold, gravity, and chemical solutions; and irradiations.

The surgical analysis of the problems of morphogenesis has been especially ingenious and revealing. The same methods used on human beings would produce Frankensteins, but the methods may be safely used with lowly organisms like the sea urchin and salamander. Fragments of the growing organism are accurately destroyed, or removed from one part and grafted into another. Limbs of the salamander are transplanted to grotesquely inappropriate regions of the body. An embryonic eye is shifted to an abdominal position to determine the ability of the rudimentary optical cells to induce the growth of a lens in surrounding tissue. A section of the embryonic spinal cord may be transected at two levels, lifted out, reversed, and replaced in position to determine whether the growing part recovers its proper orientation or polarity. Presumptive ectoderm may be grafted into mesoderm and vice versa. Tissue cells may be removed completely from the organism to be grown in the monastic isolation of tissue cultures. The cells of the embryo of one species may be lifted to fill a surgical cavity created in the protoplasm of a foreign species. The presumptive mouth of a newt may be substituted for the presumptive mouth of a toad, and so forth. And the tendency of growth to achieve expression is so powerful that an amazing array of these surgical manipulations are experimentally successful.

Although these investigations in experimental embryology are concerned with the biological environment of laboratory organisms, the mechanisms revealed throw suggestive light on the psychological problem of maturation. It has been shown that organic growth does not proceed in an absolutely predetermined and stereotyped manner. By transplanting just the right amount of embryonic tissue, at just the right time, to the right position in the body of a growing salamander, a potential eye may be converted into a gill or a gill into an eye. The conditions of surrounding tissue affect the fate of the growing part. But if the transplant is made at a later stage, the potential eye, truer to itself than to the strange surroundings, becomes an eye even on the abdomen.

There are groups of cells (in the salamander they lie within the dorsal lip of the blastopore or embryonic mouth) which have the peculiar power of directing the differentiation in neighboring cells. Such a cell group, called an organizing center, regulates the directions of development and the map of differentiation, but the cells once differentiated remain true to their chromosomal composition. Species characteristics persist. If the leg of a salamander of species

298 MENTAL GROWTH AND MATURATION §46

A is grafted into the body of a salamander of species B, the transplanted leg develops according to species A, and does not transmute into B. If the developing egg of a mammalian species C, is transplanted to a foster mother (species D), the egg does *not* take on the constitutional characteristics of species D. In sum, although the experimental analyses of development have demonstrated at every turn the responsiveness of the growth complex to external and internal conditions, these studies have also shown the existence of a profound stabilizing mechanism which regulates the degrees and the modes of the plasticity and limits the final manifestations of growth.

§46. THE STRUCTURAL BASIS OF BEHAVIOR PATTERN

In the notable investigations of G. E. Coghill (8, 10), the embryonic development of the nervous system of the salamander (*Amblystoma punctatum*) has been charted in minute detail. These studies have correlated the anatomical and physiological aspects of growth in a way which throws light on the most general principles of behavior patterning. A major conclusion is formulated as follows: "Behavior develops from the beginning through the progressive expansion of a perfectly integrated total pattern and the individuation within it of partial patterns which acquire various degrees of discreteness."

"The mechanism of the total behavior pattern is a growing thing." The nervous system dominates, integrates, and elaborates this pattern through processes of growth. But even before the embryo of the salamander has a nervous system it is a perfectly integrated organism. Its processes of tissue growth are coordinated and progress in an orderly manner under the regulative influence of organizing centers, metabolic gradients, and gradients of electro-potential. Longitudinal sensory and motor tracts are the first to emerge from these gradients while other parts of the nervous system are still in an embryonic, preneural stage of development. The nervous system controls the total behavior pattern as this pattern expands, but the preneural system of integration overlaps the neural; and individual neurones, including motor neurones, grow in an embryonic manner long after they are already functional conductors. These growth relationships demonstrated by actual microscopic studies give solid content to the concept of maturation.

The function of the nervous system is to maintain the integrity of the organism. The nervous system grows according to its own intrinsic pattern and thereby establishes the primary forms of behavior. These forms are not determined by stimulation from the outside world. Experience has nothing specifically to do with them. Coghill has shown that the primary nervous mechanism of walking (in the *Amblystoma*) is laid down before the animal can at all respond to its environment. Similarly, the sense organs are the last elements of the vestibular system to maturate. The central relation of the neurones of the postural mechanism must therefore be determined without reference to the peripheral stimulation of the sense organs concerned." "The pre-sensory growth of the cerebral mechanism may accordingly be regarded as determining what the attitude of the individual as a whole shall be toward the environment before the organism can take cognizance physiologically of its environment." The primary attitude of the organism and the initiative of attitude are thus intrinsically determined.

Behavior, however, is not stereotyped even in the *Amblystoma*. Experience has much to do in determining when and to what extent performance will take place. To provide for this "conditioning" of behavior, there is a working capital of suprasensory and supra-associational neurones. The fibers from these neurones always grow into the sensorimotor field of action, becoming consolidated with the primary structural counterpart of the form of the behavior pattern.

"It is possible also that conditioning processes are registered in structural counterparts in the sense that neural mechanisms acquire functional specificity with reference to the experience. In the counterpart of the form of the pattern, the specificity of function is fixed by the relations into which the elements grow. In the counterpart of experience, on the other hand, specificity of function is established by interaction of growth and excitation; that is to say, the excitation fixes upon the growing terminals of neurones its own mode of activation. In the conditioning mechanism in general, as in the case of the Rohon-Beard cell, according to this hypothesis, laws of growth determine the structural relation of conductors, but their specific sensitivity is fixed by the mode of excitation.

"In the motor mechanism of Amblystoma we see structural counterparts of attitudes which are released into action of definite form in appropriate situations. It is possible that in the conditioning mechanisms, also, situations organize themselves into definite structural counterparts through the interaction of growth and excitation."

§47. The Role of Maturation

On such an anatomical basis the processes of maturation and of learning may be brought into closer identification. It becomes more possible to resolve the antithesis of fixity and flexibility of response. The mechanisms of maturation rigidly conceived would lead to stereotypy of behavior, but not if there is an intimately associated mechanism for specific adaptations. These two mechanisms are not discrete, nor does environment operate on one to the exclusion of the other. They function together as a single mechanism which is constantly consolidated through the unifying processes of growth. And by growth we do not mean a mystical essence, but a physiological process of organization which is registered in the structural and functional unity of the total behavior pattern of the individual.

As far as the deeper principles and mechanism of growth are concerned, there can be no abysmal difference between the patterning of behavior in the *Amblystoma* and in the infant. Although the underlying neuroanatomical details are now more completely known for the salamander and although the neural overgrowth of the cerebrum is vastly more complex in the human organism, the elementary developmental physiology of the constituent neurones may be assumed to be essentially alike in both species. Endocrine feeding has demonstrated fundamental biochemical identities. That the basic role of maturation even in the spheres of learning may be fully recognized, it should be pointed out that the associative neural structures concerned with the highest forms of mental adaptation in man are brought to an advanced stage of developmental organization in the early fetal period, long before these structures serve their most refined functions of specific and orientational adaptation. Such anticipation in the histological "morphology" of the nervous system determines the primary attitudes, the intrinsic initiative of attitude, "the forward reference" of behavior of the organism emphasized by Herrick (25) as well as Coghill (8). In the very nature of things the quality and primary architecture of this neural mechanism must be a product of inherent growth, determined by the genes. Here lies at least the foundation of individual differences in the patterning of behavior. To this extent the factors of maturation assert their sway even in the sphere of learning.

The concrete and substantial data which have accumulated through the experimental analysis of development in the lower forms furnish a solid basis for the preliminary interpretation of the role of maturation in the patterning of human behavior. This statement assumes that the biochemistry and mechanics of human development are in a considerable measure prefigured in the growth of lower organisms. But even if we should postulate that the physicochemical system of the human cortex has distinctive characters, it is altogether unnecessary to assume that these characters are entirely unique and incomparable with the physiological processes prevailing in the neural tissues of organisms lower in the evolutionary scale.

The role of maturation in the patterning of human behavior will be briefly discussed under the following rubrics: (a) physical constitution; (b) the ontogenetic sequence; (c) developmental correspondence in twins; (d) inherited behavior characteristics; (e) the development of sensorimotor functions; (f) intellectual and affective life.

§48. PHYSICAL CONSTITUTION

The operation of maturational factors in the first structuring of the embryo has already been incidentally considered. The early period of organogenesis antedates the period when behavior patterning begins. It cannot be doubted that this organogenesis is largely controlled by maturational factors. The morphology of the organs and the order of their appearance are primarily determined by the genetic system interacting with intracellular and intercellular environmental conditions. The end products of this early growth, both normal and atypical, project themselves as constitutional and even as type characteristics throughout the later life cycle.

The projective perpetuation of such constitutional characteristics is well illustrated in hemihypertrophy. Hemihypertrophy is a developmental anomaly which produces a more or less complete unilateral asymmetric enlargement of the individual. Hemihypertrophy may be regarded as a minimal form of twinning which occurs as an imbalance of the normal embryonic process of bilateral cell division, bringing about disturbances of normal tissue development. As a consequence of these disturbances of tissue development, hemihypertrophy is frequently associated with mental defect. This rare anomaly is instructive because it provides a glimpse of the inner mechanisms of development and demonstrates that the internal regulation of the process of growth has, from the beginning, a powerful influence in shaping the characteristics of the individual (17).

There is no evidence that hemihypertrophy is due to an hereditary defect in the genes. It more probably rises out of an epigenetic factor in the internal environment, which slightly distorts the normally symmetrical processes of developmental duplication. The mechanism of normal symmetry is impaired because of some inexactness in the physical environment or some partial retardation, resulting in uneven oxygen formation (45). To what extent many problems of symmetry and asymmetry, including eyedness, handedness, and other forms of unilaterality, trace back to the period of embryogenesis is not known. The condition of hemihypertrophy, however, is very significant because it shows the importance of the maintenance of balance in tissue development. Doubtless many deviations of physical constitution trace back to this embryonic period, and, because growth is consistently integrative, such constitutional differences influence the course of behavior patterning throughout life.

§49. The Ontogenetic Sequence

Patterns of behavior in all species tend to follow an orderly genetic sequence in their emergence. This genetic sequence is itself an expression of elaborate pattern, a pattern whose basic outline is the product of evolution and is under the influence of maturational factors. The studies of Swenson (47), Avery (2), and others have shown that in the rat and in the guinea pig and other mammalian forms the behavior sequence tends to follow a time schedule. The schedule differs with species but is much alike, for individuals of the same species. The studies of Minkowski (37) and others have shown the presence of a developmental sequence in behavior patterning for the human fetus. On the basis of available records, Coghill (8) is convinced that the principle of embryological development governing this early patterning of behavior in man is the same as that in *Amblystoma*. Shirley has found uniformities of sequence in the development of human posture and locomotion (43).

Our own studies of premature and postmature infants have demonstrated a high degree of stability in both prenatal and postnatal ontogenesis when the end course of development is not interfered with by traumatic and disease factors (19). The uterus is the normal environment of the fetus till the end of a gestation period of 40 weeks. But birth with survival may very exceptionally occur as early as 24 weeks and as late as 48 weeks, an enormous range of variation in natal age amounting to 6 lunar months. Variation within a range of 3 lunar months is relatively common and yet this considerable variation does not impose a corresponding deviation on the complex of behavior. Our normative studies of both premature and postmature infants have shown repeatedly that the growth course of behavior tends to be obedient to the regular underlying pattern of genetic sequence, irrespective of the irregularity of the birth event. Refined studies will doubtless reveal that such irregularity does subtly modify many details of behavior but nothing points more comprehensively to the role of maturation than the general stability of the trend and the tempo of development in spite of precocious or postponed displacement of birth. The patterns of genetic sequence insure a basically similar growth career for full term, pre- and post-term infants. It is as though nature had provided a regulatory factor of safety against the stress of extreme variations of environment. In the mechanisms of maturation this regulation operates.

§50. DEVELOPMENTAL CORRESPONDENCE IN TWINS

Twins furnish a fertile field for the study of maturational factors. Fraternal twins tend to show the same kind and probably the same degree of differences as ordinary siblings. Jacob and Esau are a classical example of twins who differed in mental and physical traits. To what extent the mere fact of contemporaneous birth and career affects the parity of characteristics is not known. In the present brief discussion we shall first consider the problem of physical correspondence and divergence in monozygotic twins.

The identity of origin of such twins makes for similarity in stature and body type, and for detailed correspondence in the color, form, and structure of organs. The inequality in the conditions of development, however, may impose a more or less permanent difference in weight and vitality. Hence the frequency of the occurrence of a weaker twin, who yet extensively duplicates his cotwin.

F. Beckerhaus (3) studied twelve pairs of unioval twins who showed marked similarity as to hair, skin color, iris, cornea, and total refraction of eyes, and who exhibited an inherited disposition to the formation of freckles. Yet there were minute but detectable differences in respect to all these qualities.

Sano (42) found a very remarkable similarity in the disposition of the furrows of the cerebral hemispheres of the brains of identical twins who were stillborn at full term—this in spite of a difference in size of the brains.

Gesell and Thompson (22) have reported medical and anthropometric details showing remarkably stable correspondence in twin infants T and C, up to 80 weeks of age. Daily determination of weight and of temperature for 450 days as well as body measurements, dentition, and skin patterns were compared. At the age of 19 weeks the twins were sent to a hospital where a diagnosis of acute intestinal intoxication was made. On the very same day, symptoms in both twins suddenly became worse. They showed marked ashen pallor, drowsiness, and symptoms of extreme dehydration. Similar treatment was administered. A total of 400 cc. saline was given immediately, subcutaneously and intraperitoneally; 75 cc. intravenous glucose was given at the same sitting; shortly after, 150 cc. of citrated blood was given by transfusion per fontanelle; the following day 300 cc. saline was given subcutaneously. On the fifteenth of November the symptoms cleared and both patients showed decided improvement. The contrast with their appearance on admission was considered little less than remarkable. The course of convalescence in both children was similar, and they were discharged as cured at the end of 16 days. Four days prior to discharge, however, Twin C showed symptoms of acute bilateral otitis media of the suppurative type. In spite of this complication, it is significant that both children made very similar weight gains during their fortnight at the hospital. Twin T entered with a weight of 5480 grams and left with a weight of 6080 grams—a gain of 600 grams; Twin C entered with a weight of 5340 grams and left with a weight of 6000 grams—a gain of 560 grams. One day they weighed exactly alike to a gram!

Such amazing identity of reaction to an infection, and to its heroic treatment, strongly suggests that the correspondence in highly similar twins inneres in the very biochemical constitution, supplying a firm matrix for the development of correspondence in psychological make-up.

The physiological basis of behavior correspondence is clearly demonstrated in a recent study by Macfarlan (34). The hearing of middle-aged twin sisters was tested by an audiometer. A marked parallelism was shown; the hearing rose and fell across the pitch range in nearly exact correspondence.

With such a wealth of correspondence demonstrated in the physical development of twins, it becomes interesting to inquire whether there is a comparable degree of behavior correspondence in twin development. This problem, of course, is more complex. There is after all some difference between patterns of the skin and patterns of behavior. The configuration of the friction ridges of the skin is fixed for each individual in the fourth month of intrauterine life, and, unaltered, this dermal pattern is carried to the grave.

The mental characteristics of the human organism, on the other hand, are in process of almost constant change. It is impossible to seize upon stable criteria of comparison like thumb prints. Yet there is no reason to believe that the complex of mental growth is immune from those same factors which make for correspondence in the dermal patterning of sole and palm.

Twins T and C, who showed such thorough-going physical correspondence as reported by Gesell and Thompson (22) were also studied from the standpoint of psychological correspondence. Periodic developmental observations were made by individual and comparative examinations throughout their infancy. Motion picture records were utilized.

A marked degree of resemblance in behavior patterns was displayed. The correspondences in behavior patterning were literally uncountable. However, the records of 13 developmental examinations were analyzed, and 612 separate comparative ratings of behavior items were made from these records in order to determine features of correspondence and disparity. There were 99 items of minor disparity, and 513 items of identical or nearly identical correspondence. A generic and detailed parity of behavior patterns was decisively demonstrated.

In the field of pellet prehension this parity was very neatly disclosed. A small pellet, 7 mm. in diameter, was placed on a table top before each child, within easy reach. At 28 weeks both the twins, being somewhat retarded in their development, were visually unheedful of the pellet, though they definitely regarded a cube. At 38 weeks they addressed themselves in an identical manner to the pellet. The hands were placed in full pronation, the fingers were fully extended, and spread apart in a fan-like manner. The thumb was extended almost at right angles. The motion picture record of the twins' attack upon the pellet shows an almost uncanny degree of identity in the details of postural attitude, hand attitude, approach, and mechanism of grasp. At 40 weeks there was a crude raking attack upon the pellet; at 42 weeks this raking approach was replaced by a poking with the tip of the index finger. These changes in prehensory pattern occurred contemporaneously in both children.

We turn to another example of behavior correspondence in the infant Twins T and C at the age of 44 weeks. The twins were confronted with a test performance box with its three holes. The common method of approach of the two children, their preferred regard for the edge of the performance box, the fleeting regard for the holes, the exploitation of the vertical surface of the performance box by a scratching, simultaneous flexion of the digits, the failure to place a round rod into any of the holes, the brushing of the surface of the performance box with the rod, the transfer of the rod from one hand to the other, and finally an almost simultaneous peculiar, clicking vocalization in both twins—altogether constituted a very complicated behavior patterning, but one which bristled with numerous identities of spatial and dynamic detail. One can give due weight to the significance of this correspondence only by reflecting on the myriad of behavior exploitations of the situation which the twins *might* have adopted. But in spite of this multitude of exploitational possibilities, the twins were apparently under a common inner compulsion to adopt those very similarities of behavior which have been noted.

The complex nature of these behavior correspondences again suggests the fundamental role of maturation. If it were argued that extrinsic factors determine the form and the occasion of such simultaneous patterns, it would become necessary to demonstrate in detail a cunning arrangement of environment and of conditioning stimuli competent to design in duplicate the configurations of the observed behavior. How can the environment, even of twins, accomplish such architectonic miracles (21)?

Ley (33) has published an excellent monograph on *Un Cas d'audimutite idiopathique (aphasie congénitale) chez des jumeaux monozygotiques*. The subjects, two boys, A and J, age 8 years, present a remarkably synchronous developmental career with retardation in walking and in speech. They both had "convulsions" up to 2 years of age, J more frequently than A. Dentition and walking occurred late, the former at 2 years, the latter at 3½ years. At 4, both had a light bronchitis; at 5, night fears. Each pronounced his first words at 4. They were both so destructive that at 5 the parents were obliged to place them in an institution for abnormal children. At 8, they appeared normal at first sight, but upon examination were found to express themselves with the greatest difficulty, to fall frequently in walking or running, and to be unable to understand the damage they caused. They utilized the gesture language effectively with each other but did not attempt to communicate with a third person. The indications of normal reactions were excellent memories and good attention (but solely for things which interested them). Unlike aphasics, they were not timid. Physical examination results showed no sign of lesion. Asymmetry reversal was present in hair whorls, finger prints, and skull form. In play, *A* preferred the left hand, *J* the right. Upon intelligence examination, *A* and *J* passed tests which placed them at the 8 year level except for drawing and number concept. In résumé the author characterizes them as follows: they were incontestably "monozygotic," with great asymmetry reversal, and an analogy of bodily and mental development which approached absolute identity. Minute medical and neurological examination was completely negative. The essential difficulty was in the motor sphere—in spite of normal development and perfect peripheral stimulation of all their organs, they could not make certain voluntary movements. They not only learned to walk late but had difficulty with complicated movements; could not correctly articulate words; could not draw; or imitate difficult gestures. They understood the significance of drawings and gestures. Their motor difficulty consisted in a considerable retardation of development of the "praxique" functions. Great parallelism existed in the development of their intelligence, in which there were essential gaps, particularly in abstract concepts.

§51. INHERITED BEHAVIOR CHARACTERISTICS

We need not undertake any critical discussion of the complicated problem of the inheritance of mental traits. It is evident that the inborn traits of an individual can only be brought into realization through the processes of maturation. However much these traits may be specifically modified and inflected by environment, their initial manifestation will be primarily determined by maturation. That the maturational mechanism may operate with morphological precision even in the field of behavior is suggested by some of the results of Stockard's highly important experimental work in the breeding of dogs (45).

He has experimentally investigated problems of experimental morphology by the hybridization and interbreeding of pedigreed dogs. He has been chiefly concerned with the genetics and endocrinology of the somatic constitution of his dogs but his work throws striking side-lights on the developmental basis of behavior patterns. He finds in his hybrid litters assortments of temperamental and instinctive traits which indicate a well-defined hereditary determination. He finds that the general complexion of behavior in hybrid offspring tends to correlate with the shape of the cranium more than with body build.

He has bred an interesting cross between the Saluki hound and the Basset hound. The Saluki is a tall, slender, aristocratic creature that has come down through the ages (thanks to the stable genes) with a physical (and probably a psychological) pattern quite similar to that of the domesticated dog portrayed by the ancient Egyptians. The Basset hound is low flung, stocky, and short legged. Saluki, on assuming a prone position, puts out his long forelegs with a graceful extensor thrust. Basset, when he settles down, folds his short forelegs inwards with a flexor movement. And what do the strange looking, short-legged, hybrid puppies do when they take a prone posture? In spite of the anatomical grotesqueness of it, they extend their short legs as though they belonged to the ancestral Pharaoh strain. In other words, the musculature of the Basset-like extremities is controlled by the neurone mechanism of a Saluki type. This is evidence that a specific behavior pattern trend may be transmitted as an entity in spite of cross breeding, the pattern preserving integrity even under the influence of an incongruent anatomical structure derived from an alien strain. Here maturation works with a vengeance.

It is probable that in man also there are innumerable behavior characters which rest upon relatively specific pattern determiners within the individual constitution. Such inherited patterns and pattern trends as well as more generalized potencies can come to expression only through a process of maturation. Although adaptive to and responsive to environment, they are in no sense derived from the external environment.

§52. SENSORIMOTOR FUNCTIONS

In the developmental patterning of such fundamental functions as posture, locomotion, eye movements, and prehension the factors of maturation work with considerable force, in the human infant as well as in the lower animals. As already indicated, the onto-genetic sequence for such functions, though differing for species, tends to remain consistent within the species. There are individual differences, but many of these seem to arise out of variations in the original growth equipment rather than in the physical environment.

Coghill (9) doubts whether the appearance of a function like locomotion can be hastened in *Amblystoma* by exercise. Carmichael (6) found that swimming movements appeared at the appropriate time in *Amblystoma* embryos even when these embryos were completely deprived of external stimulation by an anaesthetizing solution of chloretone. Bird (4) hatched large numbers of chicks and kept them in darkness for varying periods of time. This was equivalent to specific anesthetization of the behavior pattern of pecking, for chicks do not peck in the dark. There proved to be only a small difference in pecking performance between practiced chicks and those reared in the dark; and even this small difference may have been due to differences in vitality. In the human fetus there is a comparable certainty in the progressions of sensorimotor functions, with but slight dependence upon exercise and stimula-tion in the ordinary sense of these terms.

Such lawful progressions are by no means confined to the pre-natal period. They project into the neonatal period, into infancy, and doubtless also into maturity; for maturity rests upon endog-enous factors. During the first year of life the progressional trends come most abundantly into view. In the summary accounts of the various normative situations it has been repeatedly shown that the patterns of behavior are closely linked with age. The statistical trends of both "increments" and "decrements" of infant behavior denote fundamental similarities in the order and the manner of ontogenesis. The resemblances of behavior in the same child in a dozen different situations at the same age are significant. The resemblance is a function of certain formal ele-ments in the behavior equipment at that level of maturity. These formal elements change with age, but always preserve a certain consistency, even though the infant appears always to be in a formative stage. He is; but the formativeness itself is formed by intrinsic growth factors. The influence of these factors manifests itself in the statistical trends which are so numerously apparent in the tables of behavior items presented in Chapter III.

The reader needs only refer to these tables to find illustrative data in every field of behavior—posture, locomotion, prehension, manipulation, language. The trend toward an erect head station, the trend toward upright body posture, the tendency toward combining objects, the progressive dominance of the radial digits, the emergence of the index finger for exploitive and prehensory adjustments, the increasing responsiveness to demonstration, and a host of other behavior patterns or behavior modalities might be reviewed for evidences of maturational mechanisms.

A compact normative synopsis of the pellet situation will serve here as a convenient example of developmental trends in the visual-manual field:

12 weeks	Transient regard for pellet (rarely)
16 weeks	More prolonged regard, usually delayed
20 weeks	Immediate, definite regard, sometimes with increased hand-arm activity
24 weeks	Approaches pellet with pronate hand; contacts pellet with little or no finger adjustment
28 weeks	Approaches pellet with raking flexion of fingers, without thumb opposition; occasional delayed palmar prehension
32 weeks	Approaches pellet with raking flexion but with increased thumb participation and digital prehension
36 weeks	Approaches and contacts with simultaneous flexion of fingers; prehends with defined thumb and index opposition
40 weeks	Approaches with all fingers extended; contacts with index finger and later prehends by drawing index finger against thumb
44 weeks	Promptly prehends with index and thumb and with increased obliquity of hand attitude
48 weeks	Approaches with index finger extended and lateral digits flexed; prehends with delimited plucking by index and thumb
52 weeks	Approaches and plucks pincer-wise with increased deftness

If the foregoing table is studied in perspective it shows that the development of eye-hand behavior in the infant does not consist so much in an increase of skill as in a progressive differentiation of the mechanical form of behavior. To be sure there is a trend toward economy of movement; but this is not an end result of practice but an alteration in the very pattern of response. The developmental reorganization of this pattern is outwardly a morphological phenomenon primarily correlated with changes in the inner morphology of the nervous system, and secondarily with changes in ligaments, joints, and musculature. Howsoever environment may inflect and condition the expression of the visual-motor functions, the mechanics of the behavior and the basic form of the patterns are primarily the product of maturational factors.

The prehensory patterns of normative infants have been fruitfully investigated by methods of cinema analysis by Halverson (23), and by Castner (7). McGinnis (35) has made a similar analysis of early eye movements. These studies establish in temporal and spatial detail, the lines along which visual-motor behavior is developmentally patterned. The indubitable presence of intrinsic morphogenetic determiners at the basis of visual-motor behavior forms, suggests that comparable determiners may also operate in the more concealed ontogeny of the higher thought processes.

§53. Intellectual and Affective Life

The role of maturation in the higher spheres of intellectual and moral life is, on the basis of present knowledge, difficult to determine. On theoretical grounds some may even question whether the concept of maturation can be applied to these higher and more rarefied fields of behavior accessible to introspection but not to photography. Nevertheless, if there is a general physiology of growth which governs the entire development of the individual, we may well believe that maturation maintains a role in the higher orders of thought and feeling.

Neurones grow. Laboratory investigation has shown that electro-potentials are moving factors in that growth. Axones grow away from a cathode pole (Bok's law); dendrites grow towards an active neurone or nerve bundle and cathode pole (Kappers' law). The cell body may also migrate in the same direction as its growing dendrites. Coghill (10) has emphasized the fact that neurones continue to send out (and organize) processes even after they have begun to function as conductors, and has even suggested that the creative component of thought is a form of growth. Kappers has remarked that his law of neurobiotaxis resembles the psychological law of association. E. B. Holt (27) believes "that with a very small additional consideration as to the direction in which the excitations flow, it (the law of neurobiotaxis) is the psychological law of association."

Accordingly, it is possible to posit a maturational kind of mechanism even in the spheres of symbolic thinking represented by language, thought, and moral attitudes. Granting that these spheres are elaborately influenced by social and environmental factors, they nevertheless require a substratum of maturation similar to that which underlies the simpler, sensorimotor functions like prehension.

Strayer (46) reports some valuable findings in this direction based on a study of language development in identical twins by the method of cotwin control. Both twins were given a similar course of vocabulary training in the early stage of language formation, but Twin *T* was trained 5 weeks earlier than Twin *C*. The maturity difference of 5 weeks showed itself clearly in the language behavior of Twin *C*; she responded more effectively to training and her pattern of response was more mature. There was a more rapid elimination of doubling of syllables (like *baba* for ball). This was a sensorimotor advantage (and this is of especial significance in the present connection), but there was also an intelligence advantage. Twin *C* showed less interference of associations: "She incorporated the new words more quickly into her spontaneous jargon and extended her application earlier and more widely, using them more often." These latter functions are modalities of behavior, akin to those which operate on higher levels of generalization and of reasoning. Such modalities can in no sense be explained on the basis of habit formation or of environmental moulding, however, dependent they are on social stimulation. Rather, they arise out of maturational factors which are relatively independent of specific training. We may regard Strayer's study as a virtually experimental demonstration of the existence of such maturational factors in intellectual functions.

Although generic modalities of behavior do not have a morphological configuration in the same precise sense that a method of prehension has a visible design, there is no reason why these modalities should not be represented in the nervous system by innate developmental factors which serve to incorporate the influences of the social environment. This process of incorporation is a form of growth, closely articulated with the total action system. Even thinking, or at least the creative component of thinking, as already suggested, is a growth phenomenon.

Piaget (40) has made extensive psychological studies of the child's language, early forms of reasoning, articulate concepts of physical causality and of cosmology, and the nature of moral judgment. His approach upon the problems is at once philosophical, clinical, and genetic, and in his last work he has made correlations with the literature of theoretical sociology. In his interpretations he uses biological concepts only to a limited extent and it therefore becomes interesting to inquire into his views concerning the interaction of the individual and environment. We quote a few passages which in spite of a certain abstruseness indicate the lines of his interpretation (41).

"This concordance of our results with those of historico-critical or logico-sociological analysis brings us to a second point: the parallelism existing between moral and intellectual development. Everyone is aware of the kinship between logical and ethical norms. Logic is the morality of thought just as morality is the logic of action. . . . One may say, to begin with, that in a certain sense neither logical nor moral norms are innate in the individual mind. We can find, no doubt, even before language, all the elements of rationality and morality. Thus sensori-motor intelligence gives rise to operations of assimilation and construction, in which it is not hard to see the functional equivalent of the logic of classes and of relations. . . . The control characteristic of sensori-motor intelligence is of external origin: it is things themselves that constrain the organism to select which steps it will take; the initial intellectual activity does actively seek for truth. Similarly, it is persons external to him who channelize the child's elementary feelings, those feelings do not tend to regulate themselves from within.

"This does not mean that everything in the *a priori* view is to be rejected. Of course the *a priori* never manifests itself in the form of ready-made innate mechanism. The *a priori* is the obligatory element, and the necessary connections only impose themselves little by little, as evolution proceeds. It is at the end of knowledge and not in its beginnings that the mind becomes conscious of the laws immanent to it. Yet to speak of directed volution and asymptotic advance towards a necessary ideal is to recognize the existence of a something which acts from the first in the direction of this evolution. But under what form does this 'something' present itself? Under the form of a structure that straightway organizes the contents of consciousness, or under the form of a functional law of equilibrium, unconscious as yet because the mind has not yet achieved this equilibrium, and to be manifested only in and through the multitudinous structures that are to appear later? There seems to us to be no doubt about the answer. There is in the very functioning of sensori-motor operations a search for coherence and organization. Alongside, therefore, of the coherence that characterizes the successive steps taken by elementary intelligence we must admit the existence of an ideal equilibrium, indefinable as structure but implied in its functioning that is at work. Such is the *a priori:* it is neither a principle from which concrete actions can be deduced nor a structure of which the mind can become conscious as such, but it is a sum-total of functional relations implying the distinction between the existing states of disequilibrium and an ideal equilibrium yet to be realized."

The foregoing interpretation, although too mentalistic to be readily brought into a biological discussion, indicates the presence of "a priori" factors which may be envisaged in terms of maturation. These factors become somewhat less mystical if they are ascribed to the growth characteristics of a total action system whose elementary mechanisms have been studied by direct approach. However potent and pervasive social environment may be, the basic organization of the higher thought processes is probably determined by primary ordering factors within the growing organismic pattern.

Likewise with the affective life of the infant. The primary emotions have been discussed as though they were elementary stable phenomena subject only to the changes of social conditioning. This is the implication in much that has been written concerning the emotion of fear. It seems to us that the problem has been oversimplified. Fear may be an original tendency, but it is possibly subject to the genetic alterations of maturation as well as to organization by environmental conditioning. Such conditioning may determine the orientation and reference of fears, but the mode of fearing may well undergo change as a result of maturation. Fear is neither more nor less of an abstraction than prehension. It is not a simple entity. It waxes and alters with maturity. It is shaped by intrinsic maturation as well as by experience, certainly during the period of infancy.

A discussion of the developmental aspect of intellectual and affective life should make at least brief mention of the phenomenon of invention and mental creativeness. Does maturation play a role here too? What is known about the biological process of mutation and of human variability suggests that a mechanism of maturation is requisite for manifestations of originality. Such manifestations can not be derived from the environment alone, in either children or adults. Even originative and mutational expressions of individuality emerge out of a complex of growth. Similarly the more marked differences among adults with respect to the prolongation of intellectual plasticity must have their basis in the constitutional growth potential.

§54. MATURATION AND TRAINING

There has been an increasing number of studies dealing with the effects of training on the acquisition of skill in children. The influence of age and of practice distribution on the improvement of abilities raises many questions concerning maturation factors. The contributions and bibliographies of Gates (14), Jersild (32), Hilgard (26), and Wheeler (48) may be especially mentioned.

In identical twins nature provides a stage for observing the effects of a developmental stimulus which may be experimentally confined to one twin. We have described elsewhere (22), the method of cotwin control which was first used to analyze the influence of training in relation to maturity. Having established the presence of a thorough-going similarity of a pair of infant girl twins, one twin (Twin C) was utilized as a duplicate control. Twin T was subjected to a program of daily training in climbing and in cube behavior for a period of 6 weeks, beginning at the age of 46 weeks. Twin C (reserved as a control) was deprived of all specific training in these reactions. At the age of 53 weeks Twin C was subjected to a brief period of training in climbing lasting 2 weeks. The purpose of this deferred training was to check and to extend the analysis of the interdependence of maturity factors and training factors. Twin T's early reactions to training were relatively passive, and she needed assistance at one or all of the five treads. After 4 weeks of training (age 50 weeks) she climbed the staircase with avidity and without assistance. At 52 weeks she climbed the staircase in 26 seconds. Twin C, at the age of 53 weeks, without any previous training, climbed the same staircase unaided in 45 seconds. After 2 weeks of training, at the age of 55 weeks, Twin C climbed the stairs in 10 seconds. The climbing performance of Twin C at 55 weeks was far superior to the climbing performance of Twin T at 52 weeks, even though Twin T had been trained 7 weeks earlier and three times longer. The maturity advantage of 3 weeks of age must account for this superiority.

Twin T was trained daily in cube behavior from 46 to 52 weeks of age. A day-by-day analysis of this cube behavior showed a trend toward daily changes and increments in prehension, manipulation, and exploitation. At the close of the training period, however, the cube behavior patterns of Twin C were highly similar to those of Twin T. It is suggested that the growth complex, being under the stress of continuous (diurnal) maturational changes, can not assimilate in any permanent way the effects of ordinary training or casual suggestion. The similarity in patterns of cube behavior was confirmed by a time-space cinema analysis of the prehensory reactions to cubes under experimental conditions at 42, 52, 63, and 79 weeks of age.

The method of cotwin control has also been used by Strayer (46) to analyze the relationship of language and growth and to determine the relative efficacy of early and deferred vocabulary training. Very favorable arrangements for the temporary separation of the twins and for continuous 24-hour observation were made. Twin T's training was begun when she was 84 weeks old and continued through her eighty-eighth week. Twin C's training was begun when she was 89 weeks old. Careful records of all word use and language behavior were kept; and these were later compared in quantitative detail.

The findings of the experiment indicated that the typical stages in "the acquisition of language were strikingly alike for both twins, but in practically every phase Twin C was slightly in advance of Twin T." This was attributed to the age difference of the twins during the identical (but not contemporaneous) training programs. Not only was the training which was begun with a maturity advantage of five weeks more effective than earlier training, but the patterns of response of Twin C were more mature. Strayer offers abundant detail concerning the comparative career of individual words learned by T and C, which illuminate the conditions of learning. Training does not transcend maturation.

When Twins T and C reached the age of 54 months, they were experimentally observed by Josephine Hilgard (26a), for a period of 7 months, again by the method of cotwin control. The twins well matched at the outset of the study on motor tests of scissors cutting, ring toss, walking boards (2, 4, and 6 cm. in width), digit memory, and object memory. Each twin served in part as practice and as control subject. In each comparative situation, one twin was practiced (early practice) while the other served as control; both were retested and then 3 months later the second twin was practiced leaving the previously practiced twin to serve as control. Each practice or training period was 8 weeks in length, with three sessions per week. Both twins were comparatively retested after the delayed practice, and again by way of follow-up 3 and 6 weeks later.

With the exception of the 6 cm. walking board and of the scissors test, in which one twin had a distinctively superior tech- nique, delayed practice resulted in greater gain. The curves of learning were similar to those found by Strayer. The curves of forgetting, plotted on the basis of the follow-up comparisons, showed a striking tendency for the performances to reach the same level. "That both twins 'forgot' to the same level in spite of their different attainments with practice" was interpreted to indicate the importance of general developmental factors (26a).

§55. THE RELATIONSHIP OF MATURATION AND LEARNING

The foregoing summary of various evidences of maturation leads us back to a brief consideration of the relationship of matura- tion and learning. This is, of course, a difficult problem and would demand a critical analysis of the numerous factors which operate in so-called learning: practice, forgetting, refractory phase phe- nomena, conditioning (inhibitory and remote), repetition, emo- tional reinforcement, etc. An estimate of these factors would inevitably prove the difficulty, if not artificiality, of drawing a distinction between dynamic and developmental processes. Where indeed shall the line be drawn in the border zone between dynamic psychology and developmental psychology? Would not dynamic processes which take place in a short period of time assume a devel- opmental aspect if drawn out durationally after the manner of the slowed cinema projection? And conversely, would not develop- mental phenomena simulate dynamic, if telescoped into a small span of duration?

The new formulations of learning reflect this point of view. D. K. Adams (1) characterizes learning as " . . . the process of reorganization sometimes under-gone by fields distorted by an obstructed need," and suggests that "when in such fields learning does not occur, the other sort of adaptation (change in the need) must occur." Similarly, Humphrey (28): "As biological evolution progressed, organic complexes were able to respond more and more intimately to changes in the environment, until there was devel- oped the power to make a dynamic adjustment to a highly complex four-dimensional manifold. This is the power to learn." E. B.

Holt (27) in his effort to merge genetic and dynamic aspects uses the remarkable phrase "developmental growth or learning." "Sheer growth" (whatever sheer growth may mean) is a term which has sometimes been used in contrast to "environmental moulding."

Analytically it is possible, and scientifically it is desirable, to draw a distinction between maturation and learning. The end products are blended beyond dissection; the mechanisms are alike in principle; they operate synthetically in determining the ultimate patterns of behavior; but they are not identical. Carmichael (6) suggests that "in all maturation there is learning and in all learning there is hereditary maturation." But it does not follow that they are one and the same thing; unless we grant that there are forms of maturation which are so precisely adaptive that learning is ruled out. Significantly enough, we can not conversely suppose that learning ever takes place without a maturational component. Marquis (36) in his excellent discussion of the criterion of innate behavior suggests that there is a fundamental distinction to be made as follows: "Learning represents a modification of the organismic pattern in response to specific stimuli present in the external environment at the time of the modification. Maturation, on the other hand, is a modification of the organismic pattern in response to stimuli present in the intra-cellular and intercellular environments, which at the given moment are independent of external influences."

This distinction is a defensible one, but it is unnecessary to make it hang too exclusively on immediately present stimuli. Recent stimuli also operate and emphasis should be placed on the specific nature of the adaptation to both present and recent stimuli. If the term recent introduces difficulties of interpretation, these are of a constructive character and reflect the close bonds between maturation and learning, without obscuring the difference between external and internal environments.

The intimate relationships between maturation and learning were neatly disclosed in a simultaneous comparative observation (21) of identical twins, if we may again refer to T and C. A fundamental identity in behavior responses was shown in the pellet and bottle situation. The twins were in the same crib, seated back to back, and confronting each her own examining table. The two examiners simultaneously held a small 4 oz. glass bottle in view and dropped a 7 mm. pellet into the bottle. Three trials were made with each child. The examiner, having dropped the pellet into the bottle, gave the bottle to the child.

Both children watched this dropping of the pellet with the same transfixed attention. Both children on the first trial, and again on the second trial, seized the bottle, apparently heedless of the contained pellet; but both children on the third trial (without, of course, any influence of imitation) pursued the pellet by poking at it against the glass—identical capacity to profit by experience.

In this instance we find that the correspondence of behavior patternings extends into the minute fields of specific adaptation or of learning. It may be readily granted that maturational factors primarily account for the similarity in capacity and general maturity displayed by these twins. Perhaps these same maturational factors account also for the more detailed correspondences, such as the mode of visual attention, the primary preoccupation with the bottle, and the secondary interest in the pellet. Within a brief span of time we see the spontaneous behavior patterns undergo a specific adaptation and call this adaptation learning. But the distinctive criteria of maturation and learning are not easily applied.

Let us assume that on the morrow, in the pellet and bottle situation, both children poke immediately with extended forefinger against the side of the bottle. Is this fixation of behavior due to the experience of the previous day? And shall the assimilative processes of the intervening night be regarded as maturation because the modification did not occur in immediate response to the situation, or shall it be called learning because it is virtually a specific adaptation to stimuli recently in the external environment? The fixation of the poking pattern, however, proves to be temporary, because in another lunar month without specific experience, these same twins adaptively tilt both bottle and hand, and thrust the extended index finger into the open mouth of the bottle in pursuit of the pellet. Is this incremental differentiation of behavior pattern to be attributed to maturation or to learning?

A concluding comment may here be made on *skill as a genetic concept*. The term *skill*, if used loosely can do no harm. Context and vagueness will protect the usage from mischief. If, however, the term is used critically we must exercise due caution. To begin with, the infant is never unskillful. Even when he gropes for the pellet he is performing adaptively in terms of his current equipment and very creditably. When he rakes or scoops the pellet by a swift simultaneous digit-palmar method, he may be performing *adeptly* and *efficaciously* (more efficaciously by the way than when he painfully plucks the pellet with an immature thumb-index opposition). The latter is a higher order of performance, but does not necessarily represent more *skill*, more *dexterity*, more *aptness*, *nimbleness*, *expertness*. There may even be less *deftness*. The plucking, however, is genetically a superior response, therefore we may say that it is more *clever*, meaning as the very etymology of this word suggests, a more advanced form of seizure. Even though awkward, the plucking represents a higher kind of *address* and promises later a higher level of *adroitness*. At an immature stage it is not so *neat* and *handy* nor so *efficient* as a palmar scoop but it does constitute a new and important form of hand posturing. All these italicized words are similar, but vary in connotation.

If by *skill* we mean the refinement, facilitation, and specific improvement of a given behavior equipment or an existing set of capacities, then the term is highly relative, and in infancy skill is always highly transitory. The infant is continually forging ahead because of the maturation of new behavior trends. He does not become permanently skillful as a gross manual scooper, because there emerges, without his beckoning, a propensity to prehend digitally. This new mechanics of behavior is, so to speak, a morphogenetic product comparable to the change in the profile of his nose. It is primarily a maturation phenomenon. Training and experience will in a specific and always more or less transient sense perfect, modulate, and condition; but in its basic configuration the new pattern of plucking is not the architectonic product of some mystical learning process; it is a morphological phenomenon, a topographical event in the mechanics of development.

The distinction between maturation and learning should not be pushed to pedantic extreme. We know too little for that. The processes are inevitably correlated and in some measure probably reciprocal. But for these very reasons it is desirable to enclose the word skill in judicious quotation marks and not to expand it so far that it includes all of the attainments of the infant, even those which he "acquires" through intrinsic processes of morphogenesis.

§56. MATURATION AND GROWTH REGULATION

We may look upon maturation as part of a general process of developmental regulation as well as a morphogenetic process which works toward more or less specific end results. The total complex of growth, as it were, is always meeting "problems" in the obstructions, stresses, and deficiencies of both internal and external environment. The maximum developmental success of the organism is rarely achieved but in all growing organisms there is apparently a tendency toward a maximum. We may postulate this as a developmental principle and formulate it briefly as follows: *Growth tends toward an optimum realization.*

This principle has psychological applications but it can be most concretely illustrated by examples from experimental biology. The results of the surgical alterations of a growing organism stimulate a marked tendency on the part of the structures to adapt themselves to mutilations and dislocations. For example, Detwiler (11) found that when the limb of *Amblystoma* was removed and grafted well behind its normal position, the nerve supply nevertheless organized itself in such a way as to establish appropriate function in the limb.

Speidel's study (44) of growing nerve cells showed a growth cone at the end of the fiber. The cone advances by a slow irregular flowing motion, spinning a fiber behind it. A slight temporary obstruction may cause a small thickening. A more formidable obstruction may lead to giant cones or to the formation of branches.

Boeke (5, 30) has traced the regeneration of motor end plates. He found two stages: first, the outgrowing fiber puts out exuberant, bizarre end ramifications; in the second stage, these forms disappear and a normal form is restored. Boeke remarks: "And I can imagine no other process which affords such a striking example of the elements of the different tissues as subordinate parts of the whole, to reach a given end, the restoration of the equilibrium of the organism, than this mode of regeneration of the motor nerve endings."

This whole phenomenon of regeneration gives a clue to the more intricate processes of compensatory growth and of adjustment to handicaps whereby the organism "seeks" a maximum in the sphere of behavior. Nerve tissue itself has very limited capacity for regeneration, but the nervous system as a whole plays the dominating role in preserving the integrity of the organism in the face of such handicaps as malnutrition, loss of sense organs, loss of motor capacity. The total reaction system of the individual tends to be ordered and coherent even though its resources and instrumentalities are imperfect. In many instances serious handicaps seem to be much less disastrous than one might suppose. Even grave degrees of malnutrition, correlated with excessive subnormality of weight, are usually incompetent to inflict any drastic changes upon the forms of fundamental behavior patterns and upon the genetic order of their sequence. While it is granted that certain food deficiencies, for example, in the field of calcium metabolism, definitely influence the general picture of behavior, the nervous system itself is remarkably resistant to general adversity, even to partial starvation. When certain areas of the nervous system are actually damaged by disease or injury, maturation cannot make amends, but the maturation of the nervous system seems to proceed toward the optimum in the areas unimpaired, even though lacking the stimulus of exercise of the functions controlled by the impaired areas. It is for this reason that certain clinical types of profound motor disability attain none the less considerable approximation to normality in certain patterns of behavior.

We have described elsewhere (21) the marked degree of patterned mental growth which may take place in a child suffering from severe birth injury. This child at the age of 5 years could not sit, stand, talk, or grasp, but had attained in several fields of behavior a significant approximation toward normality.

If the sources of energy on which growth depends are not stopped, as they completely are in profound idiocy, then there remains a measure of specific and general potency. This potency expresses itself in the progressive maturation of modalities and dispositions of behavior, even when normal patterns of behavior can not be consummated. Herein lies the urgency, the almost irrepressible quality, of growth. Herein lies a life tendency which works toward adjustment, harmony, and completion even in the gravely handicapped child. Accordingly there is a maximum utilization of impaired instrumentalities and impaired impressions. This tendency toward optimum development is in the individual comparable to the recognized, though poorly understood, evolutionary trend of the racial stream of life.

The organismal concept requires that the individual shall maintain an optimal or normal integrity. The phenomena of maturation suggest the presence of tenacious, stabilizing factors which safeguard the basic patterns of growth. Just as the respiration of the organism depends upon the maintenance of constant hydrogen ion concentration, so on a vastly more intricate scale, the life career of the individual is maintained by the physiological processes of growth in which the maturational mechanisms play an important role. The role is most conspicuous in infancy but it persists throughout the life cycle until the growth potential completely subsides.

§57. A BIBLIOGRAPHY

1. ADAMS, D. K.: A restatement of the problem of learning, *British Journal of Psychology* (Gen. Sect.), vol. 22, pp. 150–178, 1931.

2. AVERY, G. T.: Responses of foetal guinea pigs prematurely delivered, *Genetic Psychology Monographs*, vol. 3, pp. 245–331, 1928.

3. BECKERHAUS, F.: Über einige Zwillinge, *Zeitschrift für Augenkrankheit*, vol. 59, pp. 264–268, 1930.

4. BIRD, C.: The effect of maturation upon the pecking instinct of chicks, *Pedagogical Seminary*, vol. 33, pp. 212–243, 1926.

5. BOEKE, J.: The innervation of striped muscle-fibers and Langley's receptive substance, *Brain*, vol. 44, pp. 1–22, 1921.

6. CARMICHAEL, L.: The development of behavior in vertebrates experimentally removed from the influence of external stimulation, *Psychological Review*, vol. 33, pp. 51–58, 1926.

7. CASTNER, B. M.: The development of fine prehension in infancy, *Genetic Psychology Monographs*, vol. 12, pp. 105–193, 1932.

8. COGHILL, G. E.: *Anatomy and the Problem of Behavior*, Cambridge (England): The University Press, 1929, xii + 113 pp.

9. ———: The early development of behavior in Amblystoma and in man, *Archives of Neurology and Psychiatry*, vol. 21, pp. 989–1009, 1929.

10. ———: The structural basis of the integration of behavior, *Proceedings of the National Academy of Sciences*, vol. 16, pp. 637–643, 1930.

11. DETWILER, S. R.: Coordination movements in supernumerary transplanted limbs, *Journal of Comparative Neurology*, vol. 38, 1925.

12. DUNLAP, K.: *Habits: Their Making and Unmaking*, New York: Liveright, 1932, x + 326 pp.

13. GATES, A. I.: The nature and limits of improvement due to training, *Twenty-seventh Yearbook of National Society for the Study of Education*, pp. 441–461, 1928.

14. ———: *Psychology for Students of Education*, New York: Macmillan, 1930 (revised), xv + 612 pp.

15. GESELL, A.: The developmental morphology of infant behavior pattern. *Proceedings of the National Academy of Sciences*, vol. 18, pp. 139–143, 1932.

16. ———: The developmental psychology of twins, in *A Handbook of Child Psychology*, pp. 158–203, Worcester, Mass.: Clark University Press, 1931.

17. ———: Hemihypertrophy and twinning. *American Journal of Medical Science*, vol. 173, pp. 542–555, 1927.

18. ———: The individual in infancy, in *Foundations of Experimental Psychology*, pp. 628–660, Worcester, Mass.: Clark University Press, 1929.

19. ———: *Infancy and Human Growth*, New York: Macmillan, 1928, xvii + 418 pp.

20. ———: Infant behavior in relation to pediatrics, *American Journal of Diseases of Children*, vol. 37, pp. 1055–1075, 1929.

21. ———: Maturation and infant behavior pattern, *Psychological Review*, vol. 36, pp. 307–319, 1929.

22. GESELL, A., and THOMPSON, H.: Learning and growth in identical infant twins: an experimental study by the method of co-twin control, *Genetic Psychology Monographs*, vol. 6, pp. 1–124, 1929.

23. HALVERSON, H. M.: An experimental study of prehension in infants by means of systematic cinema records. *Genetic Psychology Monographs*, vol. 10, pp. 107–286, 1931.

24. HENDERSON, L. J.: *The Order of Nature*, Cambridge, Mass.: Harvard University Press, 1925, v + 234 pp.

25. HERRICK, C. J.: *Brains of Rats and Men: a Survey of the Origin and Biological Significance of the Cerebral Cortex*, Chicago: University of Chicago Press, 1927, xiii + 382 pp.

26. HILGARD, J. R.: Learning and maturation in preschool children, *Journal of Genetic Psychology*, vol. 41, pp. 36–56, 1932.

26a. ———: The effect of early and delayed practice on memory and motor performances studied by the method of co-twin control, Doctoral Dissertation, Yale University Library.

27. HOLT, E. B.: *Animal Drive and the Learning Process*, New York: Holt, 1931, vii + 307 pp.

28. HUMPHREY, G.: Extinction and negative adaptation, *Psychological Review*, vol. 37, pp. 361–363, 1930.

29. ———: Learning and the living system, *Psychological Review*, vol. 37, pp. 497–510, 1930.

30. IRWIN, O. C.: The organismic hypothesis and the differentiation of behavior: I. The cell theory and the neurone doctrine, *Psychological Review*, vol. 39, pp. 128–146, 1932.

31. JENNINGS, H. S.: *The Biological Basis of Human Nature*, New York: Norton, 1930, xviii + 384 pp.

32. JERSILD, A. T.: *Training and Growth in the Development of Children*, New York: Bureau of Publications, Teachers College, Columbia University, 1932, ix + 73 pp.

33. LEY, J.: Un cas d'audi-mutité idiopathique (aphasie congénitale) chez des jumeaux monozygotiques. *L'Encéphale*, vol. 24, pp. 121–165, 1929.

34. MACFARLAN, D.: Identical hearing in identical twins, *Laryngoscope*, vol. 37, p. 846. (Psychol. Abs., 1928, 2, Abs. no. 3100.)

35. McGINNIS, J. M.: Eye movements and optic nystagmus in early infancy, *Genetic Psychology Monographs*, vol. 8, pp. 321–430, 1930.

36. MARQUIS, D. G.: The criterion of innate behavior, *Psychological Review*, vol. 37, pp. 334–349, 1930.

37. MINKOWSKI, M.: Sur les mouvements, les réflexes et les réactions musculaires du foetus humain de 2 á 5 mois et leurs relations avec le système nerveux foetal. *Revue neurologique*, vol. 37, pp. 1105–1235, 1921.

38. MORGAN, T. H.: *The Scientific Basis of Evolution*, New York: Norton, 1932, ix + 286 pp.

39. NEEDHAM, J.: *Chemical Embryology.* Cambridge (England): The University Press, 1932 (3 vols.), 2021 pp.

40. PIAGET, J.: *The Language and Thought of the Child*, New York: Harcourt, Brace & Co., 1926, xxiii + 246 pp. *Judgment and Reasoning in the Child*, New York: Harcourt, Brace & Co., 1928, xiii + 260 pp. *The Child's Conception of the World*, New York: Harcourt, Brace & Co., 1929, ix + 397 pp. *The Child's Conception of Physical Causality*, Harcourt, Brace & Co., 1930, vii + 309 pp.

41. ———: *The Moral Judgment of the Child*, New York: Harcourt, Brace & Co., London: Kegan Paul, Trench, Trübner & Co., Ltd, 1932, ix + 418 pp.

42. SANO, F.: II. The convolutional pattern of the brains of identical twins: a study on hereditary resemblance in the furrows of the cerebral hemispheres, *Philosophical Transactions of the Royal Society*, London, vol. 208 (Ser. B), pp. 37–61, 1918.

43. SHIRLEY, MARY: The sequential method for the study of maturing behavior patterns, *Psychological Review*, vol. 38, pp. 507–528, 1931.

44. SPEIDEL, C. C.: Studies of living nerves. I. The movements of individual sheath cells and nerve strouts correlated with the process of myelin-sheath formation in amphibian larvae, *Journal of Experimental Zoology*, vol. 61, pp. 279–331, 1932.

45. STOCKARD, C. R.: *The Physical Basis of Personality*, New York: Norton, 1931, xviii + 320 pp.
46. STRAYER, L. C.: Language and growth: the relative efficacy of early and deferred vocabulary training, studied by the method of co-twin control, *Genetic Psychology Monographs*, vol. 8, pp. 209–319, 1930.
47. SWENSON, E. A.: The simple movements of the trunk of the albino rat fetus, (Abstract) *Anatomical Record*, vol. 38, p. 31, 1928.
48. WHEELER, R. H., and PERKINS, F. T.: *Principles of Mental Development*, New York: Crowell, 1932, xxvi + 529 pp.

CHAPTER SIX

THE DEVELOPMENTAL DIAGNOSIS OF INFANT BEHAVIOR

MENTAL growth is subject to natural laws and therefore also subject to diagnosis. Although these laws are meagerly understood, the known facts of infant behavior afford an empirical basis for the construction of diagnostic procedures which may be safely used in a clinical manner. The possibilities of clinical diagnosis and prediction of early mental growth have been concretely discussed elsewhere.* The present volume aims to set forth normative data of development in such a way that the individual study and diagnosis of infant behavior status may be made more analytic and interpretive. Biometric simplifications and applications of the data will be considered in the accompanying volume on *Norms of Infant Development.* We are now concerned with the broader aspects of the principles and scope of developmental diagnosis.

§58. PRINCIPLES OF DEVELOPMENTAL DIAGNOSIS

The concepts and principles which underlie the diagnosis of infant behavior development are outlined somewhat categorically in the following series of statements.

A. The growth characteristics of the infant are primarily determined by hereditary and constitutional factors which undergo their basic organization in the uterine period.

B. These factors do not operate independently of postnatal environmental influences, social and physical, but they determine the direction and scope of such influences.

C. Maturational factors impart characteristic trend, tempo, and general configuration to the early behavior patterning of the individual. The resultant characteristicness is amenable to cumulative diagnosis.

D. Every individual has a distinctive complex of growth; but the infant growth cycle displays fundamental sequences and progressions which are general in nature.

* GESELL, A., *Infancy and Human Growth,* Chap. VII, The Tempo and Trend of Infant Development; Chap. XVIII, The Clinical Prediction of Mental Growth; Chap. XIX, The Measurement of Mental Growth.

E. Mental growth is an orderly process of morphogenesis. The reaction system of the infant is a unitary structure which manifests itself in specific and correlated patterns of behavior.

F. Comprehensively conceived, these patterns embrace the entire organism and include the vegetative, sensorimotor, and symbolic spheres of behavior.

G. The patterns undergo progressive, ontogenetic cnanges of form and of correlation with age. These changes can be defined by objective and normative methods, particularly in the fields of posture, locomotion, prehension, manipulation, and adaptive, language, and social behavior.

H. A developmental norm is a specification of a behavior pattern or of a behavior characteristic made to serve as a criterion or as a standard of comparison in the scrutiny of a behavior status.

I. The primary use of the norm is to identify and to characterize observed behavior forms. Because of the rapidity of behavior growth in infancy, norms are essential at frequent age intervals.

J. A norm is a standardized tool for discriminative characterization. Strictly speaking, a norm is not a unit of measurement. It represents a positional value rather than an absolute value in a calibrated scale of equal units.

K. Growth is a morphogenetic process which produces changes of pattern and progressive degrees of maturity. Growth cannot be measured in the dynamic abstract. It can, however, be characterized. Growth can be examined analytically and synthetically in terms of its patterned products. Norms in a systematic series are aids to such examination.

L. A norm is accordingly used as a critical device for discovering resemblances and differences. This is comparison rather than true mensuration. But accurate comparison by means of a systematic frame of reference approximates the precision of measurement. Moreover, the characterization of behavior status can be condensed into graphic and quantitative designations.

Measurement in the physical sciences is a determination of a quantity in terms of an absolute unit. Measurement is matching against an absolute scale of units. The complex phenomena of behavior patterning yield only to a limited extent to measurement in this rigorous sense. Patterns must be appraised by a process of comparison. Observed patterns must be matched against normative patterns. Patterns may be serially arranged in organic sequence and in genetic hierarchies, but as patterns they cannot be directly projected against an absolute scale. Indirectly, however, by graphic and mathematical devices the degrees, trends, and constellations of patterns can be given quantitative expression. The task of behavior biometry is not so much to carry the concepts of the physical sciences into the biological field as to formulate the dynamic and the genetic import of the observed phenomena. In the domain of mental growth, biometry is especially concerned with index values rather than absolute values in the classic sense.

Even though such indices fail to satisfy the strictest canons of measurement, many growth phenomena may still remain within the pale of prediction. Inasmuch as all behavior growth occurs within a self-limited cycle, every product of growth has both a kinetic and a latent significance. Biometric studies can define and evaluate such significance for population groups and for age groups. Under comparable conditions, attained growth is an index of prospective growth; and theoretically it is possible to predict later growth in terms of relative probability values. Prediction is of an actuarial character if it deals only with group or population trends. Prediction becomes individual or clinical if it appraises the indicativeness of growth products in a single complex of growth observed in one or more examinations. A series of examinations of one individual may be made to yield a numerous array of data which can be treated by biometric methods.

The analytic application of multiple norms to an early sector of the growth career supplies a statistical basis for deriving a prognosis of the developmental and dynamic characteristics of the observed infant. Needless to say, such a refined biometry is not yet at our disposal, and experienced clinical judgment must determine and qualify any predictions which may be ventured. It is important, however, to point out that biometric procedures will have an unlimited field of development and refinement with the accumulation of systematic behavior data. The very nature of growth creates a constant challenge to the application of scientific methods of prediction.

With these general statements before us, we may consider more concretely the applicability of the normative data assembled in Chap. III of the present volume. These data have been presented in a wide range of ages and in elaborate detail. For the moment we are not concerned with short-cut psychometric devices which would attempt to characterize the developmental status in a simple formula. For the intensive study of individual growth conditions and for the biogenetic study of growth careers, it is more important to recognize the great variety and complexity of developmental phenomena.

The detailed normative criteria as outlined in the present volume and in the *Atlas of Infant Behavior* may be used for the analytic characterization of any given behavior picture. This is a process of comparison which demands some familiarity with infants through both direct and cinema observation. Since normative data are available at each lunar month, detailed inventories can be made at frequent intervals. As characterizational criteria, the norms may be used to ascertain and to formulate individual differences, even though the norms themselves were derived from a relatively homogeneous group. The normative import of the norms has been enhanced by cleaving to a narrow range of relatively homogeneous selection. The normative data in themselves do not furnish a picture of the individual variations in development which exist in an unselected population. We would hold, however, that the norms are serviceable for the study of such differences if we utilize the norms frankly as a medium for recording and analysis.

In the present volume no attempt is made to codify the norms into a simplified "scale." The data are presented in their complex detail which will permit both selective and comprehensive applications for research purposes and for detailed biogenetic studies of individual infants.

The behavior equipment of an infant cannot be adequately expressed in a single mathematical formula. It cannot be generalized any more than a complex landscape can be generalized by a simple formula. To be understood, such a landscape must be charted. Our developmental norms are serviceable for itemized identification of behavior characteristics and for analytic characterization. Such characterization may be varied with respect to detail and emphasis. It may cover all the behavior fields discussed in Chap. III, namely: posture, locomotion, prehension, and perceptual, adaptive, language, and social behavior.

On the basis of age norms, ratings of observed behavior may be expressed in terms of maturity levels; but a diagnosis should be formulated in a descriptive, interpretive paragraph. In their present form the norms are a system of graded items which may be used for orderly and condensed characterization of behavior status. This normative method is not adapted to mass studies, but is suited for clinical and research studies of individual development.

§59. The Limitations of Developmental Diagnosis

The foregoing discussion has emphasized the scientific feasibility of developmental diagnosis. It is important now to call attention to the numerous complications which place limitations upon our present diagnostic techniques. In spite of its remarkable integrity and consistency, the growth complex is modified by many factors which it is difficult to recognize and to appraise. Let us enumerate some of them, with brief comment.

First of all is gestation itself. This is shrouded with many obscurities. There is no reliable method for computing exactly the duration of the uterine period. We do not know how old an infant is when he is born! In clinical practice, the presence and the degree of prematurity are often in doubt. No satisfactory distinction can be made between immaturity (subnormal birth weight with full-term gestation) and prematurity (subnormal birth weight with curtailed gestation).

Birth weight and length of gestation may vary considerably in relation to such factors as age and size of the mother, race, season of conception, nutrition, and a host of other variables during pregnancy.

Innumerable developmental deviations and anomalies have their inception either germinally or epigenetically in the uterine epoch. In more or less abnormal cases infections, hemorrhage, and imbalances in symmetry regulation and organogenesis establish deviations or defect which project themselves permanently into the entire life cycle.

To an extraordinary degree, biologically speaking, the infant is already a finished product when he is born. The foundational events in the developmental drama occur on a microscopic or a chemical level and are beyond the reach of diagnostic perception. In the growth characteristics and the behavior patterning of the postnatal period, we deal with the remoter end results of uterine development.

If we could adequately know and interpret the newborn infant, the task of subsequent diagnosis would be greatly simplified. But he is almost more of an enigma at birth than at any other time in his career. During the neonatal period, the gamut of individual variations subtends its widest angle. During this period the curve of mortality reaches its highest peak. By the same token, morbidities and inequalities in nutrition, strength, and reactiveness are disproportionately frequent. Neonatal infants vary enormously in postconceptional age, in maturity, and in their adjustment to the traumatic and the physiological complications of birth. Birth injuries ranging from a benign to a grave degree occur, but their nature is often concealed. Not even convulsions furnish a true clue to the gravity of lesions which will profoundly affect later development. The whole neonatal period is inextricably bound up with medical complications which place great limitations upon behavior diagnosis but which also confer greater significance upon the implications of such diagnosis.

In a sense the infant is not fully born until after the neonatal period. But even then the factors which may modify or at least inflect the "natural" course of his behavior development are manifold. We know that of all the organs of his body the nervous system is peculiarly resistant to the adversities of disease and to hardship and deprivations in the environment. Nature has placed about him strong safeguards which insure the basic maturation of those behavior capacities which lead to maturity.

None the less we must recognize that there are innumerable combinations of malnutrition, disease, age, and constitutional predisposition which may exert temporary or permanent effects upon the manifestations and the growth of behavior. The backstrokes of acute and of chronic illness on personality characteristics must always be considered. General and specific starvation, vitamin and mineral deficiencies, disturbances of the acid-base balance of the body due to metabolic and respiratory causes, acquired and inherited allergy, diseases of the blood, lymph nodes, and ductless glands—these and many other medical complications may affect the infant both as a dynamic and as a developing organism. To this already impressive list of complicating factors must be added those of psychogenic origin—habituations, inhibitions, emotional blockings, and socialized accentuations which affect the motivations and attitudes of the infant under examination. In this lengthened list of variables must also be included the immediate circumstances of the environment and the conditions of the diagnostic test. In the discussion of the individual behavior situations, we have sufficiently emphasized the importance of those factors which determine the immediate stimulus patterns and the resultant patterns of behavior.

The mere recital of such a formidable array of complicating factors might raise doubts concerning the reliability of developmental diagnosis in infancy. But there is no adequate ground for diagnostic skepticism. In spite of a host of variables, the infant himself maintains a high degree of stability and characteristicness in his growth. His growth potentials are deeply intrenched. If it were not so, he would be too much at the mercy of all these variables and contingencies. Their effect upon him is lawfully limited by the basic integrity of his individuality. Complex as the problems of individuality are, the scope of developmental diagnosis and even of prediction remains large. Although it is impossible to assess precisely the importance of modifying factors, the improvement of diagnostic procedures will itself serve to define the degree of influence of such factors.

§60. The Medical Aspects of Developmental Diagnosis

It is evident from the foregoing discussion that disease and development are inextricably related concepts. Malnutrition is frequently an expression of disease and, conversely, diseases are constantly reflected in deviations in development. Clinical anthropology and physical diagnosis supply many keys to this fundamental interrelation, but the diagnosis of behavior is probably the master key. Behavior is at once the most integrated and most inclusive expression of developmental and of dynamic status. At every stage of the organism it is the historic end product of the life career of that organism. For this reason the scientific study of infant behavior from the standpoint of symptomatology becomes an important phase of preventive medicine in general and of clinical pediatrics in particular.

In theory, and to a significant degree in practice, society has accepted the principle that every newborn infant is entitled to medical supervision. This supervision properly focuses upon the protection of nutrition. But the problem of nutrition is so fundamental that by implication and often by actual exigency it includes the psychological and functional aspects of individual growth. The protection of the nutritional health of the child thus becomes the natural stage for a broader and equally continuous type of supervision which will take systematic account of behavior status and behavior growth.

Development is a continuous process which can be supervised only by periodic examinations. Properly used, norms of behavior development will lead to an earlier detection of preventible handicaps and to a more complete recognition of the interrelations of mental and physical welfare. An extremely large proportion of the developmental defects and deviations of children are discoverable in the first year of life. Here, as elsewhere, early diagnosis leads to prevention or to the improvement of management and control. Many sensorimotor defects, endocrine deficiencies and disturbances, mental defects, and behavior disorders are unrecognized because the supervision of the infant does not take systematic account of the symptoms of mental growth. Mental growth, like physical growth, can be supervised only through the clinical application of norms and of diagnostic criteria.

Periodic health examinations and a periodic survey of behavior patterns can be brought into association in a supervisory type of developmental pediatrics directed toward the more timely control of growth conditions. The demand for this type of pediatrics is becoming clearer, in the fields both of private practice and of public health. Systematic health supervision is only in its beginning, but in principle a revolutionary increase in medical and social control has already been achieved. How this supervisory service in infant hygiene will actually be organized no one can, of course, predict in detail. The methods of *developmental pediatrics* will naturally take shape slowly, but probably with the same steady and sound growth which has marked the advances of preventive pediatrics in the supervision of infant nutrition. In this whole field, which is now in a highly transitional stage of organization, pediatrics holds a peculiarly strategic position representing the integration of the resources of general medicine in the health protection of normal as well as sick infants.

In the next few decades research in the biological sciences will doubtless perfect new and discriminating techniques for the measurement and clinical appraisal of human characteristics, mental and physical. Such techniques will define with greater precision individual differences and susceptibilities; physiologic efficiencies of separate organs; behavior traits and trends; and, above all, the balance or correlation of different functions in the total personality.

In some systematic way these techniques, medical and biometric, are destined to be used for the better control of early human growth. How will they be applied? As separate and independent specializations? Or will they be coordinated in a form of clinical medicine which will bring the total development of the infant under periodic supervision?

INDEX

DATE

DEC 1 6 '75	
GAYLORD	